THE SPLENDID CAUSE

Neil Collins

The Splended Cause

THE MISSIONARY SOCIETY OF ST COLUMBAN
1916-1954

First published in 2009 by
the columba press
55A Spruce Avenue, Stillorgan Industrial Park, Blackrock, Co. Dublin

Cover by Bill Bolger

The cover shows the two founders of the Columbans. Edward J. Galvin, Bishop of Hanyang, baptising a child in China, arrived in Ireland in 1916 hoping to set up the Chinese mission. John Blowick joined him and was the first superior of the society. A copy of *The Far East* reveals their thinking, as the light of the gospel streams from a Celtic cross to the Chinese pagodas. Behind the photographs is a map of the Hanyang prefecture. Blowick and Galvin used it in Rome in 1919 in support of their request for a mission in a populous area. Patrick O'Connor, one of the earliest students in Dalgan, described their project in a poem as *The Splendid Cause*.

Origination by The Columba Press
Printed in Ireland by ColourBooks Ltd, Dublin

ISBN 978-1-85607-643-2

Copyright © 2009, Neil Collins

Table of Contents

Acknowledgements		6
List of tables		9
List of figures		10
List of illustrations		11
Abbreviations		13
Chapter I	Introduction	14
Chapter II	Foundation	32

CHINA

Chapter III	Mission in Hanyang 1920-1952	86
Chapter IV	Mission in Nancheng 1928-1952	138
Chapter V	Mission in Huchow 1946-1954	178

OTHER MISSIONS

Chapter VI	Mission in the Philippines 1929-1954	186
Chapter VII	Mission in Korea 1933-1954	226
Chapter VIII	Mission in Burma 1936-1954	257
Chapter IX	Conclusion	289

Appendices	300
Bibliography	310
Index	322

Acknowledgements

The author wishes to thank Brendan O'Sullivan, superior general of the Missionary Society of St Columban (2000-6), and his council, Neil Magill, Kevin O'Neill, Noel Mackey and Francis Hoare, who invited him to attempt to write the history of the society, and authorised his doing the work as a thesis. Their generous support, interest and timely suggestions provided invaluable encouragement. Members of the new council, Thomas Murphy, Trevor Trotter, John Burger and Eamon Sheridan, have been equally enthusiastic.

Credit must go to the delegates at the general chapter of the society held in Lima, 1982, who authorised the central administration 'to initiate a critical history of the society'. Following on that chapter, a succession of people undertook the creation of what is today an extremely rich archive. Ageing veterans of the missions in China were interviewed; books about and documents of the society were organised and catalogued; key selections from *The Far East* and other publications relevant to the history of the society were transcribed to zip disks. Among those who must be praised for these vital enterprises are Parig Digan, Bernard Smyth, Michael O'Neill, Michael O'Farrell, and Patrick Crowley. Donald and Helen MacInnis directed the oral history project and interviews were conducted by James McCaslin, Michael Harrison, Brendan MacHale, Martin Noone, Sean Rainey, and Parig Lehane. Christine Deegan and Kay Doran transcribed the bulk of the interviews and must represent the many secretaries whose names are not recorded. Thank you to all these, and to Dr. Charles Flynn who updated and catalogued the oral archive in a form which facilitates research.

Hugh MacMahon and James Mulroney in Hong Kong gave valuable insights. Gerard Neylon, with his encyclopaedic knowledge of China, and Daniel Troy were indispensable guides and interpreters for a visit to the church in China. Many people were wonderfully hospitable and informative during that visit: Thomas Yu and his grand-niece Yinging in Nancheng; Joseph Houston in Nanchang; Li Fuping, Li Gang, Ya Na, John Ting, Joseph Wu, Francis and Therese Sun in Huchow; Warren Kinne in Shanghai; Peter Lü in Beijing; Zeng Xianghui, Zhang Xiaojin, Zhang Wei Jiao, Zhang Hua qing and his family, and Song De Zhi in Xiantao; Zhou Wen Bing, Li Fen

Fang, Shen Ai Yun and their community in Hanyang; and Anthony Wang in Hankow.

Research was greatly assisted by the staff of: the National Archives, Kew; Cambridge University Library; and the Henry Martyn Library, Cambridge. It was deepened when Martha L. Smalley invited the author to read a paper at the Yale-Edinburgh Group meeting in 2005 where it was discussed by a small, but well-informed audience. Smalley was very patient with constructive advice for several days of exploration of the riches of the Yale Divinity School library. Claire Williamson of the Penrose Library, University of Denver, supplied important data. Willi Müller provided an introduction to Luis Cuña and the archives of Propaganda; Pádhraic O'Loughlin suggested a visit to the archives of the Irish College, Rome, where the archivist, Vera Orschel, was very informative. A paper read at a workshop in the Academia Belgica, Rome, at the invitation of Jan De Maeyer, aroused a lively argument which revealed a lack of balance in one of the main findings of my thesis.

Valuable assistance was given by people in many institutions in Ireland: by Darragh O'Donoghue in the Allen Library of the Irish Christian Brothers; David C. Sheehy in the archives of the Archdiocese of Dublin; Edward Grimes in the office of the Pontifical Mission Societies; Ger Crowley, Margaret O'Connell and the staff of the *Irish Catholic*; Eamon McCarthy in the offices of the Legion of Mary; Ciaran McConville in the Cardinal Tomás Ó Fiaich Memorial Library and Archive, Armagh; the staff of the National Library of Ireland; Penelope Woods and Etáin Ó Siocháin in the Russell Library, and Agnes Neligan and the staff of the John Paul II Library. Sisters who helped included Philomena Doran RGS, Mary Teresa Ryan RGS, and Margaret Conroy FMM. Dr Michael Smyth, Bishop of Meath, explored and photocopied sections of the minutes of the meetings of the Irish bishops 1916-20 from the archives in Mullingar. Cardinal Cahal Daly described the late Cardinal John D'Alton's account of the foundation of the Columbans and of the Legion of Mary.

The writer lived in the company of many other Columbans, active and retired, men with long experience in the regions of the society covered by this book. Their insights and comments frequently helped him to get a deeper grasp of different missions and cultures. He is very grateful for their companionship, encouragement, and wisdom. Redempta Twomey, archivist of the Missionary Sisters of St Columban, was always willing to find the answers to queries about the sisters, and the late Teresita Yu helped him to understand the church in Nancheng.

I wish to thank Professor Vincent Comerford and the Department of

History in NUI Maynooth for accepting me as a PhD student, and for giving me the constant stimulus and advice of Dr Jacinta Prunty. This book would be a paler, shallower production without her suggestions. With her it has been one of the most inspiring experiences of my life.

List of Tables

Table 2.1	Members of the Columban Congress in the Constitutions 1918-25	66
Table 3.1	Comparative statistics for the Hanyang mission, 1922-3	96
Table 3.2	Annual report, Vicariate of Hanyang, 1935-6	99
Table 3.3	Church growth, Vicariate of Hanyang, 1922-30	101
Table 3.4	Church growth, Vicariate of Hanyang, 1932-40	121
Table 3.5	Adult baptisms, Vicariate of Hanyang, 1924-39	124
Table 4.1	Church growth, Vicariate of Nancheng, 1929-35	142
Table 4.2	Church growth, Vicariate of Nancheng, 1936-41	149
Table 4.3	Church growth, Vicariate of Nancheng, 1943-49	156
Table 5.1	Church growth in the Huchow district, 1946-51	182
Table 6.1	Parishes founded by Spanish missionaries in Misamis Occ., 1776-1898	202
Table 6.2	Priests and brothers killed by Japanese in Manila, February 1945	210
Table 7.1	Church growth, Prefecture of Kwangju, 1936-46	236
Table 7.2	Church growth, Prefecture of Kwangju, 1946-51	241
Table 7.3	Church growth, Prefecture of Ch'unch'on, 1945-49	242
Table 7.4	Annual report, Prefecture of Ch'unch'on, 30 June 1951	246
Table 7.5	Church growth, Prefecture of Kwangju, 1950-55	252
Table 8.1	Population statistics by faith for the Kachin State, 1931	265

List of Figures

Figure 2.1	Map of Columban missions in China, 1920-38	39
Figure 3.1	Ecclesiastical history of the Province of Hupeh, 1684-1920	88
Figure 3.2	Map of St. Columban's mission, Hanyang, 1920-54	90
Figure 3.3	Headings for the annual report to Rome, 1937	98
Figure 3.4	Chart of church growth in the Vicariate of Hanyang, 1922-40	120
Figure 4.1	Map of the Vicariate of Yukiang 1928	139
Figure 4.2	Chart of church growth, Vicariate of Nancheng, 1929-49	141
Figure 5.1	Ecclesiastical history of the Archdiocese of Hangchow, 1575-1946	178
Figure 6.1	Map of Roman Catholic Dioceses in the Philippines, 1929	188
Figure 6.2	Map of the Columban missions in the Philippines, 1929-54	196
Figure 6.3	Map of Mindanao, 1938	203
Figure 7.1	Map of Korean peninsula	228
Figure 7.2	Chart of the Roman Catholics in Kwangju and Ch'unch'on, 1936-55	250
Figure 8.1	Map of Burma	258
Figure 8.2	Roman Catholic predecessors of the Columbans in Burma, 1535-1936	260
Figure 8.3	Map of the Prefecture of Bhamo	263
Figure 8.4	Chart of church growth, Prefecture of Bhamo, 1937-54	271

List of Illustrations

The photographs appear in numerical order in a block of 24 pages after page 160 of the text.

Plate 2.1	Priests of the Dunboyne House, Maynooth, 1914
Plate 2.2	The Council of Directors, 1917
Plate 2.3	The Far East (November, 1920)
Plate 3.1	The first group of Columbans to go to China, 1920
Plate 3.2	Irish Christian Brothers in Hanyang, 1924
Plate 3.3	Embroidery methods in Hanyang, 1925
Plate 3.4	The embroidery school, Hanyang, 1925
Plate 3.5	The first Missionary Sisters of St. Columban to go to China, 1926
Plate 3.6	Celebration for the rescue of Patrick Laffan and James Linehan, 1930
Plate 3.7	The Sisters of St. Mary, Hanyang, 1939
Plate 3.8	Peter Zhang and Joseph Seng, 1937
Plate 3.9	Peter Zhang (1915-2005), bishop of Hanyang
Plate 3.10	Roman Catholics in Hanyang, 2005
Plate 4.1	Columbans in Nancheng, 1931
Plate 4.2	Patrick Dermody and Nationalist officers in Nanfeng, 1933
Plate 4.3	Thomas McCarthy, Hengtsun, 1932
Plate 4.4	Columban sisters in Nancheng, 1941
Plate 4.5	Pupils from Catholic schools, Nancheng, with Patrick Cleary, 1943
Plate 4.6	Consecration of Patrick Cleary, 16 April 1939
Plate 4.7	Columban sisters and Thomas Ellis, 1940
Plate 4.8	Confirmation in Nancheng, 1949
Plate 4.9	Ordinations in Nancheng, 1957
Plate 5.1	Jean-Joseph Deymier welcomes Columbans to Hangchow, 1946
Plate 5.2	The parish of Nanzin, Chekiang, 1948
Plate 6.1	Columbans in the Philippines with Edward J. Galvin, 1935
Plate 6.2	Canonesses of St. Augustine and the staff of Malate school, 1933
Plate 6.3	Mariano A. Madriaga, Bishop of Lingayen, with Columban Sisters, 1939
Plate 6.4	Edward J. McCarthy and members of Student Catholic Action, 1938
Plate 6.5	John Henaghan and the first Columbans in Mindanao, 1939
Plate 6.6	Lingayen cathedral after a naval bombardment, 1945
Plate 6.7	Science class in the Philippines, 1953
Plate 6.8	Thomas Brennan with Muslim friends, 1954
Plate 6.9	Geoffrey Revatto welcomes Timothy Connolly to Sipalay, 1954

Plate 6.10   Teaching the young
Plate 7.1   Mokp'o, Korea
Plate 7.2   Florian Demange, Vicar Apostolic of Taegu with Columbans, 1933
Plate 7.3   Girls' night school, Mokp'o, 1937
Plate 7.4   Priests of Ch'unch'on interned in 1942
Palte 7.5   Harold Henry, military chaplain
Plate 7.6   Thomas Cusack and Korean friends
Plate 7.7   Thomas Quinlan arriving in Berlin, 1953
Plate 8.1   Charles Gilhodes MEP, 1941
Plate 8.2   James Stuart, Burma, 1944
Plate 8.3   Patrick Usher visits the parish of Denis McAlindon, 1950
Plate 8.4   The catechists' school, Bhamo, 1950
Plate 8.5   A Kachin family with their home shrine
Plate 8.6   Columban sisters on the Irrawaddy
Plate 8.7   Seminary dormitory, northern Burma, 1952

Abbreviations

AAS	Acta Apostolicae Sedis
AP	Archives of the Congregation for the Propagation of the Faith, Rome
APCI	Archivo, Pontificio Collegio Irlandese, Roma
CFCA	Columban Fathers' Central Archives, Dalgan Park, Navan
CFUSA	Columban Fathers' Archives, Omaha, USA
CIC	Codex Iuris Canonici
DDA	Dublin Diocesan Archives, Clonliffe
FMM	Franciscan Missionaries of Mary
FO	Foreign Office
IER	Irish Ecclesiastical Record
MEP	Les Missions-Étrangères de Paris
OBE	Officer of the Order of the British Empire
POW	Prisoner of war
PRO	National Archives, Public Record Office, Kew
RGS	Religious of the Good Shepherd
SVD	Society of the Divine Word
TFE	The Far East

CHAPTER ONE

Introduction

The Missionary Society of St. Columban was inaugurated in Ireland in 1916. Its founders planned to recruit men from among the Irish, in Ireland, America and Australia, who would establish a mission in China. There they would attempt to convert people to the Roman Catholic faith and to set up a local church complete with 'a native priesthood and episcopate'.[1] But the exclusively Irish character of the undertaking was soon diluted and the narrow focus on China enlarged. In America volunteers and supporters came from people with German and Polish names, and by 1936 there were missions outside China, in the Philippines, Korea and Burma. The enterprise became a multi-national society working in several quite distinct countries and cultures.

World War I was raging when Edward J. Galvin, one of the co-founders, first proposed an Irish mission to China in August 1916. Ireland was divided, with thousands of Irish men, enlisted in the British forces, dying at the battle of the Somme, and a thousand Irish nationalists incarcerated in Frongoch prison camp in Wales after the failed rising against British rule the previous Easter. The founding period of the new missionary society 1916-25 saw the Irish war of independence followed by civil war.

Columbans on mission in Asia were immersed in societies which were also passing through immense change. In China the nationalists led by Chiang Kai-shek defeated the regional warlords beginning in 1926 and attempted to unify the country only to succumb to Japanese invasion in 1937 and communist victory in 1949. The Philippines, Korea and Burma were colonies when members of the society first arrived, and after the devastation of the Pacific war (1942-5) became independent nations. Internally each country was torn by banditry, civil war and, in the case of Korea, the carnage of the Korean war (1950-3).

Aims

This book will examine first the vision of the Columban founders. That vision, not just the slogans of mission literature, but the broader understanding of the mandate of Christ and the task of the church, inspired them

---

1. John Blowick, 'The Maynooth Mission to China' in *The Catholic Truth Annual* (Dublin, 1917), p. 43.

to leave home and career for a most uncertain future in what was popularly termed the 'Far East'. The study will explore the sources of the vision, in the life experience of individuals and in the Roman Catholic paradigm of mission, particularly as expressed in the directives and other documents issued by Rome. Of special interest will be the influence of Irish nationalist ideas and rising cultural consciousness on the founding vision. Members of the society themselves underwent transition to new cultures, whether from Ireland to America and Australia, or more radically from western nations to the Orient. The book will ask how the system devised in Ireland to recruit missionaries and to support them fared in America and Australia, and how the original vision and missionary means were modified by experience in Asia. Other missionaries, Roman Catholic and Protestant, laboured in the same countries. It will be of interest to see how their rationale for mission and the means they used compared with those of the Columbans. The society was founded in the heyday of colonialism, and before the era of ecumenism and feminism; the book will look at the attitudes of Columbans to the people to whom they ministered, to other Christian churches and faiths like Buddhism and Islam, and to women.

The first Columbans appear to have gone to Asia, beginning in 1920, with naïve, exaggerated expectations that their methods would be more successful than those of their predecessors from other congregations. That success would be measured in numbers, especially in the numbers of 'pagans' embracing Christianity, and the editor of *The Far East* even spoke of 'the conversion of China by Ireland'.[2] Yet today, in the twenty-first century, members of the Roman Catholic Church are a small minority in China, Korea and Burma. This book will aim at an understanding of the reasons for apparent failure, hoping for insight into the wider phenomenon of Christian mission.

Historiography
Columban histories
Although the Missionary Society of St. Columban has existed for nearly a century, and been the subject of many articles and books, no full-length study of the history of the organisation yet exists. Joseph McGlade, *The missions: Africa and the Orient* (Dublin, 1967), a short account of Irish Roman Catholic missions in the twentieth century, described the foundation of the Columbans and introduced their work in Asia. Bernard T. Smyth, *The Chinese batch* (Dublin, 1994), covered the earliest years of the society, beginning with John

---

2. 'Editorial' in *The Far East*, iii (Apr. 1920), p. 50.

M. Fraser, a Canadian missionary who in 1911-2 fired many in the Irish church with zeal for mission in China, and concluding with the arrival of the Columbans in Shanghai in 1920. Smyth based his work almost completely on the documents in the central archive of the society, but did not attempt to write a critical history.

Martin J. Noone, *The Columbans in the Philippines, 1929-1950* (Manila, 1998), traced the history of the first missions in and around Manila, the expansion to Mindanao in 1938, and the post-war developments in Negros and Zambales. Noone undertook research in Seville, Madrid, London and Manila for his earlier study on the discovery of the Philippines;[3] his introductions on the Spanish and American missionaries who preceded the Columbans in Mindanao, based on that research, has proven valuable for the present work. Noone's biography, *The life and times of Michael O'Doherty, archbishop of Manila* (Quezon City, 1989), included the labours of the Columbans in several parishes in the archdiocese and as chaplains and promoters of Student Catholic Action. Francis Herlihy, author of *Swords and ploughshares, fifty years of mission in Korea* (Melbourne, 1983), was a missionary in Korea (1940-2) and used his experience, articles in *The Far East*, and correspondence and conversation with other Columbans to write a popular history of the work of the society in the 'hermit kingdom'. Patricia Brooks, *With no regrets, the story of Francis Vernon Douglas* (Quezon City, 1998), produced a thoroughly researched biography of a New Zealand Columban executed by the Japanese in 1943.

Pamphlets and booklets written by several of the founding group give important insights into their thinking and contemporary concerns. Edward Galvin, *Letters from an Irish missionary in China* (Dublin, 1916), contained four of the long letters Galvin wrote to encourage volunteers for China. James Conway and John Blowick, *The Maynooth Mission to China* (Dublin, 1916), outlined the missionary needs of China and the plan for an Irish mission. Bernard T. Smyth (ed.), *Part of the bargain, letters from and to Fr. Cornelius Tierney* (Dublin, 1963), reproduced letters of Tierney, killed in China in 1931, to Blowick and to his spiritual director. E. J. McCarthy, *Radio sermons, talks for students* (Manila, 1938), brought together twenty of the weekly radio talks McCarthy preached as a chaplain of Student Catholic Action in Manila. McCarthy dealt with topics from the church and the bible, to indifferentism, and Christian perfection.

---

3. Martin J. Noone, *The islands saw it, the discovery and conquest of the Philippines, 1521-1581* (Dublin, 1982).

Several members of the society published autobiographical accounts of traumatic periods of their lives during World War II or the Korean war. These men wrote shortly after their release, and their books are more reliable than memoirs composed long after the events described. Inevitably they gave a partial account of what happened, and frequently recorded the pain of being cut off from news of the wider scene. But they attempted to present objective accounts, even describing the humane actions and characters of some of their captors. Thomas Rillstone, *And behold we live, days of danger in wartime Burma* (Melbourne, 1946) told the story of his capture and imprisonment by the Japanese (1942-5). Francis Herlihy, *Now welcome summer* (Melbourne, 1946) covered the years from his arrival in Korea in 1940 to his repatriation in 1942. Philip Crosbie's *Three winters cold* (Dublin, 1955), telling of his experiences during the Korean War, was composed during his captivity but, since the communists confiscated both copies of his manuscript, was re-written on his release. Bernard T. Smyth (ed.), *But not conquered* (Westminster, 1958) included the memoirs of Edward McElroy, the last Columban expelled from China in 1954, and of four other priests imprisoned there 1952-3. Luke O'Reilly, *The laughter and the weeping* (Dublin, 1991) gave an eye-witness account of the communist take-over of a Columban vicariate in China. O'Reilly wrote his manuscript immediately after his expulsion from China in 1953, and asked his bishop, Patrick Cleary, and other eyewitnesses to check it for accuracy.

Several publications on the history of the Columbans were commissioned by the society. William E. Barrett wrote *The red lacquered gate* (New York, 1967), a biography of Edward Galvin, co-founder of the society, basing his work on painstaking research in the Columban archives in Ireland and America and on interviews with many witnesses. Barrett cut his original type-script at the request of society superiors who found the text too frank.[4] Patrick Cleary, superior in Nancheng (1931-52), and Barrett jointly edited the book line by line; Cleary's knowledge of events in China adds to the credibility of the final publication.

A series of books, 1976-80, by Edward Fischer are of a promotional nature and seem to have been based on articles in *The Far East* and detailed discussion with missionaries who had served there. The books include biographies of two archbishops, Harold Henry in Korea,[5] and Patrick Cronin in the

---

4. M. Claire Williamson to Neil Collins, 22 Mar. 2007 (Personal collection). Williamson states that the original typescript is 703 pages long, and the final one 574. She also identified Cleary as Barrett's co-editor.
5. Edward Fischer, *Light in the Far East, Archbishop Harold Henry's forty-two years in Korea* (New York, 1976).

Philippines.⁶ Fischer's experience as a soldier and military historian in northern Burma during World War II adds depth to his account of the Columbans in that country.⁷

Other institutional histories
Most studies in the wider field of mission history are of individual organisations and are usually denominational. Two books provide the context for the new venture in the record of the missionary thrust of Ireland and the US. Edmund M. Hogan, *The Irish missionary movement, a historical survey, 1830-1980* (Dublin, 1990), the first major overview and a monumental study, concentrated on Roman Catholic missionaries, with only brief references to Protestant mission enterprises. Hogan included Irish priests, sisters and brothers who served the Irish diaspora in Britain, North America, South Africa and Australasia. But his main interest was the mission to 'non-christian' lands, beginning with the congregations from the continent of Europe before describing the indigenous Irish societies. Angelyn Dries, *The missionary movement in American Catholic history* (New York, 1998) reviewed the colonial period (1492-1775), and missions within the United States (1820-1920) before devoting most of her volume to overseas mission in Latin America, Asia and Africa.

There are several parallel studies which served as models for the present book. Sheila Lucey's biography, *Frances Moloney: co-founder of the Missionary Sisters of St Columban* (Dublin, 1999), threw light from a female perspective on the part played by the Columban fathers in the foundation of her own congregation and on the first Columban mission in China. Patricia Jean Manion, *Venture into the unknown, Loretto in China, 1923-1998* (St Louis, 2006) used the letters, memoirs and interviews of sisters who worked closely with the Columbans in Hanyang from 1923 to 1952. Both writers illuminated key topics such as motives for mission, the unequal relations of priests and sisters, and the Columban mission in China. Jean-Paul Wiest, *Maryknoll in China, a history, 1918-1955* (New York, 1997) analysed the foundation of the Catholic Foreign Missionary Society of America in 1911 and its experience in five mission territories in China between 1918 and the expulsion of the last Maryknoller, James E. Walsh, in 1970. Wiest's book was frequently used for reference. Thomas Kiggins, *Maynooth mission to Africa, the story of St Patrick's,*

---

6. Edward Fischer, *Mindanao mission, Archbishop Patrick Cronin's forty years in the Philippines* (New York, 1978).
7. Edward Fischer, *Mission in Burma, the Columban Fathers' forty-three years in Kachin country* (New York, 1980).

Kiltegan (Dublin, 1991) described how priests, trained in Maynooth for several dioceses in Ireland but working with a religious order, the Congregation of the Holy Ghost, in Africa since 1920, set up their own society. St Patrick's Missionary Society was formally erected in 1930. Kiggins recorded the enthusiasm for foreign missions in Ireland in the early twentieth century, the difficulties in setting up a new organisation, and the methods used in Nigeria and Kenya.

Mission histories
Kenneth Scott Latourette, *A history of Christian missions in China* (London, 1929) recounted the story of missions by Roman Catholic, Protestant and Orthodox missionaries from the Nestorian monk, Alopen, in 625 to 1926. His scrupulously fair and balanced treatment of the methods used in different churches, and of the results achieved, is of lasting value. Joseph Schmidlin, *Catholic mission history*, translator Matthias Braun (Techny, Ill., 1933), as his title indicates, covered only Roman Catholic mission, but from the time of Christ to 1931, which meant that he had only limited space for each country. Yet he managed to deal with his subject in surprising detail, e.g. devoting nine pages to the Chinese Rites controversy of the seventeenth century. Stephen Neill, *A history of Christian missions* (2nd ed., London, 1986) attempted to include all Christian missions up to the Second Vatican Council. Inevitably some topics are barely mentioned, the work of the *Société des Missions-Étrangères* in Burma between 1856 and 1912 meriting only seven lines. However Neill's singular experience as a missionary and a leader of the ecumenical movement makes his volume essential reading. Bob Whyte, *Unfinished encounter, China and Christianity* (London, 1988) traced the history of Christianity in China from the Nestorian missionaries in the seventh century before devoting the bulk of his book to the fortunes of the churches since the communist victory in 1949. Samuel Hugh Moffett, *A history of Christianity in Asia, 1500-1900* (New York, 2005), while giving rather more space to Protestant missions than to those of other churches, allocated chapters on each country or group of countries, a format which facilitates comparison of the methods and successes of different organisations.

Three books on the work of Protestant missionaries in China gave more specific accounts. R. Wardlaw Thompson, *Griffith John, the story of fifty years in China* (London, 1907) wrote the biography of a Congregationalist missionary (1855-1912). Jane Wright, *She left her heart in China, the story of Dr Sally Wolfe, medical missionary 1915-1951* (Groomsport, 1999) based her biography of an Irish Methodist missionary doctor on letters home. Both

John and Wolfe were based in Hankow, across the Yangtze from Hanyang, scene of the first Columban mission. Jack Weir, 'China' in Jack Thompson (ed.), *Into all the world* (Belfast, 1990) outlined the mission of Irish Presbyterians in north-east China from 1869 to 1950.

Missiologies
Studies in missiology examine in a scientific way the principles and practice of the work of spreading the Christian faith. David J. Bosch, *Transforming mission* (New York, 1991) dealt with models of mission from the New Testament period, through several historical paradigms – of the Eastern, Roman Catholic, and Protestant churches – before attempting to map the elements of a modern missiology. Bosch influenced the choice of a chronological structure for this book, clarified the missiologies of different churches, and confirmed the insight about there being a Roman Catholic model for mission. Joseph Schmidlin, *Catholic mission theory*, translator Matthias Braun (Techny, Ill., 1931) analysed the basis of Roman Catholic missions, their subject, object, aims and means. Schmidlin clarified several aspects of the Roman Catholic approach to mission before Vatican II, such as accommodation, and the christianisation of society as opposed to simply soul-saving. Brian Stanley, *The Bible and the flag, Protestant mission and British imperialism in the nineteenth and early twentieth centuries* (Leicester, 1990) aimed at a more discerning historical understanding of the relationship between Protestant missions and British imperialism. Stanley was particularly helpful in comprehending the Protestant Evangelical doctrine of providence in history, the resentment felt by Chinese towards foreigners, and the attitudes of Protestant missionaries and the British authorities to education. Paul F. Knitter, *No other name? A critical survey of Christian attitudes towards the world religions* (London, 1985) tackled the knotty theological question of the relationship between Christianity and other world religions. Knitter presented a range of models from popular responses, through conservative evangelical, mainline Protestant, and Roman Catholic, before suggesting a theocentric paradigm in which Christ is no longer 'the norm that must judge all other norms'.[8] Michael Amaladoss, *Mission today, reflections from an Ignatian perspective* (Gujarat, 1989) used the writings of Ignatius of Loyola to explore mission in the context of Asia today. Amaladoss focused on the challenges to justice for the poor, inculturation of the gospel, and dialogue with world religions.

---

8. Paul F. Knitter, *No other name? A critical survey of Christian attitudes towards the world religions* (London, 1985), p. 145.

General histories
While 'mission' may not be indicated in the title, several general histories discuss it and provide essential background for understanding missionaries. For China Denis Twitchett and John K. Fairbank (eds), *The Cambridge history of China*, vols. xii (Cambridge, 1983) and xiii (Cambridge, 1986) were the mainstays, with more occasional reference to Jung Chang and Jon Halliday, *Mao, the unknown story* (London, 2005), and Robert Payne, *Portrait of a revolutionary: Mao Tse-tung* (New York, 1950). Teodoro A. Agoncillo, *A short history of the Philippines* (Caloocan City, 1975) gave a Filipino's account of the history of his country. Ki-baik Lee, *A new history of Korea*, translator Edward W. Wagner (Cambridge, Mass., 1984) analysed the internal history of Korea, the influence of other powers, and the place of Christianity in relation to Buddhism, Confucianism and communism. Historical background for Burma was less satisfactory. G. E. Harvey, *History of Burma* (London, 1925) stopped at 1824. No general history was available for the period 1824-1954, and the researcher depended on works such as Julian Thompson, *War in Burma, 1942-1945* (London, 2002), and Aung San Suu Kyi, *Freedom from fear and other writings* (London, 1991). Aung San dealt with the history of Burma from 1500 BC to independence in 1948, and was mainly interested in her father, Aung San, and the growth of nationalism under British rule.

Sources and methodologies
There is a wealth of primary sources for the history of the society. The principal ones are the unpublished correspondence and other documents (1912-2002) stored in the Columban Fathers' central archive in Dalgan Park, Co Meath, and the minute books (1917-2007) of the meetings of the superior general's council held with other active records in the society's headquarters at Donaghmede, Dublin. As a society of missionary secular priests the Columban Fathers dealt directly with the Sacred Congregation for the Propagation of the Faith in Rome, also known as Propaganda Fide or simply Propaganda, rather than with the Sacred Congregation for Religious. At the local level, superiors corresponded directly with bishops and priests. Documents internal to the organisation include: successive constitutions (1917-32); reports and letters from superiors in the missions to the superior general; diaries, memoirs and personal papers of individuals. Some reports were intended for publication in *The Far East*, and dealt with the progress and needs of the mission; others were confidential, detailing the failings of individuals or complaining about budget allocations.

The minutes of the meetings of the superior general's council vary from one administration to the next, sometimes recording the headings of topics discussed, at other times being remarkably detailed. Constitutions define the distinctive aim and nature of the society and determine its internal structure. In the period covered by this book, the Columban constitutions were revised five times, giving a record of the developing self-understanding of the society. Annual reports from ecclesiastical superiors on the missions to Propaganda and to the Columban central administration in Ireland relied heavily on statistics. Parishes submitted totals of members, sacraments celebrated, chapels built, catechists, and other tangible indicators of growth. While some of the figures from parishes were solidly based, e.g. on numbers of written baptismal certificates, there is more than a suspicion that returns such as the estimates for all Roman Catholics in the place are less reliable. Yet tables and graphs constructed from the statistics can be quite revealing, and will be used wherever the figures are available. They can identify phases in the mission, times of significant growth or stasis, and turning points, which must then be elucidated from other documents.

Unpublished monographs by two of the founders are of value for the historian. John Blowick wrote five volumes, covering the negotiations involved in founding a Columban mission college in Ireland, and on relations with the hierarchy.[9] He inserted the originals of all correspondence into his typescript. Edward J. McCarthy gathered materials and wrote a history of the Roman Catholic Church in Burma 'from original and other extant sources' in 1941. His original text appears to have been lost in the chaos of war and he stated that it was 'rewritten by Monsignor Patrick Usher during the war years in Mandalay (1942-1945)'.[10] Many of the original materials on which this history was based were destroyed in the fighting, making the typescript irreplaceable. The text covers the period from the arrival of the first Christians in 1519 to the beginning of the Columban mission in 1936. It raises questions about mission in a country dominated by a major religion such as Buddhism.

Incomplete personnel statistics make a regrettable gap in the sources. The society has several databases recording all living and dead Columbans, but these lists include only full members. Student probationers are not included in any databases.

The annual volumes of the *Acta Apostolicae Sedis*, the public record of the decisions and documents of the pope and the various bodies that compose

---

9. John Blowick, Longer notes (5 vols, c. 1923, unpublished MS in CFCA, Dalgan Park, Navan).
10. Edward J. McCarthy, 'The history of the Catholic church in Burma' (unpublished MS, 1941, in CFCA, BUR A-5, Foreword).

the 'Vatican', are the privileged source for information on the process for erection of new prefectures and vicariates in the missions, the dates of erection, and the civil jurisdictions included in the new mission.

Church directories vary in the information they provide. Most record the names of vicariates and parishes, the names and nationalities of priests and sisters, and brief historical notes. The volumes of J. M. Planchet, *Les missions de Chine et du Japon* (Pékin, 1916, 1917, 1925, 1927, 1929, 1931, 1933), also include the 'spiritual fruits', i.e. statistics for Catholics, catechumens, schools and sacraments. For more recent times Jean Charbonnier, *Guide to the Catholic church in China, 2004* (Singapore, 2004) can provide only tentative statistics. The *Catholic address book* (Seoul 1995), published annually by the Catholic Conference of Korea, is an essential guide for the difficult spelling of Korean names. A similar book, *The official 2006 Catholic directory of Myanmar* (Yangon, 2006), published by the Catholic Bishops' Conference of Myanmar, helps in locating parishes.

The issue of transliteration is significant for this study since the sources used a variety of methods for romanisation of Chinese and Korean names of both people and places (cf Appendix 3, pp 303-4). Columbans in China generally followed the Wade-Giles system, and this book does so too, apart from quotations and people who are alive today. In the chapter on mission in Korea the McCune-Reischauer scheme was adopted, as possibly being the best for representing the multiplicity of Korean letters and sounds.

Statistics for all the Christian churches in China since 1949 are notoriously unreliable. Those supplied by government sources cover only people and groups registered with the civil authorities. Unregistered churches, often given the misleading term 'underground', do not keep written records which could be used to prosecute their members. Researchers from agencies such as the Holy Spirit Centre in Hong Kong regularly make wide-ranging tours in mainland China, gather estimates of church membership, and extrapolate from these for reports published once a year in the centre's quarterly *Tripod*.[11] Officials of the centre claim that their totals for priests are accurate, but not those for baptised Roman Catholics.[12]

A recent addition to the sources for Columban history is The Columban Oral History Archive, completed in 2006 by Dr Charles Flynn. This includes taped interviews and life histories recorded, in the main, by elderly mission-

---

11. Tripod Staff, 'Statistics for China's Catholic Church (Nov. 2006)' in *Tripod*, xxvii (Hong Kong, Spring 2007), p. 51.
12. Interview by author with Betty Ann Maheu and Michael Sloboda, Holy Spirit Study Centre, Aberdeen, Hong Kong (6 Apr. 2006).

aries between 1969 and 2001. Each of these men served in one or more of the regions of the society.[13]

Columbans began publication of *The Far East* in Ireland in January 1918, in America in May of the same year, and in Australia in October 1920. Its avowed purpose was to attract young men to the missionary vocation and to enlist the support, by money and prayers, of others, and its editorials and articles always need to be checked as they give a selective view of the work of the society. *Pagan Missions*, the organ of the Missionary Union of the Clergy, edited by Columbans, appeared first in December 1922, was re-named *Ensign* in 1967, and continued until 1986. It was aimed at the clergy attempting to give them a deeper understanding of mission, including the work of other congregations. Despite their greater sophistication, contributions to this magazine also require careful evaluation.

Important documents consulted in other archives are listed in the bibliography. Access to the *Archivo Storico* of the *Congregazione per l'Evangelizzazione dei Popoli* in 2006 was limited by an eighty-five year rule. All papers later than 1921 were sealed.

Essential concepts

Some of the key terms in this book are no longer in common use and need to be defined. The majority of Christians when the Columban Fathers were first mooted in 1916 would have understood the term 'the missions' to mean 'the foreign missions', the countries, mainly in Asia and Africa, where the people did not yet believe in Christ. A 'mission' was a part of such a country entrusted to a religious organisation for the propagation of the faith. Many Protestant missionary societies carried on 'missions' in lands where the population was at least nominally Roman Catholic or Orthodox, although the World Missionary Conference, 1910, in Edinburgh 'implicitly declared Protestant proselytism of Roman Catholics and, rather less clearly, of Orthodox or Oriental Christians to be no valid part of Christian mission'.[14] A 'missionary' was a person sent by a church or society in the 'Christian' West on such a mission. Roman Catholic documents tended to limit the term to clerics, usually foreign priests 'sent by the Apostolic See', but occasionally extending it to include local priests also. There was some ambivalence about

---

13. The archive contains tapes, transcripts, and an index on a compact disk holding all the transcripts. A full copy has been deposited in the library of NUI Maynooth (Nov. 2006).
14. Brian Stanley, 'Defining the boundaries of christendom: the two worlds of the World Missionary Conference, 1910' in the *International Bulletin of Missionary Research*, xxx, no. 4 (Oct. 2006), p. 176.

religious sisters, brothers, and lay people, listed by John Blowick, co-founder of the Columbans, under the heading of 'auxiliary forces'. The Pope, Benedict XV, regarded sisters as giving 'eminent assistance and service to the heralds of the gospel',[15] i.e. to the 'real' missionaries. Yet the Columban sisters were recognised in 1922 as a congregation in their own right and entitled the Missionary Sisters of St Columban. Lay people were invited to 'participation … with the apostolate of the hierarchy' by Pius XI under the title of 'Catholic Action' in 1931.[16]

In Roman Catholic canon law a mission with few baptised members and depending on foreign priests was classified as a 'mission *sui iuris*'. As the numbers of converts and clergy increased the pope, at the request of the vicar apostolic of the parent territory and the superior general of the missionary congregation, and in consultation with the cardinals of Propaganda Fide, erected the mission as an 'apostolic prefecture', headed by a priest called a 'prefect'.[17] With further development, especially in the training of a local clergy, the Pope redefined it as an 'apostolic vicariate' with a bishop to lead it. The final step was when Rome erected a diocese.

Missionary aims and methods
Protestants and Roman Catholics agreed in basing their mission '*ad gentes*' on the mandate of Christ as summarised in biblical texts such as the 'Great Commission', 'Go therefore and make disciples of all nations' (Mt 28:19).[18] They used similar language to describe their aims on mission, terms like 'conversion of the gentiles' and '*plantatio ecclesiae*'. But they differed significantly on missionary methods. A fundamental characteristic of 'Protestant Christian expansion … [was] a single-minded determination to put the bible into the language of the common people as quickly as possible'.[19] Roman Catholic missionaries were slower, remarkably so given the urgent desire of the Pope, Benedict XV, in 1920 to 'promote among the children of the church, and especially among the clergy, assiduous and reverent study of the bible'. One reason was that while Protestants accepted individual interpretation of the bible, Roman Catholic teaching was that one's understanding of the biblical text must 'not overpass the limits set by the Fathers', and be sub-

---

15. Benedict XV, '*Maximum illud*' in *AAS*, xi (Rome, 1919), p. 451.
16. Pius XI, '*Non abbiamo bisogno*' in *AAS*, xxiii (Rome, 1931), p. 294.
17. Eugenio Pacelli, '*Litterae Apostolicae I*' in *AAS*, xxv (Rome, 1933), pp 232-3.
18. David J. Bosch, *Transforming mission* (7th printing, New York, 1993), p. 5, and Joseph Schmidlin, *Catholic mission theory*, trans. Matthias Braun (Techny, Ill., 1931), p. 58.
19. Samuel Hugh Moffett, *A history of Christianity in Asia* (2 vols, New York, 2005), ii, p. 260.

missive to 'the church, our supreme teacher through the Roman Pontiffs'.[20] Frequently working among illiterate people they regarded catechesis, linked to the sacraments of baptism and eucharist, as a greater priority.

All missionaries were expected to promote the formation of a local church leadership, but not all did. Pius XI, Pope in 1926, warned Roman Catholic leaders in the missions of 'the importance of building up a native clergy'. Otherwise their apostolate would 'become an obstacle and an impediment to the establishment ... of the church in those countries'.[21] The Archbishop of Canterbury urged the Danish missionaries in India in 1727 to develop a national leadership who would 'have easier access to their countrymen'. Seventy years later the eminent Baptist missionary William Carey repeated the same message in his classic text, the Serampore Covenant.[22]

Relations with members of other churches and faiths
Relations between Protestant and Roman Catholic missionaries in the field sometimes mirrored the controversial language of the Reformation. As late as 1919 the Pope, Benedict XV, described Protestant missionaries as '*ministri errorum*',[23] while some of his opponents still referred to him in words from the Westminster Confession of 1643 as, 'that Antichrist, that man of sin, and son of perdition that exalteth himself in the Church against Christ and all that is called God'.[24] Yet local circumstances such as co-operation in humanitarian work, shared dangers, and even loneliness for someone who spoke English often provided opportunities for overcoming prejudice and for genuine friendship. Protestant missionaries in China and Korea tended to work in colleges and hospitals in the larger cities while the structure of prefectures and quasi-parishes scattered most Roman Catholic missionaries in rural areas. Such physical separation lessened friction but also provided few occasions for any personal acquaintance or mutual understanding. However, there was intense resentment among Roman Catholic clerics in the Philippines where many Protestant churches, especially from America, gave in to 'the Protestant temptation to proselyte Filipino Catholics'. Charles Henry Brent, the Canadian leader of the American Episcopal Mission, was unusual in

---

20. Benedict XV, '*Spiritus Paraclitus*' in *AAS*, xii (Rome, 1920), p. 386.
21. Pius XI, '*Rerum ecclesiae*' in *AAS*, xviii (Rome, 1926), p. 73.
22. Moffett, *A history of Christianity in Asia*, ii, p. 240.
23. Benedict XV, '*Maximum illud*' in *AAS*, xi (Rome, 1919), p. 448.
24. 'The Westminster confession of faith, 1643' in Henry Bettenson (ed.), *Documents of the Christian church* (2nd ed., Oxford, 1967), p. 247.

directing 'the efforts of his missionaries to the as yet unevangelised folk in the mountains' and not to Roman Catholics.²⁵

Missionaries in India in 1910, according to Vendanayagam Samuel Azariah, 'except for a few of the very best, seem … to fail largely in getting rid of an air of patronage and condescension, and in establishing a genuinely brotherly and happy relation as between equals with their … flocks'.²⁶ Azariah complained of racism within a Christian church. A related problem was the attitude of Christian missionaries to the religions of Asia. Jacques Dupuis, a Jesuit theologian, taught Hindu and Christians students in India in 1948. Contact with them 'belied the trite negative ideas that still remained prevalent in the West about the worth or lack of worth of the other religious traditions'.²⁷

The disparaging and offensive language used by missionaries about members of other churches or faiths since Luther challenged the preachers of indulgences in 1517 is part of a wider human phenomenon, the need to belittle opponents. Jews used the word 'idolater' of Christians, Roman Catholics of Buddhists, and Protestants of Roman Catholics. The Hebrew '*goyim*', translated into English as 'people', 'gentiles', 'pagans' or 'heathens', took on a negative note because of the Jewish experience of oppression during the Babylonian Exile (587-538 BC) and the Seleucid kingdom (333-63 BC).²⁸ Margaret Preston's study of language found that the discourse of many of the charitable organisations helping the poor in nineteenth-century Dublin contained insulting words and traced it to a complex mixture of class, race, and religion adopted by Britain's elite in seeking to maintain their position at the pinnacle of power.²⁹ Preston noted that such behaviour was largely unconscious. Paolo Freire reported that in Brazil in the mid-twentieth century the rich never referred to the poor as 'the oppressed' but 'those people', 'savages', 'natives' or 'subversives'.³⁰ Milton J. Bennett sees such language and attitudes as normal in the initial experience of another culture. He claims that, 'Intercultural sensitivity is not natural. It is not part of our primal past, nor

---

25. Stephen Neill, *A history of Christian missions* (London, 1964), p. 346.
26. *World missionary conference, 1910, to consider missionary problems in relation to the non-Christian world* (Edinburgh, 1910), ix, p. 315, quoted in Jonathan J. Bonk, 'Edinburgh 1910: friendship and the boundaries of christendom' in the *International Bulletin of Missionary Research*, xxx, no. 4 (Oct, 2006), p. 170.
27. Jacques Dupuis, 'My pilgrimage in mission' in the *International Bulletin of Missionary Research*, xxvii, no. 4 (Oct. 2003), p. 169.
28. John L. McKenzie, *Dictionary of the Bible* (London, 1966), pp 302-3.
29. Margaret H. Preston, *Charitable words, women, philanthropy, and the language of charity in nineteenth-century Dublin* (Westport, Conn., 2004), p. 53.
30. Paolo Freire, *Pedagogy of the oppressed* (Penguin ed., London, 1993), p. 38.

has it characterised most of human history'.³¹ In his developmental model of intercultural sensitivity Bennett posits a continuum of stages through which people pass when they confront cultural difference. The first, ethnocentric stages are those of isolation, separation, denigration and superiority, and denigration 'may be attached to race, religion, age, gender, or any other assumed indicator of difference'.³² Peter Berger's studies of 'the reciprocal interaction of what is experienced as outside reality (specifically, the world of institutions that confronts the individual) and what is experienced as being within the consciousness of the individual',³³ are helpful in explaining the language of 'damnation', where, for example, it was a widely-held belief among Roman Catholics that Buddhists and even Protestants were damned, even though that was not the official teaching of the Catholic Church. A popularised phrase such as 'Outside the church there is no salvation', and regulations forbidding Roman Catholics to enter a Protestant church for the funeral of a friend, made a much greater impact than the nuanced theology of the institution.

Culture shock
Every foreign missionary experienced culture shock, long before the term became common currency. American and Australian Columbans found themselves in an institution which was predominantly Irish and endured irritants like conversations devoted to Irish politics or Gaelic football. However, the greatest difficulties were those involving the language, customs, and physical characteristics of the mission. After a brief 'honeymoon' stage the missionary, not knowing how to ask the simplest of questions or how to behave, felt incompetent and isolated, and commonly experienced depression and anger.³⁴

Language study was the first priority for a newly-arrived Columban, whether in China in 1920 or in the Philippines, Korea or Burma twenty years later. Teaching methods prior to 1960 were poor and many struggled to learn enough to carry out their professional duties. Columbans in China spoke with awe of Galvin's ability to read the local newspaper, giving the impres-

---

31. Milton J. Bennett, 'Towards Ethnorelativism: a developmental model of intercultural sensitivity' in R. Michael Paige (ed.), *Education for the intercultural experience* (Yarmouth, Maine, 1993), p. 21.
32. Ibid., p. 35.
33. Peter Berger, Brigitte Berger, Hansfried Kellner, *The homeless mind* (New York, 1974), p. 12.
34. Carmen Guanipa, 'Culture shock' at Amigos – Culture shock (http://edweb.sdsu.edu/people/CGuanipa/cultshok.htm) (27 Mar. 2007).

sion that such fluency was exceptional. In Burma and the Philippines men had to learn several quite different languages.

Local customs, manners and values demanded great sensitivity on the part of the foreigner. Relations with local mandarins, or with women and children, table manners, and ways of conducting business had to be learned. In densely populated areas like China and the Philippines many missionaries wrongly believed that the local people had no sense of privacy, for example private letters left on the living room table in Mindanao were regarded as public property. Living in poor, rural towns and villages where the majority were illiterate or poorly educated could lead one to feel superior especially as rural workers were unaware of their many skills, and the world economy attached little monetary value to these.

Visiting mission stations involved difficult travel, often on a pony or on foot. It was particularly arduous in the mountains of northern Burma. On arrival at a station the missionary shared the food and accommodation of the people, in many places sleeping on the floor in crowded rooms. Toilet facilities might be in the long grass or the sea. On such travels the foreigner had to be alert to health hazards such as mosquitoes, contaminated water, and inadequate food.

Structure of the book

This book opens with the foundation of the society. It attempts to assess the context within which the proposal for a Chinese mission emerged by looking at the secular press and Roman Catholic newspapers and periodicals prior to 1916, and tracing the influence on the key players of John M. Fraser, the Canadian missionary who planted the notion of such a mission. The thinking of the founders about those '*extra ecclesiam*' is contrasted with the official teaching of the church. A crucial part of the study examines the complex roles of bishops, the Vatican, established religious orders, and apostolic vicars on the missions, and the arguments that apparently swayed the officials in Propaganda Fide to grant a territory to the Columbans. In the preaching and publications used to establish the new mission, evangelical motives such as the call of Christ to teach all nations and the example of Irish missionary saints were mixed with invitations to restore 'the Irish Ireland of her ancient glory' that owed more to the myths of nationalism. This book assesses the impact of both on British and Roman authorities, on the formation of young missionaries, and in the magazine set up in 1918 to generate support from Roman Catholics in Ireland, America and Australia. The rapid evolution of the society between 1917 and 1925 is tracked by comparative analysis of the successive editions of the constitutions.

Columbans arrived in China in 1920 and the last foreign missionary was expelled in 1954. Propaganda assigned three missions in China to the society: Hanyang in 1919, Nancheng in 1927, and Huchow 1946. Given the many similarities in the physical and political context of each place, and the transfer of missionaries from Hanyang to the other two districts, it seemed convenient to do a little violence to the chronology and treat all three in successive chapters. Each chapter will include an introduction, the political and ecclesiastical context, an account of the development of the mission, and a conclusion. The main focus will be on the model of evangelisation followed in each of the three jurisdictions, the means and helpers employed, and the obstacles encountered. Parish-type structures, sacraments, catechesis, and schools, staffed by priests, sisters, brothers, teachers and catechists, were key elements in the traditional Roman Catholic approach to mission. This study examines to what extent the Columbans in each of the three jurisdictions found that Roman model beneficial or a hindrance.

Canon law obliged a parish priest to exercise the care of souls towards all his parishioners; he must regard 'non-Catholics' living in his parish as commended to him by the Lord. This 'territorial imperative' placed an enormous burden on the Roman Catholic missionary and raises the question whether there were not better ways than the constant travel in huge, scattered parishes to serve those who were already members of the church, while also searching for new entry points to reach those outside. Schools were problematic, especially when the government restricted religious instruction, and the book compares the approaches of Columbans in each mission.

The needs of women and the role of religious sisters were special questions for members of an exclusively male organisation. Protestant societies appointed single women missionaries as early as 1832.[35] This enquiry examines the behaviour and attitudes of a group of Roman Catholic priests, asking whether they recognised women with religious vows as equal partners in mission or relegated them to tasks 'that were especially reserved for women … education, medicine, and evangelism'?[36]

Propaganda Fide guided the work of missionaries and this book attempts to outline and assess its directives, the interventions of nuncios, and the reaction both of the Columban central administration and of the men in the

---

35. Moffett, *A history of Christianity in Asia*, p. 328.
36. Li Li, 'Christian women's education in China in the nineteenth and early twentieth centuries', Salem State College (http://www.samford.edu/lillyhumanrights/Li_Christian.pdf) (21 Mar. 2007).

field. In particular, it attempts to understand the instruction to pastors to remain with their flocks in time of danger.

Roman Catholic missionaries, according to Pope Benedict XV in 1919, could say that they had 'successfully completed their work and that the church had been thoroughly well founded' when 'there exists a sufficient number of indigenous clergy'.[37] Accordingly each chapter asks what success the Columbans had in forming students for the priesthood.

The sixth, seventh and eighth chapters deal with missions in three very different countries: the nominally Roman Catholic Philippines, a predominantly Buddhist Korea, and the northernmost province of Burma where the majority were animist. This study analyses the role played by church officials in assigning each mission to the Columbans, going on to explore the context, development, and results in each place, and asking if the great variety of contexts demanded innovations. It enquires how the missionaries responded to problems such as the poverty of the local people and the limited financial assistance available from the society, or the restrictions placed on Roman Catholic schools by governmental policy or by interference from Protestant missionaries. There were already local Roman Catholic priests and sisters in the Philippines and Korea when the Columbans arrived, although they were too few to meet the needs of the church. In Burma there were no Kachin priests. This book examines the responses of members of the society whether in forming a local clergy or in helping other ministers of the gospel to emerge.

---

37. Benedict XV, *'Maximum illud'* in *AAS*, xi (Rome, 1919), p. 445.

CHAPTER TWO

Foundation of the Columban Fathers, 1916-20

Millions of Chinese to be won for Christ! That was the prize that enchanted a small group of Irish priests in 1916. This chapter will explore the foundation of the Missionary Society of St Columban, the men who founded it, and their vision. It will examine the theology of mission and the missionary experience of the two main shapers of the new movement, and trace the influence of that theology and experience on the means they chose to achieve their vision. It will outline the key events of the first four years of the new mission, the actions of the founders and of those who helped them, and the obstacles they met or imagined, as all these influenced the development of the original vision and means.

The Founders
Seven Irish secular priests were the prime movers in initiating the Society of St Columban. Edward Galvin (1882-1956) was the first to go to China, in 1912, and from July 1913 wrote many, long letters to attract others to join him. Two accepted the challenge, joining him in China in 1915, Joseph P. O'Leary (1891-1974) and Patrick O'Reilly (1880-1942). A classmate of O'Leary, Edward J. McCarthy (1890-1957), was also interested and corresponded frequently with both Galvin and O'Leary, as they hammered out proposals for a dynamic, new mission. John Blowick (1888-1972), a professor of dogmatic and moral theology in St Patrick's College, Maynooth since 1914, was attracted and made plans to go to China in a few years' time. According to Blowick's notes John Henaghan (1881-1945), a priest in the archdiocese of Tuam, 'frequently thought of Father Galvin away out in China all alone, praying before the tabernacle in a lonely, pagan village', while the seventh, James Conway (1892-1977), joined the group on an impulse when he was almost killed by a horse. All were young, the oldest, O'Reilly, being thirty-six when they began the mission in 1916, and Conway, the youngest, only twenty-four years of age.

Irish awareness of China before 1916
There seems to have been little awareness of China among the majority of

Irish Roman Catholics at the beginning of the twentieth century. Newspapers published in Dublin were filled with news of the World War and local politics. The appointment by the government of the Chinese Republic of Tai Che Tcheng Ling as Minister to the Holy See was reported in the *Freeman's Journal*.[1] Readers of the *Times* of London were better informed about affairs in the Orient, from President Yuan Shih-kai's dream of a monarchy[2] to Japan's demands on China, and the murder of British missionaries. But reports on topics of a financial nature, about railways, mines, river navigation, and loans, were the most common. Articles on 'the missions', including China, appeared in *St Joseph's Sheaf*, the quarterly organ of St. Joseph's Young Priests' Society first published in 1895. The society supported the education of poor Irish students who wished to become priests. A number of these men entered the Vincentian order and, beginning in 1921, went to China. Another Vincentian, Anthony Boyle, spiritual director in St Patrick's College, Maynooth, appealed in the *Irish Catholic* in 1910 for funds for the education of Chinese priests and from then until 1923 reported regularly with accounts of money sent to bishops and their letters of thanks. Children were encouraged to give their pennies to the Pontifical Society of the Holy Childhood to save abandoned babies and some adults read articles from missionaries in the *Annals of the Propagation of the Faith*. Yet even priests knew little of China:

> We had read of her Emperors and Empresses, and had gathered a number of ideas – largely erroneous – of the customs and characteristics of her people from books written by foreigners, who resided in the Concessions or the Treaty Ports.[3]

Members of the clergy who subscribed to the *Irish Ecclesiastical Record* found mainly articles on the church in the western world. The only references to China in the first decade of the twentieth century were a letter of the Pope, Pius X, thanking the emperor, Kuang-hsü, for his gifts on the occasion of the Pope's seventieth birthday, and the announcement of the creation of the new vicariate of Kientchang [Ningyuan] in Szechwan province.

John M. Fraser

An important article, 'Prospects of the Catholic Church in China', by John M. Fraser, published in September 1911,[4] marked a new phase of information

---

1. *Freeman's Journal*, 12 July 1918.
2. *Times*, 14 Sept. 1915.
3. John Blowick, 'A new chapter of missionary history' in *The Far East*, i (Jan. 1918), p. 13.
4. John M. Fraser, 'Prospects of the Catholic church in China' in *IER*, xxx (1911), p. 277.

on China. Fraser (1877-1962), a Canadian secular priest, educated in Genoa and influenced by reading the lives of missionaries martyred in China, received permission from his archbishop to go to Ningpo, Chekiang in 1902. In 1911 he visited America, Italy and Ireland, looking for priests and money, and especially for a man who would set up a missionary seminary to supply priests for China.

Fraser used the extreme language of the period to describe the Chinese as 'idolaters'. After outlining the political and social changes in China he wrote:

> It was in Ningpo [Ningbo] that I saw, for the first time, a person committing the sin of idolatry. It was an old woman prostrating herself with great reverence before an ugly idol. I shall never forget the feeling that came over me – I was nauseated.

The statue was probably that of the Buddha, but for Fraser it was only 'an ugly idol'. He went on to appeal for missionaries to rescue the four hundred million Chinese 'from folly during life and hell after death.' No matter that he could describe them as a religious people, 'simple, honest people, having but one wife, and working from morning to night for the support of their families,' their natural virtues merely gave 'great hopes of their future conversion'. All were damned unless hundreds of Catholic priests went to rescue them. Christian missionaries of other churches were of no avail. They were 'emissaries of Satan … sowing the seed of perdition in this vast vineyard of the Lord.'

There was a sharp contrast between the theology held and preached by priests and the deeper teaching of the church. An axiom, 'Outside the church there is no salvation,' dating back to St. Cyprian (210-258), had a controlling influence, and was generalised to damn to hell all who did not believe in Christ. Yet the theology textbooks common in seminaries in the early twentieth century, such as Adolphus Tanquerey,[5] taught clearly that those inculpably outside the church could be saved. Tanquerey quoted Pope Pius IX, who in 1854 explained:

> Those who are afflicted by ignorance of the true religion, if such ignorance is invincible, have no fault in this matter before the eyes of God.

A few years later, in 1863, the same Pope reminded the Italian bishops that those who through no fault are ignorant of the Catholic faith, yet are 'ready to obey God, and live a moral and good life', will not suffer eternal punish-

---

5. Adolphus Tanquerey, *Synopsis theologiae dogmaticae* (3 vols, Tournai, 1905), i, pp 556-557.

ment, but 'can come to eternal life'.[6] That surely applied to the 'simple honest people' of China.

The Chinese Rites controversy
The contentious issue of idolatry in China, still nauseating Fraser in 1911, had disrupted the peace of the church since the Jesuit, Matteo Ricci, in 1600, had attempted to show that Chinese rites venerating Confucius and the ancestors of the family could be purely civil acts. While that may well have been true for the literati of the imperial civil service, Dominican and Franciscan missionaries, working among the common people, saw all such rites as superstitions and reported the matter to Rome in 1643. A sometimes acrimonious argument continued for the next hundred years. The Jesuits referred the question to the Emperor K'ang-hsi, who, in 1692, confirmed their interpretation of the rites as purely civil acts. But in 1704 Clement XI and the Congregation of Rites forbade acts of honour of Confucius and veneration of ancestors.[7] Further edicts confirmed the 1704 decision. However, one of Galvin's companions in China, Joseph O'Leary, disagreed, arguing that Christian missionaries should follow the method adopted by St. Patrick who 'respected the existing civilisation, Christianised it without introducing a new one'.[8] There were, O'Leary thought, a number of religious beliefs in China on which Christianity could build, among them:

> The belief in an incarnation, in a goddess who is called a 'Queen of Mercy,' in the power of Satan especially at birth, in the immortality of the human soul, a punishment and reward after death, and the power of the living to help and offer sacrifice for the dead … [and] a high code of morality.

These could be combined into one body of truths, purified, and elevated by Christianity. In general, Roman Catholic missionaries working in China were genuinely interested in accommodating the Christian faith to Chinese customs, while still obeying the ruling of Clement XI. Some had a ceremony in which Christian tablets, inscribed with words of the Emperor K'ang-hsi, were erected in the home of new Christians in place of the tablets to the ancestors. K'ang-hsi's inscription read:

> The true Cause of all things, the first Creator; without beginning,

---

6. Pope Pius IX, '*Quanto conficiamur moerore*' (1863) in Denzinger, *Enchiridion symbolorum*, p. 453.
7. Columba Cary-Elwes, *China and the cross* (London, 1957), p. 152.
8. Joseph P. O'Leary, 'Chinese superstitions' in *The Far East*, i (Feb. 1918), p. 14.

without end, Who made heaven, earth, angels, men and all things; Omnipotent, Omniscient, All-good, the true Lord and Master.

The controversy concerning Chinese Rites was finally resolved by an instruction, *Plane compertum est,* of the Congregation for the Propagation of the Faith in 1939 permitting Christians to take part in ceremonies in honour of Confucius as an act honouring a great man, and to bow before the dead or even their tablets.[9] Paul Yu-Pin, Archbishop of Nanking gave a Chinese reaction to the controversy:

> For the church to strike at these two institutions by forbidding certain ceremonies of respect to ancestors and prohibiting the usual salutations in honour of Confucius, was, in the eyes of the Chinese, an attempt to destroy our culture.[10]

John Blowick

The question of 'pagans', and the practice of idolatry, were still emotive items in June 1911 when Fraser gave a talk in St Patrick's College, Maynooth. Among the students who heard him were John Blowick, Joseph O'Leary, Edward J. McCarthy and James Conway. He made a huge impact on, among others, Blowick, who in a paper read to the Catholic Truth Society in 1917 related:

> He forced us to realise that China was a pagan nation, that priests were so few as to as to be practically powerless in their efforts to cope with the enormous task they had set themselves – the Catholicising of China.[11]

Blowick was ordained in 1913 and appointed to the Junior Chair of Dogmatic Theology in Maynooth in May 1914 (Plate 2.1). He continued to agonise about the needs of the Chinese, which may explain why in the *IER* of September 1916 he wrote an article, '*Extra Ecclesiam Nemo Salvatur*' – 'No one is saved outside the church'. The occasion of his essay was a discussion in the *IER* on whether, in canon law, it was ever lawful to celebrate Mass for a dead heretic, to which the answer was:

> The general rule, therefore, is that it is unlawful to offer Mass for the repose of the souls of those who have died members of heretical sects. The principle which seems to underlie this general regulation is that

---

9. Petrus Fumasoni-Biondi, '*Plane compertum est*' in *AAS* (Rome, 1940), vol. vii, pp 24-26.
10. Paul Yu-Pin, 'Christian influence in post-war China' in *Pagan Missions*, xx (June, 1947), p. 44.
11. John Blowick, 'The Maynooth mission to China' in *The Catholic Truth Annual* (Dublin, 1917), p. 42.

the subjective state of heretics, just as of others who are guilty of a violation of her laws, is presumed by the church to correspond to their objective position, and objectively heretics are living in a state of sin …unless there are positive and probable signs that he has lived *bona fide* in heresy …

Both Pius IX and Jeremiah Kinane, the canonist in the *IER*, agreed that the Catholic Church is the true church founded by Christ, yet the Pope would appear to have been more realistic than canon law in allowing that a Protestant might be genuinely ignorant of the validity of Catholic arguments, and by living in good faith, come to eternal life.

Blowick proposed to discuss the fate of those who die outside the church, but after his first paragraph there was no further mention of the members of other Christian churches. Instead he turned to his main interest which was 'all unbaptised persons'. He accepted two seemingly conflicting principles: that Christ founded a visible, external society for the salvation of the human race, and that the Catholic Church is that society, making membership of the church necessary for salvation; and on the other hand 'the universality of a serious divine will to save all human beings.' The problem was how to reconcile these two statements. Baptism is the sacrament of entry into the church, and those who are not baptised are not members of the church. How, then, can God have a serious will to save all? The Council of Trent in 1547 considered the problem of the salvation of unbaptised people, stating that:

> … the transfer … to the state of grace and adoption of sons … after the promulgation of the gospel, cannot happen without the washing of regeneration [baptism] or the desire for it.

But such an act of desire was impossible for infants, and after reviewing the opinions of theologians on the point, Blowick concluded that we just have 'to confess our ignorance as to the precise manner in which he puts his design [to save all] into execution'. Turning to unbaptised adults, Blowick wrote that to have the necessary, if unconscious, desire for baptism they must at least believe that God 'exists and that he rewards those who seek him.' Such faith was possible for Jews and Muslims, due to the revelations to be found in the Old Testament and the Qur'an. Even those he called 'primitives' might have such faith, because of 'the remnants of a divine revelation once made to the man who was their first ancestor and ours'. However, atheists and pantheists who through their own fault did not believe in a personal god, would be punished in hell, and:

If there be, then, *bona fide* atheists they shall never gaze upon the infinite beauty of God, face to face, but they will probably be the companions of those infants who die without the saving laver of regeneration.

In this final sentence of his article Blowick consigned unbaptised children and *bona fide* atheists to Limbo. It seems reasonable to interpret his 'atheist and pantheist' as including many of the people of China, since in the theology of his time educated Confucians and Buddhists were thought to be atheists, and Taoists were pantheists. He hoped to go to China to save some of them.

Edward J. Galvin in China, 1912-16
Having aroused such ferment in John Blowick, John M. Fraser proceeded to recruit Edward J. Galvin for mission in China. Galvin, a young Irish priest on loan to the diocese of Brooklyn, was already thinking of going as a missionary and saw the series of events that had led him to Brooklyn, and to his meeting with Fraser in January 1912, as the guidance of Providence. Even so, his instant decision to go with the Canadian priest to China, 'with the hope of saving the souls for which Christ died,' was remarkable. Two months later the two priests arrived in Shanghai on their way to Hangchow (Figure 2.1) in the vicariate of Western Chekiang.

But the situation Galvin found in China was very different from what his reading in the Brooklyn Public Library had led him to expect. His time was taken up by caring for the existing groups of Catholics, with no time for reaching out to others. 'Of the pagans I know very little, beyond this that they are very polite.'

> Our Vicariate is almost as large as Ireland and we have only twenty missionary priests. The pagan population is eleven million ... We have about eleven thousand Catholics and probably two thousand catechumens ... You can readily see how miserably small the number of our priests is when you take into account that our Catholics are scattered through an immense territory.[12]

The few French Vincentians, with a handful of Chinese priests, were already unequal to the task, and Galvin foresaw a large falling off in the numbers of priests from France due to a series of anti-clerical laws passed by the government in Paris between 1901 and 1905. Since 'all the houses of the Lazarists [Vincentians] are closed except the mother house in Paris and a

---

12. Edward J. Galvin to Malachy Eaton, 20 July 1913 (CFCA, G-1:2).

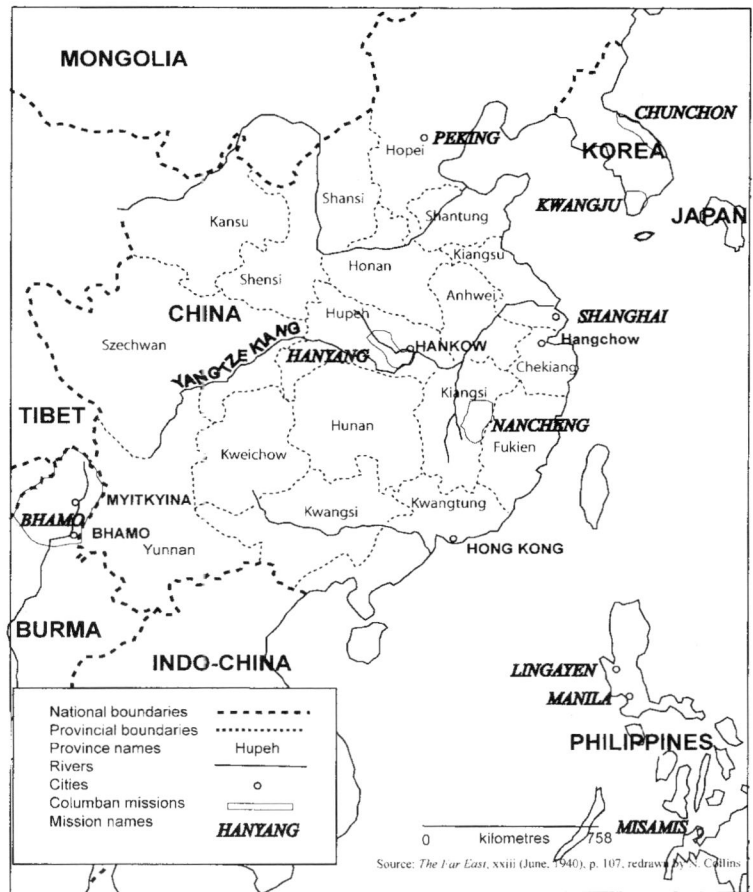

Figure 2.1 *Columban missions in Asia 1920-38*. Edward J. Galvin went to Chekiang in 1912. The Congregation for the Propagation of the Faith invited the Missionary Society of St Columban to go to Kweichow in 1918, but Galvin persisted in asking for a populous province such as Hupeh, preferably including the city of Hankow.

house in Dax,' there would be fewer vocations for their order, and for the missions. When many French priests were called home in 1914 to serve in the army in the First World War the personnel situation became even more desperate.

Galvin's concept of mission centred on the role of the priest, as minister of the sacraments and of the word of God, and helped by auxiliaries such as nuns and catechists. Canon law laid down pastoral methods which were essentially the same the world over. The parish priest was charged with administering baptism and the other sacraments, with preaching the

Catholic faith,[13] and with the catechetical instruction of the Christian people, whether by himself or by 'pious lay people.' Converts, Galvin found, were attracted by the church ceremonies and by the lives of the people:

> Our converts generally come at first to the church to hear the sermons, then they begin to enquire about the church and finally to be admitted to the catechumenate. Sometimes a few are converted in a village, and soon the whole village follows their example. That case is rare. Many are brought to the church by the good lives and example of our Catholics.

However, Galvin's work in China was beyond anything he had experienced in Brooklyn. Parishes were huge, 'equal in size to a home diocese'. In the neighbouring vicariate Fraser and a Chinese priest were looking after an incredible 'one thousand towns and villages'. One priest would remain in the parish centre while the other would go out for a month, visiting mission stations, staying a day or two in each place.[14]

> Unfortunately he cannot visit them very often, perhaps once or twice a year. You can easily see how little a priest can do during a stay of a few days. There may be a hundred or two hundred Catholics and perhaps the same number of catechumens. Their people have only a faint idea of their religion. Most of them can neither read nor write.[15]

Since most parts of the sacraments were in Latin and incomprehensible to the people the priest had to spend much of his visit preaching and teaching both the Catholics and the catechumens who were preparing for baptism. Confession, which is largely a dialogue, in Chinese, between priest and penitent, would show him how successful his teaching had been.

> I stayed in that place four days, had the Catholics recite their catechism, heard one hundred and thirty confessions, had one hundred and eighty communions, preached before Mass and again at night prayers (about 7.00 p.m.). I visited every family within a radius of three miles, saw the homes of the catechumens and made sure there were no idols hanging around, talked, laughed, told stories and drank tea.

Since the people were illiterate they learned their catechism by chanting the questions and answers together led by a catechist, in many cases without

---

13. *CIC* (Rome ,1919) canons 462, 1327 and 1333.
14. Edward J. Galvin to Maynooth students, 1915 (CFCA, G-3:17).
15. Edward J. Galvin to Sister Stanislaus Desmond, 15 July 1914 (CFCA, G-3:7).

comprehension. However, the priest had to encourage them by listening to their recitation. The confessions which followed must have taken Galvin hours as he conscientiously tried to ensure even a minimum of faith and understanding. Communions at that time were commonly before and after Mass rather than an integral part of the eucharist. The priest also checked that catechumens had removed all 'idols' from their homes. These might be simply tablets to their parents or statues of a god. General pastoral practice demanded that they be thrown out.

Proper religious formation became one of the themes in the letters which, from July 1913, Galvin wrote to priests, sisters and students in Ireland and in America. In a typical report in December 1914 he lamented the little knowledge of religion, the inadequacy of catechists, and the special difficulties faced by women:

> In all these chapels most of the Catholics are men. Very few of the women are baptised. The men can read a little. The women not a word. They find it difficult, bound up as their feet are, to walk to the chapel. In the home the mother is always busy and can't study.

During a visit to one mission station an old woman approached him, wanting to go to confession in preparation for receiving communion. Galvin began:

> Very well, we will run over the catechism together. Now tell me what do you receive when the priest gives you Communion. She thought a little. A piece of bread she said. I explained as well as I could but she didn't seem able to follow very clearly. She didn't know when the bread was changed into the Sacred Body and Blood of Our Lord.

Normally in confession the woman would have requested a blessing, confessed her sins, and made an act of repentance for them, but in the special situation of China Galvin felt he had to check if she understood what she was doing. Since she was confessing before communion, he asked her about both sacraments. She understood neither. For her the Eucharist, which for Catholics is the body and blood of Christ, was only a piece of bread.

The question of clerical numbers was, for Galvin, the main problem. There were too few priests, and he set himself the task of recruiting more, from Ireland. Beginning in July 1913 he sent a barrage of long letters, up to fourteen pages each, and as many as twelve in a day,[16] to seminaries, and to priests who could spread the message of the needs of the church in China.

---

16. Edward J. Galvin to James O'Connell, 1 Nov. 1913 (CFCA, G-1:3).

He laid special emphasis on English-speaking priests because he saw schools and colleges where English was taught as an important means of reaching out to non-Christians. The French missionaries had colleges, but could not teach English.

> The business language of the East is English. Our priests don't know it …The Protestants have a flourishing College where English is well taught and they have crowds of students. Think of the influence that gives them with the better classes who will afterwards have so much say in shaping the Republic.

His argument about the effect of Protestant education was prophetic and in the 1931 *Who's Who in China* thirty-five percent had been educated in Protestant schools and colleges.[17] The massive stream of letters was effective and in the middle of 1914 he could tell his mother:

> Things here are moving ahead fast. Money is coming in pretty well and I have many letters from priests and students looking for information about China. I never thought I would do so well.

Proposal for an Irish vicariate in China
At the end of 1915 two priests arrived, Patrick O'Reilly and Joseph O'Leary, and in the months that followed, even though O'Leary was assigned 150 miles from the others, they carried on an intense discussion on how to ensure a steady flow of priests for China. O'Leary's friend and classmate, Edward J. McCarthy, joined in the argument by letter, and in April 1916 wrote to O'Leary to send Galvin home to start 'a Chinese mission college in Ireland for an Irish vicariate' in China. A vicariate is an ecclesiastical territory not yet erected into a diocese, usually because it has not enough priests of its own. Only the Holy See could set up a vicariate or name the vicar apostolic to lead it. However, any bishop had the power to set up a mission college, though he must consult Rome. Two American priests, Thomas F. Price and James A. Walsh, founded a seminary in the US for foreign missions in 1911. They gained the approval and support of the archbishops of America in April 1911, and of the apostolic delegate, Diomede Falconio, in May, with the result that Gerolamo Gotti, prefect of Propaganda, gave the project his approval in July.[18] The three Irish missionaries in Hangchow decided that Galvin should follow the American example and go to Ireland 'to get the Irish bishops to sanction the project of establishing an Irish Vicariate with an Irish bishop'.

---

17. *Who's who in China* in Bob Whyte, *Unfinished encounter* (London, 1988), p. 133.
18. Gerolamo Gotti to William Gibbons, 3 July 1911 (AP, Vol. 601, p. 202).

The emphasis on an Irish vicariate came from Edward J. Galvin's impatience with the ways of the French. In 1919 Benedict XV had criticised missionaries in China, many of them French, for keeping Chinese priests as 'a lower class' with 'no bishops to govern nor priests to teach their own countrymen', and for promoting 'the business of their own country' rather than the kingdom of Christ.[19] But Galvin's letters from China mention only the problems arising from the recall of priests at the beginning of World War I, the lack of English language in Catholic colleges, and poor catechetical formation. It is in his correspondence on his journey home that more outspoken criticism appears. The French in Japan were 'slow, stick-in-the-mud', and looked down on Japanese priests. Priests in Canada told him that French bishops were 'trying to force wearing soutane at all times, just like in China', and that 'Catholics are never visited'. But most remarks are general, like those of the priests in Chicago who 'all spoke of French difficulty and even said what we wanted was an Irish diocese'. An Irish vicariate, headed by an Irish bishop, would be able to introduce 'Irish' methods like the ones Galvin had known in Brooklyn, with smaller parishes, more priests, schools where English was taught, and properly trained and supported catechists. 'Priests in bundles and Sisters galore is my conviction.'

America was probably not included in Galvin's plan for an Irish mission when he left Shanghai for Ireland in June 1916, other than as providing financial support. He travelled via the US because the First World War made the European routes unsafe. But as he talked to priests in San Francisco, Chicago and Brooklyn about his ideas they assured him, 'An Irish diocese for China will strongly appeal to every priest of Irish blood all over the world'. He met some women who were thinking of going to China and he encouraged them, realising that he needed American priests and sisters if the mission was to be successful in the US. His vision was still of an Irish mission, but it was expanding, as his own emphases make clear:

> ... some way must be thought out TO BIND Ireland, America and Australia together in this work. Ireland has the vocations. Australia and US have the funds and some vocations too. We must not confine it within the four seas of Ireland but try to make it the work of the Irish race ... both now and in the future most of the assistance will come from the Irish abroad and they must be BOUND CLOSELY to us.[20]

---

19. Benedict XV, '*Maximum illud*' in *AAS*, xi (Rome, 1919), pp 445-447.
20. Edward J. Galvin to Joseph O'Leary, 16 Aug. 1916 (CFCA, G-1:33).

Galvin was well aware that he might be accused of poaching vocations and support from the new Catholic Foreign Mission Society of America at Maryknoll, New York. One of his advisers, Dr Peter Yorke, warned him not to speak about his plans to anyone in New York, and to be especially careful of James A. Walsh, co-founder of Maryknoll. Yet he realised that, given the extreme poverty of China, the Irish vicariate needed financial support, which could not come from Ireland alone.

Appeal to the Irish hierarchy
Galvin's most urgent concern was to gain the support of his own bishop in Cork, Dr Daniel Cohalan, as well as that of influential Irish churchmen like Monsignor James MacCaffrey, vice-president of Maynooth, and Michael Logue, Cardinal-Archbishop of Armagh. On arrival in Dublin in August 1916, after a brief call on Thomas Ronayne, a priest who had been writing to him in China, he went straight to Cork, where he told the bishop of the situation in China and of his plans. He described the meeting for Joseph O'Leary, still in China:

> I opened up to him re affairs. LISTENED ATTENTIVELY. Sad at things, but when I made the proposal he jumped at it, caught it up and started to say how, when, where, and what should and could be done. [Punctuation added]

The bishop was so impressed by the 'sad' state of China, and by Galvin's proposal that he gave him an enthusiastic letter of introduction to Cardinal Michael Logue, the leader of the Roman Catholic Church in Ireland, in which he outlined the proposal for an Irish vicariate in China and a college in Ireland. Early in September Galvin could send a letter, telegraphic with excitement, to O'Leary:

> Saw Mickey [the Cardinal]. Said good work. Suggested committee of representative priests be formed. McCaffrey's idea too.[21]

Clearly the cardinal recognised that Galvin was practically unknown to the Irish bishops and priests, even though McCarthy had published his letters from China in *The Irish Catholic*, hence the suggestion of a committee of priests representative of various dioceses, to draw up a proposal to the Roman Catholic hierarchy. An impressive group composed of men from the four ecclesiastical provinces of Ireland, and headed by the Bishop of Cork, met on 2 October 1916 and drafted a lengthy document, outlining the needs

---

21. Edward J. Galvin to Joseph O'Leary, 8 Sept. 1916 (CFCA, G-1:37).

of the church in China, the interest of a number of priests in working there, and the generous contributions Ireland had been making in recent years for the education of Chinese priests, before proposing that the bishops take steps to establish an Irish vicariate in China, and a mission house in Ireland to supply priests for it.

The bishops needed assurances that there were already enough volunteers to form the basis of a permanent structure. A Maynooth Mission to India in 1838 had failed because there was no organisation at home to guarantee a steady supply of priests.22 John M. Fraser, in 1911, had proposed a college for China, and Cardinal Logue had even offered him a house, but there was no one to establish and run a seminary and the project came to nothing. While still in China, Galvin thought that either Monsignor James MacCaffrey or Malachy Eaton might resign their positions in Maynooth to head the new mission. At his first meeting with Thomas Ronayne in August 1916 he told him what he needed:

> He wants a man of position, a man whom the bishops will support and back by practical approval, to come forward as head of the whole affair.

Ronayne had good news for him, for John Blowick was thinking of going to China. The leader of the organisation had been found. In the first weeks of September Henaghan and Conway joined the group and others showed great interest. There were plans for a 'paper' or magazine, to reach out to the people of Ireland. And McCarthy and Galvin were house-hunting in Dublin. The Bishop of Cork even suggested a name, 'The Maynooth Mission to China'.23 It seemed that the committee would have a solid proposal for the bishops when they met in Maynooth on 10 October 1916.

Fear is a surprising and persistent undercurrent in the documents dealing with the founding of the Society of St Columban. Galvin worried that the French in China would hear of his proposal for an Irish vicariate and, through their contacts in Rome, move to block it. When Eaton and Conway proposed 'The Irish Mission to China' as a more inclusive name for the society, Blowick was afraid to antagonise the Bishop of Cork, author of the name 'The Maynooth Mission to China'. Yet despite all their attempts to avoid creating opposition they offended the Roman Catholic Archbishop of Dublin, William J. Walsh (1841-1921), who felt that a college was being founded in his diocese behind his back.24 Blowick approached the archbishop, through his

---

22. Edmund M. Hogan, *The Irish missionary movement 1830-1980* (Dublin, 1990), p. 27.
23. Edward J. Galvin to Joseph O'Leary, 30 Sept. 1916 (CFCA, G-1:40).
24. Edward J. Galvin to Joseph O'Leary, 11 Oct. 1916 (CFCA, G-1:42).

secretary, Michael Curran, on 16 September 1916, giving a full account of the plans for the society, and saying that they were anxious to place the proposed college in Dublin. At the end of September he wrote to each bishop, outlining the scheme for a vicariate in China, suggesting that the necessary money could come from America, proposing a college in Ireland, and listing the names of the committee suggested by the cardinal. Archbishop Walsh responded on 3 October warning:

> Certainly no bishop who happens to know anything of the enormous difficulties brought upon the diocesan authority here by All Hallows College, until it was placed under the control of a recognised religious body, would think of allowing a similar community to set up in his diocese.[25]

Walsh became Archbishop of Dublin in 1885. Six years later he was faced with a rebellion among the staff of All Hallows College, founded by secular priests in 1842. The Irish bishops solved the problem by handing the college over to the care of 'a recognised religious body', the Vincentians, in October 1891.[26] The archbishop was hardly unreasonable in refusing to welcome an amorphous group like the Columbans. They, of course, planned to go through the canonical process, beginning as a society of diocesan right approved by a bishop, and eventually of pontifical right authorised by the Holy See, and a recognised religious body at either stage. Perhaps that is why the group of representative ecclesiastics, in presenting its memorial to the Standing Committee of the Bishops on 9 October 1916, mentioned that there were two or three houses in the Terenure district of Dublin which could serve as a mission house. Apparently the archbishop was furious. According to Dr Patrick O'Donnell, Bishop of Raphoe, he immediately wrote to Cardinal Logue complaining that the Columbans proposed to enter the archdiocese of Dublin without his permission.[27] And it was among several objections he raised at the meeting of the Standing Committee. Patrick McSweeney, Professor of English in Maynooth, gave the bad news to Blowick who immediately wrote to Curran, the archbishop's secretary, reminding him of his visit to the archbishop's house on 16 September, and how he had given Curran a full account of the plans for the new mission. He went on to ask Curran to 'set the matter right as soon as possible'. Curran replied next day, saying that

---

25. William J. Walsh to John Blowick, 3 Oct. 1916 in Blowick, Longer notes , v, p. 21 (CFCA, P. 2).
26. Kevin Condon, *The missionary college of All Hallows 1842-1891* (Dublin, 1986), pp 167-190.
27. Blowick, Longer notes, v, p. 23.

he had told the archbishop all about the Chinese mission project on the day after Blowick's visit, but that Walsh had reacted to the committee's memorial by writing to the cardinal, who replied that he 'appreciated the archbishop's resentment at to the Terenure project being started without consulting him.' Remarkably Curran went on to assure Blowick:

> From beginning to end your name was never mentioned, nor are you the person held responsible for the omission.

If Blowick was not held responsible, who was? The most likely candidate is the Bishop of Cork, chairman of the preparatory committee.

The Standing Committee of the Roman Catholic Bishops met on 9 October 1916 and, Blowick believed, was at the point of rejecting the scheme for a new mission, mainly because of the points raised by the Archbishop of Dublin. However the Bishop of Raphoe, Dr Patrick O'Donnell, suggested that they invite Blowick to explain the situation in person. In his presentation Blowick asked for two things, permission to appeal throughout the country and to found a college for the Chinese missions. He made it clear that the Columbans would be subject to the bishop of the diocese where the college was located, and to the bishops in general. Having been warned of the mood of the meeting, he did not ask the bishops to use their influence in procuring a vicariate in China. In any event this would have been premature until such time as the society had enough men and money to staff it.

> However, after about half an hour's talk with the bishops the Cardinal said they were prepared to grant their approval for the two things which I had asked, namely, the making of a collection in the country and the foundation of a mission college in Ireland.

The memorial drawn up by the committee of prominent clerics was laid before the full body of the bishops on 10 October 1916 informing them that:

> ... a vigorous movement, of which the heart is Maynooth College, has grown up among young Irish ecclesiastics to go forth and carry the light of the gospel to the Chinese ... The bishops were rejoiced and thankful to God for this new and striking evidence of the continued life of the ancient Irish missionary spirit.[28]

After careful consideration the bishops approved the project and issued a statement to the press, drafted by the Bishop of Cloyne, Dr Robert Browne.[29]

---

28. Minutes of the general meeting of the Irish bishops, 10 Oct. 1916 (Archives of the Irish bishops, Mullingar).
29. *Irish Times*, 11 Oct. 1916. Cf. Appendix 1, p. 399.

Blowick regarded that statement as the foundation charter of the Society.

A nationwide collection was the first priority for Blowick and his four companions. Without money they could not buy or run a college. Galvin began the appeal in Cork on 22 October 1916. In early November, less than a month after the bishops' approval, McCarthy wrote to O'Leary:

> For the next two Sundays I and six or seven priests of Cork will preach in different parishes to give the people an interest in the movement ... Fr Blowick is in the Northern Province, Fr Conway in the East and Fr Hennegan [sic] in the West. Fr Galvin is a 'winger' at the back of every man who wants him for a special occasion with a flourish of trumpets.

For the next year the five were constantly on the move, assisted by professors from Maynooth,[30] priests from religious orders, and from almost every diocese in Ireland. As well as preaching, Blowick handled correspondence with bishops about the appeal, or acknowledging the donations that came pouring in, as well as letters to Michael O'Riordan, rector of the Irish College in Rome, who would help him in dealing with the Vatican. Many bishops devoted part of their Lenten pastorals to supporting the mission, typically reminding the people of the Irish missionaries of the sixth and seventh centuries, and of the Irish in the nineteenth century who had helped in building up the church in Britain, America and Australia, and of

> the countless millions of a mighty empire that still sits in the darkness of Paganism and the shadow of eternal death.

McCarthy, who had already shown his gifts as a propagandist in getting Galvin's letters from China published in *The Irish Catholic*, produced a lantern slide show and two or three sermons. He wrote to O'Leary:

> If you want money move their hearts and you can only do that by praising up the Irish Faith, getting sentimental about 'the wrongs of ould Ireland', putting a halo of glory and heroism about lads like you and Galvin, comparing your sacrifice to that of the patriots who died for Ireland.

Realising how cynical that sounded, he hastened to assure O'Leary that he was quite sincere about Irish faith and O'Leary's heroism. Such propaganda was effective and by May 1917 Galvin could predict that by the end of the year they would have £40,000. Even better news was that seventeen

---

30. Edward J. Galvin to Joseph O'Leary, 28 Jan. 1917 (CFCA, G-1:58).

priests and twelve students had volunteered, and that sisters were interested.[31] With money and volunteers flowing in it was time to set up a college, the second step in their plan to found a society to supply priests for China.

Negotiations with Rome, 1916-17
According to the Code of Canon Law of 1917 only a bishop has the power to found a religious congregation or society, and he must consult the Holy See. Consequently Cardinal Michael Logue forwarded the decision of the Irish bishops to the Vatican, through the hands of O'Riordan, rector of the Irish College, Rome. O'Riordan presented the letter in December 1916,[32] to the Congregation for the Propagation of the Faith, the body responsible for the missions of the Roman Catholic Church in places, like China, where the hierarchy had not yet been established. There was no response. In May 1917 O'Riordan sent a message to Blowick, 'Come out [to Rome] and come quickly'. Blowick later discovered that someone had reported to Rome that the new mission was merely an excuse for priests who didn't want to serve as chaplains in the British army:

> They said we weren't genuine missionaries at all. We were a bunch of Sinn Féiners who were providing a decent front for priests that didn't want to go to the army.[33]

Vatican officials appear to have believed also that the Sinn Féin party in Ireland was the same as the Bolshevists in Russia and, when Blowick and Galvin arrived in Rome on 12 July 1917, greeted them with the cry, '*Bolscevici*'. There were even rumours in Maynooth that Propaganda might take control of the project out of Irish hands. James MacCaffrey wrote to John Hagan, Vice-Rector of the Irish College, before Blowick and Galvin returned with the letters of approval:

> If the Propaganda insists on putting in an Italian or foreign superior the project is ruined. It appealed to the people as being an Irish National Mission and unless it remains that it will be disastrous. Urge that as strongly as you can.[34]

However, with the help of O'Riordan and Hagan, and 'commendatory letters' signed by Michael Logue, the two young priests convinced

---

31. Edward J. Galvin to Joseph O'Leary, 2 May 1917 (CFCA, G-1:72).
32. Michael O'Riordan to Propaganda, 24 Dec. 1916 (AP, Vol. 601, p. 26).
33. John Blowick, Talk to students, 1968, p. 11 (CFCA, P. 2, p. 11).
34. James MacCaffrey to John Hagan, 23 July 1917 (Archivio, Pontificio Collegio Irlandese, HAG1/1917/ 61).

Propaganda 'that the undertaking [was] *bona fide* and real'. Domenico Serafini, Prefect of the Congregation, gave them two letters for Cardinal Logue and the Irish bishops, one dated, fictitiously, 13 June 1917, welcoming the:

> ... founding in Ireland of a college for the Foreign Missions where young men called to the priesthood, may be trained by suitable discipline for apostolic work among infidel peoples.[35]

Benedict XV 'ordered [Serafini] to signify to you [Logue] his most cordial approval of it, and desired me to add in his name a wish that the new work might be started with alacrity'. Significantly the congregation, with its wider view of the needs of the church, changed the wording of the Irish bishops' proposal from 'a mission house or college for ... the propagation of the Catholic Faith in China' to 'a college for the Foreign Missions'. Monsignor Camillus Laurenti, the Secretary of the Congregation, told them to open the college immediately and to draw up a constitution for the society. A second letter to Cardinal Logue stated:

> As a consequence there is nothing to hinder a beginning being made from now in putting the project into execution, commencing with the erection of the college, under the guardianship of the Bishops, and especially the Ordinary of the place where the college is to be established. Care will be taken to draw up a provisionary scheme of rules and give the institution at its inception suitable organisation and solid discipline.[36]

The language suggests that Blowick told the congregation of the concerns of the Archbishop of Dublin for it spells out the canonical position of the proposed college as 'under ... the Ordinary [bishop] of the place where the college is to be established', as well as demanding that 'the institution' have 'suitable organisation'. To that extent it would be a recognised religious body and perhaps meet Walsh's objections. Accordingly a meeting of the committee of prominent ecclesiastics on 25 September 1917 instructed Blowick to write to the archbishop again requesting permission to establish the college in Dublin. Blowick summarised the Roman letters and, diplomatically, acknowledged that the archbishop's earlier objections were easily understood before presenting the request of the committee:

---

35. Congregation for the Propagation of the Faith to Michael Logue, 13 June 1917 in *AAS*, ix (1917), p. 395.
36. Domeneco Serafini to Michael Logue, 18 July 1917 in Blowick, Longer notes, v, pp 39-40.

But now that the Holy See has granted approval and has commanded the formation of a Society whose subjection to the diocesan authority has been clearly defined in Canon Law we take the liberty to approach Your Grace again in the belief that the difficulties which existed at the time the previous request was made have ceased to exist or, at least, will have ceased after the approval of the Constitutions.[37]

The final point in Blowick's letter was that the committee wished the college to be in Dublin for two reasons: to be near a university, and to be in or near the capital since the society had now assumed the nature of a national mission. A reply came from the archbishop, noting, with regret, that 'the project of the Chinese Mission … has not received the sanction of the Holy See', and remarking that he thought he had made it plain that he could not authorise the establishment of any college in his diocese.[38] Perhaps he meant the canonical approval of the Holy See which would make the mission a society of pontifical right, but this would be granted only after a number of years when the constitutions of the new society had been tested by experience. Archbishop Walsh continued to snipe at the society. Blowick quoted Michael Higgins, Auxiliary Bishop of Tuam, who told him that at the October 1917 meeting of the Roman Catholic Bishops Walsh claimed that the Columbans would be sent to Japan. 'They will not be sent to China, and if you want to know the reason, ask the Vincentians.' It may be that Walsh was quoting a Vincentian source here, for some members of that order were afraid that the Columbans would be given part of the vicariate of Monsignor Faveau, a Vincentian, where Galvin, O'Leary and O'Reilly had worked. Laurenti, the Secretary of the Congregation for the Propagation of the Faith, had indeed suggested to Blowick and Galvin, during their visit to Rome in July 1917, that the Columbans 'leave ourselves free to be sent to other places than China and he expressly mentioned Japan.' But at no stage did anyone in the congregation rule out a mission in China. When, in December 1919, Blowick remarked to Laurenti, that 'it was said at the beginning of our work by a prominent archbishop at a public meeting of the bishops that you would never let us go to China.' Laurenti interjected, 'Ah! Yes, Walsh … It's very sad.'[39] This suggests that the archbishop had no inside knowledge of the plans of the congregation, and that his objections came from pique rather than principle. But his opposition had a major impact on the development

---

37. John Blowick to William J. Walsh , 30 Sept. 1917 in Blowick, Longer notes, v, p. 41.
38. William J. Walsh to John Blowick, 4 Oct. 1917 in Blowick, Longer notes, v, p. 43.
39. Report of John Blowick and Edward J. Galvin, 7 Dec. 1919 (CFCA, CN A-1:21).

of the society since he prevented the Columbans from sending their students to a university.

A mission college

A college somewhere in Ireland was essential, both as the headquarters of the society and for the formation of students volunteering for China. As early as 9 October 1916 Canon James J. Ryan offered a house and land near Thurles, Co Tipperary, but when he added onerous conditions about payment of taxes, excluding future lease or sale, and even asking for shooting and fishing rights, the advisory committee turned down his offer. Other suggestions were considered by the committee. The Bishop of Cork offered a wing of the seminary at Farranferris from which students could attend University College, Cork, while for their theology, he suggested, they might be sent to Propaganda College, Rome, but the other members of the committee thought that:

> The sending of the students to an already existing college either in Ireland or abroad would have the effect of injuring the mission in the future by making the whole project less tangible and less concrete.

They resolved that there should be a distinctively Chinese Mission College in Ireland. Still other houses were considered, some belonging to landlords who refused to negotiate with priests. In October 1917 Galvin and Blowick inspected Dalgan Park, an old Georgian building with a large farm near Shrule, Co Galway. The location was wrong from several points of view: far from any university, twenty miles from Galway city and twelve miles from the nearest railway station but, wrote McCarthy, it 'was at the time the only suitable place we could find in Ireland.'[40] The property was leased on 10 December 1917, and the first students arrived on 29 January 1918. Thomas O'Dea, the Bishop of Galway, by a decree issued on 28 June 1918, and a religious ceremony on the following day, erected the Maynooth Mission to China as a diocesan society, with St Columban's College, Dalgan Park, as its headquarters.[41]

The new college had a curriculum similar to that of other seminaries, and students laboured at manuals, the neo-scholastic Latin textbooks that were in common use before Vatican II. In dogmatic theology they studied Adolphus

---

40. Edward J. McCarthy, 'Life of Father Henaghan', p. 6. (MS in Columban Archives, Omaha).
41. Thomas O'Dea, *Decretum*, 28 Jun. 1918 (Dublin Diocesan Archives, Walsh Papers (1919), 386/6).

Tanquerey, a systematic, internally coherent presentation of Catholic doctrine. Augustino Lehmkuhl, in moral theology, laid out the principles of a moral life, expounding the ten commandments and the duties connected to the different sacraments. These books were designed to produce priests who in preaching would give the doctrine of the Roman Catholic Church, and in hearing confessions would be prudent and compassionate guides. Rather than preparing missionaries who could meet and respect people of other faiths, the curriculum trained them for controversy with 'Christians living outside the Roman Catholic Church' who were regarded as 'adversaries'. Other religions were briefly described and then dismissed, for example Islam was not from God as it could not be said that Mohammed:

> ... was the legate of God: for he pretended to be pious, he was clearly ambitious, he used criminal slaughter, he was aflame with the most foul lust in polygamy and adultery. These all indicate with certainty that he was the herald, not of the holy God, but of the evil devil.[42]

The rigidity and dogmatism encouraged by such works was further strengthened by the oath against modernism required of all candidates for ordination:

> I ... firmly embrace and accept all and everything that has been defined, affirmed, and declared by the unerring *magisterium* of the church, especially those chief doctrines which are directly opposed to the errors of this time.

Yet Dalgan was a place of enthusiasm, drawing its inspiration from Irish nationalism, the missionary saints of the sixth to eighth centuries, and the heroism of penal times, expressed in the language of a new crusade for Christ. Many of the priests and students who came from Maynooth had belonged to the Irish-speaking 'Columban League' there.[43] Irish competed with English in daily conversation, and the rosary was recited in Irish. In his train journeys around Ireland in 1917 Blowick read Patrick Pearse's account of Scoil Éanna,[44] and when asked about the origin of the 'Dalgan Spirit', a blend of egalitarianism, sincerity and enthusiasm, said that it was simply putting that book into practice.[45] Pearse used 'the national factor' to inspire his pupils, because:

---

42. Adolphus Tanquerey, *Synopsis theologiae dogmaticae* (3 vols, Tournai, 1937), i, p. 382, '... non dicere licet eum fuisse Dei legatum: nam pietatem simulavit, ambitione claruit, fraudibus et caedibus criminosis usus est, foetidissima exarsit libidine in polygamia et adulterio'.
43. 'Another distinguished priest joins the Chinese mission', *The Far East*, ii (July 1919), p. 9.
44. Patrick Pearse, *The story of a success*, ed. Desmond Ryan (Dublin, 1917).
45. Frank Chapman, 'John Henaghan' in *Columban Intercom*, xx Oct. 1998, p. 103.

> ... it addresses itself to the most generous side of the child's nature, urging him to live up to his finest self. I think that the true work of the teacher may be said to be to induce the child to realise himself at his best and worthiest ...

By emulating models like Cúchulainn and the Fianna warriors of Irish mythology, and Robert Emmet, a United Irishman executed in 1803, the pupils would grow in a spirit of self-sacrifice, immense brotherly charity and loyalty. Similarly Blowick wanted Columbans to be generous idealists. In language reminiscent of St Columban's, 'At the first word of a senior, all on hearing should arise and obey',[46] the students' rules of Dalgan in 1917 stated:

> The Students shall obey with cheerfulness and promptness the Superiors placed over them in the College. They shall rise promptly at the given signal and attend punctually at the various exercises throughout the day.

Students were also to observe, in their relations with one another, the greatest charity and forbearance. A key idea in Pearse's educational programme was the role of the teacher as 'fosterer', to nurture the elements of character already present in the pupil, as had been done in the Ireland of the Fianna. For that he must know his pupils. In regulations drawn up in 1919 for the government of the college Blowick, reminding the staff how Christ called his disciples friends, charged them:

> ... to treat all students of the College with that respect, consideration and fraternal love which is calculated to develop their characters, to inspire loyalty and confidence and to cause them to take a personal interest in the welfare of the College and of the Society.[47]

Staff and pupils lived together, sharing the same food, with none of the distance that was common in other colleges. Since students could not play cards neither could the professors. For a while the staff even gave up smoking, as a good example for the students. Students would keep the rules, 'not to satisfy your own sense of honour but because this is God's will'. Professors would not supervise examinations, nor would they use punishments such as the 'clipping', the postponement of orders, then practised in St Patrick's College, Maynooth. Blowick attempted to make the students feel that they were joint-proprietors of the college and the society to the extent that some

---

46. Columbanus, '*Regula monachorum*' in G. S. M. Walker, *Sancti Columbani opera* (Dublin, 1970), p. 123.
47. Regulations for the government of St Columban's college (1919), p. 1 (CFCA, CA F-3).

even admitted to being homesick for Dalgan while on summer holiday with their family by the sea.

The Far East

The Far East, the magazine of the society, appeared first in January 1918. John Henaghan, the editor, inspired his readers with articles from missionaries in China, and with a stirring mixture of Irish nationalism and Catholic crusade. In his editorials he returned constantly to the identification between Irish, Catholic and missionary. Ireland, he said, 'must recover that ancient missionary spirit if she is really to be the Irish Ireland of her ancient glory.'[48] The very cover of the magazine in 1920 proclaimed the same message (Plate 2.3). A Celtic cross with Christ at its centre is surrounded by poor imitations of Celtic spiral decoration. On the arms of the cross are the names of Irish missionaries of the sixth to eighth centuries, Columbanus, Gall, Vergilius and Rumold. Above and below the arms are pictures of Patrick lighting the Easter fire on Slane, a grieving Columcille looking back to Derry, a priest at a penal Mass rock, and a Christ-figure pointing across the sea to the pagodas of China and bearing a banner with the text, in Latin, 'Go teach all nations'. Underneath are three texts: in Latin, 'To go on pilgrimage for Christ', attributed to St Columban; in English the words of Christ, 'The harvest is great but the labourers are few'; and in Irish, 'To the glory of God and the honour of Ireland.'[49] Embedded in the design are several of Henaghan's favourite themes, the golden age of Irish missionaries, the martyrs of penal times, and the call to modern missionaries to preach the gospel in China. Henaghan frequently used the language of crusade, describing the priests and students at the opening of the new missionary college on 7 February 1918 as:

> ... a bodyguard around the Person of Christ, an advance party to spy out the ground in this undying war to push the standard of the Cross into the farthest outposts of heathendom.

Like Fraser and Blowick he had a pessimistic view of the 'heathendom' that was China:

> That vast, restless mass of sweltering souls stretching out before us, rotting in sin, living, yet hardly living; the despair, the wretchedness, the misery; the dark rites amid the smoke of horrible sacrifices; the children doomed to suffering, even in their mothers' womb; the degrad-

---

48. See, for example, John Henaghan, 'Editorial' in *The Far East*, i (Apr. 1918), p. 1.
49. Front cover, *The Far East*, iii (Nov. 1920).

ation of the people, men, women and children; what a sight for men and angels.

Protestant missionaries were seen as a threat. One can almost hear Henaghan's envy in his description of the resources available to them, their schools, clinics and hospitals. Introducing the idea of a Catholic Student's Mission Crusade, he compared the lack of concern among Catholics with the activities of the Protestant Volunteer Crusade. Roman Catholic missionary magazines in the early years of the twentieth century regularly used the generosity shown by Protestants to stir up like support for Catholic missions. In an article entitled, 'Danger of the Protestant Propaganda', in the *Annals of the Propagation of the Faith* in 1920, the writer quoted from the annual report of the Society for the Propagation of the Faith in New York, 1915, showing a huge increase in Protestant missionaries from 1815 to 1915. From 175 men and no women in 1815 there were 25,000 men and 6,000 women in 1915. A year later the annals quoted from the *Catholic Bulletin* of Beijing:

> Let us not be either intimidated or discouraged at the thought of the vast funds at the disposal of Protestant Missionaries of which their journals so constantly boast.[50]

Henaghan trumpeted the superiority of Columban missionaries who stayed with their people during the Chinese Nationalist Revolution of 1927, while Protestants fled. Yet his vision was not limited to the myths of resurgent nationalism or the prejudices of his day. Central to the Celtic cross on the cover of *The Far East* was Christ, and in his editorials Henaghan followed the great feasts of the church year, from the 'unutterable tenderness of Bethlehem' to 'the fullest expression of his compassion and yearnings' on Calvary, challenging all, the student preparing to go to China and those who at home will, 'lend their support to the missions among pagan peoples'.

Founding a society
The cornerstone of Galvin's plan, to bind together an Irish vicariate in China and the college in Ireland, was, in the language of the canon law of 1917 'a society of men ... living in common without vows'.[51] There are five 'books' in the Code of Canon Law first published in that year, the second of which is entitled *De personis* and deals with the members of the church. This book is divided into three parts: on clerics, on religious, and a rather small section

---

50. 'Protestant aid in China', *Annals of the Propagation of the Faith*, lxxxiv (Dublin, 1921), p. 110.
51. *CIC,* Book II, Title XVII.

on the laity. Religious are members of religious orders and congregations who take public vows of poverty, chastity and obedience, while secular clergy do not. A society like the Columbans, 'a society of men living together without vows' is placed, rather oddly since they are secular priests and brothers, in the section dealing with religious. When Blowick and Galvin visited Rome in July 1917 in support of their proposal for an Irish vicariate in China and a college in Ireland, they went to the Congregation for the Propagation of the Faith. The Secretary of the congregation, Camillus Laurenti, instructed them to 'form themselves into a Society with a Provisional Constitution approved by the Irish Hierarchy'. He advised them to get copies of the constitutions of such foreign missionary societies as the Mill Hill Fathers. According to Galvin they visited Mill Hill and the Paris Foreign Missionaries. St Joseph's Society for Foreign Missions, Mill Hill, was founded by Fr Herbert Vaughan in 1866 and approved by Cardinal Wiseman.[52] *Les Missions Étrangères de Paris* (MEP) was formed by Frs Francois Pallu and Lambert de la Motte in 1658[53] and authorised by the Congregation for the Propagation of the Faith. The Columbans followed the same procedure as Mill Hill, in accordance with canon law. They submitted their constitutions to the Bishop of Galway for his approval, Dalgan Park being in his diocese. He, in turn, applied for permission to the Congregation for the Propagation of the Faith, since he was erecting a missionary group. His application included necessary information, the name of the originator of the new society, the motive that impelled him, the name of the society, the good works it was designed to do, and its means of support. Once erected by the bishop, the new body became a society of diocesan right. When it set up houses in other dioceses it came under the jurisdiction of the bishops there too, all of whom would have to approve any changes to the institution. Seven years later, in 1924,[54] when the constitutions of the society had been tested by experience and necessary changes made, the society applied for Roman approval or a 'decree of praise', and became a society of pontifical right.

Constitutions
The constitutions of a religious society set out its specific purpose, and guidelines for achieving it. While all Roman Catholics are bound to love God and

---

52. 'St Joseph's Missionary Society' at Mundus (http://www.mundus.ac.uk/cats/37/ 268.htm) (14 June 2004).
53. Raymond Rossignol, 'The Paris Foreign Missionaries' at The Paris Foreign Mission Society (www.rc.net/malaysia/collegegeneral/MEP.htm) (9 July 2004).
54. Council of directors, minutes of meetings (1917-1925), 7 June 1924 (Columban central house, Dublin).

their neighbour, and to follow the teaching of the church, the members of a religious body are called to do so in a particular way, whether by contemplation, in teaching or nursing, or as missionaries, depending on the special foundational grace or 'charism' of the group. Constitutions, typically, begin with the purpose, nature and spirit of the organisation, before legislating about qualifications for membership, methods of admission, formation, government, way of life, sickness and death, departure from the society, and mundane matters like personal possessions and society property.

Blowick and his companions were attracted by the ideals and structure of the Paris Foreign Missionaries. *La Société des Missions-Étrangères*, founded in 1658, was a society of secular priests,[55] and had as its main aim to accelerate the conversion of the 'pagans', not only by preaching the gospel, but above all by preparing suitable Christians to become priests:

> ... so as to form in each country a clergy and hierarchical order such as Jesus Christ and the apostles established in the Church.

In this the society was following the instruction given by the Congregation for the Propagation of the Faith to the vicars apostolic, Pallu and de la Motte, in 1659, 'to educate the youth so that qualified priests are provided and consecrated by you.' The society aimed at setting up, eventually, a church like that in France with dioceses each led by a bishop, and staffed by secular priests. That would involve sending priests from a seminary in Europe, until such time as there was an indigenous clergy. Since a bishop would govern each vicariate or diocese, the only other authorities that were seen to be necessary were the council of directors of the seminary in Paris. There was no superior general with authority over the entire society.

The Columbans followed the model of *La Société des Missions-Étrangères* in making their first constitutions. Blowick wrote to Galvin in September 1917:

> I am about to begin the drafting of the Constitutions and I think your assistance at every step is indispensable. Could you come here within the next few days?

He wanted all the members of the group to see and approve of the constitutions before they were sent to the Roman Catholic bishops at their meeting in October 1917. Titled, in the actual text, 'Provisional Constitutions of the Foreign Mission Society of Ireland', they were indeed very provisional. The society had two other editions, in 1918 and 1919, before the Cong-

---

55. *Règlement de la Société des Missions-Étrangères* (Rome, 1890), no. 23.

regation for the Propagation of the Faith made it a society of pontifical right and issued yet a fourth set of constitutions on 5 July 1925.[56] Even these were '*ad experimentum*', and some changes were made in the General Chapter of 1931, before the Congregation approved a definitive set on 14 March 1932.

Since Rome's approval of June 1917 was only for 'a college for the Foreign Missions', and not specifically for China, the first article of the 1917 constitutions stated that 'the end of the Society is, in general, the propagation of the gospel in pagan countries'. A letter from the Congregation for the Propagation of the Faith to Cardinal Logue in March 1918 announced that Benedict XV agreed that the new college should have the cultivation of the Chinese missions as its principal end, and a second edition of the constitutions, approved by the Bishop of Galway for the erection of the society on 29 June 1918, gave the name of the society as 'The Maynooth Mission to China'[57] and the principal end as 'the evangelisation of China'. The 1925 constitutions were edited in Rome by Fr Copere, a member of the Marist order, and added, 'besides the sanctification of the members' to the principal end. In service of the principal end special duties were laid down in the constitutions. The *MEP* had three special tasks, in order of importance, the formation of a local clergy, the care of the existing Christians, and the conversion of pagans.[58] Columbans adopted these in their 1917 constitutions, borrowing even the wording of the French society, but placing care of the existing Christians first. Both the *MEP* and the Columban constitutions outline a missionary strategy. The Paris Foreign Missionaries saw the setting up of a local clergy as the primary aim, since priests, by their own preaching and by formation of catechists, were the main agents of evangelisation, as well as being the ministers of the sacraments. Yet 'pagans' would be attracted by the lives of ordinary Christians, hence care of Christian families and communities was second only to the provision of priests. Galvin, however, intended 'to work more intensively', using schools and infirmaries, which would serve 'both pagan and Catholic and would make many converts'. Hence the 1918 Columban constitutions spoke of:

> ... the furnishing to these same Christians, as well as to the pagans,

---

56. *Constitutiones Societatis Sancti Columbani pro Missionibus apud Sinenses* (Dublin, 1932), p. 3.
57. Constitutions of the Maynooth Mission to China (1919), Ch. I, no. 1 (CFCA, CA F-3).
58. 'Voici, en conséquence, l'ordre des fins qu'ils doivent se proposer: i, dans les lieux où il y a déjà des chrétiens, former et élever à la cléricature les sujets qu'ils en trouveront capables; ii, prendre soin des chrétiens existants; iii, travailler àa la conversion des infidéles, en sorte qu'ils préferent, autant que les circonstances le permettront, le premier objet au second, et le second au troisième.' *Règlement de la Société des Missions-Étrangères*, Ch. I, no. 3.

primary and higher education; the founding and equipment of hospitals.

By 1925 the society was in some financial difficulties which may explain why the founding of hospitals was no longer mentioned.

The 1917-19 editions of the constitutions of the Columban Fathers state that 'the Society is not a religious order or congregation. Its members take no vows, but they take an oath ...' Blowick supported this in 1917 by adding a note:

> The Secretary of this Congregation [for the Propagation of the Faith] explained to us orally that vows are forbidden to members of the Society but that, to ensure solid organisation, all the priests should take an oath of the same nature as that taken by the members of the Foreign Missionary Society of Paris ...

Blowick even placed canons 673-681, those dealing with societies without vows, as a preface to the constitutions. In 1918 an article was added on cultivating 'the spirit of prayer, self-sacrifice, and the detachment which is becoming in apostolic missionaries ... [and] the spirit of charity as the distinguishing mark to the pagans and heretics among whom they work....' Obedience was inserted in this list in 1919, and members were asked to 'walk faithfully in the footsteps of their patron, Saint Columban, and of the great Missionary Saints of Ireland'. They were also, in accordance with the spirit of canon 125, to spend one half-hour daily in mental prayer, visit the Blessed Sacrament, and say the rosary. Prior to 1925 there was no special probation year for new members. Priests were not finally admitted to the society until they had proved themselves over three years, while for students the probation period lasted until their ordination. A spiritual year (for lay brothers it was two years) was introduced in 1925, the wording of the article borrowed straight from canon 565, on the novitiate of religious. The heart of the year was the spiritual exercises of St Ignatius of Loyola, a retreat lasting thirty days. At the end of the probation period each candidate who was considered suitable was aggregated by taking an oath binding him, in 1917:

> ... to remain ... in the Society; to undertake any office, mission or duty assigned to him by the Council of Directors or the Holy See, and to continue in such office, mission or duty till he is removed, recalled or changed by the Council or the Holy See.

In 1919 there was an additional clause:

... to obey any order of the Superior or of the Rector or Director to whose charge he is immediately committed, given in accordance with the Constitutions, or with the nature, purpose and spirit of the Society.

In the editions of the constitutions from 1917 to 1919 the member swore that he would stay in the society for life. A three-year period of temporary aggregation was introduced in 1925, and this could be extended for another year. Final aggregation, for life, followed. There seems to be some tension between the language of 1919, demanding obedience 'in accordance with the Constitutions,' a phrase which appears to place some limit on the authority of the superior, and that of 1925, where a chapter on the obligations of members lays down that:

In all matters that directly or indirectly, explicitly or implicitly, are covered by the Constitutions members of the Society are bound to give their Superiors the same kind of obedience that children in a family give to their parents. Hence the Superiors as God's representatives enjoy true authority; they can even give orders binding under pain of grave sin, but this power Superiors should use only rarely and with the utmost prudence ...

Even though a limiting phrase 'matters ... covered by the constitutions' is still included it is qualified by 'directly or indirectly, explicitly or implicitly', and especially by reference to the obedience of children and pain of grave sin. It is close to expecting blind obedience especially when the final sentence reads:

And indeed the same family spirit demands that members should promptly carry out the will of the Superior not only when he gives an order but even when, as often happens, he merely recommends or lets his wishes be known.

The language is reminiscent of the idealism and enthusiasm of Pearse's description of Scoil Éanna or of Blowick's vision for the college in Dalgan. But there is an overlay of juridical terminology, 'explicitly or implicitly' and 'grave sin' that suggests the regimentation of a large institution rather than the spirit of a family.

The form of government envisaged by the founding group was far from such an authoritarian model. According to Edward J. McCarthy they adopted a style of decision-making by consensus from their first meetings in 1916. Writing to Joseph O'Leary he said, 'Our policy is to merge every individual fancy when it comes to a question of the *bonum commune*.' Looking back, more than thirty years later, he remembered:

> ... a general tendency among us from the outset to try out something that would be as far removed from the character of a religious order as we could have it. In doing this we eliminated a central personal authority and established instead a kind of *quintumvirate*.

In the constitutions of 1917 and 1918 the society was governed by a council of five directors (Plate 2.2): John Blowick (1888-1972), Edward Galvin (1882-1956), John Henaghan (1881-1945), Edward J. McCarthy (1890-1957), and James Conway (1892-1977), five young, strong characters. As McCarthy had told O'Leary in June 1917, they based their constitutions as far as possible on those of the Foreign Missionaries of Paris. In 1923 an annotation was made to that letter, in what may be Blowick's hand, 'This was done at first. Later it had to be changed. Would not work.'[59] Part of the problem was that Blowick, who drew up both sets of constitutions, was himself hesitant to exercise any personal authority, even though, as president of the board, he had a casting vote. Galvin went to the US in November 1917. That left four directors in Dalgan. By March 1918 the minutes of the meetings of the council show that regularly no decision could be reached. The votes were equally divided and the council was deadlocked. In July 1918 Galvin wrote from Omaha, Nebraska, that he wanted the name 'The Maynooth Mission' changed. In Ireland the name had been a passport assuring them of a welcome in most parishes, but in America it was perceived as an obstacle to their work. Even before Galvin left Ireland:

> Jim Conway and Mc[Carthy] said I should call it the Irish Mission in order to avoid giving offence to the All Hallows men and men from other colleges in the States.

Most of the Irish priests working in the US were from colleges other than Maynooth, seminaries like All Hallows and St Patrick's College, Carlow. In minor seminaries there was 'the bishop's examination' or some other means for selecting those 'good enough' for Maynooth. Those who wished to become priests, but were not selected, went to one of the other seminaries, and some might feel resentment. Galvin proposed another name, 'The Irish Mission', for the society. On 18 September McCarthy left Ireland for the US and Cornelius Tierney (1872-1931) replaced him on the council. Less than a month later McCarthy wrote to Blowick, also calling for a new name:

---

59. Edward J. McCarthy to Joseph O'Leary, 14 June 1917 (CFCA, P. 24), annotation 4.

You have no idea of the set that the American priests have on Maynooth. No pastor would leave us inside the door if we were running a Maynooth show. All the Maynooth priests that I met in Brooklyn and New York assured me of this. Even 'The Irish Mission' is out of the question here in America. As long as we are running under that name we will be regarded as intruders as we are at present.[60]

He went on to tell how at a Mass half the congregation were Poles, Germans or Bohemians, and that he got more subscriptions for the American edition of *The Far East* from them than from the Irish. The matter was so serious that Galvin, O'Leary and he decided that 'either the name must be changed over there [in Dalgan] or that we be erected here [in Omaha] as a distinct society called the "Chinese Mission Society"...' McCarthy cabled the council on 26 October 1918 saying that it was absolutely necessary to call the society the Chinese Mission Society. The reply of the council was sent by Tierney on 31 October 1918, saying that Blowick was in hospital and that in his absence the council had consulted a canon lawyer, Jeremiah Kinane, in Maynooth, who pointed out that only a congress of the society could change the name. Tierney added that the Irish people, on whom the society depended, would be against such a move, as would prominent Maynooth professors like James MacCaffrey and Kinane. A furious McCarthy wrote to Blowick:

> I promise you that some of your 'big men' over there wouldn't be long changing their views, once they got the fog of Maynooth prejudice off their eyes. You might at least consider the opinions of men who are working out here rather than the opinions of men like MacCaffrey and other 'big men' whose almighty authority Corney Tierney throws at us.

The intensity of McCarthy's anger can be attributed in part to his mercurial character. But experience of group dynamics in the last forty years has shown that passionate suspicions are typical between groups that have shared interests, an element of competition, and insufficient communication. Not really knowing what the other group is thinking, each tends to fantasise, negatively, about the motives of the other. McCarthy was so enraged that he wrote to the council and to Blowick demanding not just a change in the name, but in the structure of the council itself. 'In other words, the government of the society by a body of men each having an equal vote is not practical.' Instead he proposed a very monarchical system in which 'all the author-

---

60. Edward J. McCarthy to John Blowick, 13 Oct. 1918 (CFCA, USA A-1).

ity of the society must be placed in the hands of one man,' who would have consultors in each country, whose advice he could follow or not 'just as he wished'. And he warned Blowick that Galvin was going to a congress or chapter of the society, which had just been called, with that programme, to change the way the society was governed. In reply Blowick said that he had been opposed to the constitutions in question from the beginning:

> I could not persuade myself that government of a society by a council of equal votes would not soon be proved to be an impossibility. I gave expression to that but the other view was so unanimous that I saw there was no good impressing it ... You remember, the declared policy was to take away from any individual any pretence of authority.[61]

But he questioned McCarthy's proposal 'to have one man who is really a Pope in the society'. Instead he suggested that it would be better 'in certain of the graver questions to have him bound to follow the Council'. When the congress met on 8 June 1919, and produced a third edition of the constitutions, it laid down that:

> The authority to govern the Society shall be vested in a Superior. He shall be assisted by a Council ... The Superior shall have supreme authority to govern the Society in all matters, except in so far as these Constitutions require a consultative or decisive vote of his Council.

When a consultative vote was required, the superior had to really listen to the advice of the council, but could decide to act against it. In matters where a decisive vote was required he had to follow the decision of the majority. A decisive vote was needed in major questions such as interpretation of the constitutions, disputes between a member and the society about the rights and obligations of the member, admission and dismissal of members, foundation of houses, and accepting vicariates where members would work. However the name was not changed. Galvin wrote to McCarthy:

> The canonical name 'Maynooth Mission' is not changed. It couldn't be carried in Congress. The fellows all admitted the US difficulty ... but yet they felt that in changing it they would be tampering with the very foundations of the Society and they couldn't in conscience vote for it.

However an amendment was made allowing that:

> ... the Superior and his Council, with a decisive vote, shall have

---

61. John Blowick to Edward J. McCarthy, 31 Jan. 1919 (CFCA, CA F-3).

authority to allow civil incorporation or registration as a Trust under the name of the Chinese Mission Society, or The Irish Mission to China, whenever circumstances shall, in their opinion, require it.

The Congregation for the Propagation of the Faith introduced a new canonical name in the 1925 constitutions, 'The Society of Saint Columban for Missions to the Chinese.' However the civil title in Ireland remains 'The Maynooth Mission to China Inc.' to this day.

One concern of the 1919 congress was that all members of the society should be represented on the superior's council, with one councillor selected from the men working in the US, one from Ireland, and a third from either country. Looking ahead to the time when the society would have a mission in China, the congress added 'a representative of the priest members working in each Vicariate or Prefecture in China,' followed by the intriguing sentence:

> In the event of the canonical erection of a House in South America, Oceania, or South Africa, the priest members of the Society who may be labouring in any of these spheres shall be entitled to have a representative on the Superior's Council.

It is quite remarkable that the congress could envisage missions in South America, Oceania, or South Africa, since Blowick consistently maintained that 'our Society is for Chinese missions, that such are the orders of Rome,' and that in 1928 the superior and council would turn down an invitation from the Congregation for the Propagation of the Faith to undertake a mission in India, partly on the grounds that the principal end of the society was the preaching of the gospel to the Chinese people.

Ordinary members were, and are, also represented at the congress, chapter or assembly of the society. The Code of Canon Law of 1983 explains the place of a chapter in the life of a religious organisation:

> In an institute the general chapter has supreme authority in accordance with the constitutions. It is to be composed in such a way that it represents the whole institute and becomes a true sign of its unity in charity. Its principal functions are to protect the patrimony of the institute ... and to foster appropriate renewal in accord with that patrimony. It also elects the supreme Moderator, deals with matters of greater importance, and issues norms which all are bound to obey.

The earliest mention of a congress in society documents was in the constitutions of 1918, where its role was simply to make 'alterations and amplifications in these constitutions'. Election of the council of directors was by all members of the society. In 1919 the general membership lost that right and congress ruled that:

> The only powers which Congress shall possess shall be: to make an examination into the administration of the outgoing Superior and his Council ...; to elect a new Superior and his Council; to designate a First Councillor; and to make amendments, alterations, or amplifications in the Constitutions. It shall have no executive power.

There was a significant change in the role of the chapter in the 1925 constitutions. It still elected the superior and council, and reviewed 'the more important affairs of the Society', but it could only 'enact statutes in conformity with the Constitutions,' not amend or alter them. Once the society was of pontifical right, only the Congregation for the Propagation of the Faith could change, or interpret, the constitutions. Membership of the congress, and of most subsequent chapters, tended to be tilted towards people in authority because of the number of ex officio members. When he was drawing up the 1918 constitutions, Blowick expected the next congress to be in 1921. However Galvin called an extraordinary congress in 1919, when the society had not yet developed to the stage projected by Blowick for 1921. It is worth comparing what the framers of each set of constitutions mandated and could reasonably expect (Table 2.1).

Constitutions	Superior	Council	Bursar	Directors	Ex Officio	Elected
1918	1	4		1	6	3
1919	1			1	2	5
1925	1	4	1	4	10	5

Source: Constitutions of the Society of St Columban (CFCA, CA F-3).
Table 2.1 *Members of the Columban congress according to the constitutions 1918-1925*. The Constitutions drawn up in 1919 had a more democratic balance between superiors and elected delegates. Propaganda imposed a more authoritarian structure in 1925.

Those authorised by the 1918 constitutions were the five directors, any vicar apostolic who was a member of the society or his delegate, any priest member who was in charge of a mission, and three priests elected by the men on the 'pagan missions'. It was wishful thinking to expect to have a vicar apostolic or even a prefect by 1921, but reasonable to plan for a superior and representatives from China. No provision was made for delegates elected by members outside China, but Patrick Cleary, then professor in Dalgan, attended, and there may have been greater balance between official and elected delegates. The 1919 constitutions certainly reversed any trend towards domination by *ex officio* members, including in the next congress vicars apostolic, the future director in China, the outgoing superior, and one member elected by the men in each house or vicariate. There were still no vicars or prefects when the congress met in 1924, but the new constitutions of 1925 were in the hands of the seven delegates, and the three members of the superior's council were authorised by Rome to take part in the elections. Such democratic tendencies disappeared in 1925 which laid down that the chapter would include the superior general, his four councillors, the bursar general, regional superiors, and delegates elected by the members whether on the missions or in regions outside the missions. By 1931 there would be a bursar general, and directors in Ireland, USA, Australia, and China. The tilt towards *ex officio* members had increased.

As secular clergy priests of the society, from the earliest constitutions in 1917, were 'entitled to retain for their personal use *honoraria* for Masses they celebrate' as well as money or gifts given 'for their personal use'. All members were entitled to full maintenance, medical care, and even burial 'in a becoming and edifying manner'. In 1925 members were reminded to use 'temporal goods' in a spirit of apostolic poverty, rejecting superfluous or expensive things and being content with 'the standards of poor people in similar station in life'. The article was written, perhaps, by someone ignorant of the Spartan living conditions of missionaries in China.

The United States of America
Edward Galvin's plan when he arrived in Ireland in August 1916 was to found a college to supply priests for a vicariate in China. Camillus Laurenti, in the Congregation for the Propagation of the Faith, insisted that he found a society for that purpose. By the end of 1917 the society was a reality, the college was about to open, and negotiations for a vicariate had begun. He had long been impatient to explore the insight that had come to him in America in 1916 that 'Australia and US have the funds and some vocations too.' In October 1916, less than two weeks after the Irish Roman Catholic bishops had given their approval for the new mission, he wrote to Blowick suggesting that some of the priests should go to the US. But the task of making the Irish people aware of the needs of China and getting their support for the society was so huge that by January 1917 he had 'decided not to go to US until September when we hope to have finished Ireland.' Once that work was practically completed, on 20 November 1917 he left Kingstown (Dún Laoghaire) together with Matt Dolan, a priest from the diocese of Kilmore who joined the society in 1918. They arrived in New York ten days later. The archbishops of New York,

Washington, Boston, Chicago and Philadelphia made them welcome and gave them permission to seek support in their dioceses, but Galvin was 'keen on opening an office in some central place ... From that office we would probably issue an American edition of *The Far East*.' His long search took him west until he reached Omaha, Nebraska, where Jeremiah J. Harty, who had been a bishop in the Philippines, gave him permission to set up the American headquarters of the society, and publish the magazine, in his diocese.[62] The first issue of the magazine appeared in May 1918, using the very Irish cover of the Irish edition and much of the same content. A year later, with Edward J. McCarthy as editor, the Irish cover was replaced by a picture of Christ in the agony in the garden, never to reappear. In November 1918 Galvin, McCarthy, and Alphonsus Kerr moved into 'a fair-sized frame house with three or four acres of orchard and garden.' More that thirty years later McCarthy remembered Galvin, ever the visionary, saying, 'Wouldn't it be fine if we had a few students here now?'

The canonical status of the Columban society in the American church was a more urgent concern. Of course they had been made welcome by Archbishop Harty but, Galvin wrote to Blowick, 'Harty may be moved any day,' and his successor might not be so hospitable. In canon law a society of diocesan right, like the Columbans, founded in one diocese, cannot formally set up houses in another diocese without the consent of the bishops of each place. With the permission of the Bishop of Galway, Archbishop Jeremiah J. Harty formally announced on 14 December 1918:

> Wherefore, we hereby consent to and decree the establishment of this house of the Society of the Maynooth Mission to China – to be known as St Columban's Mission House – in this Diocese of Omaha in the State of Nebraska ... We also approve and bless the project, now entertained by the founders, of establishing in connection with the work of the Society in this Diocese a seminary for the education of missionaries for the missions in China.[63]

Despite its establishment in Omaha, many ecclesiastics saw the society as in essence an Irish organisation, and some questioned its right to collect funds in America. Cardinal James Gibbons invited representatives of Roman Catholic missions, hospitals, charities, educational institutions, and press to a meeting at the University of Notre Dame in July 1919, to coordinate all

---

62. Edward J. Galvin to John Blowick, 22 Mar. 1918 in Bernard T. Smyth (ed.), 'Galvin and Galvin-related letters, 1912-27' (CFCA, P. 1), p. 98.
63. Decree of Archbishop Jeremiah J. Harty, 14 Dec. 1918 (CFCA, USA A-1).

these activities for the welfare of the church on a national level. At the first meeting of the committee for home and foreign missions 'Father Walsh and Monsignor Kelley went into a head-on verbal collision on their respective ideologies.'[64] James A. Walsh was a co-founder of the Catholic Foreign Mission Society of America, also known as the Maryknoll Missioners, while Francis C. Kelley headed the Catholic Church Extension Society, which raised funds for priests in poorer areas of the American home missions, particularly the south and west. Walsh advocated:

> ... first priority for struggling 'missionary societies' which shouldered the fullness of the mission effort including vocations and seminaries, over 'mission aid societies' which did nothing more than collect and distribute money.

Kelley saw this as an attack on his society and a sub-committee was formed to sort out the matter. The sub-committee proposed the formation of an American Board of Catholic Missions, to include both the Extension Society and Maryknoll, but excluding 'foreign collecting agencies.' Since the Columbans were still such a foreign collecting agency McCarthy wrote to Blowick:

> Now at the present time we are nothing more than missionary beggars in this country and we must take into account the American attitude and try to meet it. Under the new scheme there are but two courses open to us, either establish a college here in the States and educate American boys or, failing that, clear out.

McCarthy had already acted, having bought a large farm at a little town called Bellevue, without waiting for permission from the superior. The first three students arrived days before the foundation stone of the new seminary was laid on 8 September 1921. Dedication of the new college, St Columban's, Omaha, followed on 29 June 1922 and it opened with eleven students on 1 September 1922. Canon law prescribed a system for educating candidates for the priesthood, with 'minor' seminaries for second level 'science of letters', and third level 'major' seminaries for those studying scholastic philosophy and theology. The Columban students from America would undertake their philosophy studies in Omaha, but would go to Ireland for theology. McCarthy wanted a minor seminary also. Vocations to the priesthood were few in the US, due, he was told, to the state schools system.

---

64. 'Reminiscences of Edward J. McCarthy', 1950, (unpublished MS in St Columban's, Omaha) p. 24.

There is naturally not the same faith among the older people taught in the state schools and the home atmosphere is not one that would foster vocations to any extent.[65]

While the situation was improving thanks to the building of parochial schools, and an increase in vocations was already noticeable, McCarthy claimed that many boys of high school age were exposed to the 'dollar lure' during their vacations, and lost interest in the priesthood. An Irish Christian Brother, who had worked in schools both in Ireland and in the US, impressed McCarthy.

He told me that if you can safeguard the average American boy he is better stuff for the priesthood that the Irish boy. They are, he said, getting fine material themselves, and holding them because they never leave them home.

McCarthy proposed that the Columbans in America should provide a residential high school for boys who had an interest in becoming missionaries. St Columban's Preparatory College, Silver Creek, New York, opened formally on 7 October 1924.

Australia
Galvin's plan of August 1916, to involve Irish people everywhere in the support of the new Chinese mission, included the Irish in Australia. In November 1918 the council of directors instructed Blowick to write to Daniel Mannix, Archbishop of Melbourne, to request permission for a collection in Australia. Mannix was president of St Patrick's College, Maynooth, 1903-1912, when all the first Columbans were students there, and on receipt of the letter at Easter 1919, he replied immediately:

What I would suggest to you is this. The Archbishops of Australia and New Zealand will hold their annual meeting in Melbourne in October next. Send a formal general appeal in time for that meeting and I am confident that you may count on a sympathetic response.[66]

The choice of a Columban representative to respond to this invitation was excellent. Edward Maguire had been professor of theology in All Hallows Missionary College, Dublin, before joining the society in 1919, and since many of the priests in Australia were graduates of All Hallows he could

---

65. Edward J. McCarthy to John Blowick, 13 June 1919 (CFCA, USA A-4:3).
66. Daniel Mannix to John Blowick, Easter Sunday 1919 (CFCA, P.2).

expect a welcome from them. Together with James Galvin, ordained the previous year, he sailed for Melbourne in December 1919. Australia was still formally a mission territory under the jurisdiction of the Congregation for the Propagation of the Faith, for although it had a canonically erected hierarchy the church there was 'somewhat unfinished', in that it could not yet provide enough priests of its own. Despite the potential competition, the two Columbans were welcomed for a mixture of reasons, some linked to the war of independence then raging in Ireland, and expressed, perhaps, in anti-British terms:

> Many have been prompted to help us out of sheer admiration of Ireland's pluck. The spectacle of a little nation, battling for its very life and bleeding from a thousand cruel wounds, undertaking the spiritual conquest of a country which contains half the pagans of the whole world has made many an Australian heart beat fast and brought us a host of letters, some of which I would be happy to publish if they were just a little less 'political'.[67]

Two young Melbourne priests, Romuald Hayes (1892-1945) and Luke Mullany (1897-1970), joined the society in July 1919. An Irish priest, Thomas Ryan, arrived from the US at the same time, and all five began the mammoth task of making appeals. Like McCarthy in America, Maguire felt that the name 'Maynooth' in their title could be an obstacle, calling it, instead, 'The Irish Mission to China'. The first Australian edition of *The Far East* appeared in October 1920, and a year later, on 5 December 1921, the society opened a house in Melbourne, as 'residential offices for *The Far East* and prospective novitiate for a new congregation of sisters.' At the blessing ceremony both Maguire and Archbishop Mannix made speeches, and a close reading of Maguire's words suggests that he wanted permission to recruit priests from the Australian church. After fulsome praise of the Australia that 'has made our mission her own,' he continued:

> I have stated more than once that, up to the present, we have never asked for volunteers for China. But from the very first, volunteers have come forward unsolicited. Young women, especially, came forward in great numbers to assist us as teaching and nursing sisters. What were we to do in regard to these volunteers? Turn them down? We could not do it.[68]

---

67. 'Australia's gift to China', *The Far East* (US ed.), iii (July 1920), p. 150.
68. 'Our missionaries open a house in Australia', *The Far East* (Australian ed.), ii (Jan. 1922), p. 10.

There appears to be a sub-text. Young women, especially, were volunteering, implying that there were male volunteers also. Was the society to turn them down? Maguire's answer in relation to women applied with equal force to young men. 'We could not do it.' In October 1921 Maguire had reported that there were rumblings of discontent about 'these Chinese missionaries from Ireland,' and 'Australians going to China to make room for Irish priests.' It seems that in his speech at the house-blessing Maguire was asking for permission to recruit candidates for the priesthood, but in a way which would not embarrass the archbishop. Mannix replied in similar style, ending a witty speech by:

> ... expressing the hope that God would continue to bless the labours of the Chinese Missionaries, and that Dr. Maguire's anticipations in regard to the new house ... would be fully realised.

It was enough. Two Australian women arrived in Ireland in February 1922, to join the first group of postulants in a new congregation, the Missionary Sisters of St Columban, and in 1923 there were four Australian men in Columban colleges in Ireland. A further step towards making Australia a mission-sending region of the Columban Fathers was taken when, in November 1925, the superior general's council agreed that it should admit probationers, who would do their probation year in Essendon, Victoria. The first two students began there in 1926, and in December of that year *The Far East* openly invited students to come to 'Australia's first foreign missionary seminary,' for the beginning of the scholastic year, on 1 March 1927. Ironically the Columban Sisters, with limited personnel and financial resources, made no foundation in Australia while Essendon seminary grew and the first ordination took place there in 1933. At the congress of the society in 1924 Maguire was elected as a member of the superior general's council, which entailed living in Dalgan Park. Romuald Hayes, an Australian, was appointed director of the Australian region, continuing in that post until he was made Bishop of Rockhampton in 1932.

Further negotiations with Rome 1918-20
The purpose of the missionary college in Ireland and the houses in America and Australia was to provide priests for an Irish vicariate in China. Only the Pope, advised by the Congregation for the Propagation of the Faith, can set up or divide vicariates or prefectures apostolic. While Propaganda itself took the initiative in sending out the first vicars apostolic in the seventeenth century, more usually the suggestion to divide an ecclesiastical territory came

from the vicar apostolic of the place. Edward Galvin's was a third approach, with a missionary society making the first overture, by-passing the vicar in China, and going directly to Rome. He knew that the older missionary orders would resist his plan to set up an Irish vicariate, especially since he wanted one of their best missionary areas, a densely populated district with a large city, where schools and colleges would be viable. Not being conversant with Vatican procedures, less than two weeks after the Roman Catholic bishops of Ireland had given their approval to found the new college, Galvin suggested to John Blowick that he ask Michael O'Riordan, rector of the Irish College, to find out, 'What are the conditions on which Rome would give us a vicariate?' A second question was whether some of the priests already working in the area would remain for a year or two to help the new missionaries. On receiving O'Riordan's reply in March 1917 Galvin wrote to Joe O'Leary in China:

> Rome has replied per O'Riordan saying SURE OF VIC [vicariate] and O'Riordan says study geography of China. Joe, look up and find out what you can about Hankow [Hankou] … Study Hankow fully, make out your report and send on direct to Blowick. Also drive home the point that being put at the back of God speed would be fatal.[69]

The city of Hankow (Figure 2.1) in the vicariate of Eastern Hupeh lay at the centre of one of the most populous areas of China, quite unlike the thinly-populated mountains 'at the back of God speed,' that Galvin feared. Hupeh province was divided into three vicariates, West, North, and East, each staffed by Italian Franciscans. In 1920 Eastern Hupeh had a population of 16,000,000, of whom 39,000 were Catholic. The vicar apostolic was Monsignor Gratien Gennaro, who had thirty-one foreign and twenty-two Chinese priests. Galvin's priorities, and his suspicions of the missionaries in possession in China, appear in a report to O'Leary, on 21 March 1917, on the occasion of a letter from Monsignor Faveau, vicar of Hangchow, and Galvin's bishop in 1912:

> Faveau wrote me, a few days ago, a very nice letter saying how glad he was to hear of the work and inviting us to Chu Chow and Ching Wa, The idea is to offer us a part lest we take the whole by force. Faveau is convinced we are after his diocese. If we went in such a place we'd never be heard from. There is no important town and the place is thinly populated. It wouldn't work.

But Galvin planned to 'sing dumb about it, for if once it got out we

---

69. Edward J. Galvin to Joseph O'Leary, 10 Mar. 1917 (CFCA, G-1:63).

would be packed off there right away' by the Irish bishops. Instead he was researching a forceful case to present to Rome and in May 1917 wrote to O'Leary:

> I spent all day yesterday here looking over maps and geography, and found things complicated. The Hankow vicariate would be hard to divide. I think the only possible division would be to give us Hankow and Hanyang cities and three prefectures and give the present bishop Wuchang and two prefectures. I fear that is too much to hope for ... The people in Rome are strongly in favour of us; our Protestant argument is a strong one.

The reference to a 'Protestant argument' introduces what was to become a major theme. Benedict XV had not yet written his apostolic letter on the missions in which he referred to Protestant missionaries as 'ministers of error,' but Galvin knew that the threat of such missionaries would carry weight in the Vatican. In June 1917 he returned to his main concern, thanking O'Leary for maps of Hupeh, and agreeing with him that they should ask for Hankow:

> My point is to have Hankow no matter how small the territory that may go with it, and in drafting our demands to Rome we shall go on the lines that for our special line of work imperative to have big city, that we don't go for large diocese and intend to work intensively.

Galvin was aware that his proposal would be countered by Gennaro, the vicar apostolic, and by the Franciscan superior in Rome. Even though Gennaro's priests were too few to staff the vicariate properly he would fight to keep the whole territory. This seems to be the background for a cryptic letter of Galvin to O'Leary:

> By the way, and this is news. Rome knows the game that is being played in China. Riordan [sic] had a talk with high official who told him in a nutshell nearly everything I told you when you came to China. Riordan says for that reason all Rome is taking a deep interest in us. The information this official gave Riordan surprised me. I thought they didn't know the game so well.

Rome was very concerned about the chronic shortage of priests in China, especially during the world war, and O'Riordan advised Galvin and Blowick that 'the question of vicariate is easy especially at present seeing that every vicariate in China is and will be so much in need of priests.'

However, despite the shortage of priests in China, the Congregation for the Propagation of the Faith demanded suitable preparation for the new missionaries:

> … before a separate mission is assigned [they] should begin under the jurisdiction of some vicar apostolic, as is the normal custom in similar cases, until they learn the language and customs of the people … Then a separate mission can be set up, to be entrusted to them under their own prelate.[70]

The congregation added that the vicar of Kweichow [Guizhou] wanted missionaries, and proposed that the Columbans go there. Edward J. McCarthy sent the news to Galvin in America, and received a vehement response, 'Kweichow is out of the question. I wouldn't consider it for a moment.' Galvin described Kweichow as thinly populated, mountainous, and malarial, with not a single city worthy of note. He went on:

> You know, Ned, how anxious we are to have a chance of opening schools, colleges and hospitals. Kweichow gives us absolutely no chance to do that. That must be your chief argument against it. Kweichow gives us no chance of doing what Rome admits we are needed for, viz. to counteract the influence of heretics. Our English language would be of no use to us.

Galvin consistently argued to have Hankow as the capital of the Irish vicariate, but for a moment he admitted to McCarthy that they might not get it. In that event he would settle for a place somewhere else in the vicariate of Eastern Hupeh, close to Hankow. Blowick responded to the letter of Propaganda in similar vein:

> We wish most humbly to observe that this project originates from the desire to supply to the Chinese missions priests who by using the English language can supply an antidote both to the works and writings of the heretics who use this language to convert both pagan and Catholic Chinese to their heresy. This seems to be the primary and principal reason for this project of ours …[71]

Since there were few 'heretics' in Kweichow, to assign the Columbans there would mean that their special skill, in speaking English, would not bear adequate fruit. Blowick's 'Protestant' argument seems to have made an

---

70. Congregation for the Propagation of the Faith to Michael Logue, 26 Mar. 1918 (CFCA, CN A-1:1).
71. John Blowick to Propaganda, 5 June 1918 (AP, Vol. 601, p. 130).

impact in Rome. In the archives of Propaganda the passage of his letter just quoted was side-lined in red. Blowick went on to propose that the Holy See send the Columbans to the vicariate of Eastern Hupeh, supporting his request by citing the huge population, the few priests, and the two hundred and thirty Protestant missionaries with hospitals, schools and even a large university. These statistics were also marked with a red pencil by someone in Propaganda. Columbans, Blowick argued, could use the English language 'in teaching and promoting the true faith, in opening schools, in setting up hospitals, and perhaps also, after some time, in establishing a university.' An intriguing memorandum written by someone in Propaganda for William Van Rossum, Cardinal Prefect of the Congregation, supported Blowick's application for permission for the professors of theology, philosophy and scripture in Dalgan to read forbidden books, saying that they:

> … should have access to books written by Protestants on these matters in view of the fact that we shall be in constant conflict with the ideas put forth in such books while in Cinà [China].[72]

The anti-Protestant arguments of the Columbans attracted the attention of British postal censors in the tense period following the Easter Rising of 1916, and during the Great War. Like the Vatican officials who greeted Blowick and Galvin with the cry, 'Bolscevici', the censors were convinced that the Maynooth Mission to China was an anti-British, Sinn Féin conspiracy. An intelligence report written in 1919 began:

> In the summer of 1916 our attention was first aroused by a number of ecclesiastical pamphlets which were being sent to Ireland, treating of the success of Protestant (British and American) Missions in China. Maps and diagrams were given showing the extent and preponderance of Protestant teaching … and the Irish were insistently urged to do their utmost to combat this advance of British influence.[73]

The censor confused 'Protestant' with 'British', and on this basis found further evidence to fit his false premise, in the support for the new mission from 'Sinn Féin priests' and 'pro-rebel bishops' in America, or in the description, by Blowick and others, of the society as 'a national mission'. Where Blowick used the word 'national' in the context of generating financial contributions from the whole Irish nation, censors construed it in the political

---

72. Pro-memoria of Gulielmus M. Van Rossum, 23 Mar. 1919 (AP, Vol. 643, p. 638).
73. 'Maynooth Mission to China', 1918, (National Archives, Public Records Office (PRO), Kew, FO 371/3699 (1919-1920), p. 555).

sense as 'nationalism', and accused the society of 'aiming at the recognition of Ireland as an independent power'. The report concluded that 'the mission can be nothing but a menace to England in China'. A second communiqué was also impressed by 'the undeniably anti-English character of the whole enterprise'.[74] When Columbans tried to arouse students to support for the 'cause' of the gospel they were understood to be 'stirring up enthusiasm for the greatest cause on earth, i.e. Ireland'. The support of American bishops with Irish or German names, or of Irish nuns who were 'bitter haters of England' convicted the mission by association as 'a virulent and successful Anti-English activity.' A more sophisticated memorandum was quoted in the intelligence report of the Shanghai Intelligence Bureau in August 1920 arguing that:

> In spite of fears expressed there is apparently no reason to suspect any political motive either in the selection of the priests or in the place they are destined for.[75]

However, a civil servant in London added a note saying that 'the priests are probably Sinn Féiners'. The Shanghai report was included in a special Foreign Office file on Bolshevism.

Propaganda, once Blowick and Galvin succeeded in persuading it that the Columbans were not a Sinn Féin or Bolshevist plot, proceeded, in June 1918, to write to Graziano Gennaro, vicar apostolic of Eastern Hupeh, and to Cimino Serafino, minister general of the Friars Minor, since Gennaro was a Franciscan. Bernardino Klumper replied for Serafino, saying that he couldn't respond until he had heard from Gennaro, while Gennaro needed 'to consult my council and the Minister General'. Despite such delays the Congregation for the Propagation of the Faith sent a confidential letter to Blowick, in January 1919, to say that:

> ... this Sacred Congregation, having received the replies of the Vicars Apostolic of the region of Hupeh, and the Minister General of the Order of [Friars] Minor, ... is now negotiating to have a territory designated, where the principal institutes of the Protestants are, which will be given to you to cultivate.

Despite its authority, Propaganda had to negotiate diplomatically with influential people such as the Franciscan vicars apostolic, and their superior,

---

74. 'The Maynooth Mission to China, Aug. 1918-May 1919' (PRO, FO 371/3699, pp 560-563).
75. 'Maynooth Mission, Summary, 22nd April', 1920 (PRO, FO 371/5341, p. 207).

the minister general, in Rome. Indeed, like any bureaucracy dealing with worldwide affairs, it depended on reports from vicars and, in this case, the head of the Franciscan order. The replies giving the state of the mission in Hupeh would reveal a shortage of priests, and the congregation could then propose that a section of the vicariate be given to the new society. But in February 1919 the Franciscans had a counter suggestion, that additional priests were needed in North Hunan rather than in Eastern Hupeh. Blowick responded in March 1919, saying that although Hunan was larger than Hupeh the population of the latter was 34,000,000 as compared with 22,000,000. Discussions dragged on all through 1919 and in May Blowick wrote to John Hagan, the vice-rector of the Irish College in Rome, asking why the delay in granting a district in China. 'The whole country is daily asking for the reason of the inexplicable delay.' Propaganda counselled patience, pointing out that they had sent Blowick's proposals to Hupeh, but that it took five or six months to post a letter to China and receive a reply. In October 1919 Gennaro, the vicar apostolic, offered seven counties in the lake and marsh area in the south of his vicariate. Before that message reached Ireland Blowick drafted a strong letter, which was approved by the Standing Committee of the Roman Catholic bishops of Ireland at their October 1919 meeting, and signed by Cardinal Michael Logue. They complained that it was now three years since they had given their approval for the mission and described the huge response of the clergy and people of Ireland. Blowick had given the congregation's letter of 19 May 1919 to the bishops, but since then they had heard nothing. Pointing out the danger that the delay might make the people doubt the whole project, the bishops asked Rome to send the Columbans to China as quickly as possible, and to give them Hankow.

Finally, in November, Blowick could tell McCarthy:

> Rome has written to me to say that Bishop Gennaro has consented to give us the city of Hanyang with a certain piece of country around it … I am going to Rome next week to see what we can do to hasten a settlement.[76]

Galvin accompanied Blowick to Rome in December 1919 where they had a series of meetings with officials of the Congregation for the Propagation of the Faith. The most remarkable, on 6 December 1919 with Monsignor Camillus Laurenti, Secretary of the Congregation, was so heated that

---

76. John Blowick to Edward J. McCarthy, 18 Nov. 1919 in William E. Barrett, *The red lacquered gate* (New York, 1967), p. 132.

Blowick wrote a lengthy verbatim record the following day, and both he and Galvin signed it. Laurenti began:

> You are going to China to see Monsignor Gennaro and to enter into negotiations with him about his giving you some suitable vicariate. Perhaps when you are there you can also see the Bishop of Canton. He is the Visitor of the missions in China. He may be able to suggest a suitable Vicariate. There are many places in China where you can get a vicariate. Propaganda cannot say to the Franciscans, 'Go away!' They are now many years in Hupeh; they have works there not to be despised.[77]

The Columbans were young and untried, he argued. Let them begin small, like the mustard seed, and show what they could do, like Maryknoll and the Salesians. Galvin replied:

> Maryknoll after eight years had only four men. We have got twenty. Look in this map at the bit of territory that Monsignor Gennaro has offered. It is impossible – all water, swamps, etc. We can not take it.

Laurenti agreed that it was small and too unsuitable but that, in negotiations with Gennaro, it could be modified. However:

> You are dreadfully exclusive. You always ask for Hankow as if there were Protestants nowhere else. Why are you so exclusive? Why make the success of your Mission depend on one city?

The audacity of the response of the two young priests, one thirty-nine years old, the other only thirty-one, to a man shortly to become a cardinal, is astounding. Presumably it was said with some lightheartedness:

> Not exclusive by any means. We will take Shanghai, or Canton, or Peking, or Tientsin. All we want is a city suitable for the work we are going out specially to do, and which you admit is the work which suits us especially, namely to counteract the influence of Protestantism, and Hankow is their citadel.

After discussions lasting an hour and a half Laurenti pointed to the map of Hupeh which they had brought with them[78] and pleaded:

> Will you suggest on that map some more reasonable place; some place which is suitable for you, even though it may be less suitable. We can-

---

77. Report of John Blowick and Edward J. Galvin, 7 Dec. 1919 (CFCA CN A-1:21).
78. Map of Hupeh (Shanghai, 1911) (CFCA, CN A-1).

not allow you to Hankow till your have grown and proved what you can do.

The map showed the city of Hanyang and the surrounding county clearly marked as '*Oblatum*' (Offered), since Monsignor Gennaro had already agreed to that. But the Columbans still wanted Hankow, on the northern side of the Han, and the section of the civil prefecture of Hanyang that lies around Hankow, and the neighbouring prefecture of Tehngan were marked *Territorium Petitum A* (Requested Territory A). Their second preference, *Territorium Petitum B,* included the part of Hanyang prefecture south of the Han and the prefecture of Nganluh. Three days later Galvin wrote to McCarthy, 'We got our Vic.'

In strict canonical terms the territory assigned to the Columbans did not become a vicariate until 1927. However the term 'vicariate' was used in letters and, with journalistic licence, in *The Far East*. In 1924 the area was made an apostolic prefecture.

Only an alert canon lawyer would have noticed a similar inaccuracy when *The Far East*, in January 1920, announced that Galvin and Blowick 'have returned from Rome with the news that the Maynooth Mission has been granted a large diocese in the very heart of China.' But they were being premature. All that Gennaro had granted was the city of Hanyang and the surrounding hsien (county). The Congregation for the Propagation of the Faith temporised, giving its approval 'to the going of some of your missionaries to China', there to place themselves in dependence on

> … the Vicar Apostolic of Eastern Hupeh until your territory is erected into a distinct mission, … another difficulty seems to arise out of your petition for the Prefecture of Nganluh and half of the Prefecture on Hanyang, because in these places old Christianities exist.[79]

The civil Prefectures of Hanyang and Anlu, called Nganluh by the congregation, contained a number of villages that had been Christian for several hundred years. Since these were the fruit of the labours of the Franciscans and their predecessors, and the principal source of local vocations to the priesthood and religious life, Gennaro, understandably, would have liked to keep them. Rather than offend the Franciscans the congregation advised:

> Therefore, it is best for you to send your missionaries immediately to Hupeh and that they should take up their residence in the city and dis-

---

79. Propaganda to John Blowick, 12 Dec. 1919 (CFCA, CN A-1:23).

trict of Hanyang which is granted to you by the Vicar Apostolic without controversy ... Then, too, you can more easily discuss the matter of a more extensive territory with the Vicar Apostolic, and this Sacred Congregation will always favourably consider your wishes.

Hanyang

The Columbans appear to have assumed that they would eventually be given, in addition to Hanyang city, the part of the prefecture of Hanyang south of the Han river, and the prefecture of Anlu. Certainly *The Far East* in January 1920 celebrated the grant of the territory by the Congregation for the Propagation of the Faith with a triumphant editorial in which Henaghan gave a geographical description of the new mission, laced with rhetorical flourishes:

> At last the momentous word has come from Rome. An Irish vicariate has been established in China. The wire flashed across Europe the tidings that a definite field in the vast vineyard of Christ in China had been assigned to Irish missionaries. The reveille has sounded; the door has opened; out yonder is the battleground for Christ.

The same issue of *The Far East* included an article by Ignatius Ying, professor of Chinese in Dalgan Park, giving details of the geography and population of Hupeh and of the Hanyang-Anlu areas in particular. By October 1920 both the Irish and American editions of *The Far East* could publish maps of the new mission. But when John Blowick returned to Rome in December 1920, having escorted the first band of Columbans to China, and gave the congregation a long report on what he had seen there, he still argued that the Columban mission should include Hankow. He described the city as divided in two, the foreign concessions and the Chinese city. Four priests lived in the foreign concessions, but they were the procurator and the vicar general of the diocese, both engaged in administration, and two retired Chinese priests. In the Chinese city, with a population of 800,000, there was just one old Chinese priest. A letter from Edward Galvin to Blowick, written in September 1920, may explain Gennaro's reluctance to part with Hankow. Two Franciscans came to Hanyang for lunch, the vicar general and Roger Covi, the procurator. Covi told how, after the Boxer Uprising in 1900, France had forced the Chinese government to pay huge indemnities to the Roman Catholic missions and that the religious orders had invested the money in the Foreign Concessions. These were the areas like Hong Kong and Hankow wrung from China by England, France and the other powers after the 'opium' wars of 1839-42 and 1856-60.

Covi says that all the missions taken together own about from one third to one half of the Hankow concessions. Gee Whiz and he says he thinks the same is true in all the other concessions, but about Hankow he has first hand information for he is the man who is doing the business for the most of the missions there ... It explains to some extent the hatred which the educated Chinese have for Missions and ... why we have made such slow progress.

Of course the orders would plead that they used the income to build churches and schools, and to support their missionaries and catechists. Galvin's criticism was not about the investments, and in 1926 the superior general of the Columbans, Michael O'Dwyer, told the council in Ireland that 'he would strongly advise the Prefect [Galvin] to invest a certain percentage annually as a foundation for the missions'. But clearly a man like Covi, true to his vow of poverty, objected to the scale of the investments in Hankow, and to the way in which the money had been obtained. The wrangle about the location of the new mission dragged on into 1921 when Gennaro began to look for Franciscans from the US, and Galvin did extensive tours of the counties offered by Gennaro and of the prefecture of Anlu desired by the Columbans. In a thirty-nine page report on Anlu, where he saw practically every neglected Catholic community, he recorded a visit to a Wesleyan missionary couple called Rowley in the city of Anlu. They made him welcome and, having lived for several years in the counties offered by Gennaro, advised Galvin not to accept them. Agreement on the territory to be given to the Columbans was not reached until November 1921. Two years later, in December 1923, Pius XI separated three new apostolic prefectures, Hanyang, Wuchang and Puchi, from the vicariate of Hankow. The apostolic prefecture of Hanyang would include:

> ... the civil sub-prefectures of Hanyang, Mienyang, Tsienkiang, Tienmen, Kingshan, and Anlu, as well as the part of the sub-prefecture of Hanchwan between the Han and Yangtzekiang rivers.[80]

Departure
Propaganda had given its orders during the visit of John Blowick and Edward Galvin to Rome in December 1919, ushering in a period of intense activity for the Columbans. A meeting of the superior's council on 21 December 1919 discussed the men who would go to China. Three of them were still students; the council called them to the priesthood, and they were ordained on 2

---

80. Pius XI, 12 Dec. 1923, '*Quo christiani gregis*' in *AAS* (Rome, 1924), xvi, p. 36.

February 1920. Blowick would accompany the group to China, and had much to settle before they left on 19 March 1920. Since the college at Dalgan Park was over-crowded another house was bought at Cahiracon, Co Clare. Michael O'Dwyer, newly admitted to the society, was appointed rector of the Cahiracon college, which would be called St Senan's, and house the first and second year students. On the eve of the departure for China, one of the items discussed by the council at its final meeting was a congregation of sisters.[81] Blowick had first mentioned 'auxiliaries ... teachers, nurses and doctors,' and possibly a congregation of nuns, at a meeting in Dublin in October 1917. From May 1918 he had been in correspondence with Lady Frances Moloney about founding a congregation,[82] but pressure of work and lack of funds delayed the project. Now, rather belatedly, the council judged that the time was ripe. Clifton House, on the Cahiracon property, was suitable as a novitiate. Cleary, the rector of Dalgan Park, was instructed to ask the Bishop of Killaloe for permission to set up the new congregation in his diocese. The final item of business on 18 March 1920 was to place Cleary in charge while Blowick, the superior, was away. Next day the new missionaries left for Dublin and Liverpool, and for China.

Conclusions
The founding years 1916-1920 established that the motive for setting up a new missionary society was to save the souls of 'pagan' Chinese who would otherwise be damned to hell, despite the teaching of the church that all who lived a moral and good life could come to heaven. In service of that salvific goal, missionaries worked to build a church modelled on their home diocese. Edward Galvin found that priests were so few in China that they were forced to concentrate on the needs of those already Roman Catholic, doing the rounds of mission stations, with no time for adequate catechesis, or for evangelisation. He wanted more intensive methods, with a smaller, less scattered vicariate, well staffed with priests, sisters, and catechists, and with schools and clinics which Protestant missionaries used so successfully. The schools would teach English to attract ambitious Chinese parents, but their main business would be to produce Roman Catholics who really understood their faith. Galvin had a special concern for the Christian education of women, usually illiterate and house-bound.

An Irish vicariate in China, and in Ireland a society with a college and

---

81. Council of directors, minutes of meetings 1917-1925, p. 29.
82. Sheila Lucey, *Frances Moloney, Co-Founder of the Missionary Sisters of St Columban* (Dublin, 1999), p. 152.

magazine, were necessary components of such an ambitious project. The college would educate priests, and the magazine would generate both volunteers and funds. Galvin's vision grew quickly to encompass the support of Irish emigrants in the US and Australia. An initial emphasis on Irish nationalism, linked to the theme of crusade, would continue among the students in Dalgan Park and in *The Far East* magazine, but experience in America would broaden the thinking of the men assigned there. Blowick and others wanted to place the Irish college near University College, Dublin, although others argued for a purely missionary college. Opposition from William Walsh, the Archbishop of Dublin, defeated the university plan, and the seminary was opened in a remote spot in the west of Ireland. Such isolation, and the liberal ideas of John Blowick, contributed to the creation of a special egalitarian, enthusiastic atmosphere. Chinese language and history, taught by Ignatius Ying, were added to a rather dogmatic curriculum, similar to that in other colleges.

The first group of Columbans drafted constitutions for the new society, stressing that they were secular priests, not religious, and incorporating their experience of working together by consensus. However, when the superior's council became deadlocked on a number of important issues, a congress of the society in 1919 gave the superior greater powers. Other parts of the constitutions preserved the note of being secular clergy: new members took an oath, not a vow; priests could keep the honoraria they received for Masses; all members were to be represented in meetings of congress, the supreme legislating structure in the society. In practice superiors consulted widely on new departures such as the founding of the Missionary Sisters of St Columban. Galvin's plan was for a vicariate in a populous area of China. That meant forcing a vicar apostolic to give up a more developed part of his territory, rather than a less promising section. Galvin and Blowick had to work through Propaganda, and negotiations were slow and acrimonious.

Opposition to the new society came from the Archbishop of Dublin, from officials in Propaganda, from the Franciscans in charge of the area targeted by the Columbans, and from the British wartime censors. The attitude of Walsh, the Archbishop of Dublin, has still to be explained. That of Propaganda and the British censors was due to the confusion of politics and religion. The Franciscans were reluctant to part with places where they had worked and died, hoping, like Mr Micawber, that something would turn up, whether a new flowering of vocations in their home countries, or extra Franciscan forces from America.

Language occurs as a significant thread in the foundation period, determining attitudes and responses, and obstructing any new thinking. Priests daily prayed such texts as 'God of truth, you hate those who serve worthless idols', and understood them to be literally true. In that context the use of words such as 'idolater', 'pagan', and 'herald of the evil devil', in theology textbooks or *The Far East*, made it difficult to believe that good Buddhists or Muslims could be saved, and released huge, misguided energies for mission. When the Pope himself described Protestant missionaries as 'the ministers of error' he was trapped in and reinforcing the intolerance which viewed Protestants as competitors, and even adversaries. A further strand, the language of nationalism, combined with that of persecution and crusade, inhibited balanced judgement for the missionaries who used it, and for the British censors who read it. Roman officials tended to confuse 'Sinn Féin' with 'Bolshevism', and British Intelligence placed the Maynooth Mission to China and Bolshevism in the same reports. It is difficult not to construe the delay in founding the Columban Sisters as a result of classifying them as 'auxiliary forces' to the priests who would be the main agents of mission.

Yet, despite all obstacles, volunteers for the new society came forward, the money was given, a college was founded in Ireland, magazines were published in Ireland, the US, and Australia, and the process for founding the Missionary Sisters of St Columban was initiated. Blowick, and especially Galvin, must have boarded the ship for China in 1920 with a sense of achievement.

CHAPTER THREE

Mission in Hanyang, 1920-1953

The first group of Columbans arrived in China in June 1920, led by John Blowick (1888-1972). His companions were Edward J. Galvin (1882-1956), the superior in China, and Owen MacPolin (1889-1963), who joined the society from the diocese of Dromore in 1919. Their task was to open a new mission in Hanyang, a small city on the banks of the Yangtze river in the densely-populated province of Hupeh. There were already some Roman Catholics in the area, fruit of the labours of a succession of missionaries over several hundred years. Galvin had a plan for more intensive methods of evangelisation. This book will follow the efforts of his team to implement that plan, and will be organised around two major pivotal moments, the floods and civil unrest in 1931, and the entry of Japan into the Second World War on 7 December 1941. For the first ten years the Columbans made slow progress, but in the second decade there was a remarkable growth in the Roman Catholic Church in Hanyang, while the conditions during world war and civil war made the final years a time of endurance.

Initially the Columbans moved into existing parishes, but soon they opened new ones, built churches and schools, and trained catechists. Three doctors joined the mission, and members of three congregations, the Irish Christian Brothers, the Sisters of Loretto from Kentucky, and the Missionary Sisters of St Columban, founded by John Blowick and Lady Frances Moloney (1873-1959), came to co-operate in the work. Their contribution will be assessed. Galvin invited the sisters to China because of the special needs of women, and this will be a significant theme in this chapter. Inevitably the mission met obstacles. These and the changes they entailed affected the whole society. Financial difficulties arose and the society could not find the money for its commitments in Ireland, America, Australia and China. The study will examine the causes for the crisis, the remedies tried by the leadership, and the effects on the work of evangelisation. China's volatile politics was another source of difficulties, and the research will look at dangers from war and bandits, the implications of the unequal treaties of the nineteenth century for missionaries, and the effect of government policies about education, especially after the capture of Hupeh by the Nationalist government in 1926.

The first Columban mission in China will be the focus for much of the chapter but events there had an impact on, and were affected by, the rest of the society with its ambitious building programme in several countries and the foundation of the Columban Sisters. After the communist victory in 1949 the civil authorities at first obstructed the work of foreign missionaries, and in 1953 expelled the last Columban from Hanyang. Churches were taken over for secular use, Christians imprisoned or even killed, records destroyed. It is difficult therefore to assess the overall effect of the Columban mission, but some evaluation will be attempted.

The political situation in China in 1920
John Blowick, Edward Galvin and Owen MacPolin arrived in Hankow, Hupeh province, China on 26 June 1920, to prepare the way for thirteen others waiting in America. They found a country divided among powerful generals. After the downfall of the Ching Dynasty (1644-1912) a republic was declared on 1 January 1912 with Yuan Shi-k'ai as president. But when Yuan attempted to make himself emperor in December 1915 the military governors in several provinces rebelled, and for the next ten years regional warlords, in continually changing alliances, controlled different sections of the country. Hupeh province was under the jurisdiction of the central government, and until 1926 the Columbans lived in relative peace. There were, however, attacks and kidnappings by bandits, and unrest among workers and students. Many Chinese resented the humiliation of their country in the nineteenth century by the major powers, especially Britain and France. These defeated China in two wars in 1842 and 1856, and in subsequent treaties imposed a system of 'treaty ports', areas controlled by foreign governments, and exacted the right to protect, not only missionaries, but Chinese Christians.[1] Hankow, just across the Yangtze river from the mission in Hanyang, one of the treaty ports, 'had its foreign settlements, British, French, and Japanese, each a small town in itself, managed by its own nationals and completely independent of Chinese rule.' Educated Chinese bitterly resented the 'unequal treaties' and treaty ports, and were hostile to all foreigners, including missionaries.

The Roman Catholic Church in China
The Roman Catholic Church in China in 1920 was still organised as in a mission country since Catholics were few and, more critically, there was an insufficient number of Chinese priests. All those in positions of leadership in the church, such as bishops and superiors of religious orders, were foreign

---
1. Kenneth Scott Latourette, *A history of Christian missions in China* (London, 1929), pp 271-277.

missionaries. China was divided into forty-nine vicariates entrusted to eleven different missionary congregations, a vicariate being a territory not yet developed enough to be made a diocese. Macao, a diocese under Portuguese rule, was staffed by secular priests. Italian Franciscans had been in Hupeh as early as 1684, but by 1759 the only priests in the two provinces of Hunan and Hupeh were four French and three Chinese Jesuits. A French Vincentian, John Gabriel Perboyre, worked in Hupeh in 1838 and was executed in Wuchang in September 1840. However, in the middle of the nineteenth century the Congregation for the Propagation of the Faith at Rome decided to entrust each vicariate apostolic to only one congregation. Franciscans were made responsible for Hupeh, as well as Hunan, Shensi, Shansi and Shantung. An Italian Franciscan was vicar apostolic of the combined provinces of Hupeh and Hunan from 1838 to 1856, when Hupeh became a separate vicariate (Figure 3.1).

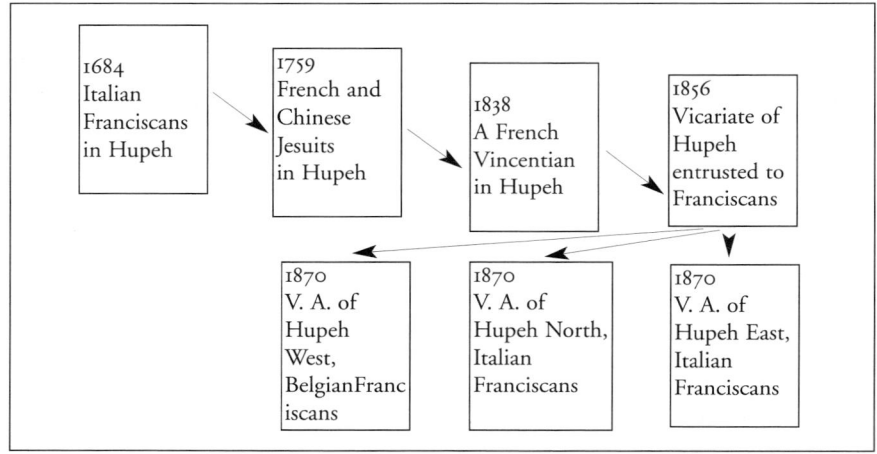

Source: J.M. Planchet, *Les Missions de Chine et du Japon* (Pékin, 1916) pp 159-160.
Figure 3.1 *Ecclesiastical history of the province of Hupeh, 1684-1870*. Franciscans, mostly Italian, were still in charge of the vicariate of Eastern Hupeh when the Columbans arrived in 1920.

In 1870 Hupeh was divided into three, with Belgian Franciscans in the west, and Italians in north and east. Hupeh province is in the very heart of China, at the junction of the Yangtze Kiang, flowing from west to east, and the railway lines to Peking in the north and Canton in the south. It was surely because of its centrality that Archbishop Celso Costantini, the apostolic delegate appointed in 1922, based himself in Hankow, one of the three cities making up the megalopolis of Wuhan, rather than in Peking or Shanghai. The cities of Hankow, Hanyang and Wuchang had a combined population of 2,800,000 in 1920, while the whole province of Hupeh had 27,176,241 inhabitants, giving a population density of 146 per sq. km, less than that of Kiangsu, with 338, but making it the fifth most crowded of the eighteen provinces of China.² Such a density of population made the district ideal for the intensive missionary methods, with more priests and schools, envisaged by the Columbans. Edward Galvin hoped that the Chinese part of Hankow city would be assigned to the society, partly for an urban apostolate but also as an educational centre where he 'might put up a middle school and perhaps a university if necessary'. He had been researching Hankow since March 1917, using maps and information sent by Joseph O'Leary, and also Planchet's *Les Missions de Chine et du Japon*, a Catholic directory first published in Pékin in 1916 and biennially from 1917. By May 1918 he could write to Edward J. McCarthy:

> So Ned my second suggestion is that we ask to be sent for the present to the Vicariate of Eastern Houpe [Hupeh] where Mgr Gratien Gennaro is vicar. He has 16,000,000 pagans, 37,000 Catholics, and only 49 priests.

These statistics differ slightly from those in *Les Missions de Chine et du Japon* for 1917, suggesting that Galvin was quoting that book, but from memory. He got detailed information on Protestant schools and colleges in Wuhan in March of 1919 from the 'China Mission Year Book 1915' published in London. From these sources he would have known that the vicariate of Eastern Hupeh comprised five civil prefectures, listed by Planchet as Outch'ang, Tehngan, Hanyang, Nganlou [Anlu], and Houangtchow.

The mission in Hanyang

Hanyang, the first mission territory entrusted to the Columbans in China (Figure 3.2), was finally defined by the Congregation for the Propagation of the Faith in November 1921, and included Hanyang city, half the prefecture of Hanyang, and the prefecture of Anlu, but not Hankow.³ While much of Hupeh was mountainous the Columban area was largely in the fertile basin of the river Han, with 5,000,000 people in an area of 8,500 sq. miles (22,015 sq. km), giving a density of 227 persons per sq. kilometre. Most of the inhabitants were farmers or fishermen or in related occupations, although the city of Hanyang was home to an iron and steel works, a military arsenal, cotton mills, silk filatures, and immense timber yards. Sientaochen and Shinti were described as 'very active commercial centres, and each has a population of nearly 100,000'. On his arrival in June 1920 Edward Galvin 'knew as little about Hanyang as he did about Tibet,' and began to build up a detailed

---

2. Luigi Gramatica, *Testo e atlante di geografica ecclesiastica e missionaria* (Bergamo, 1927), p. 90.
3. Edward J. Galvin to John Blowick, 27 Dec. 1921 (CFCA, China Correspondence: 045).

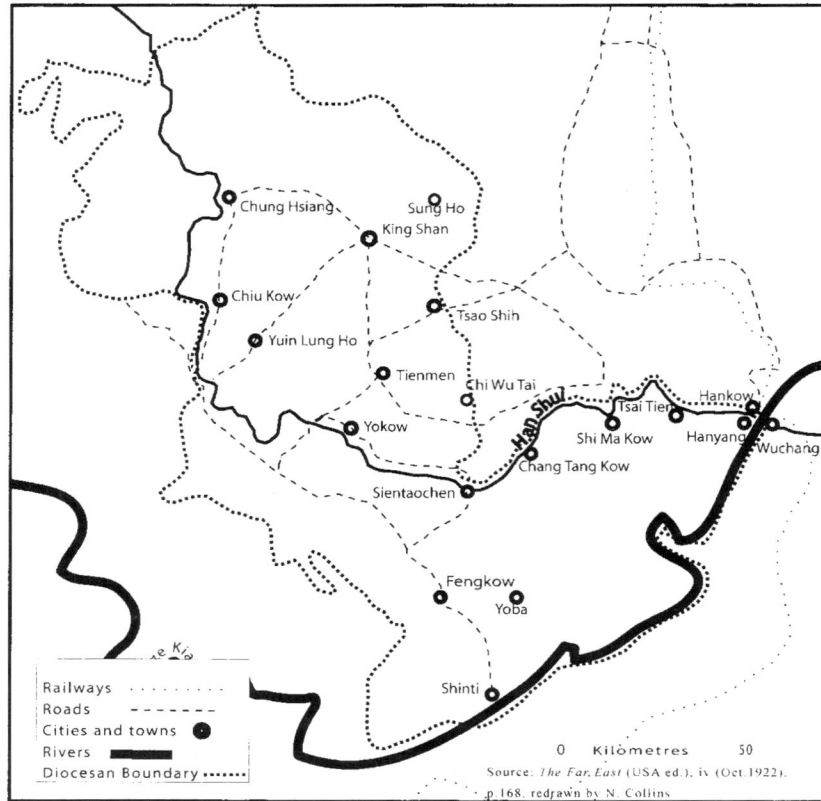

Figure 3.2 Map of St Columban's Mission, Hanyang, 1920-1954. Hanyang is one of three cities making up the metropolis of Wuhan. In 1920 the first group of Columbans remained in the city and its immediate vicinity. The Pope, Pius XI, created the apostolic prefecture of Hanyang in 1923, enabling the missionaries to spread through the entire territory.

account of the area. There had been no resident priest in the city of Hanyang since 1900, and Blowick was told that there were only about forty Catholics there. Galvin estimated the number of Catholics in the mission as a whole to be 15,489 as of 15 August 1921,[4] drawing the figures from the annual report of the Franciscans to the Congregation for the Propagation of the Faith. Most Roman Catholics in China lived in rural towns and villages, not in cities such as Hanyang:

> While they were also present in the larger cities where the Protestants were concentrated, the Catholics emphasised work in the more rural areas, sought the conversion of entire families or villages, attempted to

---

4. Edward J. Galvin, Census, 27 Mar. 1922 (CFCA, CN A-4).

build integrated local Catholic communities, and tended to restrict their educational efforts to the children of converts only.⁵

Galvin explored the prefecture of Anlu in May of 1921, consulting priests and even a Methodist missionary couple. He visited sixty-three 'christianities',⁶ making detailed notes on them and sixteen other communities, and finding a distressing situation. The nine Franciscan priests assigned to the area echoed the message of one of their number, an American, Patrick Gilgan:

> He insists that he is not able to do the work alone. He has asked the bishop for another priest and has been asking for years, he says, but the bishop has no priest to send him, and so the neglect goes on.

There were villages where almost all the people were Catholic, some for four or five generations, others made up of recent converts who were not yet baptised. Generally the priest visited only once a year, but for the mountain villages in the northwest of the prefecture Galvin's assessment was:

> There are forty families of converts, which came in last year, but the priest never came here and there is neither school nor chapel.

Thirty-three places had a chapel, usually decrepit, and only ten had a Catholic school, mostly with only nine or ten pupils. With no catechist or teacher in most villages, Galvin was not surprised to be told of hundreds of people who had become 'perverts', meaning, in the parlance of the time, people who had abandoned the church.

Many members of the long-established orders such as the Franciscans did not want to hand over part of their territory to newcomers like the Columbans. They believed that in granting a vicariate to their congregation Rome had given them a '*ius commissionis*' or 'right of entrustment', almost a property right. The Congregation for the Propagation of the Faith, as late as 1929, reminded missionaries that:

> When the church entrusts some region to an Institute to be evangelised it does not intend to relinquish that tract of land wholly and completely to the care of that Institute. Obeying the divine command … it retains the principal part, the total government of the mission, to itself, expecting from the helping Institute the generous aid of evangelical workers and the means to do the work.⁷

---

5. Albert Feuerwerker, 'The foreign presence in China' in Denis Twitchett and John K. Fairbank (eds), *The Cambridge history of China*, (15 vols, Cambridge, 1983) xii, pp 167-8.
6. Christianities: the term used in Roman documents for 'groups of Christian families'.
7. Gulielmus M. Van Rossum, '*Instructio*' in *AAS*, xxii (Rome, 1930), p. 111.

There was no 'right of entrustment'. Rome 'governed' the territory, and the religious order simply assisted. But at the local level many believed otherwise. However, some welcomed the new missionaries when they arrived in June 1920. Cassian Kleinenbrouk, a Franciscan, wrote:

> I am very glad to hear that you and two Rev. arrived some days ago. *Sit nomen Domini benedictum!* And I cry out: You are welcome my Rev. Frs!! I send my boy to invite you and your confreres. Kindly come to me, for I have a big residence and a nice church and you will find a good confrater.

A note added to this letter says that Kleinenbrouk died a month later, on 1 August 1920. 'He died of disease caught in spending himself for his stricken people.' The Franciscan procurator in Hankow, Roger Covi, also made the three Columbans welcome, in practical ways such as finding houses for them at Bai Ya Tai, Hanyang. Other people were less pleasant. The procurator of the Paris Foreign Missionaries in Shanghai barely spoke to them, but complained to Ignatius Ying, their professor of Chinese:

> He told Mr Ying Junior that we behaved unpardonably in daring to approach Rome without first getting Monsignor Gennaro or some other Vicar Apostolic to ask for us.

The bishop, Gratien Gennaro, was initially cold but after a few minutes 'became quite kind and friendly'. He was still negotiating with Rome about the new mission and had sent his latest offer to the Congregation for the Propagation of the Faith a few months previously.

> But he has objected, he said, to our getting Ngan Lu [Anlu]. It was the heart of the vicariate and his losing it would mean the ruin of the vicariate for the reason that it contains the old Christians and most of the seminarians come from there.[8]

According to Planchet, in 1916, 21 of the 51 priests in the vicariate were Chinese, evidence of Gennaro's efforts to build up the indigenous priesthood. Since old christianities were the most likely source of vocations to the priesthood his reluctance to hand the area over to another congregation was more understandable.

---

8. Diary of John Blowick, 27 July 1920 (CFCA, P. 2).

Priorities for the new Columban mission
Edward Galvin and his companions arrived in Hanyang in June 1920 (Plate 3.1) with clear instructions, inserted in the constitutions of the society by a congress in June 1919:

> The Society shall have for its principal end the evangelisation of China in accordance with the teachings of the Holy Roman Catholic Church. In particular it sets before its members as special duties the spiritual care of existing Christians … the furnishing to these same Christians, as well as to the pagans, primary and higher education; the founding and equipment of hospitals; the work of increasing … the number of native Roman Catholic bishops, priests, brothers and nuns; and, finally, the conversion of pagans …

Galvin expected to establish, eventually, a fully equipped, self-sustaining Roman Catholic diocese, with 'parishes' where the existing Catholics could hear the word of God and receive the sacraments; with schools and hospitals, which would serve both Christians and 'pagans'; and with a seminary and religious congregations to provide Chinese leaders for the church. The final duty was 'the conversion of pagans'.

Language study was the first priority for the other members of the first team of Columbans who arrived in Hanyang on 24 August 1920. Rome expected that:

> … all should live in the same place to learn the language and customs … When however the missionaries of the institute will be sufficiently instructed in the language and customs of the people of the place they can gradually substitute for the missionaries of the Minor Fathers [Franciscans] in the various stations and works already existing in the same territory.[9]

The new arrivals lived with Galvin in Bai Ya Tai, Hanyang until in December Galvin succeeded in buying, through the sub-manager of the Iron and Steel Works, a failed Baptist hospital which became his headquarters. By early January 1921 the new men were ready to go out to 'the missions' Since the only territory that had been granted so far was the county (*hsien*) around Hanyang, the Columbans went to other stations 'as guests of the Franciscans'. Their guest status meant that they could make no improvements, and when Galvin visited each priest in April 1921, making a list of

---

9. Congregation for the Propagation of the Faith to John Blowick, 12 Dec. 1919 (CFCA, CN A-1:23).

priests' houses, churches, and schools to be built, he sent the details to John Blowick, with the handwritten warning, 'Not for publication.' Presumably he didn't want the Franciscans to read it, considering that the places surveyed were still under their jurisdiction. The Franciscans trained the young Columbans until:

> In September 1922 the Vicar General of Hankow ... deemed our priests fit to take complete charge of the territory assigned to us by the Sacred Congregation for the Propagation of the Faith. Hence, all the Franciscan Fathers, with one exception, have been withdrawn from that territory and from that time our priests have been in complete charge.[10]

The Columbans, once they had 'complete charge' began to set up a network of central stations which by January 1923 covered the entire district assigned to the society. Even in a lonely town such as Yen Shi Kang in the far north of Anlu they found Catholics who were prepared to walk 180 li (ninety-six kilometres) to celebrate great feasts like Christmas. To reach out beyond their Roman Catholic flocks the priests would open schools:

> Our plan is to open a number of good primary schools as soon as we can. It is the quickest and cheapest way at our disposal and at present the only way by which we can reach the people . Next Sept we must have a number of brothers and sisters here at any cost to take charge of primary schools. It is our only hope. We can't go round Hanyang on the soap box ticket.[11]

Galvin's dismissive remark about 'the soap box ticket' referred to preaching to passers-by in the streets. Christ preached to the Jews in their synagogues, and Paul to Greeks on the Areopagus. But there were conflicting opinions about following their example literally in the twentieth century. Writing in 1919 the missiologist Joseph Schmidlin judged:

> Neither in the case of primitive nor of civilised pagan races, would it be practicable or serve much purpose (at least under present conditions), for a missionary to appear suddenly in the streets or squares and proclaim Christ in a loud voice, even though in certain circumstances such an immediate introduction might be advantageous.[12]

---

10. Edward J. Galvin to Celso Costantini, 5 Mar. 1923 (CFCA, CN A-8).
11. Edward J. Galvin to Joseph O'Leary, 9 Aug. 1920 (CFCA, China Correspondence: 018).
12. Joseph Schmidlin, *Catholic mission theory*, trans. Matthias Braun (Techny, Ill., 1931), p. 366.

A Congregationalist missionary, Griffith John, working in Hankow in the previous century, believed that 'the [missionary] method *par excellence* is the daily heralding of the gospel in the chapels and the streets'. Wesleyan preachers in Hankow in the twentieth century found it 'impossible to preach in the crowded street itself, so they set up their own preaching rooms', opening off the streets where the tired could rest and listen to the word of God. 'Sometimes people went away, unmoved, but sometimes they listened and were converted.' Propaganda enjoined the preaching of the word of God to 'pagans', but did not specify street preaching.[13] A few Roman Catholic missionaries, like the Vincentians Vincent Lebbe and Anthony Cotta, had gone beyond

> traditional ministries of instructing catechumens and visiting the poor and the sick … to launch new ways of reaching Christians and non-Christians. In 1911, for instance, in Tianjin, Lebbe thought of opening public lecture halls as a way of getting into the life of the city and bringing the church before the public … In 1912, with the help of his friend and well-known literary figure Ying Lianzhi, he began publishing *Guang Yi Lu* (The Royal Way), the first Chinese Catholic weekly.[14]

Lebbe was an exceptional linguist. Perhaps the Columbans in Hanyang were less gifted for although they preached to both 'faithful and unfaithful', Galvin's main hope for evangelical outreach lay in the schools. These schools taught Christian doctrine as well as Chinese reading and writing. They were open to members of other faiths 'provided, of course, that they agree to attend instructions and Christian Doctrine classes just like the Catholic children'. More Columbans arrived in 1921 and 1922, enabling Galvin to give the apostolic delegate comparative statistics of personnel and church building in the Hanyang mission under the Franciscans, and after the Columbans took charge in September 1922 (Table 3.1, p 97).

The new chapels built by the Columbans were small structures, usually in the village christianities, and holding no more than 400 people. In larger towns Roman Catholics were few. Cornelius Tierney estimated the population of Shinti to be about 40,000 with only 150 Catholics, and, while a large central church would be necessary in the future, a smaller chapel was sufficient and could become a school later. But the statistics show the Columban emphasis on education, with a four-fold increase in the number of schools

---

13. Gulielmus M. Van Rossum, '*Epistola*' in *AAS*, xiv (1922), p. 292.
14. Jean-Paul Wiest, 'The legacy of Vincent Lebbe' in *International Bulletin of Missionary Research*, xxiii (Jan. 1999), p. 34.

	Franciscans	Columbans
Priests	15	31
Schools	27	97
Pupils	437	2,708
Teachers/Catechists	32	139
Chapels	72	115
Churches	4	4

Source: E.J. Galvin to Celso Costantini, 5 Mar 1923 (CFCA, CN A-8).
Table 3.1 *Comparative statistics for the Hanyang mission, 1922-3*. The figures show the Columban emphasis on intensive methods, with many priests and schools.

and teachers or catechists, and an even greater leap in the figures for pupils. Canon law imposed a strict obligation, especially on bishops, to have Catholic schools built, but many missionaries still questioned their value. According to Blowick, Gennaro, the vicar apostolic:

> … did not approve of educational establishments, as they were of little to no avail for making conversions.[15]

Yet even Gennaro tried three times, in 1914 and 1915, to get Irish Christian Brothers for his schools. The Congregation for the Propagation of the Faith urged Blowick to implement this aspect of canon law, writing in November 1921:

> … since evangelisation of the infidels, spiritual care of the Christians, and assiduous preaching and catechetical instruction, especially through schools, are the first duties of missionaries, I commend to you before all the building of churches and schools in each station …

The existing Roman Catholic schools were of a low standard, unlike the 'many fine establishments run by Protestants'. Latourette observed:

> In education, the church was only here and there beginning to modify the policy long pursued. Most of the primary education was still for the purpose of teaching the children of Christians the catechism with the rudiments of reading and writing …[16]

Galvin knew that some educated Chinese pagans admired 'the church and her doctrines but since she consists largely of coolies' they could not join her. He was determined to reach out beyond the poorest classes and saw good schools as the way to do so. However there were few able Catholic teachers, and those who knew English easily got positions in foreign firms at salaries

15. Diary of John Blowick, 27 July 1920 (CFCA, P. 2).
16. Latourette, *A history of Christian missions in China*, p. 555.

the mission could not match. So until teaching sisters and brothers arrived from abroad Galvin was forced to bring one of the young priests, Thomas Quinlan, back from a parish to St Columban's primary and middle school in the city of Hanyang. With the assistance of a Chinese teacher who had good English, Quinlan's students achieved excellent results, but Galvin needed all his priests for parish ministry.

The Roman paradigm of mission

Missionary superiors were obliged by canon law to submit annual and quinquennial reports on the state of the mission. These reports tended to reinforce the clerical model of evangelisation that the Columbans derived from their home dioceses, their seminary training, the society's constitutions, and the practice of their predecessors. Faithful to the *Code of Canon Law* the reports centred on the work of bishops and priests. The *Prospectus Status Missionis,* the official form for the mission's annual report to Propaganda (Figure 3.3), reveals the shape of the congregation's thinking. Beginning with the name and location of the vicariate, the society, and the bishop, the main part of *Prospectus* had nine sections covering religious personnel, lay mission workers, the population, ecclesiastical subdivisions, sacred buildings, works, schools, changes in the number of Catholics, and 'life and spiritual fruits'. A final page asked for an account of the finances and property of the mission. The population was broken down into Catholics, catechumens, Eastern Orthodox, Protestants, Jews, Muslims and 'Pagans'. Possible subdivisions of a mission territory were districts, parishes or quasi-parishes, primary stations (with a resident priest) and secondary stations. Sacred buildings, churches and chapels, were categorised as holding more or less than 400 people. Hospitals, dispensaries, orphanages and newspapers came under the heading of works or, in the quinquennial report, 'Institutions useful for the spread of the faith'. The importance attached to schools was indicated by placing them in a section of their own, which included everything from elementary to teacher training schools as well as institutes for training catechists and catechumenates. In 'Changes in the number of Catholics' were listed: the number of Roman Catholics in the preceding and current years; the increase through baptism of adults and infants, but not of people baptised in danger of death; increase through immigration or other cause; and decrease by death, emigration, or some other reason. Life and spiritual fruits covered: baptisms in danger of death; communions whether in fulfilment of Easter duty or of devotion; marriages, both between Catholics and between Catholics and non-Catholics; missions preached to the people; and retreats.

PROSPECTUS STATUS MISSIONIS 1937

Name of mission, society, bishop, vicar delegate.

1. **Religious Persons:**
    - Priests: number, congregation, nationality.
    - Brothers
    - Sisters
    - Seminarians: major, minor, preparatory, or abroad.
2. **Lay Workers:**
    - Catechists
    - Teachers
    - Baptizers: to baptize children in danger of death
    - Doctors & Nurses.
3. **Population:** Total, Catholics, Catechumens, Orthodox, Protestants, Jews, Muslims, Pagans.
4. **Ecclesiastical Divisions:** Districts, Primary Stations, Secondary Stations.
5. **Sacred Buildings:** holding more than 400, holding less.
6. **Works:**
    - Hospitals, dispensaries, orphanages
    - Newspapers.
7. **Schools:**
    - Elementary, Middle, Higher
    - Professional schools
    - Teacher training schools
    - Training schools for catechists
    - Catechumenates.
8. **Changes in the number of Catholics.**
9. **Life and Spiritual Fruits:**
    - Baptism in danger of death
    - Easter Communions
    - Communions of Devotion
    - Marriages between Catholics
    - Mixed Marriages
    - Missions preached to the people
    - Retreats.

The Possessions of the Church:
1. Immovable goods: buildings and land
2. Movable: Money, animals
3. Mortgages, debts
4. Income: from investment, Pontifical Works, and offerings from foreigners
5. Expenditures: maintenance, travel, seminaries, works of the Mission, etc.

Source: Annual Report for the Vicariate of Hanyang, 1937, trans. N. Collins (CFCA, CN A-4).
Figure 3.3 *Standard headings for the annual reports to the Congregation for the Propagation of the Faith.* These reports were submitted each year by every vicar and prefect apostolic on the missions 1917-65.

Financial accounts listed: estimated value of buildings; money in a bank or elsewhere; mortgages and debts; as well as details of income and expenditure for the year.

Edward Galvin prepared for the annual *Prospectus Status Missionis* to Rome by compiling statistics from each parish in a separate report (Table 3.2), a copy of which he sent to the superior general. These accounts show

Parish	Priests in Charge	Catholics	Adults	Children of Catholic	In Danger of Death	Catechumens	Deaths
CITY OF HANYANG							
St. Columban's	Rev. Jeremiah Pigott	864	100	30	734	61	20
St. Mary's	Rev. Joseph Hogan	903	180	38	84	56	31
St. Rosalia's	Rev. James O'Rourke	503	31	22	4	71	12
Holy Family	Rev. Paul Hughes	193	15	4	5	18	4
OUTSIDE CITY OF HANYANG							
Shinti	Rev. Hugh Sands	459	197	18	419	190	7
Tsai Tien	Rev. Patrick Maguire	240	76	2	27	127	1
Hwang Kia Shan	Rev. Thomas Powers	1,193	59	50	10	125	45
Sientaochen	Rev. Ulick Burke Rev. G. O'Collins	8,162	91	145	99	200	71
Chang Tang Kow	Rev. Timothy Leahy Rev. Dominic Wang	4,233	393	113	26	254	78
Mo Wang Tsui	Rev. James Vallely	1,833	142	74	16	959	8
Feng Kow	Rev. Titus Seng	1,750	247	18	45	200	44
Liu Kia Ho	Rev. James Collins	742	37	24	7	110	26
Yu Pa	Rev. James Chu	861	71	33	32	505	8
Shin Yuen Tze	Rev. Martin Croffy	1,179	31	80	21	394	19
Kuo Kia Tsui	Rev. P. O'Connell. Rev. Thos. Tracey	2,271	32	51	6	165	74
Tsien Kiang	Rev. A. McGrath	1,015	33	40	36	1,020	32
Yo Kow	Rev. Robert Staples	1,137	54	27	26	740	19
Tien Men	Rev. M. McCarthy	882	440	12	13	692	9
Peng Shih Ho	Rev. T. O'Rourke	1,746	3	80	1	85	69
Chi Wu Tai	Rev. Henry Collins	1,319	75	41	28	50	54
Tsao Shih	Rev. James Loughran	917	53	32	21	569	20
Yung Lung Ho	Rev. John Mackey	1,907	35	35	10	920	83
King Shan	Rev. Joseph Grimley Rev. P. Hennessy	1,466	91	23	21	466	58
Sung Ho	Rev. Paul Chang Rev. J. McMullan	2,067	107	19	157	755	53
Kao An Lao	Rev. Wm. Holland	1,055	51	24	23	748	44
Yen Tze Kang	Rev. J. McNamara	1,128	15	35	14	197	53
TOTALS		35,025	2,671	1,070	1,885	9,677	942

Source: Annual Reports, Vicariate of Hanyang (CFCA, CN A-4)

Table 3.2 *Excerpt from the annual report, vicariate of Hanyang, 1936-7.* Statistics from this report were used by Edward Galvin in preparing his annual report to Rome.

that the principal structure for the evangelisation of Hanyang was a cluster of mission stations termed in canon law a quasi-parish. Each priest recorded: numbers of Catholics and catechumens; totals of those celebrating the sacraments; and attendance at catechumenates and schools. Diocesan institutions were noted on the last page. The constitutions of the society did not mention mission stations, yet the Columbans in China viewed their task in a parish-type framework, and understood their work to revolve around the sacraments and Christian instruction. After the name of the primary station and the priest or priests assigned there, the first six columns presented statistics to do with the growth of the community, mainly through baptism of adult converts and children of Roman Catholics. Babies and victims of cholera or other plagues who were baptised in danger of death were not counted as additions to the church on earth. The figure for catechumens included people interested in becoming Christian, but not yet under instruction. Statistics for the dead were subtracted from church totals. Roman Catholics were required to confess their sins and receive communion at least once a year, during Lent or the Easter season, a practice described as 'fulfilling their Easter Duty'. The columns on these two sacraments are divided into 'annual', or in fulfilment of the canon law, and 'devotional'. Priests regarded the number of those who did not fulfil their Easter duty as an important indicator of the vitality of a parish or mission station. Catechists kept lists of all the Roman Catholics in a village, and of those who did not make an annual confession. The final columns dealt with Christian instruction, through the schools and catechumenates.

Ten lean years, 1920-30

Statistics for the years 1922-30 show a steady growth until 1926, and then a crisis (Table 3.3). One reason for the sudden drop in numbers of Catholics was that the Society of St Columban had been expanding too rapidly, buying property and erecting buildings in Ireland, America, Australia and China. A conference or general chapter in June 1924 recommended that the new superior general, Michael O'Dwyer, 'should endeavour with all his strength to put the finances of the Society on a solid foundation'. Men were recalled from China to make fund-raising appeals in Ireland and America, new buildings or property were unthinkable, and in China the parish schools were closed. The total number of boys in schools in Hanyang dropped from 3,886 in 1923-24 to 338 in 1927-28, and that for girls from 794 in 1922-23 to 105 in 1927-28. Since many of the schools served as catechumenates at night, the numbers of men and women under instruction also fell, even though people

	1922-23	1923-24	1924-25	1925-26	1927-28	1929-30
Catholics	14,719	17,614	18,597	18,571	16,663	17,233
Baptisms: Adults	1,082	1,149	502	413	186	311
Children of Catholics	501	734	715	607	570	530
In Danger of Death	270	216	201	188	186	139
Catechumens	6,607	10,182	7,609	6,085	2,837	
Deaths		365	259	443	465	
Extreme Unctions	400	296	287	372	292	298
Annual Confessions	7,986	8,867	9,160	9,045	7,270	7,180
Devotional Confessions	20,348	31,919	30,405	31,544	31,931	37,657
Annual Communions	7,866	8,829	9,053	8,969	7,283	7,110
Devotional Communions	31,575	45,750	42,832	46,197	56,267	68,742
Easter Duty Unfulfilled				4,155	3,888	3,912
Confirmations	70	58	270	1,156	88	85
Marriages, Catholic	85	155	93	105	157	79
Marriages, Mixed	75	129	144	107	79	79
Men under Instruction	1,146	635	0	85	460	422
Women under Instruction	301	281	0	0	99	744
School pupils: Boys	3,278	3,886	2,223	901	338	562
School pupils: Girls	794	606	650	285	105	54
Catechists, Male	186	162	71	156	140	104
Catechists, Female	26	20	11	27	23	25
Priests	32		31			
Virgins	60	38	34	42	33	46
Primary Stations	15		15			

Source: Annual Reports, Vicariate of Hanyang (CFCA, CN A-4(SR))

Table 3.3 *Church growth in the vicariate of Hanyang, 1922-30.* While all these statistics were reported to Rome, numbers for adult baptisms and annual communions were regarded as the best indicators of the health of the church.

seeking to enter the church, listed as 'catechumens', still came in thousands. Catechists employed by the mission numbered 212 in 1922-3 and only 88 in 1924-5. Galvin acknowledged the society's financial crisis and, reluctantly, accepted the need to close the schools. However the annual report for 1925-26 was so bad that he wrote to O'Dwyer complaining:

> Look over the headings Inconfessi (the people who should have made their Easter duty and didn't). Look at our adult baptisms . We must spend more on instruction ... I should have said that these inconfessi

are chiefly due to the fact that they don't know anything and are afraid to face the ordeal of Confession.[17]

The political situation also affected the mission. Figures for the total number of Roman Catholics showed an increase between 1922 and 1924, and a sharp decline over the next four years, coinciding with the period of unrest surrounding the arrival of the left wing of the Kuomintang army in 1926. Many nominal Roman Catholics left the church.

A medical mission
John Blowick, in the vision of the mission in China he had outlined in 1917, recognised that the Columbans could not achieve their goal without co-workers:

> Hence, to have a complete Irish Mission, a body of teaching religious is a necessity – teaching nuns and brothers, and that too for the wealthier as well as the poorer classes … Besides the teaching body, there is another auxiliary of the first importance for our Missions. It is the medical one … It is an old and very wise axiom that the best way to get at the soul of a pagan is through the body.

Two doctors and a medical technician volunteered. Dr Robert F. Francis from Indiana arrived in Hanyang 28 January 1921, followed a few months later by Dr P. J. O'Donoghue of Madras, India, and Mr Otto Scheuerman from Rochester, New York, who had served in the medical department of the American army. Galvin reported on the medical mission on St Patrick's Day 1923, that:

> Dr Francis is located in Hanyang and looks after the sick in the southern part of our district. Mr Scheuerman is located in the central part, and Dr O'Donoghue looks after the northern section.

The three medical professionals treated 10,008 patients in the year 1923-24. However, despite efforts to make the medical work self-supporting, the superior general of the Columbans and his council in November 1924 decided to withdraw Dr. Francis from China. Before they could act Francis suffered a nervous breakdown, and had to return to America. O'Donoghue served over three years in Hanyang, going to Burma in 1925 where he studied for the priesthood and was ordained for the vicariate of South Burma in 1934. Neither was replaced. Francis McDonald, a doctor and a Columban priest,

---

17. Edward J. Galvin to Michael O'Dwyer, 26 Oct. 1926 (CFCA, CN A-4).

arrived in China in 1925, but since canon law forbade priests to practise medicine, he served as a parish priest until a crisis arose in 1931. Scheuerman remained in China for twenty-two years, working as a medical aide, a supervisor of construction, and a bookkeeper, until the Japanese expelled him in 1943.

The Irish Christian Brothers
The first teachers to join the Columbans in China were the Irish Christian Brothers. Blowick wrote to Patrick Hennessy, superior general of the Brothers, in February 1921:

> For the present our priests are doing their best to teach in the schools but they have not, of course, been specially trained for this work ... [and] the people of the district have come enormous distances asking us to send them priests to minister to them. So, you see, without the aid of Brothers a great deal of work must be neglected.

Blowick asked for six brothers 'who would take charge of our schools in China.' Galvin's idea was that a brother in every parish directing the schools would leave the priest free for evangelisation and sacramental ministry, and Blowick had tried, in vain, to find Franciscan brothers for school work. Indeed Galvin had ambitious plans for further expansion of the parish structures, publishing a budget for building expenditure in the American edition of *The Far East* in October 1922, listing priests' houses, chapels and schools in twenty-four places. But the superior general of the Christian Brothers could send just four men, who arrived in December 1921, one from Australia and three from Ireland (Plate 3.2). They found that the Columbans had four schools in and around the city of Hanyang, Quinlan's high school and three primary schools. After studying Chinese, in February 1922 the brothers took over the management of two of the primary schools and the high school.[18] The first hint of a difference between Galvin and the brothers came in July 1922. No suitable site for a college had been found when:

> Towards the end of July Father Galvin informed us that he had decided on starting a boarding college to be opened in temporary premises at Pei Ya T'ai [Bai Ya Tai] on the first of September.

The houses at Bai Ya Tai, used by the Columbans for their language school, were unsuitable for the brothers' college since they were 'only jerry-

---

18. Alban O'Donoghue to Mark McCarthy, 27 Feb. 1922, in W. A. O'Hanlon, 'Christian Brothers in China', in *Christian Brothers Educational Record* (1975), p. 103.

built and are out of repair and the Brothers are only monthly tenants of the proprietors of the Ironworks'. However, since there was no alternative site, the brothers obeyed and opened St Columban's College, offering, in its prospectus, Catholic doctrine, Chinese literature and history, English, world history, geography, commercial subjects, physics, chemistry, and mathematics, subjects which:

> ... will enable students who so desire it to pass the Matriculation of Entrance Examination of any of the Universities of China, America, or Europe.

In reality, the superior, Patrick Harty, admitted, 'There is very little chance for the average Chinese boy to get to the university.' However 'they can get good positions in Hankow if they have anything like a decent education,' which included English and western arithmetic with its bewildering pounds, shillings and pence, ounces, pounds and stones, instead of the Chinese decimal system. Relations with Galvin improved. O'Donoghue, the most prolific writer among the brothers, reported to Gregory Hogan, assistant of their superior general, in September 1922:

> Father Galvin leaves all ... to ourselves. Indeed in everything he could not be more considerate. His dictum is: that's your job; I have mine. Since we came he has been in everything most liberal with us, and has never interfered in anything. He is scrupulously careful in this respect.

Indeed Galvin must have been well satisfied with the results of the brothers' work. Committed by their constitutions to 'the instruction of youth, especially the poor, in religious knowledge',[19] the brothers saw their chief objective in China as making their Catholic pupils better Christians and helping 'pagan' pupils who wished to become Catholics to prepare for baptism. These were Galvin's priorities also. And the quality of their teaching of English and foreign arithmetic attracted 'pagan' pupils, just as Galvin had envisaged. He wrote, approvingly, to Blowick:

> The order and discipline of the whole place is delightful ... All boys, without exception attend Mass each morning ... I go there every Saturday at 10 a.m. to hear confessions ... All the boys receive Catholic instruction each morning for half an hour.

Galvin had no reservations concerning the compulsory attendance of all

---

19. *Constitutions of the Brothers of Christian Schools of Ireland* (Rome, 1923), p. 11. (Allen Library, Dublin).

boys, Roman Catholic or of other faiths, at religious instruction or Mass, and his only requirement, in January 1923, was that when a boy wished to become a Catholic 'you must have obtained the permission of the parents for the baptism'. However if a boy was the only Christian in his family he would find it difficult to grow to maturity in the faith, and in 1924 Galvin gingerly changed that policy. After a series of meetings with Harty, the superior of the brothers, Galvin ruled that the priests 'would baptise no more of our boys unless the parents also came into the Church'. O'Donoghue complained that the new policy was unreasonable since at the time the Columbans had no catechumenate in the city of Hanyang, and consequently no converts among the parents of Hanyang boys seeking baptism. The ruling frustrated the brothers in their chief objective. Galvin seems to have acted hesitantly in this matter, perhaps sensing the brothers' resentment at clerical interference.

In matters like compulsory religious instruction and worship and also corporal punishment the brothers ran the school as they would have done in Dublin, and seemed reluctant to accept the wisdom of even a seasoned missionary like the Irish Franciscan, Maurice Connaughton, in China since 1915. A clash between clerics and brothers threatened in August 1926 when Connaughton passed on the instructions of Costantini, the papal delegate, forbidding the compulsory attendance of students who were not Roman Catholic at religious instructions or worship, and also forbidding the slapping or beating of boys.[20] Since the government in Peking and the advancing Nationalists both prohibited compulsory religious instruction, the delegate was simply complying with that policy.

Galvin and the brothers also disagreed on the management of primary schools. He had expected some of them to become involved in the rural parish schools. In March 1923 he reported that the Columbans 'have ninety-seven schools, one hundred and thirty-nine teachers, two thousand seven hundred and eight pupils'. Blowick wrote in *The Far East* in March 1922:

> It is too bad that, whereas the Christian Brothers have undertaken for us the higher education in China, we have, so far, been unable to find any volunteers for what is really more vital and more essential – the primary education.

The statement alarmed the brothers in Hanyang. O'Donoghue told Hogan:

---

20. Maurice Connaughton to Alban O'Donoghue, 11 Aug. 1926 in O'Hanlon, 'Christian Brothers in China', p. 224.

> We have been asking ourselves here what exactly does he mean. For you can realise that a system in which the primary schools would be in the hands of another institute would leave us in a difficult position.

Yet clearly the brothers had no plans to oversee the primary schools of the mission themselves for when more brothers arrived, four in 1923 and a further three in 1925, the order took on, not Galvin's primary schools, but the Catholic college, a second level institution, in the new prefecture of Wuchang, across the Yangtze from Hanyang. Indeed they had been looking further afield. In May 1923 O'Donoghue wrote to Hogan:

> We have had Changsha [in the province of Hunan] in our eye for a long time ... We knew that it was one of the most important Protestant strongholds in China – perhaps *the* most important. We anticipated that there existed a pressing need for a Catholic college ...

A month later Thomas O'Donnell, president of All Hallows Missionary College in Dublin, and a Vincentian, presented an even more attractive appeal to the superior general of the brothers in June 1923, for two brothers to teach English in the Vincentian school in Peking. To have a community there, in a province which produced one third of all the vocations in China, must have been tempting, but the appeal was rejected. O'Donoghue commented, 'We were sorry to lose Peking.' Instead, in April 1925 the general council of the Christian Brothers voted to send three brothers to the college in Wuchang.[21] There was a clear conflict of interests between the two groups, the Columbans wanting brothers to oversee the parish schools, and the Christian Brothers concerned to have second and third level schools from which they could hope to recruit Chinese members for their congregation. It appears that these differences were not discussed openly, and Galvin continued to support the college in Hanyang. Writing to the new superior general of the Columbans, Michael O'Dwyer, in March 1925, he said that the Iron Works were selling the Bai Ya Tai property. Together with Patrick Harty and the superintendent of the Iron Works he had gone over every foot of the ground a number of times. Could the society buy it? O'Dwyer referred the appeal to the bursar, Owen MacPolin, who replied with a detailed accounting of society finances and the opinion, 'I therefore cannot recommend the sanction of the proposed 70,000 taels by the Society at the present moment.'

---

21. 'Acts of General Council', 29 Apr. 1925, in O'Hanlon, 'Christian Brothers in China', p. 179.

Political unrest, 1925-7

Political turmoil 1925-1927 caused the Christian Brothers to withdraw from China. A nationwide protest, called the May Thirtieth Movement, began when a British officer in Shanghai, on 30 May 1925, ordered his Chinese and Sikh police to fire on a crowd demonstrating against the unequal treaties and the military rulers of China, killing four and wounding many. Anti-foreign riots broke out in many cities including, on 11 June 1925, Hankow, where more Chinese were killed and wounded.[22] Students from the Catholic college in Wuchang joined the protests, going on strike. The Christian Brothers took over the administration of the college three months later, in September 1925. Unknown to the brothers, the Anti-Christian Student Federation saw the change of management as an opportunity, and orchestrated a year of anti-foreign strikes in the college by students, teachers and manual labourers. When the Kuomintang army captured Wuhan in September 1926 the Nationalist government introduced regulations for private schools, three of them conflicting with the educational practices of the Christian Brothers:

4. Private schools cannot have foreigners as presidents, but under special conditions foreigners may be appointed as advisers.
6. Private schools must not have compulsory religious courses or do religious propaganda work in the classroom.
7. Attendance at religious services in private schools must be voluntary.[23]

Several brothers felt that the sixth and seventh regulations were contradictory to their rule, which laid down:

> ... that they endeavour to promote the spiritual good of the neighbour by the instruction of youth, especially the poor, in religious knowledge, and their training in Christian piety.

Nationalist demonstrators broke into the British Concession in Hankow in January 1927. There was further anti-foreign violence when the Kuomintang armies captured Nanking on 24 March 1927, and British and American gunboats on the Yangtze shelled the city in support of their nationals. War between China and the foreign powers, Britain, France and Japan, seemed imminent. The Columban director in Hanyang, John O'Leary, advised Harty, the principal of St Columban's College, to open the school,

---

22. Patrick Harty to Jerome Hennessy, 25 June 1925 in O'Hanlon, 'Christian Brothers in China', p. 192.
23. 'Educational conditions under the Nationalist government', in O'Hanlon, 'Christian Brothers in China', p. 269.

but he refused and on 22 February 1927 the brothers left for Shanghai. O'Leary admitted that school work was difficult:

> But we do not want to give anything up until we have to; and mission work in China would cease in no time if men were to run away from trouble as these men have done in Hanyang.

Three months later O'Leary changed his opinion and wrote, 'I now believe that they were right in their decision not to open school.' O'Donoghue sent a cable to the superior general, Hennessy, on 24 February 1927: 'EVACUATED SCHOOLS IMPOSSIBLE YEARS ADVISE TEMPORARY WITHDRAWAL CHINA CABLE MARISTS SHANGHAI.' Many other missionaries took refuge in Shanghai. In April 1927 Galvin wrote to his priests:

> There is a grave danger of war between the Powers and China, there is also danger of a clash between the communists and anti-communists ... It is the opinion of all of us here that no matter what comes, we cannot desert our people ... In a critical time like this when it is a question of a priest giving his life, I do not believe it is the proper thing for me, at present, to order him to remain with his people .... Therefore, I ask the following: I ask the pastor, first, to stay with his people. If he is unwilling to volunteer – and remember, he is quite free – I ask the assistant ...[24]

Three of the Christian Brothers remained in Shanghai to see if conditions would allow them to return to Wuhan, the rest returned to Australia and Ireland. But in May, O'Donoghue judged that 'There is no hope whatever of our being able to resume work for another twelve months at least,' and recommended that they be withdrawn temporarily from China. They sailed on 20 June 1927. On 13 July the Kuomintang government outlawed the Chinese communist party and the political situation in Wuhan eased, allowing the missionaries to return. The religious orders that were prepared to follow government regulations gradually reopened their schools. However, the Christian Brothers did not return to China even though O'Donoghue's cable to Hennessy, and all other correspondence, indicated that they regarded their departure from Hanyang as a temporary measure.

Galvin had become disillusioned about education in China, according to John O'Leary, believing that the Columbans would do better by trying to

---

24. Edward J. Galvin to the priests of Hanyang, 27 Apr. 1927 in Bernard T. Smyth, 'Galvin and Galvin-related letters', (CFCA, P.1) p. 170.

instruct adult Chinese in the Catholic faith. In June 1927 O'Leary wrote to O'Dwyer, the Columban superior general:

> I do not know where I am in the matter of education in China. We have no schools at all now. All the energy is being put into catechumenates.[25]

Catechumenates taught adults, not children. O'Dwyer responded in July 1927 insisting that Rome wanted Catholic schools, for 'even though immediate results are disappointing, the schools make for the ultimate [success] of the church.' But O'Leary found that both Galvin and Quinlan, previous director of the Columban high school, were 'very much in favour of severing the connection with the Brothers'. Quinlan's reason was:

> … that the expense of providing for them will be too heavy for the Society, that the work they do will not be worth that expense, and that under the leadership of Bro. O'Donoghue it is likely that our relations with them will not be pleasant.

Galvin wrote to Michael O'Dwyer in October, advising him not to bring the brothers back to China. He believed that the priests could run the college in Hanyang, and would ultimately be a greater success than any brothers. In his opinion:

> A brother is trained in such a way that he sees only the boy at the desk; an ordained priest's zeal reaches out to the pagan parent of the boy and he knows, almost by instinct, that it is a matter of supreme importance to bring the parent into the church in order to safeguard the faith of the boy.

It is a feature of dedicated people that they tend to focus on their own field of endeavour, the teacher in the classroom and the priest in the parish. But clearly the Columbans in Hanyang, because of different priorities in evangelisation, and limited resources, would not initiate an invitation for the brothers to return.

The Sisters of Loretto at the Foot of the Cross

Sisters had an important place in Edward Galvin's original plan for the mission in China. Two days before his first meeting with John Blowick on 4 September 1916 he could already tell Joseph O'Leary of his broad vision of 'Priests in bundles and Sisters galore.' A year later, at a public meeting in

---

25. John O'Leary to Michael O'Dwyer, 5 June 1927 (CFCA, CN A-5).

Dublin in October 1917, Blowick envisaged 'a new congregation of nuns whose vow would be the medical care of the sick in pagan countries'. Initially the energies of Columbans had to be focused on appealing for funds and recruits, setting up the new college, and sending the first bands of priests to China. But by March 1921 one of the men in Hanyang, announcing a school for boys, wrote:

> Our school has been opened. We have accommodation for a hundred children. Our one regret is that we cannot do something for the many girls of school age.

Blowick appealed to Mother Gertrude Chamberlain, superior of the Irish Sisters of Charity, saying that 'we are badly in need of about 12 sisters in China next September'. Since the Sisters of Charity decided not to go to China, Edward J. McCarthy, in Omaha, wrote to Blowick in September 1921 asking if 'you or the Council have any deep rooted objection to taking Sisters from an American Order'. If not, he offered to try 'to get what I consider the best and most progressive order in America', the Sisters of Loretto at the Foot of the Cross,[26] founded in Kentucky by a Belgian missionary, Charles Nerinckx, in 1812. Blowick, already over-worked and in poor health, was unable to tackle the question of the Loretto sisters just then, but the following March McCarthy felt free to open negotiations with Mother Praxedes Carty, their superior general:

> Father Galvin, in China, wrote me recently to say that their mission had reached the stage where it was impossible for them to do any effective work unless we could get some order to take up educational work, and he suggested the Sisters of Loretto ... Our Superior-General, Father Blowick will be in the United States at Eastertime ... One of the reasons he is coming at this time is to endeavour to find an order here in America who will take up this work.

The Loretto sisters, according to the first article of their constitutions, were founded 'for the good of the neighbour through Christian education and instruction of the youth, principally through the parochial schools'. But they understood this to mean the parochial schools in America. Opening a mission in China was a major decision, which Mother Praxedes referred to their general chapter. On 22 July 1922 she wrote to McCarthy:

> You have doubtless ere this received my wire of the 20th instant, as follows: 'Votes of the General Chapter were in favour of Chinese

---

26. Edward J. McCarthy to J. Blowick, 2 Sept. 1921 (CFCA, CN A-5).

Mission.' ... My connection with the matter now ceases, and you will take up the affair with the new Superior General, Mother Clarasine Walsh.

Blowick and his council would have liked six Loretto sisters for Hanyang 'at the earliest possible moment'. But the Loretto order had to ask the Roman congregations of Propaganda and for Religious for permission to go to go to China, and to undertake work not prescribed by their constitutions. Blowick thought that their mission in China would involve more than education, and:

> ... that unless the Sisters are prepared to undertake other work, such as the visiting of the poor, the care of the sick, and the like, it would scarcely be worth their while coming to China with us.

The Congregation for Religious agreed a change in the Constitution of the Loretto sisters, on 7 February 1923. In addition to education they would also 'visit and give spiritual and material assistance to the poor and sick'. A further addition, authorising them to go to the foreign missions, was deemed to be unnecessary. A formal agreement between the Sisters of Loretto and the Columbans was signed on 7 March 1923. In it the sisters contracted to send six volunteers within the year, and to pay for their passage and their support in China. The Columbans undertook to 'provide a home and school or schools for the said Sisters of Loretto at the Foot of the Cross'. McCarthy announced the good news in the March issue of *The Far East*, spelling out that:

> The Sisters will take over the supervision of girls' education and will establish a number of primary schools, together with a high school and college at Hanyang.

A remarkably mixed group of six sisters left the motherhouse in Kentucky on 12 September 1923, three American, one Irish, one from Holland, and one from Bohemia, Czechoslovakia. Their first languages included Dutch, Czech and Spanish. On their arrival in Hanyang on 19 October 1923 Galvin wrote an exuberant letter to a Loretto sister in Kentucky:

> We are now 53 all told, 39 priests, 4 of whom are Chinese, 8 Brothers and, last but by no means least, 6 Sisters all the way from Kentucky. Out here we have so many nationalities that there can be no doubt about our Catholicity. We have an Indian doctor and an American doctor, an English priest, if you please; a representative from Czecho-

Slovakia and another from dear little Holland and then, it goes without saying of course, that the Irish are swarming all over the show.

Galvin also reported their arrival to Blowick, and in the same letter sounded a warning, 'All the priests are well, but the brigandage trouble is still acute and is causing all of us a great deal of worry'. John O'Leary, director in China from 1924, reported an even more imminent threat to the mission of the sisters. There were long delays in negotiations for a plot of land where the Columbans proposed to build a convent:

> But that only puts us into a greater difficulty, for even if the Society could build them a convent, I do not see how it could build and support a school for them at present. And that school would not be worth much to the mission.

O'Leary didn't have the money to build and support a school, but even in 1924 seems to have doubted the value of the school, presumably as an instrument for the conversion of the Chinese. Other Roman Catholic authorities in China in 1923-1924 had questions about schools. Monsignor Celso Costantini, the apostolic delegate, complained in a pastoral letter in March 1923 of schools which had a reputation for good results in the humanities, languages and economics, 'But conversions are not many, even rather few'.[27] Costantini expected church schools to produce Christians, not just good examination results. However, the first plenary council of the bishops of China in 1924 affirmed:

> Christian schools seek to cultivate piety among the faithful and to propagate the faith among infidels, and they are to be valued as one of the most apt means of evangelisation, even if not many conversions of pagans come to fruition in them.

Columbans, faced with growing commitments in Ireland, America, Australia and China, and a limited income, had to evaluate each work in light of their primary goal, 'the preaching of the gospel according to the teaching of the Holy Roman Church to the Chinese people'. Galvin's immediate concern, in inviting the Loretto sisters, was the Christian education of women. He had mentioned this anxiety frequently during his earlier missionary work in Chekiang province in 1914. A crisis in 1921 forced him to act. Blowick described the emergency:

---

27. Celso Costantini, *Epistola ad vicarios apostolicos*, 19 Mar. 1923 (CFCA, China Correspondence: 064).

Owing to the great floods caused in our district in China last year our Fathers have had to provide work and shelter for 300 Christian women.

Each summer, in July or August, the Yangtze rose, swollen by the melting snows of Tibet, and usually augmented by rain in the inland provinces. Dykes protected the land and the people, and could contain a rise of up to fifty feet, provided they were in good repair. The dykes broke in 1921, thousands were drowned, and the survivors driven from their homes. Christian mothers begged Galvin to help their daughters who were forced to sleep out on the open hillsides near the city.[28] Faced with starvation, fathers of families had nothing to sell but their daughters. Galvin found shelter for 300 women, but faced the problem of feeding them. His solution was to have some of the women trained to support themselves by producing priests' vestments, and in the spring of 1923 he founded an embroidery school. The vestments would be sold in America through the publishers Benzinger Brothers. 'At the school, there would be time for religious instructions. These young women would make good Christian wives and mothers.' Later, when the refugees had gone home, priests continued to send girls from the country missions, so that they could have solid religious instruction. Girls would stay there for two years before returning to their village. Galvin wanted the Loretto sisters to take over the management of the school (Plate 3.3). A priest, quoted in *The Far East* in March 1924, announced:

> The six Sisters have arrived. They have taken charge of a work which we were only just trying to keep going.

However, the Columbans had contracted to build a school or schools for the sisters, clearly meaning schools for general education. The embroidery school was more of a factory or workshop (Plate 3.4), and while three sisters learned skills like managing workers and dyeing silk threads, only one was free to open a small primary school. An editorial in *The Far East* of August 1924 lamented that there were vacant lots on either side of the sisters' dwelling, but:

> … land is at a prohibitive price within the city gates. It costs £10 for one fong, that is for ten feet square. It would cost £1,000 to buy the ground before ever a stone is erected. And a larger school is necessary if the Sisters' work is not to die.

---

28. Sister Clementia Rogner, 'A memorable day in Hanyang' in *The Far East*, xxiii (Apr. 1940), p. 70.

Mary Jane McDonald, the superior of the Loretto community in Hanyang, discussed the educational limitations of the embroidery school with Galvin and in July 1925 reported to her superior in Kentucky:

> Today we outlined a plan by which the commercial work would become secondary and the religious and educational primary. Under such conditions there is no reason in the world why we should not take it over.

Michael O'Dwyer, superior general of the Columbans, while on visitation in China in 1926 wrote to his council concerning the society's agreement with the sisters:

> In a letter of a few days ago, explaining the financial state of the Society to the Council, I mentioned as one of the obligations the contract with the Loretto Sisters … I instructed the Prefect [Galvin] to ask the Sisters if they would be satisfied to have a home at the Embroidery and to be given charge of same in place of school.

The Loretto sisters, while still hoping for a high school, agreed to manage the embroidery school, improving it by additions like new dormitories, and searching for new products and markets. A catalogue produced in 1932 announced:

> The School specializes in Church embroidery, but embroidered novelties of all sorts, such as lingerie, kimonos, scarfs, baby dresses may be made to order.

Numbers in the school varied, sometimes dropping to around 100, but in times of war or flood rising to three times that total, and the sisters guided it through many calamities until the American citizens among them were interned in 1942. They also helped feed thousands of refugees from floods or war, nursed victims of cholera and smallpox, and their letters home frequently reported the joy they experienced in baptising 'dying infants, cholera victims, mortally wounded soldiers, and old people on the verge of death'.[29] Mary Jane McDonald finally got her wish in 1933, running a high school for girls, but in Shanghai, at the invitation of the Jesuit fathers. Galvin still wanted to provide higher education for girls, but could not find the money to pay for it.

---

29. 'Letters from Loretto', *The Far East* (US ed.), xvi (Feb. 1933), p. 11.

The Missionary Sisters of St Columban

Members of a third religious congregation, the Missionary Sisters of St Columban, joined Galvin in Hanyang in 1926. Founded by John Blowick and Lady Frances Moloney (1873-1959), widow of Sir Alfred Moloney, former Governor of the Windward Islands, West Indies, the congregation was erected by Dr Michael Fogarty, Bishop of Killaloe, on 10 September 1924.[30] In a talk on the Maynooth Mission to China given in October 1917 Blowick had outlined the history of the mission and the immensity of the task it faced, before predicting that the society would need the help of:

> teaching nuns and brothers.... [and] a new congregation of nuns whose vow would be the medical care of the sick in pagan countries, whose members would be properly qualified in medicine, surgery and midwifery.

Frances Moloney responded to his call. Since the death of her husband in August 1913 she had been attracted to the religious life, and to medical work on the missions. When she approached Blowick in June 1918, he responded, 'It seems to me as if you were the person chosen by God to set on foot a new congregation or order'.[31] The Columban superior general's council considered the proposal for a Catholic ladies' medical mission on 9 December 1918 and agreed:

> Regarding Lady Moloney's scheme for the establishment of a Catholic ladies medical mission, it was unanimously deemed of highest importance to our mission. A general guarantee was given her that our Society would accept their services when we got a Vicariate in China. The consideration of relations between the two societies was postponed.

Blowick sent the council's commitment to Moloney the following day, describing her proposal as 'the forming of a body of ladies for the purpose of nursing, teaching and medical work in our districts in China'. By the insertion of the word 'teaching' he kept open the possibility that her organisation would have 'a branch for higher education'. In an article in *The Far East* of January 1919 Blowick stressed the need for a ladies' medical mission, pointing out that:

> Protestant doctors and nurses are literally flocking to China – at the present moment there are 200 lady doctors in China, while we have not even one ... We have appealed for lady doctors as well as for nurses.

---

30. Michael Fogarty, *Decretum Erectionis*, 10 Sept. 1924 (CFCA CA A-12).
31. Sheila Lucey, *Frances Moloney, co-founder of the Missionary Sisters of St Columban* (Dublin, 1999), p. 154.

Galvin had a very different proposal to that of Moloney and Blowick. He, and the priests in China, sent a ten-page reply to questions from the council of directors about the nature and role of the new congregation. According to Galvin they envisaged sisters who would live out in the country parishes:

> They would teach the girls, instruct women converts, go short distances from their convent ... and instruct the women who for one reason or another may not be able to leave their homes and come to a Catechumenate.[32]

Secular education in the parish primary schools would be in the hands of Chinese teachers, supervised by the Sisters of St Columban. To live in rural towns they had to be 'physically strong and prepared to rough it if necessary', and while able to learn Chinese,

> ... to my mind for the kind of work that I have outlined above, the sisters do not require any very special training or qualifications, beyond an ordinary National School education.

Galvin's primary concern, going back to his experience in Hangchow (1912-16), was that converts to the Roman Catholic Church, mostly illiterate people, should be thoroughly instructed in their faith. To help with women converts he wanted sisters who, in his opinion, need not be highly educated. But he did not recognise that a congregation composed of graduates of the national schools would not be equipped to undertake other roles in the mission of the church, and perhaps would be unable even to govern itself. His plan for the medical side of the mission was for 'one sister in each district to have a good knowledge of nursing', not any special training, but just enough to manage until a doctor arrived. As for Blowick's appeal for lady doctors, Galvin judged that:

> Lady doctors are not, I think, practical. In practice men doctors do not want to work with lady doctors. To put it frankly, they cannot agree, so at least the doctor here assures me, and I have got the same view from a Protestant lady doctor.

This remarkable statement would appear to have been contradicted by the experience of female doctors, like the Methodist, Dr Sally Wolfe from Cork, who served in Hupeh from 1915-1951. Her letters suggest that she was able to work with male doctors, foreign and Chinese.[33] Galvin was not quite

---

32. Edward J. Galvin to John Blowick, 1 Feb. 1922 (CFCA, CA A-12).
33. Jane Wright, *She left her heart in China, the story of Dr. Sally Wolfe* (Groomsport, 1999) pp 45 and 76.

so dismissive about having the Columban Sisters take charge of a high school, but suggested that perhaps that should be left to an American order. Michael O'Dwyer, Blowick's successor as superior general in Ireland, had a broader image of the Columban Sisters, for in drafting a letter to the Congregation for Religious for the Bishop of Killaloe in 1924, he wrote:

> The congregation also proposes to its members as special duties: to exercise spiritual and bodily care for the Christians in the missions to which they are sent; to provide primary and higher education for the Christians and pagans living in those places; to help the poor and afflicted; to teach Christian doctrine, especially to women and girls; and finally, to labour for the conversion of pagans.

O'Dwyer emphasised the educational, pastoral and catechetical work of the sisters; any medical mission is covered by the vague 'bodily care for the Christians'. He did not mention lady doctors, because canon law still forbade religious 'without an apostolic indult, to practise medicine or surgery'.[34] Blowick hoped for a change in the law, but the sisters had to wait until 1936 before the Congregation for the Propagation of the Faith announced, with questionable accuracy, that it was accustomed to grant the necessary indult, and also gave permission for sisters to act as midwives.[35]

The first five Columban Sisters went to China in September 1926 (Plate 3.5) to run a catechumenate for women and a dispensary. They spent several months of their first year in Hanyang learning Mandarin, and then had to seek refuge in Shanghai when tensions between the National Revolutionary Army of the Kuomintang under Chiang Kai-shek and the foreign imperial powers made war a real threat. Galvin wrote in April 1927:

> There is a grave danger of war between the Powers and China, there is also danger of a clash between the communists and anti-communists. From almost every Vicariate priests and sisters are being evacuated, or have already gone to Shanghai.

Galvin ordered the sisters to Shanghai. But when peace returned in 1928 he resurrected his plan for the sisters to go to the country parishes. He explained the need to O'Dwyer:

> The priests and myself discussed the situation yesterday at a general conference and every man has his tale of woe – perversions, indifferent Catholics, Catholics who know nothing or practically nothing …

---

34. *CIC*, canons 139, 592.
35. Petrus Fumasoni Biond., 'Instructio' in *AAS*, iii (1936), pp 208-9.

I have found and so have the priests that where a woman or two in a little mission was instructed she held the place, or if under pressure it perverted, she was in most cases mainly responsible for bringing it back.

Galvin wanted the Columban sisters 'to go to the country' to train the women, and he proposed to build two central catechumenates, in places that 'are fairly safe', and to place four sisters in each. He suggested Sientaochen for the southern counties and either Yokow or Yuin Lung Ho in the north. Unfortunately on 21 November 1929 bandits burned Yuin Lung Ho. But Sientaochen had never been attacked, so on 16 April 1930 five sisters arrived there to staff a catechumenate and dispensary. Nine days later, on 25 April 1930, the Sixth Communist Army over-ran the town. Two priests were held by the communists, but by the most amazing good fortune the five sisters, with Bishop Galvin and two other priests, escaped. Such unsettled conditions restricted the work of the sisters to the city of Hanyang, ending, for the moment, Galvin's vision of having them in every parish.

Orphanages
One of the works of mercy carried on by missionaries, at the behest of the Holy See, was the running of orphanages. The Association of the Holy Childhood provided support for:

> … the redemption and Catholic education of heathen babies who have been abandoned by their parents or have been exposed to death as often happens in certain lands.[36]

Missionaries in the field were divided about the value of orphanages. Some regarded 'the erection of orphanages as one of the "most radical" means of spreading the faith' since the children would be brought up as Catholics. Others felt that if the money spent on an orphanage was used instead for the salaries of catechists these would bring in many more converts. Supporters of both points of view were blinkered by the dominant model of mission which saw evangelisation as more important than love of neighbour. Preaching the word of God or establishing the church were the primary tasks of missionaries. Schools, hospitals and orphanages were considered as 'indirect missionary means' and those who staffed them as 'auxiliary' affording 'eminent assistance and service to the heralds of the gospel'. The criterion for mission was

---

36. Pius XI, '*Rerum Ecclesiae*' at Papal Encyclicals online (http://www.papalencyclicals.net/pius11/p11REREC.HTM) (12 Jan. 2004), p. 5.

no longer, 'I was hungry and you gave me food.' Galvin shared that thinking, opposing orphanages both from his desire to attract Chinese of higher classes to the church, and because of the economic situation of the society:

> John [Blowick] and I ... decided to cut out the S. Infantia [Holy Childhood] and all such charitable stunts for the present at least, as they would tie us up with the lowest kind of coolie class and put a burden on us which we couldn't bear ... I spoke to several prominent Chinese and they all without exception said that the great objection fairly decent men had to becoming Catholics was that in the church there was nothing but paupers.[37]

He was still against having 'an orphanage of the Holy Childhood type' when he explored the new mission in Jiangxi in 1928, thinking that 'a young Society like ours had not the means to take up that work to any extent'. The plight of young Christian girls, evacuees from floods in 1921, forced him to provide shelter, but he tried to make the project a self-supporting embroidery school. By 1932 he appears to have mellowed, writing to O'Dwyer:

> We are about to open an orphanage in Ying Wu Dzou for Christian boys whose fathers have been killed by the Communists and bandits, and who are now, many of them, thrown on the world ... Our idea is to give these boys a trade, and so try to set them up in life.[38]

Vicariate, 14 July 1927

The Columbans in Hanyang in 1930 must have felt disappointed at the results of all their work and sacrifice. Their more intensive efforts in opening parishes, building churches and schools, providing the sacraments, and instructing converts brought only modest results. A Roman Catholic flock of 14,719 in 1922 grew to only 17,233 by 1930. Numbers of those seeking baptism or under instruction fell, and many left the church. Doctors and Irish Christian Brothers had come and gone. Financial restraints meant that the society could not build schools for the Sisters of Loretto, and communist armies made it impossible for the Columban Sisters to go to rural parishes. Yet in 1927 Propaganda recognised that since the erection of Hanyang as an apostolic prefecture in 1923 'it had received greater increase', prompting the Pope, Pius XI, to make it an apostolic vicariate.[39] He appointed Galvin as

---

37. Edward J. Galvin to Joseph O'Leary, 9 Aug. 1920 (CFCA, China Correspondence: 018).
38. Edward J. Galvin to Michael O'Dwyer, 1932 in *The Far East* (Australian ed.), xiv (Mar. 1932), p. 15.
39. Pius XI, '*Venerabilis frater*' in *AAS*, xix (Rome, 1927), p. 404.

vicar apostolic. The apostolic delegate, Celso Costantini, together with Eugene Massi, vicar apostolic of Hankow, and Odoric Tcheng, vicar apostolic of Puchi, ordained him as titular bishop of Myrina,[40] and vicar apostolic of Hanyang, on 6 November 1927. Odoric Tcheng was one of six Chinese bishops ordained by Pius XI on 28 October 1926, the first Chinese bishops since Luo Wenzao in 1685, and the first step in creating an indigenous hierarchy.

Spectacular church growth, 1932-40
Galvin's annual printed reports for the years 1932-40 described spectacular increase in the vicariate of Hanyang, seen most strikingly in a chart of church growth (Figure 3.4).

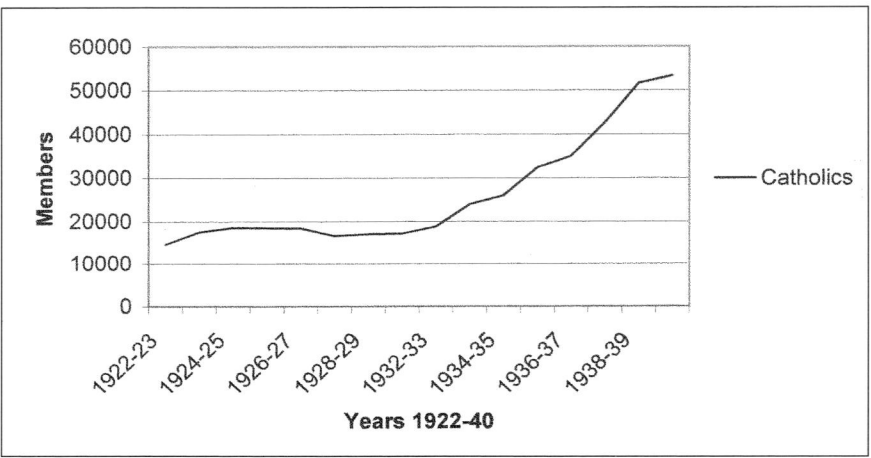

Source: Annual Reports, Vicariate of Hanyang 1922-40 (CFCA, CN A-4).
Figure 3.4 *Church growth in the vicariate of Hanyang 1922-40*. The number of Roman Catholics remained almost static until after the flood in 1931. Then it rose spectacularly

The numbers of Roman Catholics, of catechumens seeking baptism, of those under instruction, and of actual baptisms all increased sharply after 1931. Totals for people not making their Easter confessions dropped, while statistics for confessions, communions, and catechists rose steadily (Table 3.4). Growth in church membership was consistently greater than the number of adult and child baptisms, and comparison of the statistics shows that more men and women were under instruction than were being baptised. This suggests that some were poorly-instructed Catholics, perhaps people who had

---

40. As a vicar apostolic Galvin was not bishop of Hanyang. A vicar apostolic was made titular bishop of a defunct see. Myrina is in Turkey, in the ecclesiastical province of Ephesus.

left the church, and were returning. The missionaries were overwhelmed by the mass of new converts.

An amazed Galvin reported in November 1932 that:

> All the pagan community ... are loud in their praise of the work [the church] did during these terrible years, and especially last year when our priests worked day and night to feed the thousands of starving people ... The Sisters handed over their convent to the refugees, and every day they worked with the priests in a huge refugee camp where 100,000 starving people were huddled together. This work of charity brought the mission of the church very clearly before the mind of every pagan ... with the result that whole countrysides have come to us to signify their intention of becoming Catholics. In the history of this Vicariate there never was such an extraordinary influx.[41]

1932-3	1934-5	1935-6	1936-7	1937-8	1938-9	1939-40
Catholics	18,885	26,000	32,428	35,025	42,660	51,544	53,338
Baptisms: Adults	3,820		6,040	2,671	7,915	9,056	4,130
Children of Catholics	730		977	1,070	1,187	972	1,797
In Danger of Death	1,175		2,932	1,885	1,989	5,625	1,158
Catechumens	26,513	18,364	18,527	9,677	34,486	37,012	10,682
Deaths	1,645		970	942	899	991	1,475
Extreme Unctions	465		677	679	581	643	744
Annual Confessions	11,559		19,539	20,616	23,972	28,036	27,353
Devotional Confessions	69,447		106,282	108,667	110,381	101,640	107,346
Annual Communions	11,505		19,572	20,451	23,863	28,891	28,214
Devotional Communions	120,237	177,373	179,683	178,860	129,124	167,159	
Easter Duty Unfulfilled	1,138		1,409	2,076	1,733	1,411	
Confirmations	1,229		131	4,182	2,675	126	
Marriages, Catholic			157	202	186	176	
Marriages, Mixed			213	227	214	301	
Men under Instruction	3,989		3,953	1,729	3,484		
Women under Instruction	3,412		4,270	2,114	4,959		
School pupils: Boys	1,625		4,278	2,693	1,614		
School pupils: Girls	599		211	343	229		
Catechists, Male		302	102	148	271	138	202
Catechists, Female		76	54	56		53	
Priests		38	41	41			46
Virgins							
Primary Stations				26		26	

Source: Annual reports, Vicariate of Hanyang (CFCA, CN A-4).

Table 3.4 *Church growth, vicariate of Hanyang 1932-40*. Galvin boasted of the huge increase in numbers but he was aware that many converts received inadequate instruction. Had it not been for the Pacific war and the communist victory of 1949 normal parish life and worship would have supplied the missing formation.

41. Edward J. Galvin, 'Peace after years of turmoil' in *The Far East*, xvi (Feb. 1933), p. 27.

The rush of people wishing to enter the church, Columbans believed, was due to the example given by priests, sisters and catechists in the years since 1927, and especially during the apocalyptic devastation when, in 1931, the Central China Flood inundated seventy thousand square miles, forcing twelve million people from their homes. Hanyang, at the confluence of the Yangtze and Han rivers, was engulfed. Galvin described, on 31 July 1931, how:

> It has rained steadily for over a month; there is eight feet of water in the Su Wan [Columban] compound … It is five feet deep in all the houses. So far as I can gather … about two thirds of the Vicariate is inundated and the rice crop is ruined. There is three feet of water in Hankow concessions and boats are plying about the streets there … Nothing like it has been experienced in 60 years.

Refugees poured into the few high parts of the city of Hanyang, most of them camping on a ridge called The Black Hill or near the Columban compound. The majority had nothing to drink except 'the putrid water around,' this bringing, inevitably, dysentery, cholera, and death. All the priests, sisters, and lay workers were given a brief instruction in tropical medicine and spent their days distributing medicine or giving anti-cholera injections.

> The Dispensary was extra busy. Every morning each priest came and got a basket with different medicines. Each basket had several jars with the name of the medicine, also the disease it was for … We had different coloured papers for each medicine. Some of our girls helped and the Virgins were there.

Galvin estimated that they 'had baptised some 4,000 pagan children and had dispensed medicine to well over 100,000 stricken people'. When a relief organisation, The Hanyang National Relief Company, was set up several priests worked with it, erecting shelters and distributing food. However,.a year later, in November 1933, attempting to explain the leap from an annual average of 800 baptisms to a colossal 3,820, Galvin made no mention of the great flood, focusing instead on the work and sufferings of the priests and sisters in the years of communist anarchy:

> The cause of this great influx of souls is, under God, to be sought in the years of chaos that have just passed, the years when Communism reigned supreme and when no man's life was safe … Our priests and Sisters went amongst them every day, shared their burdens, relieved their distress and won their gratitude.

The left wing of the Kuomintang and the communist party 'supported a vituperative anti-Christian movement'.⁴² Communist-led peasant unions, and KMT soldiers, repeatedly attacked missionaries when they captured Hupeh in 1926. In the chaos of civil war bandits were free to kidnap people and even to burn whole towns. Conditions became even worse when Chiang Kai-shek attacked the communists in Shanghai on 12 April 1927, beginning a process to drive them out of the Kuomintang. In June a telegram from Stalin ordered the communists to break off contact with Chiang Kai-shek. They retreated to the countryside and by 1930 in Hanyang:

> The whole country district was under Soviet rule; not quite half a dozen towns remained under the control of the Central Government.

Priests and Christians were under constant threat in rural parishes of Hanyang, and in neighbouring vicariates. The Bishop of Ichang, two priests, and three Chinese catechists were murdered in October 1929. Five Franciscans, including the Bishop of Laohekou, were captured on 16 May 1931, two dying in captivity. Several Columbans were kidnapped. Galvin personally carried the ransom for two priests, Patrick Laffan and James Linehan, prisoners of the communist Sixth Army for seven months (Plate 3.6). His exploit embarrassed the superiors in Ireland since he travelled on *HMS Mantis*, a British gunboat. In all these years of danger, Galvin and his priests acted on the principle 'that we could not desert our people',⁴³ and the fruit of their sacrifice, the bishop believed, was the huge influx of converts.

There are other possible explanations for the rapid growth of the Hanyang church after 1932. Timothy Leahy, pastor of Chang Tang Kow, one of the parishes where growth was greatest, admitted that many were drawn by a dole of thirty-five Chinese cents allocated weekly by Galvin to each Roman Catholic refugee during the floods of 1931, even though Leahy explained that there was no more money. However, Aedan McGrath argued that where people were so poor that even a day off work meant hunger:

> ... if you brought people into a catechumenate, to spend six weeks learning a bit of doctrine, that you had an obligation in justice to give them the equivalent in rice or in money.⁴⁴

Priests in some parishes avoided that dilemma by conducting catechum-

---

42. C. Martin Wilbur, 'The nationalist revolution: from Canton to Nanking, 1923-28' in *The Cambridge history of China*, xii, p. 596.
43. Edward J. Galvin to Michael O'Dwyer, 27 Apr. 1927 (CFCA, China Correspondence:169).
44. Daniel Fitzgerald, Interview by author, 20 Feb. 2004.

Parish	1924-5	1928-9	1932-3	1935-6	1936-7	1937-8	1938-9
Hanyang	33	46	90	318	109	83	252
St Mary's			50	444	180	112	857
Wu Shen Miao				228	31	2	139
Ying Wu Chow				101	15	8	325
Tsai Tien				50	76	50	508
Shinti 3		652		197	351	175	
Feng Kow		2		502	247	89	164
Chang Kia Kow							52
Yo Pa	9	8	365	323	71	384	151
Chang Tang Kow	23		544	1,358	393	3,120	3,204
Mo Wang Tsui					142	2,024	1,963
Sientaochen	37	22	500	361	91	230	38
Chi Wu Tai	6	9	26	201	75	89	42
Kuo Kia Tsui	16	1	384	287	32	57	60
Yung Lung Ho	12	1	132	176	35	2	16
Tsao Shih	37	93	64	113	53	34	0
Yien Dz Gong	102	4	19	78			
Sung Ho	106	32	45	225	107	103	4
Pao Shan Kiao			520	267			
Tai Lin Meao	9	85					
Kao An Lao	42	8	46	184	54	32	100
Hwang Kia Shan	66	4	166	216	59	76	337
Yo Kow	1	9	170	349	54	131	48
King Shan		18	47	131	91	64	1
Tsien Kiang				128	33	109	213
Liu Kia Ho					37		
Shin Yen Tze					31	296	232
Tien Men					440	156	175
Peng Shih Ho					3	14	0
Yen Tze Kang					15	25	0
Total	502	342	3,820	6,040	2,671	7,915	9,056

Source: Annual reports, Vicariate of Hanyang (CFCA, CN A-4(SR)).
Table 3.5 *Adult baptisms, vicariate of Hanyang, 1924-39*. While the greatest increase in the number of baptisms was in Chang Tang Kow and Mo Wang Tsui, there was also significant growth in the city parishes: Hanyang, St. Mary's, Wu Shen Miao and Ying Wu Chow.

enates at night, so that people could work in the day. According to the detailed annual reports for Hanyang between 1924 and 1939 all missions grew. The number of primary stations went from fifteen in 1924 to thirty in 1939, although in a few cases the 'new' parish was simply a change of centre. Totals for adult baptisms increased dramatically (Table 3.5). The most striking results were in Leahy's Chang Tang Kow and Mo Wang Tsui, part of Chang Tang Kow until 1936. Faced with the unprecedented mass-movement toward the church in Chang Tang Kow in 1932 Leahy and his assistant, James Chu, changed the method of dealing with catechumens:

> The old system, which had been tried and tested by hard and often sad experience, was … not to accept more converts than you could reasonably hope to absorb, with the limited personnel, money and native help at your disposal. We decided … to accept everyone.[45]

Whole communities asked to become Christian. Leahy described the process:

> One of the most influential men in each village takes the names of each family which he copies into a respectable notebook. A Chinese letter is then written in ornate style … Both letter and register of prospective Catholics are then brought to the priest accompanied by a deputation of the village potentates. The priest makes the next move … opening a school … A contract is entered into whereby no family is entitled to send its children to the day-school unless the father and mother also come in the evenings and learn the Catechism and prayers.

Chinese villages were generally made up of families who were related to each other, even sharing the same surname, so that the village might be called simply 'The Village of the Lees'. In some cases the whole village decided to become Christian, by some unrecorded process, in others only some of the inhabitants embraced the new religion. Social pressure was undoubtedly a factor. Leahy admitted that:

> Sometimes the motives of our newly enrolled villages were in question; always the motives were mixed and indeed more material than spiritual, but the great thing was that they entered at all and gave you the opportunity to open day and night schools, visit freely, and instruct them.

Galvin was concerned that instruction might not be adequate but, using indicators like the number of people not making their Easter confession, judged that it was sufficiently thorough. He sent extra priests to the area, as well as foreign and Chinese sisters, to help with the instruction. Others, at least in hindsight, thought that the process may have been rushed. In an interview recorded in 1987 Henry Collins, pastor of the neighbouring mission of Chi Wu Tai, commented:

> I would say this, that we possibly baptised them too quickly and there

---

45. Timothy Leahy, *Beyond Tomorrow* (Dublin, 1968), p. 40.

was no follow up because we had no sooner baptised them than we were kicked out ... I don't think they got good instruction. They had enough to be baptised, but then there was no follow on ... with the sacraments ... we didn't get time to consolidate our people.[46]

However, the number of adult baptisms in both Chang Tang Kow and Mo Wang Tsui increased ten-fold in 1938 and 1939, dropping again in 1940. Dan Fitzgerald remembered that after the Japanese attacked China on 7 July 1937, 'to be associated with foreigners was a way of having a certain amount of protection' from the Japanese. His observation is supported by similar, if less spectacular, expansion in other threatened dioceses. Adult baptisms in Hankow, for example, rose from 1,845 in 1938 to 4,164 in 1939, and in Wuchang from 935 to 2,476.[47] Wuhan was captured on 26 October 1938. Fear of the Japanese was a motive for conversion everywhere, but the methods used by the Columbans in Chang Tang Kow and Mo Wang Tsui amplified the results.

World War II
Almost all the Columbans in Hupeh were expelled from the rural parishes by the Japanese after Pearl Harbour in December 1941. American and Australian members were interned in Shanghai. Some Irish priests were taken to a concentration camp in Hankow, the Japanese thinking they were British. Many parishes were without a priest for several years. One pastor who remained was able to protect 1,500 women and children from the Japanese soldiers who were given three days to rape and plunder the town of Tsien Kiang. Many of the refugees became Christian through the efforts of the Legion of Mary,[48] a newly introduced lay organisation. Missionary work in the city of Hanyang came to a halt. Galvin reported:

> Even to move around here necessitated a pass to which one's photo was attached. We had to pass surly sentries with fixed bayonets, who could express no idea except by means of a grunt. Under these circumstances, mission work became quite impossible.

Inevitably some of the new Christians fell away in the face of the anti-Christian campaign conducted by the Japanese. Galvin was so concerned about the young communities where pre-war instruction was incomplete that almost as soon as peace returned he went, with Peter Zhang and two Chinese sisters,

---
46. Interview with Henry Collins, 14 Feb. 1987 (CFCA, P.145).
47. Leading vicariates in China according to adult baptisms (CFCA, CN A-4).
48. Interview with Aedan McGrath, 24 Jun. 1993 (CFCA, Oral history archive).

on 1 November 1946, to the mission of Dou Wan, an old christianity in the parish of Chang Tang Kow, their base for the next three months. Zhang wrote:

> After a few days we were ready to start our real work. The bishop went to one village, and I went to another ... Confessions, sermon and Mass took about three hours. Usually after Mass there were some children to be baptised and some marriages to be straightened out ... After supper in the evening the Catholics assembled for night prayers and an instruction.[49]

Even Zhang, young and newly returned from abroad, found it extremely hard work, but Galvin was 66 years old, and had endured near starvation and, for the entire final year of the war, daily and nightly air-raids. A priest who knew how much privacy meant to him remembered the cost of his dedication to instruction:

> And the bishop and Peter Chang [Zhang] and the two Chinese sisters, they went up to that area ... living in Chinese houses and eating Chinese food, and coping with the rats and coping with the Chinese in on top of you day and night, and no privacy, and no nothing.

Zhang remained in Dou Wan until June 1947 when he was appointed pastor of Chang Tang Kow, with four Irish assistants. They found that some villages had remained faithful. Other groups of villagers who had weakened under persecution came back to the practice of their faith. The schools of the parish re-opened and had five hundred pupils. When the communists captured the area in February 1948 the priests fled to Hanyang city. Six, including Zhang, returned to communist-occupied Mo Wang Tsui, Chang Tang Kow and Sientaochen for a few months in late 1948 and early 1949, but had to leave again when, on 1 October 1949, Mao Tse-tung proclaimed the People's Republic of China.

Foundation of the Sisters of St Mary

Evangelisation of women required women catechists and, the Columbans believed, sisters. As early as 1922 they envisaged having nuns who would live and work in the rural parishes, and not just in the more protected cities. But the near capture of five Columban sisters in Sientaochen in 1930 made Galvin reluctant to assign foreign women away from Hanyang. He decided to found an order of Chinese sisters in 1939. A nucleus already existed, the Virgins of St Mary. The first Chinese plenary council of 1924 had legislated for such virgins, describing them as women who:

---

49. Peter Chang, 'My first mission' in *The Far East* (US ed.), xxix (Dec. 1946), p. 14.

> ... remain virgins in their own homes, and serve the mission under the direction of the bishop or missionaries ... They receive no support from the mission, nor take any vows except those which, purely for devotion ... a confessor chose to allow.

Galvin had already met the 'Virgins of Purgatory' in Hangchow in 1915. Virgins served in the parishes of Hanyang, acting as catechists, caring for the village chapels, baptising children, and sometimes helping the priest to escape from bandits or communists. A number were martyred. There were many women among the refugees from the floods of 1931 and, as always, Catholic mothers appealed to the bishop to take in their grown daughters. The Columban Sisters gave him their new convent, into which he packed three hundred women. When more came he bought some Chinese houses and filled them too. Among the refugees was a young virgin called Paula Wu whom he placed in charge, calling the buildings St Mary's. After the floods a group, the Virgins of St Mary, continued to live there, running a catechumenate and a dispensary. Galvin had long 'believed that the women would be the salvation of China, and that the church should concentrate on them'. On 25 March 1939 he transformed the Virgins into a new congregation,[50] the Sisters of St Mary (Plate 3.7), which would train the women and girls in the countryside. He said:

> If we haven't decent mothers, we can't have decent families ... We foreigners must get out of the picture. We must realise that we cannot do the work for them; we must train them, and fast, and get them on their own. We will never see the end of this; all we are doing is planting the seed.

The Congregation for Religious released two Sisters of Loretto, Justa Justyn and Clementia Rogner, from the Loretto rule temporarily in 1939, 'for the most important work of their ... years in China' to train the new order. Galvin was initially blind to the limitations of the virgins. All except one were uneducated. In the opinion of one Loretto sister:

> If he had accepted girls with education they would never have consented to move in and live and go down low with these girls who had no education. He was afraid that the presence of girls with education would make the others unhappy and discontented. In the beginning too, some of the priests had the old-fashioned idea that if these girls

---

50. Sister Clementia Rogner, 'A memorable day in Hanyang' in *The Far East*, xxiii (Apr. 1940), p. 70.

knew their prayers and doctrine, that would be sufficient; they could go and teach others.

One day Galvin was shocked to hear an exasperated Loretto sister, Justa Justyn, complain about the impossibility of 'teaching a bunch of illiterate people'. Afterwards he often referred back to the incident saying, 'You saved the day, the day you said that. You must have been inspired the day you lost your temper and said it'. Only then did he realise that after their novitiate the Chinese sisters would need high school and further education. Once they became Sisters of St Mary he sent them to high school in Hankow, and later to train as nurses and teachers.

Chinese priests

Chinese priests, not just sisters, were necessary if the church in Hanyang was to reach full maturity. The task of the Columbans was not just to convert the people to the Christian faith but to provide them with 'a diocesan structure equipped with its own clergy'. Benedict XV declared that:

> Finally, the point on which all those who rule over missions must fix their principal attention is to educate and instruct members of the sacred ministry from among the people with whom they live, for in this is contained the principal hope of new churches.[51]

According to Benedict, when 'there exists a sufficient number of indigenous clergy' the foreign missionaries would 'have successfully completed their work', and he envisaged their superiors transferring 'these chosen soldiers of Christ to the rescue of another nation from the hands of the devil'. The Pope deplored that:

> … there are regions in which the Catholic faith has been introduced for centuries without any indigenous clergy being as yet to be found there, except of a lower class.

Columbans, from their earliest provisional constitutions of 1917, saw 'the work of increasing … the numbers of native bishops, priests, brothers and nuns' as part of the purpose of the Society.' Galvin could write in 1922:

> A Seminary for the education of native priests is an obvious necessity in this Vicariate. If China is to be converted, we must rely ultimately on Chinese priests to do the greater part of the work.[52]

---

51. Benedict XV, '*Maximum illud*' in *AAS*, xi (Rome, 1919), pp 444-445.
52. Editorial notes, *The Far East* (Australian ed.), v (Nov. 1922), p. 1.

Surprisingly neither the Columbans in China nor their superiors in Ireland seem to have done anything about providing such a seminary. Technically the mission in Hanyang remained part of the vicariate of Eastern Hupeh until it was set up as a separate prefecture in December 1923. Four Chinese priests, educated by the Franciscans in the seminary in Wuchang, were ordained for Hanyang in May 1923, but the apostolic delegate, Celso Costantini, assigned two of them to the newly created, all Chinese, prefecture of Puchi. Titus Seng and Paul Zhang remained in Hanyang. The superior in Ireland and his council discussed a large donation for 'a seminary in the Prefecture of Hanyang', given by an Australian donor in September 1924. They debated whether it should be a Columban or a diocesan seminary. Interestingly they decided that it would be 'a house of the society for the training of aspirants to membership in our society as priests'. However by May 1925 the Columbans faced such a financial crisis that the council was forced to change its mind and conclude that the 'seminary in Hanyang should not be a society one'. But the training of Chinese priests does not seem to have been a high priority for Galvin, and he was unaware that there were students from Hanyang in the Hankow seminary until, in 1926, he received two letters from Monsignor Eugenio Massi, Bishop of Hankow. One letter announced that two young men were shortly to be ordained. The other was a substantial bill for the upkeep of the two students, and that of several others, in both the major and minor seminaries. Costantini, the apostolic delegate, reproached Galvin for the failure of Columbans to foster Chinese vocations to the priesthood:

> At that conference in Hankow, he gave me a call-down because we didn't have a seminary, especially in view of the fact that Propaganda had given us a field so fruitful in vocations, and that we were doing nothing to develop them.[53]

Galvin ordained Dominic Wang, one of the students from the Hankow seminary, in 1928, and James Chu soon afterwards. A junior seminary was set up in Hwang Kia Shan in 1928. The twenty-four boys, all around fourteen years old, studied Chinese language and literature, Latin and mathematics as well as prayers and doctrine. Rectors from twelve vicariates met in Hankow in 1933 and decided that while each ecclesiastical district would have its own minor seminary there would be one, regional major seminary. They tried 'to secure uniformity ... in programmes and methods of working' in the minor seminaries. Boys would enter a preparatory college at twelve years old and

---

53. Edward J. Galvin to Michael O'Dwyer, 26 July 1926 (CFCA, China Correspondence: 158).

remain for two years. Minor seminary lasted for seven years, and major seminary for six, a gruelling course.

In so far as possible, the choice of students would be made from the families of 'Old Christians'. These with traditions of a hundred, perhaps hundreds of years of Catholicity behind them, would be more likely to appreciate their great privilege and be much more likely to persevere.[54]

Particularly promising students were sent to Rome. Peter Zhang and Joseph Seng (Plate 3.8), from Hanyang were chosen by the apostolic delegate in 1937 to study in the college of Propaganda Fide where they were ordained in 1942. John Kao graduated from the major seminary in Macao in 1950 and was ordained by Galvin. Another student, Joseph Yu, was sent to Rome in 1948. Ordained in 1954 he could not return to China and, with the permission of his bishop, Galvin, ministered in Australia. These eight priests were a very modest contribution to the future of the church in China. Clearly the Columbans, when they first went to Hanyang in 1920, had not foreseen a Chinese church which would have to survive without foreign help within thirty years. Blowick's vision was that:

The sending of European and American missionaries to China must continue for a very long time to come. It must only cease when there are, in China, sufficient numbers of Catholics to warrant a sufficiency of native priests.[55]

Aggressive nationalism in Japan and in China was the context of Galvin's 1939 remark,[56] 'We foreigners must get out of the picture'. But even though he saw that westerners would soon be unwelcome in Asia his priority was to lay a foundation of solidly Christian communities which would be the seedbeds of vocations. However, he treated his Chinese priests equally with the foreign ones, promoting them to be parish priests, with Irish or American assistants. While he rarely criticised other missionaries, on one occasion he remembered the arrogance of French priests in Chekiang 1912-1916:

This incident led Bishop Galvin to speak to Sr M. Justa of the shabby treatment he had received in Chekiang. They were made to feel not wanted, that they were intruders; that it was wrong for them to be in

---

54. Jeremiah Pigott, 'About Chinese seminaries', in *The Far East* (US ed.), xvi (May 1933), p. 101.
55. John Blowick, 'The Maynooth Mission to China' in *The Catholic Truth Annual* (Dublin, 1917), p. 43.
56. Interview with Sister Justa Justyn and Sister Clementia Rogner, p. 20.

China which belonged to the others. They received bad food, had bad rooms; the Chinese priests received shabby treatment ... His experience there led him to insist on a different attitude towards the Chinese, priests, sisters and laity.

Japanese surrender in 1945 brought the promise of peace. Galvin felt that the Kuomintang armies with the support of the western powers would defeat the communists. The Pope erected the hierarchy in China on 11 April 1946,[57] changing the vicariates there to full dioceses. Archbishop Antonio Riberi, the new papal internuncio to China, came to Hanyang on 1 April 1947 to install Galvin as the first residential bishop. Some priests were able to open schools. Archbishop Cushing of Boston provided funds for a Loretto high school for girls. It opened on 15 October 1947. Galvin wrote:

> One of my long-cherished dreams was to open a middle or high school in the city of Hanyang to educate girls in the vicinity. This dream has materialised at last ... But finally, with the financial assistance of Archbishop Cushing of Boston, we were able to outfit the school as required by government regulations ... The principal of the school is Sister Isabel, a Loretto Sister who is Chinese.[58]

Since Chinese law demanded that the principal of a school be a Chinese, Isobel Huang was principal of the Loretto school and James Chu was in charge of the three grade schools in Hanyang. Sisters of St Mary were already staffing a dispensary, and in the next three years, with members qualified as teachers and nurses, would run both schools and a maternity ward. The situation seemed so hopeful that Jeremiah Dennehy, superior general of the society, sent a letter to his council in March 1949.

> It revealed that Bishop Galvin was anxious to have as many as possible of his priests [on home leave] back in Hanyang, as he considered conditions very suitable for mission work.

But it was a false promise. Galvin wrote a month later, in April 1949, to say that 'a grave situation was developing in Hanyang, which prompted him to reverse his decision ... asking his priests to return'.

Communist victory, May 1949

The communist army of Lin Biao captured Wuhan on 16-17 May 1949. Next

---

57. Pius XII, '*Quotidie nos*' in *AAS*, xxxviii (Rome, 1946), p. 301.
58. Edward J. Galvin, 'A high school for Hanyang' in *The Far East* (US ed.), xxxi (Feb. 1948), p. 2.

day Galvin and a priest, Martin Croffy, were arrested briefly in the street. Dennehy, the superior general in Ireland, and his council tried to maintain normal structures, appointing new Columban officials for China on 5 November 1949. Early in 1950 indoctrination classes began for all Chinese. Fr James Chu returned from the ordeal of a three-week, enclosed course so shaken that he asked Daniel Fitzgerald to go over the teaching of the church on God, the soul, and the afterlife.[59] Priests visiting Hanyang city could not get back to their parishes, and the superior general had to transfer them to other countries. The government took over the Loretto sisters' school in September 1950, and the last two foreign members of the community were expelled from China on 23 November 1951. Galvin released all the Chinese sisters from their vows and sent them to their homes on 18 February 1951. Charges were brought against Galvin in September 1952:

> You have opposed and obstructed the establishment of an Independent Church in China. You have brought into being a reactionary organisation called the Legion of Mary. You have engaged in anti-patriotic propaganda against the government. You have destroyed the property of the people.[60]

Three days later, on 17 September 1952 he was expelled, leaving Peter Zhang in charge of the diocese. Hugh Sands, the last foreign priest in Hanyang, was deported in January 1953.

Conclusions

An evaluation of the Columban mission in Hanyang between the arrival of the pioneer group in 1920 and Galvin's expulsion in 1952 must examine what became of the priests, sisters, and lay Catholics left behind. From 1951 Chinese Roman Catholics came under increasing pressure to join the Three-Self Movement.[61] The bishops in China and Pius XII condemned this movement as an attempt to set up a national church.[62] For most Chinese Roman Catholics, loyalty to the Pope and priestly celibacy became powerful symbols for the entire Christian way of life. Of the priests of the diocese of Hanyang Joseph Seng promoted the Legion of Mary, and died in a

---

59. Interview with Daniel Fitzgerald, 28 Sep. 2005 (CFCA, Oral history archive).
60. Report of Edward J. Galvin, 25 Sep. 1952 (CFCA, China Correspondence: 458).
61. John Tong, 'The church from 1949 to 1990' in Edmond Tang and Jean-Paul Wiest (eds), *The Catholic church in modern China* (New York, 1993), pp 9-11. The Three-Self Movement proposed a church that was self-governing, self-supporting, and self-propagating.
62. Pius XII, '*Cupimus imprimis*' in *AAS,* xxxxiv (Rome, 1952), p. 155.

Communist prison in Shanghai on 10 January 1953. An oral message reaching Hong Kong in 1956 stated that:

> Two Columban priests (Chinese) were executed at 9 pm on November 2nd. One Loretto Sister (Chinese) was executed at 9 pm on November 2nd.

The report was erroneous. Paul Zhang, thought to have been one of the priests mentioned, died later in a labour camp, while the Loretto sister, Isobel Huang, survived until December 1998. Peter Zhang was imprisoned from 1955-1979. Immediately after his release Zhang found work as an English teacher in Sientaochen, but used his freedom to search for his flock. He wrote guardedly to a Columban priest in Hong Kong:

> About our *sacerdotes, tres mortui sunt in carcere,* one got married and one turn-coat. All the younger sisters got married, only five old ones are alive.[63]

Three priests, Paul Zhang, Titus Seng, and Joseph Seng, died in prison. Presumably the 'one turn-coat' refers to a priest who joined the Chinese Catholic Patriotic Association. Zhang was ordained Bishop of Hanyang (Plate 3.9) in the 'underground' church by Bishop Lu Zhensheng of Tianshui, Kansu province, in 1986,[64] and led a thriving church near Sientaochen until he died on 12 October 2005. Yao Fei, a 'registered' priest loyal to Dong Guangging, the government-appointed Bishop of Hankow, was assigned to the former cathedral in Hanyang. In 2006 four priests, one elderly and three young, served Peter Zhang's communities in the rest of the diocese.

Most of the Sisters of St Mary, released from their vows by Galvin, got married, but several wished to continue as sisters. The community came together again after the rise of Deng Xiaoping 1981. In 2006 two of the original Sisters of St Mary were still alive, and had been joined by six young sisters. Living in the city of Hanyang they were under the jurisdiction of the Bishop of Hankow, but were clearly loyal to the Pope.[65] Another, quite separate, community, also called the Sisters of St Mary, worked with Peter Zhang's priests in the Sientaochen area. A photograph in *Frontier Evangelization*, the Columban magazine in Korea (Plate 3.10), in 2005 shows an amicable group which includes Chinese Roman Catholics, some registered with the Bureau of Religious Affairs and others unregistered, welcoming members of two of

---

63. Peter Zhang to Edward McElroy, 3 June 1979 (CFCA CN A-5).
64. Thomas Glennon, Report on China visit, 12 Jan. 1989 (CFCA, CN A-5).
65. Interview by author with Zhou Wen Bing, Brigid, Hanyang, China (21 Apr. 2006).

the organisations that worked in Hanyang before 1954, an American Loretto and an Irish Columban father.

Accurate statistics for the number of Roman Catholics in China do not exist. The government gives a figure of 5,000,000,[66] but that does not include members of the 'underground' church. A more accurate estimate of 12,000,000 comes from The Holy Spirit Study Centre in Hong Kong.[67] However, members of the study centre admit that even that figure is very doubtful. 'Unregistered' priests do not keep baptismal records, since these could be used by the government to prosecute Catholics. *The Guide to the Catholic church in China 2004* gives a total of 60,000 Catholics for Hanyang, the same figure recorded in the 1997 edition. The history of persecution in China in previous centuries would suggest that, while members of 'old christianities' would endure under communist pressure, many newer Christians would not. A visit to China in April 2006 revealed that the Roman Catholic communities in Chang Tang Kow and Mo Wang Tsui, where thousands entered the church between 1935 and 1939, had become tiny in number. However, the 'old christianity' of Dou Wan had barely a hundred members, raising doubts about the suggestion. Yet a Chinese sister described how, when she accompanied one of the priests to Shinti, people 'who had not seen a priest for thirty or forty years came crying'. Even more striking was the affection for long-dead Columbans shown by people in every place visited. It seems that the Roman Catholic communities in Hanyang, small, struggling, yet remarkably sturdy, are the fruit of the Columban mission there.

The Columbans went to Hanyang in 1920 for 'the evangelisation of China', which involved 'the spiritual care of existing Christians', 'the furnishing to … Christians [and] … pagans … education … [and] hospitals', 'increasing the number of native Roman Catholic bishops, priests, brothers and nuns', and 'the conversion of pagans'. One of the findings in this chapter is that this plan was a model laid down by Rome in canon law and various reports. Columbans in Hanyang were guided by the model and only on rare occasions realised that their experience contradicted it, for example when Galvin doubted the value of orphanages, or Joseph O'Leary proposed that Christianity build on Chinese beliefs.

At first the society poured men and money into Hanyang, building churches and schools, and bringing in doctors, brothers and nuns as co-workers. However, it was a very expensive programme, and the donations

---

66. Yan kejia, *Catholic Church in China* (Beijing, 2006), p. 3.
67. Tripod staff, 'Estimated statistics for China's Catholic church (October 2005)' at Holy Spirit Study Centre (http://www.hsstudyc.org.hk) (23 Mar 2006).

from Ireland, America and Australia were not enough to fund it. Following the society's general congress of 1924, a system of budgeting was introduced. Faced with a choice between schools and catechumenates, and with government policies on religion in schools, Galvin had second thoughts about education as a means of gaining converts. Results for the first ten years were disappointing.

The Roman Catholic population trebled from 18,885 in 1932 to 53,338 in 1940, although the failure of the college of the Irish Christian Brothers meant that there were few educated Catholics. Galvin consistently aimed at forming Christians who understood their faith and, with the priests and sisters of the mission, was ever pragmatic in exploring ways of achieving that goal. They used schools and catechumenates. To care for a flood of converts they devised an extended period of instruction that would continue after baptism. Galvin drew up a new catechism, and sent all available priests, sisters and catechists to the parishes most affected. But the Japanese war stopped almost all catechesis, before the experiment had been tested. When the communists came to power many converts drifted away.

Galvin recognised the special needs of women, and the role of women of faith in Christian communities, while he was still in Chekiang. In Hanyang successive plans, involving first the Loretto Sisters and then the Missionary Sisters of St Columban, were only partially successful. Due to the risk of kidnapping he could not station foreign women in rural areas, moving him to found a congregation of Chinese sisters. Yet, for a long time he, and other Columbans, failed to recognise that sisters, whether foreign or Chinese, should receive a secular education. At least part of the reason appears to be the vision that classed women as 'auxiliaries' to the 'real' missionaries, the priests.

Columbans, in common with other missionaries, and even the Pope, used language which reveals class,[68] sectarian, ethnocentric,[69] and sexist attitudes. Galvin, and some Chinese friends, did not want a church in which 'coolies' and 'paupers' pre-dominated. The Christian Brothers regarded Changsha as a Protestant 'stronghold'. People who left the church were called 'perverts'. In the acts of the first plenary council of China in 1924 Buddhists, Taoists and Confucians were described as 'infidels' and 'pagans', while Pius XI called

---

68. Margaret Preston, 'Discourse and hegemony: race and class in the language of charity in nineteenth-century Ireland' in Tadhg Foley & Seán Ryder (eds), *Ideology and Ireland in the nineteenth century* (Dublin, 1998), pp 100-112.
69. Milton J. Bennett, 'Towards ethnorelativism: a developmental model of intercultural sensitivity' in R. Michael Paige (ed.), *Education for the intercultural experience* (Yarmouth, Maine, 1993), pp 21-67.

them 'heathen'. In the anti-communist hysteria of the 1950s a Columban shuddered at 'the thought of the prolonged and barbaric tortures which only communists and Orientals could think up', and remembered how an American sister, Clementia Rogner, poured holy water over a communist inquisitor, to exorcise the devil. Benedict XV praised missionary sisters, comparing them to the 'women, who, from the very first days of Christianity, have been accustomed to afford eminent assistance and service to the [male] heralds of the gospel'. Such language limited the missionaries' ability to think creatively.

All foreigners were expelled from Hanyang 1949-54 and the local church went through a prolonged period of testing. When Deng Xiaoping came to power in 1981 a much reduced church re-appeared, men and women who recognised Galvin, the Columban fathers and sisters, and the Loretto sisters as their fathers and mothers in Christ.

CHAPTER FOUR

Mission in Nancheng, 1928-1954

Columbans were invited to take a second mission in China, the civil prefecture of Kienchang in the province of Kiangsi, in November 1927.[1] It was a hazardous time and place for a new venture. Chiang Kai-shek had broken with the Communists in April 1927. In response Mao Tse-tung established a military stronghold in the Chingkang mountains in Hunan, followed, in January 1929, by the creation of the Central Soviet straddling the Kiangsi-Fukien border, just to the south of the Columban mission.

The first Christian missionary to enter Kiangsi was the Jesuit Matteo Ricci who lived in the provincial capital, Nanchang 1595-1598. In the seventeenth and eighteenth centuries priests from several orders, Jesuit, Dominican and Franciscan, ministered in the province until, in 1838, a French Lazarist (Vincentian) was appointed vicar apostolic of both Chekiang and Kiangsi. A separate vicariate of Kiangsi was set up in 1846, again in the care of the Lazarists. The same order remained in charge of each of the divisions of the province in 1879 and 1885, when the vicariate of Kiangsi Oriental was created. This was renamed the vicariate of Yukiang in 1920. The whole province (Figure 4.1) encompassed 180,000 sq. km. and had a population of 24,466,800, giving a density of 136 per square km. However, Edward Galvin reported:

> In common with almost the whole of Kiangsi [Jiangxi] Kienchang is mountainous throughout … Small and narrow valleys, for the most part, wind in and out among these mountains, and in the valleys are the villages where the people who till the fields live.

The Bishop of Yukiang estimated the population of Kienchang at 1,500,000 in 1928, but this figure would change dramatically in subsequent years, to 1,100,000 in 1935, and only 570,000 in 1937.[2] Patrick Cleary, made prefect apostolic in 1933, carefully noted that all these figures are unreliable. In his report in 1935 he gave the estimated area of the mission as 7000 sq. km. Two years later he entered an exact 8696.67 sq. km. However, the statistics, even though questionable, indicate a huge drop in population. Infant mortality was

---

1. Edward J. Galvin to Michael O'Dwyer, 7 Nov. 1927 (CFCA, CN A-1:56).
2. Annual reports of the vicariate of Nancheng (CFCA, CN A-4).

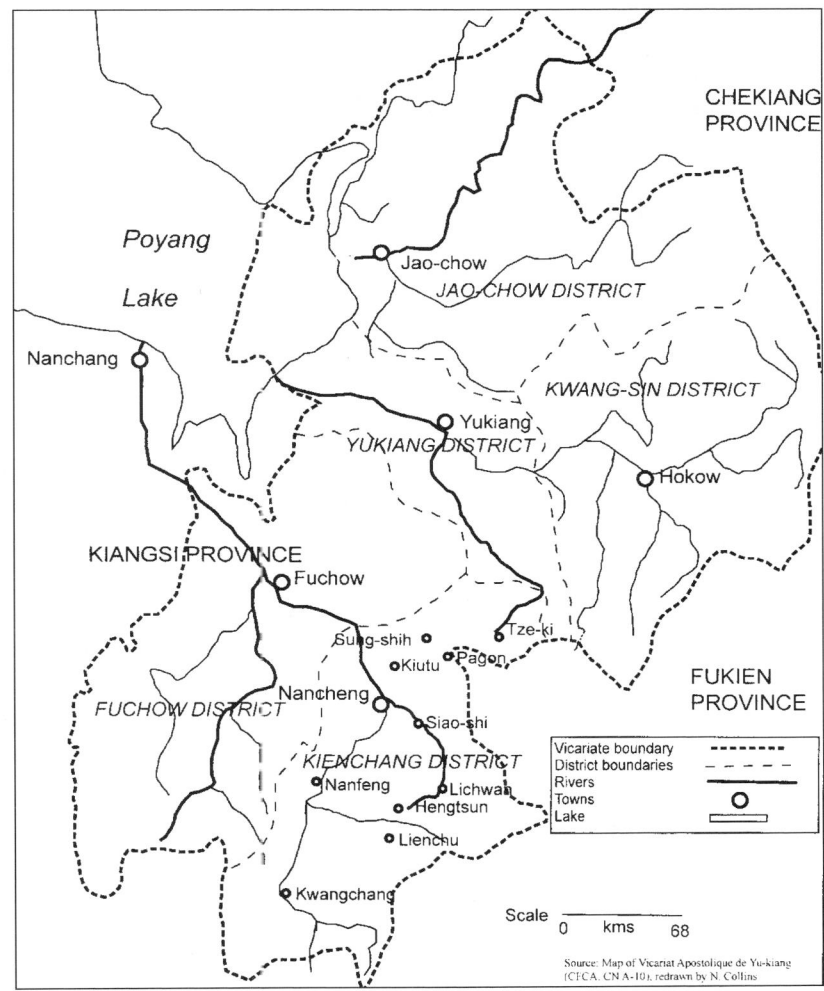

Figure 4.1 *Map of the vicariate apostolic of Yukiang in Kiangsi province, China, 1928.* Jean-Louis Clerc-Renaud, vicar apostolic of Yukiang, invited the Columbans to staff the district of Kienchang. The Pope, Pius XI, made the Columban mission a vicariate in 1938 and his successor, Pius XII, created the diocese of Nancheng, with Patrick Cleary as the first resident bishop, in 1947.

very high at the time of Edward Galvin's initial visit in 1928. But the principal cause must have been the raids from the communist bases, and the five encirclement campaigns waged by Chiang Kai-shek on the Central Soviet between 1931 and 1934.

A Columban mission in Kiangsi, 1928
The process of inviting the Columbans to Kienchang seems to have begun with a proposal by the vicar apostolic of Yukiang, Jean-Louis Clerc-Renaud, to the apostolic delegate, Celso Costantini, to separate two apostolic prefectures from his vicariate. One would be staffed by Chinese priests. Costantini, through Galvin, asked the Columban superior general to provide priests for the other. Galvin commented that:

> It appears from what the Delegate told me that the policy of Propaganda is that the Delegate and the parties concerned come to an arrangement concerning the division of Vicariates and then refer the matter to Prop. for approval.

Clerc-Renaud and two American Lazarists met Galvin and another Columban, John McGrath, from 11 to 14 January 1928 to negotiate the division. They agreed: that the boundaries of the new mission would coincide with those of the civil prefecture of Kienchang (Figure 4.1), and include the five sub-prefectures of 'Tze-ki hsien, Nan-cheng hsien, Li-toan hsien, Nan-fong hsien, Kwang-chang hsien'; that the Columbans would have their own director but that the Lazarists would supply an adviser for the first six months; that the Chinese parish priests would stay, also for six months; that two Chinese seminarians, shortly to be ordained, would be attached to the mission; and that all buildings and their furniture would 'follow their own district'. The only sticking point concerned the '*bona mobilia*' money. In canon law the Columbans were entitled to a share that would be judged a 'due proportion' by the ecclesiastical authority making the division. But the vicariate was poor, and the new Chinese prefecture apostolic would not have the sources of funds available to the Columbans. Clerc-Renaud asked that they adjourn overnight, saying, 'I will consider the question before God and I will give you what in my conscience I consider to be just.' Galvin spent the night trying to judge what a due share would be. In the morning Clerc-Renaud offered 30,000 taels. 'I ran it into dollars as quickly as I could,' wrote Galvin, 'and I decided to accept it without any further ado.' Typically, Galvin inspected as many parishes as he could before sending O'Dwyer a detailed report on population, distances, and the dimensions and condition of the church buildings:

> Let me say at the outset that the largest compounds and the finest churches and residences I have seen in China are in the Kienchang district. The *bona immobilia* [buildings] is a tremendous asset and the priests who go down there will have practically no building at all to do … We have nothing at all to compare with them in this Vicariate.

Eleven Columbans, led by Cornelius Tierney (1872-1931), were transferred from Hanyang to Kienchang in 1928. On their way through Nancheng, the provincial capital, two were delayed by a procession. 'It was the march of five communists to execution.' Soldiers of the Kuomintang occupied many church buildings in the new mission. A communist force of 3,000 attacked Kienchang at the end of August 1928, almost capturing the town before nationalist reinforcements put them to flight. There were frequent rumours of impending assaults in the succeeding months, and news of the deaths of missionaries in neighbouring provinces. In such a tense situation the Columbans began wrestling with a dialect different from that in Hanyang, opening new parishes, trying 'to get all poorly instructed Catholics to come to our schools for Christian Doctrine', and visiting the mission stations. Annual reports sent to Rome between 1929 and 1949 give an outline history of the mission.

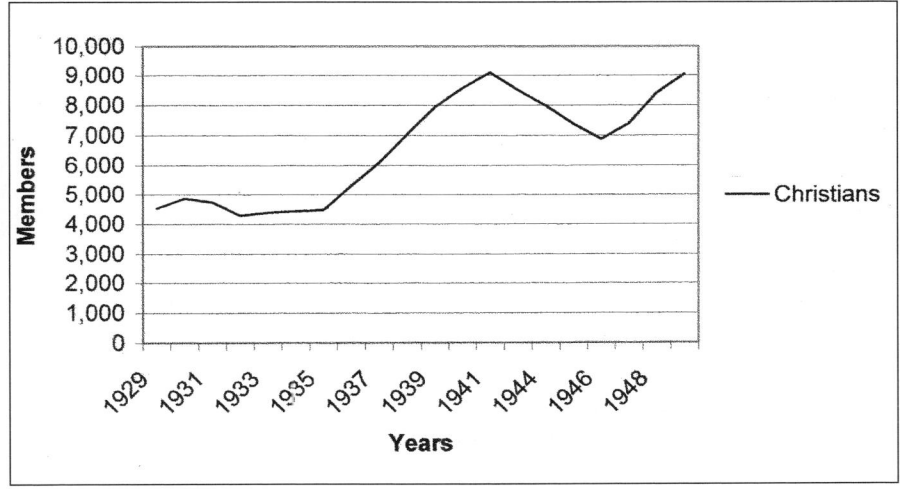

Source: Annual reports, Vicariate of Nancheng (CFCA, CN A-4).
Figure 4.2 *Church growth in the vicariate of Nancheng, 1929-49.* The church shrank while communist and nationalist armies fought in Kiangsi (1930-4). Then followed a period of steady growth until World War II. When peace returned in 1945 there was a short time of recovery before the communist victory in 1945.

Columbans in Nancheng never experienced the same flood of converts as in Hanyang in the period after 1931. Instead statistics for the number of Christians in Nancheng show that the church grew in time of peace and lost members in war (Figure 4.2). Key indicators for the years between 1929 and 1935, such as the numbers of Christians, catechumens, adult baptisms, annual baptisms and communions, climbed initially, then dropped, before recovering sluggishly (Table 4.1). For the next six years, 1936-1941, the numbers of

Christians, of annual confessions and of communions rose steadily. During the third period, 1942-1949, there was a steep decline and then a recovery.

Towards the end of 1928 the priests were assigned to five parishes, to begin their work of preaching and sacraments. Despite government regulations which forbade the teaching of religious doctrine in schools some Columbans opened state registered schools in 1929, and found that the 'regulations were not vigorously enforced'. Articles sent to *The Far East* spoke of tours of mission stations and even a visit from the superior general.

Mission in the shadow of Mao Tse-tung's soviet, 1929-34

But a cable reached Columban headquarters in Ireland on 23 July 1929 stating that Timothy Leonard had been murdered by bandits. Leonard, one of the first band of Columbans to go to China, was captured while saying Mass in

	1929	1930	1931	1932	1933	1934	1935
Christians	4,539	4,869	4,735	4,294	4,395	4,443	4,476
Catechumens				174	409	356	
Adult Baptisms	65	148	69	71	64	327	468
Missions Preached				91	9		142
Sermons given				722	195		
Annual Confessions	1,977	2,256	1,710	1,767	1,038	1,701	2,438
Devotional Confessions	6,666	17,133	14,024	12,634	9,667	19,265	20,402
Inconfessi			432	499	65	260	392
Annual Communions	1,940	2,218	1,716	1,744	1,068	1,695	2,467
Devotional Communions	14,589	36,531	32,020	29,924	28,205	43,670	47,681
Prayer Schools							41
Pupils							1,468
Elementary Schools	13	24	23	16	8	36	41
Pupils	430	621	487	496	299	883	731
Priests (Foreign)				19	24	21	23
Priests (Chinese)				2	2	2	2
Seminarians (Prep.)				6	11	14	19
Seminarians (Minor)							4
Seminarians (Major)						1	1
Central Stations							12
Out-Stations							80
Population		1,500,000					1,100,000

Source: Nancheng Annual Reports (CFCA, CN A-4).
Table 4.1 *Church growth, vicariate of Nancheng, 1929-35*. The number of Roman Catholics in Nancheng remained fairly static during this troubled period, which is quite remarkable given the huge drop in total population.

his parish of Nanfeng, taken to the mountains, and killed on 17 July 1929.[3] At a trial his communist captors accused him of breaking the law, in that 'he had practised religion and that furthermore his church had "hooked on" with the Kuomintang'. He was found guilty and stabbed to death. The same communist force, one thousand strong, captured Nanfeng again in September 1929. Michael Moran and John Kerr, forewarned, had escaped to Kienchang. On their return they found the church daubed with slogans, 'Kill the Priests', and 'Kill the Catholics'. The mandarin's residence and the Protestant church had been burned, but the military arrived before the raiders could fire the buildings of the Catholic church. Still the other priests tried to carry on normally. Peter Toal wrote about a three day retreat conducted by Fr Luke Teng for his teachers and catechists in the town of Kiutu, in the northern part of the province. Even in the southern parishes of Lienchu and Lichwan Cornelius Tierney and Edward Byrne celebrated midnight Mass at Christmas 1929. Tierney wrote:

> I am happy to inform you that we here in Kiangsi passed a quiet Christmas. The bandits and the soldiers left us alone and the result was very encouraging. All over this district there was a marked increase in the numbers coming out to the Sacraments.

However, reports of kidnappings of missionaries came from all parts of China, and for the first time *The Far East* began to mention Protestant victims. Rev Mr Sandy, a Wesleyan Methodist, was captured near Hankow on 13 December 1929, and the mission board of his church refused to pay any ransom. Even more remarkably a Roman Catholic priest, Aloys Baumeister, paid twenty pounds for the release of the Rev Mr Smith, a Protestant, in Kweichow province. National politics affected Kiangsi and the Columban mission in May 1930. Patrick Dermody reported on the effects of:

> … the war between the North represented by Yen Shi Shan [Yen Hsi-shan] and Feng Yu Shiang [Feng Yü-hsiang] and the Nanking Party … The soldiers from every place round here with the exception of Nan Feng have been drafted away quite a long time ago … A short time ago I heard [that the communists] had their agents near Lien Chu where Fr Duffy is.

The communists seized the opportunity to attack major cities, Mao Tse-tung attempting to take Nanchang, capital of Kiangsi, at the end of July 1930 and P'eng Te-huai occupying Changsha in Hunan.

---

3. Patrick Dermody, 'Seized on the altar' in *The Far East*, xii (Oct. 1929), p. 219.

On 14 November 1930 Cornelius Tierney, the superior of the Columban mission (Plate 4.1), was captured by a communist force in the town of Shang Tang Hsu where he was supervising some building work for the pastor, John Kerr. There seem to have been some former Christians among his captors for:

> He was stripped of his clothes, his hands were bound and he was brutally scourged. Afterwards they threw a soldier's red cloak around his shoulders, and all this time he was being mocked. How often he was scourged is not known; some say every day, others only once or twice. While he was receiving this terrible treatment, he kept praying continuously.[4]

Tierney was released early in January 1931 but, having walked about twenty miles towards safety, was re-captured by another band. He died while still a prisoner on 28 February 1931. Chiang Kai-shek launched three encirclement campaigns between December 1930 and October 1931 aimed at annihilating the communists in southern Kiangsi. Armies swept through several Columban parishes and the forces of Mao Tse-tung occupied and ransacked Nanfeng and Lichwan. The priests had to flee, but needed to rush back to protect churches, residences and schools from occupation by nationalist armies. Typically they found that, while new Christians had been affected by weeks of communist propaganda, 'the old Christians were of course quite uninfluenced by the Red doctrines and are wonderful in their thanks to God'.[5] John Kerr, who remained near Shang Tang Hsu hoping to ransom Cornelius Tierney, praised his teacher, Yang Mao, who disguised himself as a carpenter, entered the city, and even brought a note from the captive priest. Kerr was protected by some of his people:

> I owe my life to the old man who harboured me all during this reign of terror. He and his family were running a terrible risk in giving me shelter, for the Reds were encamped on each side and once they passed by his door … I had always two or three Catholics with me. They never left me, night or day, even when we slept on the hills or in the outhouses. I think it speaks well for the pagans, too, that though they nearly all knew where I was, no one ever gave me away.

The Japanese invasion of Manchuria on 18 September 1931 forced Chiang Kai-shek to wind up the third encirclement campaign in Kiangsi. Mao Tse-tung was unable to take advantage of the respite. Instead, his strategy of guerrilla warfare came under attack in the communist party and he was replaced

---

4. John Kerr, 'How Father Tierney was captured' in *The Far East* (US ed.), xiv (Feb. 1931), p. 15.
5. Edward Byrne, 'The reds in Lichwan' in *The Far East*, xv (Jan. 1932), p. 10.

by Chou En-lai. When the new director of the Kienchang mission arrived in December 1931 he found a largely peaceful province. Patrick Cleary (1886-1970) was professor of moral theology in St Patrick's College, Maynooth, before joining the Columbans in 1918 to become rector of St Columban's College, Dalgan Park. Shortly after his arrival in Kiangsi he wrote:

> You may have seen very alarming accounts in the papers of the position of affairs in Kiangsi. So far as this place is concerned there is absolutely no truth in them. Nan Feng is strongly held by Government forces (there are two divisions down there), and so long as Nan Feng holds out there should be no danger in the rest of the district.[6]

The priests began to rebuild, except in the parish of Lichwan which was 'in the border-land of the Red area'. Relative peace continued through 1932 until August when the communists captured Nanfeng and threatened Kienchang. A second communist raid, beginning on 17 October 1932, again drove the priests from the less secure parishes. Chiang Kai-shek launched a fourth campaign (Plate 4.2) against the Kiangsi Soviet in April 1933, followed by an even more savage, scorched-earth assault from October 1933 to October 1934, during which 'over a million peasants of Kiangsi were starved to death or killed'. The Kuomintang armies captured many towns, but Cleary reported, 'There has been no effort made to clear the surrounding countryside and I do not consider it safe to send men up there at present.' However, the government's tactics of 'slow advances, fortifying every place as they moved' and 'building roads as they go' brought victory. Priests were able to return to their parishes, but Cleary explained to O'Dwyer in his report for the year ending 30 June 1934 that:

> ... only two parishes were available for work during the entire year, and even in those two it was not safe to visit the out-missions till late in the Spring. A third parish opened shortly before Christmas, the others gradually from the end of March ... The vast bulk of the baptisms were secured among the refugees who had fled into Kienchangfu and Nanfeng.

Rebuilding

Columbans returning to their parishes, in some cases after an absence of a year and a half, found much to do. Buildings had been damaged or destroyed and furniture burned, mainly by the Kuomintang armies (Plate 4.3):

---

6. 'Editorial notes', *The Far East*, xv (May 1932), p. 97.

Hengtsuin was literally pulled down and used for fortifications by the regulars. They simply dug it up from the foundations. Curiously enough if our losses had been confined to what the Reds did on their last trip they would have been comparatively small.[7]

Slowly schools were re-opened, and the patient work of instruction and sacraments began again. Edward Byrne returned to Lichwan after eighteen months and rebuilt the church. But when two villages requested that he send catechists he could afford only one. He opted for the one where fourteen families wished to enter the church. In the other there were only seven, and it must wait until he had more money. Cleary had plans, dividing parishes and moving men to new assignments.

Columban Sisters
Cleary was so hopeful that peace would finally come that, despite the doubts of some of his council, he wrote to Propaganda on 29 July 1934 for permission to erect a convent for the Missionary Sisters of St Columban in the city, re-named Nancheng. The sisters arrived 17 March 1935 (Plate 4.4), five from Hanyang and three from Ireland,[8] to operate a school and an orphanage. Columbans in Kiangsi inherited an orphanage built by an outstanding Vincentian, Anthony Tamet in 1902. Many of the children were not strictly orphans, but girls who had been abandoned by their parents. Baby boys were rarely destroyed:

> The birth of a male child is a source of joy to a Chinese father ... On the other hand, the birth of a baby girl is regarded as little less than a misfortune, and few parents allow all their female children to live.

More girl babies were killed or abandoned in times of war when farmers could not plant rice and other crops, and the presence of soldiers increased the number of mouths to be fed, forcing up prices. Michael Moran described how:

> In normal times you find one now and again, but in the past few days five baby girls have been left at the door of the compound ... Then we send for a woman willing to nurse them. And such women are hard to find at times ... Those [babies] whom we accept we send on to our mission headquarters in Kienchang, as soon as they are able to handle a bowl and chopsticks by themselves. Of all great works of charity I think picking the helpless foundlings off the street is the greatest.[9]

---

7. Patrick Cleary to Michael O'Dwyer, 23 Apr. 1934 (CFCA, China Correspondence: 297A).
8. 'A sister's diary', *The Far East*, xviii (July 1935), p. 152.
9. Michael Moran, 'Saving the babies' in *The Far East* (US ed.), xv (Jun. 1932), p. 13.

There were municipal orphanages, 'endowed and maintained by the town council from taxes raised for the support of foundlings'. Moran visited the one in Nanfeng, finding it run by 'a few old pagan grey-beards'. It was a huge place, with over one hundred rooms, all empty. His host explained:

> Before the Boxer Rising [in 1900], when you priests had no church in Nanfeng we got very many orphans. But after the Rising you built a big orphanage and then the people went there with their orphans. From that on we got very few, and now we get none at all.

The Columban Sisters took over the management of the Kienchang orphanage in 1935, caring for more than one hundred children. Those who were old enough attended classes in the sisters' primary school. One sister boasted in 1937 that the pupils she had entered for public examinations had all graduated, and would move to a state-run middle school.[10] Sadly, many of the children who came to the orphanage were already sick and malnourished, and died as a result, or in epidemics such as measles or cholera. Cleary regarded orphans as 'an uneconomic proposition'. Some money for their support came from the Association of the Holy Childhood, founded in France in 1843 'to save from death and sin the many thousands of children that in pagan countries like China are neglected by their parents and cast away to die unbaptised'. The subsidy from that association covered only part of the maintenance of such orphans, and there was no financial help at all for the 'Catholic-born babes whose parents would have sold them to pagan families'. Cleary knew that the money needed to support five or six girls would pay a catechist, who could be expected to produce more than five or six baptisms. Other priests, like Moran, were more positive about the orphanage, supposing that the girls would marry Catholic husbands. That wasn't always possible, and the young wife might have to live under the control of a mother-in-law who was not a Christian.

> But once she is dead then the young wife becomes a mighty power for good or evil in her new home. In external affairs the husband may be master, but in the home she rules. He may be an angel, but that never seems to affect the family; the children follow the mother.

A woman who had the faith and courage to live up to what she had received in the mission school would turn her family into a flourishing Catholic community. One Columban remembered a girl called Mao Yu. Her father married her to a 'pagan'. The priest did not see her for some years, but

---

10. 'School examinations in Kienchang', *The Far East*, xx (Dec. 1937), p. 275.

asked the other Catholics to visit her. Then one day she came to his house. He inquired about the husband. 'She answered, with a glint in her eye, that her husband would do whatever she told him,' and asked for a catechism to take back with her.

A period of growth, 1935-41
The turning point in the civil war in Kiangsi was a decisive battle in Kwangchang, the southern-most Columban parish, in April 1934. For another six months the communists engaged in guerrilla warfare, 'for diversionary purposes', to gain time for the organisation of the Long March of October 1934. When the main force evacuated the central soviet in Kiangsi they left small guerrilla forces behind, and these were occasionally a threat to the missionaries. But, for the first time since the arrival of the Columbans, Cleary was able to assign two priests to Kwangchang parish. From 1935 to 1941 the Roman Catholic church in Nancheng grew steadily (Table 4.2). The most striking statistics are those for population. Cleary noted that the figure of 1,100,000 for 1935 was merely an estimate, and wondered if those for 1937 and subsequent years came from a census in 1935. The 1,175,000 in 1936 is extremely doubtful. Yet the area had been devastated by war. In a letter accompanying his 1937 report to the Holy See, Cleary explained:

> Our people have suffered almost intolerable tribulations and, as is evident, within ten years half the population has been wiped out, and the remaining part has been plundered incessantly.

Priests again began the patient rounds of mission stations, searching for Christians who had fallen away, examining catechumens, sorting out marriages that had been contracted in their absence, helping the destitute, baptising, and saying Mass. Even in 1936 the countryside remained so unsettled that they were warned not to remain in the hills more than two or three days. Yet Cleary was optimistic:

> ... the disastrous times up to ... March of 1934 gave the work a terrible set-back from which it is now barely recovering. Some parishes are now very promising; one had practically no movement though there is a decided improvement in the old Christians. A large number of people throughout the Prefecture who had not been to the Sacraments for years have now been brought back within the last two years.[11]

Many adults wished to enter the church, their numbers limited only by

---
11. Patrick Cleary to Michael O'Dwyer, 4 July 1936 (CFCA, China Correspondence: 316B).

	1936	1937	1938	1939	1940	1941
Christians	5,290	6,092	7,028	7,939	8,564	9,093
Catechumens	1,990	2,425	1,938	1,618	1,326	1,650
Adult Baptisms	764	936	1,080	1,004	757	806
Missions Preached	218	340	322	419		
Sermons given						
Annual Confessions	3,059	3,927	4,564	5,033	5,471	
Devotional Confessions	31,578	40,700	49,359	53,675	54,163	59,858
Inconfessi	271					
Annual Communions	3,066	3,948	4,578	5,236	5,457	5,719
Devotional Communions	80,755	95,524	113,485	123,186	126,014	142,234
Prayer Schools	61	92	82			
Pupils	1,737	3,102	2,491	211	333	490
Elementary Schools	27	29	25	33		
Pupils	907	1,040	1,151	1,212	1,174	1,318
Priests (Foreign)	23	25	28	26		
Priests (Chinese)	2	2	2	3		
Seminarians (Prep.)	27	30	32	28	23	23
Seminarians (Minor)	8	10	16	14	19	17
Seminarians (Major)	1			2	2	2
Central Stations	13	12	12	12		
Out-Stations	88	92	92	92		
Population	1,175,000	569,066	569,066	569,066		

Source: Annual Reports. Nancheng (CFCA, CN A-4).

Table 4.2 *Church growth, vicariate of Nancheng, 1936-41*. Statistics for Roman Catholics and adult baptisms show steady growth. Equally significant are the numbers for students for the priesthood, indicating a sustained effort at building up the local clergy.

the budget available to fund the instruction of catechumens. There was no mass movement like the one in Hanyang, yet sometimes whole villages sent representative men to the priest:

> … bringing the *gwan-hao* (the long strip of red paper containing a eulogy of the Catholic religion, together with the names of intending converts), and asking for a teacher.

Conversions always involved the 'giving up their idols, their ancestral tablets, and other superstitious objects' to be burned. But sometimes, 'for the edification of others', the event became a piece of theatre for the whole village, as in the case of a Taoist priest:

> Mr Hen, the village tinsmith, was like a jack-in-the-box, jumping for joy. My catechist collared the idol by the scruff of its neck, Mr Hen bundled the tablets into a bamboo dustpan, and so the procession began … First came myself, followed by the catechist with the idol hanging over his shoulder . Then came the tinsmith, his arms full of tablets … The ex-priest followed in the rear, a little shy on finding himself sharing in this unrehearsed liturgical ceremony.[12]

The incident seems to reveal a complex of attitudes. Perhaps Mr Hen had suffered from the ridicule of his Taoist neighbours, and was indulging in some revenge; the catechist showed that he despised the Taoist image and religion; and the Roman Catholic priest sensed the humiliation felt by the new Christian, but regarded that as a small price to pay for advertising his new faith. Priests constantly searched for points of entry into such Buddhist and Taoist villages, occasionally resorting to unusual stratagems, as when one man pretended to be lost while out hunting.

Schools

Schools remained the preferred method. Chiang Kai-shek spent much time in Kiangsi during the campaigns against the communists. While there he gave a great impetus to the New Life Movement, which he inaugurated in 1934, aimed at producing 'a militarised society, strictly disciplined and unconditionally obedient to the Leader's will'. His constant emphasis on the necessity for education brought pressure on the Columbans in the province to opt for state-registered schools (Plate 4.5) rather than those concentrating on doctrine:

> The local authorities must have a certain percentage of schools and attendants, and they look askance at mere doctrine schools which take away their boys. The law is that they can claim those boys for their schools up to the age of 18. The Doctrine School cannot be called a 'school' in law, and does not meet their requirements.[13]

Initially Cleary was slow to register any school, because doctrine could be taught only outside school hours. The priests were even more reluctant. But he found that officials were very friendly and gave him great freedom once he had registered, and informed O'Dwyer, 'I am convinced that there is no alternative of any value down here in Kiangsi, whatever may be said of other

---

12. James Griffin, 'The old Taoist priest' in *The Far East*, xix (Oct. 1936), p. 224.
13. Patrick Cleary to Michael O'Dwyer, 17 Dec. 1935 (CFCA, China Correspondence: 312A).

places.' The boys' school in Nancheng produced no converts directly, but it gave the missionaries access to the parents of the boys, some of whom entered the church. Cleary's seminarians, at the preparatory stage, attended it, and it gave them a solid foundation. Yet he remained ambivalent about registered schools:

> ... for the schools problem is a continual nightmare. If only we had the money we could capture the education of the Prefecture, and even without it we are being forced into registration here and there.

Medical mission

A medical mission in Nancheng became possible in 1934 with the arrival of Dr John J. Sherry, who opened a dispensary. The annual reports of the vicariate recorded numbers of consultations, beginning with 19,267 in 1935. Two Columban sisters took over the work when Sherry moved to a leper settlement in Kwangtung province in 1935. Their ministry won the admiration, not only of the poor, but even of members of the ruling class. They were called to attend the seriously ill sister of a government official. When she recovered the official was so overcome with gratitude that he presented the sisters with a *pien-tze* (a memorial scroll). An embarrassed sister reported on how the testimonial was brought to the dispensary, accompanied by the city band playing the Chinese anthem:

> Then, with a great many bows and much speech-making the testimonial was carried in procession to the dispensary, where it was hung in the most prominent place in the waiting-room. It is about six feet long by two feet wide and it records the name of Mother Mary Columban and the other Sisters who attended the sick girl.[14]

The priests of Nancheng parish bought an old Chinese house as a hospital for men in the autumn of 1938. With no funds available to make the necessary changes and repairs they appealed to the priests in the other parishes to help with any money they could spare from their own work. It was so poorly equipped that someone remarked, 'Its medicine cupboard has more keys than medicines.' Doctor Otto Homberger, a refugee from Nazi Germany because of his Jewish descent, arrived as its physician in 1939.[15] He was joined by Doctor Teng, some Chinese nurses and, always, the sisters. There was no money for a hospital for women, who were cared for in the dispensary in the sisters' compound. The Japanese army destroyed the hospital

---

14. 'The sisters' harvest', *The Far East* (US ed.), xxii (June 1939), p. 10.
15. 'The sisters write', *The Far East*, xxii (July 1939), p. 155.

in June 1942, but as soon as they withdrew the sisters gathered up what medicines and food that had not been destroyed or looted:

> Our hospital was no more, but we turned every available classroom and dormitory into sick wards and set out tables on the verandahs with medicines and dressings for the sick who were able to move around. Fortunately, we had a large stock of rice … to feed the half-starved refugees who flocked to us for help.

After the war the hospital was re-built and Cleary, a student of the letters of St Paul, called it St Luke's.

Apostolic Vicariate and the Sino-Japanese war
The mission in Nancheng had grown, from 4,539 Christians in six parishes in 1929 to 7,939 in twelve parishes by 1939. Following its normal practice the Congregation for the Propagation of the Faith recognised the development by making the district an apostolic prefecture on the 29 November 1932, including 'the civil sub-prefectures of Nangcheng, Tzuhi, Nanfeng, Lituan, Kuanchang'. The Pope, Pius XI, erected it as a vicariate on 13 December 1938, and at the request of Michael O'Dwyer, superior general of the Columbans, officially changed the name from Kienchang to Nancheng.[16] Cleary was consecrated bishop on 16 April 1939 (Plate 4.6). Normally three bishops take part in the ordination of a new bishop, but the Sino-Japanese war had cut Nancheng off from the Yangtze valley, so:

> The [Papal] Bulls contained the power to dispense from the presence of the assisting bishops … there was no hope of getting two for the 16th. The assistant priests were Father Dermody and Father Luke Teng. Mgr O'Shea consecrated.

Travel was still possible, but extremely difficult. Sister Michael Mongey was transferred from Hanyang to Nancheng in May 1940, sailing down to Shanghai on a Japanese passenger boat, then by ship to Hong Kong, where she flew over occupied China to Ganzhou in the south of Kiangsi, to finish an epic journey by bus.[17] But the war reached beyond the front lines. Cleary complained in August 1939 that:

> … during the last three months air-raids and the fear of air-raid provided a very disturbing factor in the people's minds especially in the cities. School-work was particularly unsatisfactory as classes could be

---

16. Pius XI, *'Praefectura apostolica de Kienchang'* in *AAS*, vi (Rome, 1939), pp 98-9.
17. Sister Michael Mongey, 'Reminiscences', 1964 (MS in CFCA, P.14, p. 70).

held only in the mornings and evenings.... Just now we are in the throes of a fearful epidemic of cholera.

Remarkably Cleary had many plans. He applied, in early 1940, to the civil authorities for permission to open a middle [high] school. There were already 'six pagan ones in the district with a membership of about 2,500'. Only about twenty-five Roman Catholics attended them, and he saw that 'in a few years we will be an uneducated coterie in the middle of a rather well-educated community'. Building construction was cheap and he reported:

> This year we shall have completed three lovely new residences and have a fourth well advanced. They will cost between £75 and £80 apiece. During Easter Week I blessed a new solid brick church in Luki. It cost about £200. Another is going on in Father Moran's parish and a third in a new parish that Father Lucey is opening ... We have a school in Luki, an extension of Kaopi church and school, and sleeping quarters for the school in Lichwan also on hands.

Cleary also composed a new catechism, and had it translated into the spoken language of the vicariate. The official catechism was too difficult for simple converts. Galvin had produced one in Hanyang, but Cleary commented that:

> ... it would not give sufficient instruction for a sparsely populated district like ours. One can baptise a whole series of villages on a lower standard than is required where isolated families are to be dealt with, for supplementary instruction is possible in the former case but not in ours.[18]

World War II

All such plans and projects were frozen shortly after the Japanese attacked Pearl Harbor on 7 December 1941. The presence of a Chinese military garrison made Nancheng a target for frequent Japanese air-raids, and there was a constant influx of refugees, many of them sick or wounded, from the neighbouring provinces. Roman Catholic German missionaries in the vicariate of Shaowu, Fukien province, to the east of Nancheng, were interned by the Chinese in April 1942. Cleary was appointed apostolic administrator, and sent six priests to staff the parishes until the Germans were freed in August. American bombers attacked the Japanese mainland on 18 April 1942, flying on to land behind Chinese nationalist lines. The Japanese retaliated by raids into Chekiang and Kiangsi, destroying bases which could be used in future

---

18. Patrick Cleary to Michael O'Dwyer, 22 Aug. 1940 (CFCA, China Correspondence: 359A).

attacks on their home islands. One plane crashed about fifty miles from Nancheng, but the crew jumped safely, and was guided to the Columbans, which made the city a target:

> In the summer of the same year, the Japanese made punitive raids into our part of China. Any place where the fliers had been was destroyed, some completely, some partially. They came to Nancheng and destroyed the city entirely.[19]

The Japanese captured Nancheng after a night of shelling, on 11 June 1942, and occupied it for a month of wanton destruction and murder. 'When they left, Nancheng city was a smoldering ruin, in which only eighteen houses stood intact.' One of the buildings destroyed was the hospital, but although fires had been set in the buildings in the priests' and sisters' compounds someone extinguished them. Despite the efforts of the bishop to explain that the Columbans were Irish and neutral, the soldiers ransacked the priests' house and the convent, stealing all money and clothing, smashing delft, furniture and equipment, and constantly threatening to shoot or stab the missionaries. Three sisters and Thomas Ellis were taken out and marched up a hill at the back of the compound. Sister Michael Mongey remembered:

> When we reached the top there was a high official there who questioned Father Ellis and said, 'You have been helping our enemies' … From our elevation we could see soldiers killing men down in the valley. Then they took Father away a bit from us and told him they would shoot him.[20]

Ellis and the sisters were again in peril when, toward the end of the occupation, they opposed soldiers who demanded the Chinese Virgins. A soldier fired at Ellis, the bullet just missing. At that the shooter said that he had never seen such brave people, and shook the hand of the priest. Nancheng's ordeal continued from 12 June to 9 July 1942. Cleary reported:

> Nancheng city is literally no more. North-east Kiangsi is a wilderness. On the west bank of the Fu from here to Fuchow there is not an unburnt village. There are hundreds of farmers in the Vicariate whose farm implements have been smashed or burned, even their plows. Since the Japanese left, we have been treating anything from 200 to

---

19. Robert D. Degnan, 'The 14th Air Force remembers the Columban missions in China' in *The Far East* (US ed.), xxix (Oct. 1946), p. 2.
20. Mongey, 'Reminiscences', p. 75.

300 a day, mostly the poorest of the poor. We have to live from hand to mouth.[21]

Refugees began to return and the missionaries helped with re-building homes, feeding the starving, and caring for the sick. As winter approached Cleary appealed to Paul Waldron, the Columban superior in the USA, for the 'thousands of families in Nancheng who have no bed-covers for the winter; who have lost their padded wearing apparel'. The war had interrupted postal and financial communications between China and Ireland. Cleary complained to O'Dwyer in December 1942:

> I have not had a line from Navan (Columban headquarters since 1927) for about eighteen months ... It seems to me that you do not realise how serious the situation is for us here. We have got only a thousand pounds from you during the whole year, and the Japanese tore up over £900 of that. The Sisters have not got a penny. Were it not for [some money from] America we should probably have had to sell out everything to save the priests and sisters from starvation.

Fortunately the missionaries still had a lot of rice, and were able to offer a meal, and some medical attention, to poor refugees. But from the middle of 1942 until the end of the war, the poverty of the people and of the missionaries limited all the usual work of the vicariate. Cleary was rather apologetic when he wrote to Patrick O'Connor in May 1945:

> But catechetical work is out of the question ... The people have no time for study in the midst of their struggle for existence ... priests are trying to do just what Our Lord did – going around doing good.

The annual reports show a decline in numbers of Christians, confessions and communions from 1942 until 1946 (Table 4.3), with the spaces for listing catechumens left blank.

In the parishes the priests continued to do the twice-yearly rounds of the 'missions' to the out-stations, the gatherings of all who would come to the parish centre for the four great feasts of Christmas, Easter, Pentecost and Assumption, the sick-calls and other ceremonies. Unable to conduct catechumenates they 'concentrated on giving our Catholics an extended training'.

---

21. Patrick Cleary, Annual report for year ending 30 June, 1942 (CFCA, CN, A-1).

	1943	1944	1945	1946	1947	1948	1949
Christians	8,505	7,979	7,376	6,885	7,396	8,402	9,037
Catechumens					745		
Adult Baptisms	166	161		271	692		647
Missions Preached					370		
Sermons given							
Annual Confessions	4,566	4,044		3,655			
Devotional Confessions	34,898	32,196		35,942			59,807
Inconfessi							
Annual Communions	4,558	4,035		3,658	4,099		5,182
Devotional Communions	83,318	84,151		91,287	103,303		125,40
Prayer Schools					9		
Pupils					112		
Elementary Schools					25		
Pupils	1,043	1,289		1,392	1,531		1,164
Priests (Foreign)					28		
Priests (Chinese)	4				4		
Seminarians (Prep.)	33	13		5	7		5
Seminarians (Minor)		18		16	14		17
Seminarians (Major)		1		5	7		
Central Stations					13		
Out-Stations					110		
Population		450,342	420,000		400,000	482,535	

Source: Annual reports, Vicariate of Nancheng, CFCA, CN A-1

Table 4.3 *Church growth, Vicariate of Nancheng, 1943-9*. The most important statistics for the future of the church in Nancheng are those for Chinese priests and major seminarians, students soon to be ordained.

Spiritual retreats

Retreats, for catechists and teachers, for schools, and for whole parishes at Chinese New Year, were a feature of Columban ministry in Nancheng, first mentioned in a letter of Timothy Leonard's written to his uncle in 1929, six days before he was killed:

> One of the greatest consolations I had during the year was when the *pusillus grex* [little flock] insisted, if you please, on making a seven days' Retreat under my direction. The spirit with which they entered into it!

A more common form of retreat was one of 'three whole days of it in perfect silence and with so much devotion and zeal'. Even in peaceful times it was remarkable that men and women gave up three days' wages to spend time in silent recollection and prayer, and even more wonderful when they did it in the extreme poverty during the Japanese War. In the parish of Kaopi in 1944 the retreat was given by Father Luke Teng, professor in the seminary in Nancheng. After a ten-mile cycle and a twenty-five mile hike he was met by an enthusiastic crowd and firecrackers:

> The program for each of the three days was [Mass], three lectures, two rosaries, the Stations of the Cross, two periods of spiritual reading in common, with evening prayers and Benediction closing the day … In fact they asked for even more – another rosary and reading at meals.[22]

Teng conducted similar retreats in Nancheng itself for the Catholic students in the state high schools. For three days he spoke to them of 'the fundamental truths of Catholicism'. Normally the students were 'isolated individuals swamped in the pagan schools they attended,' but in the retreat they experienced themselves as 'a body … a force in spreading the gospel'. Cleary reported that between five and six hundred people attended three retreats in Nancheng, Kiutou and Kaopi at the Chinese New Year in 1944, a figure that suggests that perhaps ten per cent of the 7,979 Roman Catholics in the vicariate as a whole participated in such spiritual exercises, an indication of a strong, internalised faith and great desire for spiritual growth.

Care of refugees

However, care of poor refugees was the principal ministry in Nancheng, and in a parish like Kwangchang, the furthest from the Japanese. Catholics who could not afford to rebuild their homes were housed in the church. Even before the Japanese raid in 1942 Thomas Ellis (Plate 4.7) had begun what became known as 'The Works', a group of small industries producing candles, booklets on Christian doctrine, rosaries, medals, crucifixes. He gave employment to 'down-and-outs … to save them from making idols and paper-money for a living'. When the Japanese withdrew from Nancheng in July 1942, leaving the city destroyed, life for the survivors during the next nine months was a nightmare:

> … a long-drawn, disheartening struggle against sickness, destitution, and famine. Money was not arriving from home, and it seemed as if

---

22. Bernard O'Neill, 'Firecrackers sound retreat' in *The Far East* (US ed.), xxvii (Oct. 1944), p. 6.

the Mission would have to look on helplessly at the hopeless misery which surrounded it. Fortunately the American Advisory Relief committee came to our assistance, and Father Ellis, together with the other priests and sisters, flung himself whole-heartedly into the work.[23]

Ellis, with 'Sisters Baptist [Connolly] and Malachy [McPolin] began visiting the people in what had once been their homes'. The poor received direct relief, food, clothes and bedding. 'The Works' employed two hundred women in weaving cloth and making cloth shoes and stockings. An amused Columban Sister told how an elderly woman and her daughter tried to persuade Ellis to put them in his spinning department, but he was forced to refuse, as the place was already full. A few days later he found the pair firmly established, working away, quite unperturbed by his visit. In addition to relief work he tried to carry on the regular services of the parish, and in the bitter winter of 1944 visited the mountain missions. On his return:

> ... he slaved in the hospital with a crush of 80-90 derelicts who were flung on his hands in an appalling condition with frost-bite, relapsing fever and other diseases; at one time he had seven corpses on hand because he could get nobody to bury them ... To crown all he personally conducted two Retreats for the people of Nancheng ... and next day set out for Nanfeng to conduct another there.

On the second day of the retreat in Nanfeng Ellis collapsed with typhoid. His friend, Dr Homberger 'fought a losing battle for the priest's life', and he died on 8 March 1945. The people of Nancheng regarded him as a saint.

Chinese priests
A key indicator of the success of a vicariate, more vital than an increase in the number of Christians, or even their growth in faith and in service of others, was the provision of leaders from among the members. Benedict XV's teaching was clear:

> Finally, the point on which all those who rule over Missions must fix their principal attention is to educate and instruct members of the sacred ministry from among the people with whom they live, for in this is contained the principal hope of new churches.

Columbans in Nancheng regarded the training of Chinese students for the priesthood as a priority. When negotiating the agreement to set up the

---

23. Patrick Cleary to Michael O'Dwyer, 18 Apr. 1945 (CFCA, China Correspondence: 364J).

mission, in 1928, Galvin asked the bishop, Jean-Louis Clerc-Renaud, for two seminarians who were about to be ordained as diocesan priests. The two, Philip Chou and Luke Teng, agreed to serve in the mission. However, the vicariate must produce its own priests, and arrange for their education. From 1932 the annual reports included the number of seminarians. Boys at the preparatory and high school stages studied in Nancheng itself; more advanced students went to the regional seminary in Kiukiang. But when the Japanese captured Kiukiang in 1938 travel from Nancheng, in Free China, was so hazardous that Cleary undertook the training of two major seminarians in Nancheng:

> As for myself, I am just the major seminary! Kiukiang is out of the question, so I have two boys on my hands – one a theologian and the other a philosopher. I do nearly all the teaching myself and I have begun to grow fat on it!

Cleary ordained the theology student, John Chang, in 1939.[24] The second seminarian, James Yang, having done his entire course in Nancheng, was ordained on 20 December 1942. A third priest, Joseph Peng, followed on 6 August 1952, the ceremony being held in secret, in the presence of only a handful of people. Just before the communists took control in China. Cleary sent four others to a seminary in Genoa, where they were ordained in 1953. Unable to return to Nancheng they served in Taiwan and Fiji. Zhou Jishi, Archbishop of Nanchang, ordained three others, secretly in a bedroom, on Palm Sunday 1957. One of the three died, but since 1990 Peter Xie Yunsheng has been ministering in Yingtan, in the diocese of Kiukiang.

Thomas Yu (Plate 4.3), who was attracted to the priesthood by the example of Thomas Ellis, and spent thirty-three years in prison and labour camps,[25] is parish priest in the former cathedral in Nancheng.

Sisters

Cleary contemplated founding a diocesan congregation of sisters. By 1937 interested girls were grouped in a distinct section in the grade school run by the Columban Sisters in Nancheng, and in the autumn of 1938 they were regarded as candidates for the native sisterhood:

> ... one ... was taken on to help Sister Campion [McCarthy] by teaching drawing and needlework. We have three other prospective native

---

24. Photograph, *The Far East* (US ed.), xxvi (Dec. 1943), p. 4.
25. Interview by author with Thomas Yu, Sheshan seminary, Shanghai (June 1990).

Sisters here and four have been sent to Shanghai. Of the three here, two teach in the catechumenate, while the third helps in the dispensary. One of those now in Shanghai is anxious to enter Carmel.

The Japanese war delayed the project of a diocesan sisterhood, and when peace returned four of the interested women had already joined existing congregations. Cleary feared, in March 1946, that the best of the remaining group would join the Columban sisters, and that 'the rest … would not be fit to form an independent native community'. He suggested a compromise in June 1946, proposing that the women would become Sisters of St Columban, but that they remain in Nancheng, even for their initial formation:

> I did not raise the question of the Native Sisterhood with Mother Patrick [Moloney, Mother General of the Columban Sisters]. There is a nice little group of girls rising up, and if there were a sensible and sympathetic Mistress of Novices there does not seem to be any reason why they should not be moulded into good Sisters of St Columban.

The Columban sisters did not accept Cleary's compromise, making the Chinese sisters members of a diocesan annexe of an international congregation. Instead three of the young women, including Teresita, a sister of Thomas Yu, sailed to Ireland in 1949 to enter the Columban novitiate. The Yu family came from the village of Kiutu, an old Christianity founded by two Jesuits, Father John da Rocha and Brother Paschal Mendez, who entered Kiangsi in 1618. In 1948 two thirds of the 700 inhabitants were Roman Catholic, and there had been a priest in every generation of the Yu clan. Another brother, Joseph, a teacher, translated Cleary's catechism into *t'u-hua*, the dialect spoken in Kiutu. Two of the three Chinese women became professed sisters but the coming of the communists made it impossible for them to return to China. They worked in America, Teresita in a primary school run by the Columban Sisters in Los Angeles until, in 1974, she was assigned to Hong Kong. Changes in China following the death of Mao Tse-tung in 1976 made it possible for her to visit her family in May 1979. Even then an article in *Columban Mission*, the renamed magazine of the Columbans in the US, used pseudonyms to describe her meeting with Thomas, the brother she had last seen as a seminarian in 1947.[26] She retired to the Columban Sisters' convent in Wicklow, Ireland in 1999.

---

26. 'At long last – voices out of China past', *Columban Mission*, lxiii (Feb. 1980), pp 3-5.

Source: Far East Office, Dalgan Park, Navan.

Plate 2.1 Priests of the Dunboyne House, St Patrick's College, Maynooth, 14 May 1914.
Sitting: Edward Maguire, Patrick Cleary, Michael O'Dwyer, Owen MacPolin.
Standing: Edward McNamee, Michael Daly, John Hanly, Pat Cahalane, John Blowick, E. O'Callaghan.
Maguire, Cleary, O'Dwyer, MacPolin and Blowick joined the Maynooth Mission to China.

Source: Far East Office, Dalgan Park, Navan.

Plate 2.2 The council of directors of the Maynooth Mission to China, 1917, with Matthew Dolan and James O'Connell.
Front row (L. to R.): Edward Galvin, John Blowick and John Henaghan
Second row: Matthew Dolan, Edward J. McCarthy, James O'Connell and James Conway.

Source: The Far East, iii (November, 1920), cover.
Plate 2.3 *The Far East.* Irish motifs dominating the front cover of the Columban magazine signalled the mixture of nationalist and religious themes that inspired missionaries to go to China and people at home to support them with their prayers and financial contributions.

Source: Far East Office, Dalgan Park, Navan.
Plate 3.1 The first group of Columbans to go to Hanyang in 1920.
Front: M. McHugh, E.J. Galvin, J. Blowick, J. Dawson.
Second row: T. Quinlan, O. MacPolin, R. Ranaghan, E.J. O'Doherty, J. P. O'Brien, C. Tierney, T. Leonard, M. Dolan.
Rear: J. Crossan, A. Ferguson, A. McGuinness, W. O'Flynn, M. Mee.

Plate 3.2 The Irish Christian Brothers, Hanyang, China, 1924.
Front: Alban O'Donoghue, Nicholas Kealy, James Dougan;
Second row: Pancras Howlen, Dionysius Hamill, Justin Roberts;
Rear: Gregory Barrett, Patrick Harty (superior).

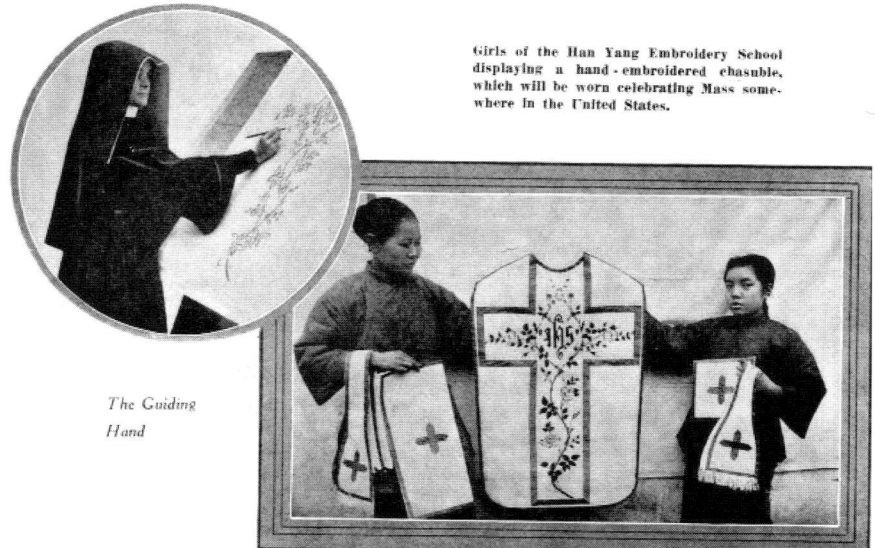

Source: *The Far East (US ed.), ix (Feb. 1926), p. 25.*

Plate 3.3 Embroidery methods in Hanyang, 1925. A Loretto sister, Justa Justyn, drew a design, here the vine surrounding IHS, symbols for Jesus and the eucharist, to be embroidered by the Chinese women on the chasuble worn by a priest at Mass.

Plate 3.4 The embroidery school in Hanyang, 1925. Galvin wanted the school to train young women who would be good Christian wives and mothers. Mary Jane McDonald, superior of the Loretto sisters, argued for a more general education. Since it had to be self-supporting the institution was a workshop rather than a school.

Plate 3.5 The first Missionary Sisters of St Columban to go to China in 1926.
Sisters Philomena Woods, Theophane Fortune, Finbarr Collins, Agnes Griffin,
Lelia Creedon, Patrick Moloney;
Fathers C. Donnelly, J. Blowick, J. Hogan, A. Ferguson, M. Fallon, J. Loftus and J. Linehan

Plate 3.6 Celebration for the rescue of Patrick Laffan and James Linehan from communists in 1930. Laffan and Linehan are seated on extreme left and right. Their ransom was carried up the Yangtze by Galvin on *HMS Mantis*, a British gunboat, thanks to the cooperation of the British consul in Hankow, W. Russell Brown (standing between Galvin and Thomas Quinlan).

Source: Far East Office, Dalgan Park, Navan.
Plate 3.7 The Sisters of St. Mary, Hanyang, 1939. The new congregation was founded by Edward Galvin and trained by Sisters Justa Justyn and Clementia Rogner. Galvin believed that the future of the church in China depended on well-instructed Christian women.

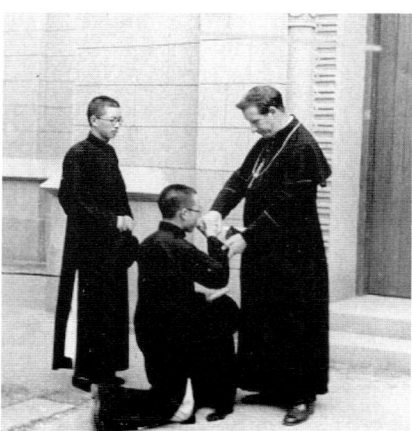

Source: Far East Office, Dalgan Park, Navan.
Plate 3.8 Peter Zhang and Joseph Seng say goodbye to their bishop, Edward J. Galvin, Hanyang, 1937.

Source: Zeng Xianghui, Hanyang.
Plate 3.9 Peter Zhang (1915-2005), Bishop of Hanyang, imprisoned 1955-79, and ordained bishop 1986.

Source: Frontier Evangelization (Seoul, Autumn 2005), p. 20.

Plate 3.10 Roman Catholics in a rural church in Hanyang, 2005. The woman crouching is the superior of a community of sisters who are registered with the Bureau of Religious Affairs, the two standing on the left, and the elderly man in front of them, are sisters and a priest in the 'underground' church.

Source: Far East Office, Dalgan Park, Navan.

Plate 4.1. Columbans in Nancheng, with Michael O'Dwyer, superior general, in 1929.
Seated: Thomas Quinlan, Michael O'Dwyer, Cornelius Tierney, Luke Mullany.
Standing: Edward McManus, unidentified, Patrick Dermody, John Kerr, unidentified, Michael Moran.

Source: CFCA, CN A-5.
Plate 4.2. Patrick Dermody with officers of the nationalist garrison in Nanfeng, Kiangsi, 1933. The troops were part of the fourth encirclement campaign of Chiang Kai-shek against the army of Mao Tse-tung.

Source: Far East Office, Dalgan Park, Navan.
Plate 4.3. Thomas McCarthy in the parish of Hengtsun, Kiangsi. The church was demolished by Kuomintang troops in 1933 to construct block houses against the forces of Mao Tse-tung.

Source: *Far East Office, Dalgan Park, Navan.*

Plate 4.4. Missionary Sisters of St Columban with pupils from the girls' school in Nancheng, 1941.
Seated: Francis Monaghan, Veronica Murphy, Michael Mongey, Berchmans Dooley.
Standing: Malachy McPolin and Baptist Connolly.

Source: *CFCA, CN A-5.*

Plate 4.5. Pupils from the boys' and girls' schools, Nancheng, on the steps of the cathedral, 1943.
Seated in the centre are Joseph Flynn, John Chang, Patrick Cleary, James Yang, and Bernard O'Neill.

Source: CFCA, CN A-5.
Plate 4.6. Consecration of Patrick Cleary as Apostolic Vicar of Nancheng, 1939. John O'Shea, Vicar of Kanchow (left of centre), ordained Cleary (centre), assisted by Luke Teng (left of O'Shea) and Patrick Dermody (right of Cleary).

Source: CFCA, CN A-5.
Plate 4.7. Sisters Baptist Connolly, Michael Mongey and Francis Monaghan with Thomas Ellis in Nancheng, 1940. The city was destroyed in June 1942.

Source: *CFCA, CN A-5.*

Plate 4.8. Patrick Cleary administering confirmation. The assisting priest was James Yang, ordained 1942. Standing between Cleary and Yang was Thomas Yu, who became a priest in 1957, after the Columbans were expelled from China.

Source: *CFCA, CN A-5.*

Plate 4.9. Ordinations in Nancheng, 1957. Zhou Jishi, archbishop of Nanchang, secretly ordained three priests. *Front row:* Luke Teng, Thomas Yu, Peter Xie, Joseph Wu, and James Yang. *Back:* John Chang, Philip Chou, and Paul Yu.

Source: Far East Office, Dalgan Park, Navan.
Plate 5.1. Jean-Joseph Deymier, archbishop of Hangchow, welcomes the Columbans to his diocese, 1946.
Standing: Jerome Halliden, James Hughes, Paddy Rowan, Owen O'Kane, William Sheridan, John Flynn, Michael McConnell and John Casey.
Seated: Fr. Yang, Jeremiah Pigott, Deymier, Fr. Tsu Feng Chin, Fr. Bao.

Source: CFCA CN A-5.
Plate 5.2. The parish of Nanzin, Chekiang, 1948. Many of the parishioners were fisherfolk who lived on their boats on the many canals of the district.

Source: Far East Office, Dalgan Park, Navan.

Plate 6.1. Columbans in the Philippines during the visit of Edward J. Galvin in 1935.
Seated L to R: John Lalor, John Henaghan, Edward J. Galvin, Patrick Kelly (superior), and Peter Fallon;
Standing: Samuel Sheehan, Thomas Connolly, Michael Donoher, Gerald Cogan and Joseph Monaghan.

Source: CFCA, RP A-5.

Plate 6.2. Michael O'Doherty, Archbishop of Manila, welcomes Columban superior general Jeremiah Dennehy to Malate school, run by the Canonesses of St. Augustine, in 1948. Gerald Cogan was the parish priest of Malate.

Source: *The Far East*, xxii (Dec. 1939), p. 274.

Plate 6.3. Mariano A. Madriaga, Bishop of Lingayen-Dagupan, welcomes the Missionary Sisters of St Columban to his diocese in 1939.
Seated: Columcille McCormack, Alberto Zobala, Madriaga, Samuel Sheehan, Francis de Sales Hogan.
Standing: Monica Finn, Vianney Shackleton, Teresa Devins, Aloysius Lenihan, Bernadette Connolly.

Source: *CFCA, RP A-5.*

Plate 6.4. Members of Student Catholic Action, University of the Philippines, Manila, with Edward J. McCarthy in 1936. These young university students were volunteer catechists, teaching religion in the secular schools in the city.

Source: Far East Office, Dalgan Park, Navan.

Plate 6.5. John Henaghan visiting the first Columbans in Misamis Occidental, 1939.
Seated: Frank Chapman, Joseph Grimley, Denis Murphy, Peter Fallon, John Henaghan, Tom Callanan, Olan Healy, Dick Brangan.
Standing: Frank McCullagh, James Corrigan, Vincent McFadden, Patrick Cronin, Martin Noone, Bill Hennessy, Gerald Byrne.

Source: Far East Office, Dalgan Park, Navan.

Plate 6.6. The cathedral in Lingayen in 1945. A three-day naval bombardment by American forces prior to invasion destroyed the roof and the interior. All Japanese forces had already withdrawn.

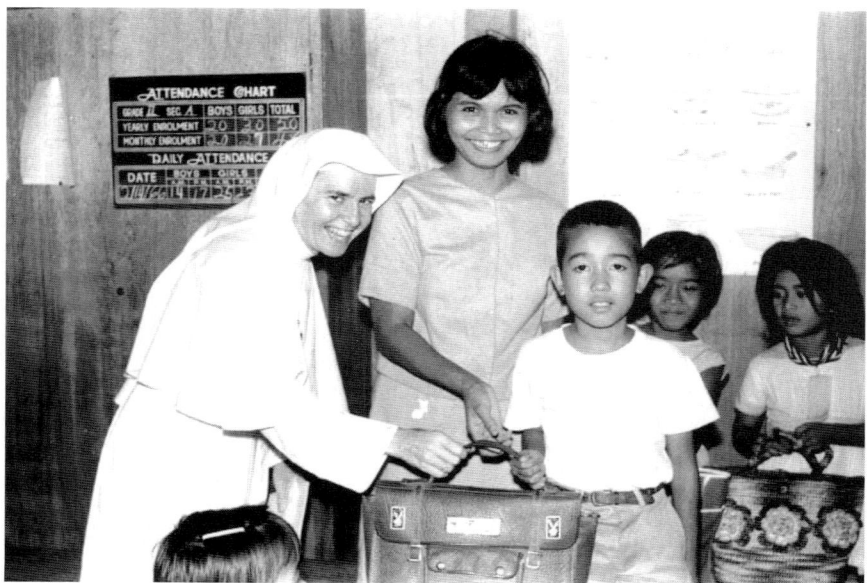

Source: *Far East Office, Dalgan Park, Navan.*

Plate 6.7. Sr Clement Sheehy arrives for class in the elementary department of Immaculate Conception College, Ozamiz. The sisters took over the elementary school in 1940 and added a high school. In 1941 they fled from the Japanese. After the war they rebuilt, and in 1946 opened a college department.

Source: *The Far East, xxxvii (Apr. 1954), p. 9.*

Plate 6.8. Thomas Brennan with Muslim friends. The population of his parish of Dansalan (Marawi) and of the province of Lanao del Sur on the island of Mindanao was predominantly Maranao, a Muslim tribe.

Source: Far East Office, Dalgan Park, Navan.
Plate 6.9. Geoffrey Revatto welcoming the Columban superior general, Timothy Connolly, 1954. Revatto's rectory in the remote mining parish of Sipalay, Negros, was a simple nipa hut.

Source: Far East Office, Dalgan Park, Navan.
Plate 6.10. Kieran Heneghan, pastor of San Antonio, Zambales, with children from a local school. Catechists or members of the Legion of Mary taught them catechism.

Source: Far East Office, Dalgan Park, Navan.
Plate 7.1. Mokp'o, Korea. Mokp'o was the headquarters of the first Columban mission in Korea before the outbreak of the Korean war in 1950.

Source: Far East Office, Dalgan Park, Navan.
Plate 7.2. Florian Demange, vicar apostolic of Taegu, with the first group of Columbans in Korea, 1933.
Seated: Thomas D. Ryan, Owen MacPolin (superior), Demange, Patrick Dawson, Patrick Monaghan.
Standing: Harold Henry, Jerome Sweeney, Gerard Marinan, Brian Geraghty, Thomas Neligan, Daniel McMenamin.

Source: The Far East, xx (July 1937), p. 152.

Plate 7.3. Girls' night school in Mokp'o, Korea, 1937. The school offered Christian doctrine, reading, writing, and sewing for three hours each night.

Source: Far East Office, Dalgan Park, Navan.

Plate 7.4. A Japanese propaganda photograph of priests of the prefecture of Ch'unch'on interned in 1942. *Front:* Brian Geraghty, Thomas Quinlan, Pat Brennan. *Second:* James Maginn, Frank McGann, Tony Collier (giving the victory sign). *Third:* Pat McGowan, Phil Crosbie, Tom Neligan. Fourth: Paddy Deery, Frank Herlihy, James Doyle, Frank Gallagher, Hubert Hayward.

Source: The Far East (US ed.), xxxiv (Dec. 1951), p. 5.
Plate 7.5. Fifty Columbans, including Harold Henry (centre), served as military chaplains in the wars of the twentieth century. One, Patrick McMahon, was killed in Normandy in 1944.

Source: Far East Office, Dalgan Park, Navan.
Plate 7.6. Thomas Cusack and Korean friends. In 1950 Cusack was arrested by North Koreans in the company of Patrick Brennan and John O'Brien. All three were taken to Taejon prison. It is thought that they were massacred along with the other prisoners before the communists withdrew.

Source: Far East Office, Dalgan Park, Navan.

Plate 7.7. Thomas Quinlan arrives at Gatow airfield, Berlin, 27 April 1953. Quinlan spent thirty-two months as a prisoner of the communists in Korea. Together with six Britons he was welcomed by Mrs. H. B. Nixon of the US High Commission, Major General C. F. C. Coleman, British commandant in Berlin, and the band of the Royal Scots Fusiliers.

Source: Far East Office, Dalgan Park, Navan.

Plate 8.1. Charles Gilhodes MEP, 1941. Beside the bearded Gilhodes are Patrick Usher and Edward J. McCarthy. *Columbans in second row:* William Kehoe, Bernard Way, Thomas McEvoy, Thomas Dowling, Lawrence McMahon, James Foley, Michael Barry. *Third:* James Devine, Frank McManamon, Edmund McGovern, Kevin Flatley, Malachy Lyons.

Source: Edward Fischer, Mission in Burma, p. 84.

Plate 8.2. James Stuart, seated right, with General Frank Merrill of Merrill's Marauders, during the guerrilla campaign in Burma in 1944.

Source: Far East office, Dalgan Park, Navan.

Plate 8.3. Patrick Usher visits Momauk, parish of Denis McAlindon, in 1950. McAlindon was pastor of Kachyihtu during World War II, evading the Japanese. The heavy silver ornaments were typical of the ceremonial dress of Kachin women.

Source: Far East Office, Dalgan Park, Navan.

Plate 8.4. The catechists' school, Bhamo, 1950, on the occasion of a visit by Jeremiah Dennehy, Columban superior general. Seated: Bernard Way, Dennehy, Patrick Usher, John Howe and Edmund McGovern.

Source: Far East Office, Dalgan Park, Navan.

Plate 8.5. A Kachin family show their devotion to the Sacred Heart of Jesus and to Our Lady by setting up a shrine in their home.

Source: Far East Office, Dalgan Park, Navan.

Plate 8.6. Missionary Sisters of St. Columban in Burma. The sisters normally worked in Myitkyina, teaching in school. However, Sisters Ita O'Mahoney and Maureen Griffin were often invited to parishes along the Irrawaddy.

Source: Far East Office, Dalgan Park, Navan.

Plate 8.7. The dormitory of a seminary in northern Burma. Columbans selected boys from the families of teachers and catechists and gave them a preparatory year in Mogok before sending those who had a vocation to the priesthood to the minor seminary in Mandalay.

The final months of war

Foreign missionaries of all denominations in Kiangsi appear to have expected a Japanese offensive in the province in early 1945. In the years since the previous incursion in 1942 the Columbans had entertained many American airmen, and could expect harsh treatment from the Japanese, so Cleary made plans:

> Should we be threatened with occupation I shall send the Sisters up to Luki. It is completely out of the line … I would also disperse the priests through the country missions, though I would probably remain here myself to try to save the buildings.[27]

Members of the Chinese Inland Mission in both Kiangsi and Fukien left for western China, as did the American Vincentians in the vicariates of Kiukiang and Ganzhou. Japanese advances normally followed good lines of communication, such as railways, but in late January 1945 they moved from Hunan into southern Kiangsi, to occupy the airfield at Suichuan and destroy another at Ganzhou. Cleary, normally optimistic, spoke of 'a moment when I almost despaired of being able to carry on', and suggested to O'Dwyer that 'I'm getting stale. It is high time to get your eye on a successor.' Yet, in the same letter he was planning for the end of the war, asking O'Dwyer to think of establishing a technical school, and warning that:

> We shall want a big number of priests immediately after the war … Most of the districts are now being run as one-man parishes. There are no substitutes to give them the rest and change they require. Moreover, the majority of the men are now overdue for home leave.

Cleary could see the toll that the sufferings of the war had caused to the missionaries. Poor diet left them prone to sickness, and in the cold winter of 1944 their clothes were rags, and their footwear made from old tyres. The terrible plight of the people weighed heavily upon them. Sister Michael Mongey, who had witnessed the disastrous floods in Hupeh in 1931, wrote to the mother general, Patrick Moloney, in Ireland:

> There is a great deal of poverty this year, more than I ever saw since I came to China. Starving people flock to our gates; many have to be put into the sick ward, and all need clothing. The Bishop will not have anybody turned away while he has a dollar left.[28]

---

27. Patrick Cleary to Timothy Connolly, 24 Jan. 1945 (CFCA, China Correspondence: 364G).
28. Sister Michael Mongey to Mother Patrick Moloney, Dec. 1944 in *The Far East*, xxviii (May, 1945), p. 36.

Edward McManus, stationed in Kunming as Cleary's procurator and channel for communication between Nancheng and the Columbans in Ireland and America, detected a querulous note in the letters of the men in China, 'showing that no matter what they say, the last few years have been a considerable strain'. When news reached Cleary that six Columbans had been killed by the Japanese in the Philippines, one in May 1943 and five in February 1945, his first concern was for Sister Francis Monaghan, sister of one of the murdered priests, and stationed in Nancheng.[29] And he worried about the Columbans still in areas under Japanese control:

> I hate to contemplate the possibilities in Shanghai and Hanyang in [case] of an open conflict. I have tried to send a message of warning to Bishop Galvin, but I do not know whether it will get through. I have not heard directly from him for a couple of years ...

Oddly, the Columbans in China did not mention, in the extant correspondence, the dropping of the atomic bombs on Hiroshima and Nagasaki in August 1945 and the Japanese surrender in September, yet these constituted another turning point in their mission.

Japanese surrender, August–September 1945
Letters from Nancheng to Ireland in 1945 kept returning to the problem of personnel. Many priests were long overdue for vacation, and Cleary hoped that older men who had been at home when the war began would return as soon as possible. Apart from Thomas Ellis none of the Nancheng priests had died or was seriously ill; in Hanyang one priest died, and many were sick physically or mentally.[30] The comparison suggests that the rigours of war were greater in Hupeh, occupied by the Japanese and bombed by the Americans, than in Kiangsi. A second, ominous theme was the danger of civil war. Nicholas Cody, the regional bursar, stationed in Shanghai explained that at the end of 1945:

> There is a ring of communists and guerrillas between the Japanese and Chungking (Chinese Nationalist) armies. As far as this area, i.e. Shanghai-Nanking, is concerned the Chungking forces cannot pierce this ring, so they have to rely on airborne troops to come and take over from the Japanese.

---

29. Patrick Cleary to Michael O'Dwyer, 31 May 1945 (CFCA, China Correspondence: 364L).
30. William McGoldrick to Michael O'Dwyer, 3 Sept. 1945 (CFCA, China Correspondence: 365).

The two topics, of re-organisation of the church and the military threat from the communists, recurred at different levels for the next four years. Immediately after the war it was impossible to get passage from Europe to the Far East, and the first reinforcements for the weary missionaries, five priests and two sisters, arrived only in August and October 1946. Two of the priests were veterans who had previously served in Nancheng, but the others were neophytes who could say Mass, in Latin, but needed to study Chinese before they could engage in any kind of evangelisation. Ten other young priests reached Nancheng early in 1947, and were placed in parishes where 'they will study the language under the supervision of their respective pastors'. McGoldrick, superior for the region of China, and based in Shanghai, warned O'Dwyer that Cleary had more priests than he needed, unless he was to open new parishes, 'but prospects would hardly repay the expense of building new churches and residences'. It is unclear whether 'prospects' refers to the small number of converts or threat of invasion.

Strengthening Roman Catholic defences, 1946-8

The Roman Catholic church was strengthening its defences, and looking for allies, against communism at the highest levels. Pius XI had condemned 'bolshevistic and atheistic communism' in 1937.[31] His successor, Pius XII, moved to encourage nationalist China as a barrier to communist expansion. First he instituted the Roman Catholic episcopal hierarchy in China on 11 April 1946.[32] Prior to that date the bishops and archbishops in China were vicars apostolic, delegates of, and deriving their authority from, the Pope. After tracing the history of the church in China from the mission of John of Montecorvino in the thirteenth century, and giving a detailed list of all the ecclesiastical territories, especially those ruled by Chinese bishops, together with numbers of Christians, priests and religious, the Pope stated that the time had come to erect the hierarchy, thus making the leaders of the church 'residential' bishops, deriving their authority from Christ. They became:

> ... successors of the Apostles and by divine institution are placed over the particular churches which they govern with ordinary jurisdiction under the authority of the Pope.

The pope's decree raised the church in China to the same level as it had 'in the other nations of the Catholic world'. In a further move, Pius XII, on

---

31. Pius XI, '*Divini Redemptoris*' in *AAS*, xxix (Rome, 1937), p. 66, '... *de quo minaci periculo loquemur; de communismo sciticet bolscevico, quem vocant, eodemque atheo...*'.
32. Pius XII, '*Quotidie nos*' in *AAS*, xxxviii (Rome, 1946), pp 301-313.

6 July 1946, appointed Archbishop Antonio Riberi as the first apostolic internuncio to the government in Nanking. Previously the Vatican representative in China was an apostolic delegate, dealing only with bishops and church affairs. With Riberi's appointment, and that of a Chinese minister to the Holy See, Dr Wu Chin-hsiung, China and Rome were establishing diplomatic relations. In Kiangsi the immediate effect of the new arrangements was the installation of a Chinese archbishop, Zhou Jishi, in Nanchang, the provincial capital, in October 1946. Zhou asked the Columbans for some priests, one as his personal secretary, and another to take charge of the middle school in Kiukiang, and he wished 'to hand over the North-West portion of his diocese to the Society'. Riberi, the internuncio, also needed personnel:

> The Nuncio is very keen on establishing the Legion of Mary in China and called here yesterday to see if we could lend him Father Aedan McGrath to tour the country as his delegate. He had already heard of Aedan's success in running the Legion.[33]

The Legion of Mary, founded in Dublin in 1921, helped lay people to develop spiritually and to become involved in the apostolate of the church. Through it the nuncio hoped 'to enlist many of the zealous laity in the apostolate of making the church better known and loved in China'. Riberi also planned to reorganise the seminaries in China, and wanted Columbans to staff a central minor seminary for Kiangsi. Cleary sensed, on a visit to Nanchang in June 1947 for the enthronement of the archbishop, that the Chinese government would press the nuncio for the appointment of more Chinese bishops as vacancies arose, and suggested to O'Dwyer that the Columbans re-open 'the question of admission of Chinese priests into the Society', or at least those who could be considered '*episcopabiles*', possible bishops.[34] The topic of accepting Chinese men as members of the society does not seem to have been formally discussed by the Columbans since 1924.

The Archbishop of Nanchang, Zhou Jishi, presided at the ceremony of raising Nancheng to the status of a diocese when he installed Cleary as resident bishop on 7 October 1947.[35] Since Cleary was already a bishop there might have seemed to be little of substance in the change. Yet it was seen as the crowning of the growth of the mission, through all the labour and trials,

---

33. William McGoldrick to Michael O'Dwyer, 12 Feb. 1947 (CFCA, China Correspondence: 389A).
34. Patrick Cleary to Michael O'Dwyer, 9 June 1947 (CFCA, China Correspondence: 391B).
35. Hugh Bennett, 'Dr. Cleary becomes bishop of Nancheng' in *The Far East*, xxxi (Mar. 1948), pp 40-41.

since the first two Jesuits, John Da Rocha and Paschal Mendez, established a christianity there in the seventeenth century. With the return of more settled conditions in 1946 the Columbans in Nancheng predicted further increase, since many people were interested in the church:

> This looks like a good year as far as conversions are concerned. Here in my parish, Lichwan ... we have upwards of one hundred under instruction, mostly in the country districts. During the past few days, many people in the town have come to ask for catechisms and wanted to be instructed.

There was even hope of converts from the mandarin class. One of the civil dignitaries present at Cleary's installation as bishop was Yang Ta-Ching, prefect of Nancheng city, a catechumen who, together with his wife and family, would be baptised in 1948. A few experienced priests returned from vacation, and the younger men slowly acquired 'an imperfect mastery' of Chinese, and began the search for 'lost sheep', before 'undertaking a campaign for the conversion of the pagans'. Cleary could report growth in 1947, for the first time in five years, with a net increase of 511:

> The figure in itself is not very big, yet it marks a very definite turn in the tide, and I have every hope that, if peace continues, each succeeding year will see a notable increase in that figure.

Cleary's optimism was tinged with that note of caution, 'if peace continues'. There was peace in Kiangsi, and the government forces were, up to that point, winning the civil war in Manchuria and the north of China. However, a communist force of about 4,000 moved into the diocese of Hanyang in December 1947, bringing the war to the Yangtze, the only barrier to southern China. Despite that news the most pressing matter in letters between Cleary and Dennehy was hyper-inflation and the setting up of a bureau in each mission to raise funds from the friends whom priests knew in America.[36] Both society and church authorities were attempting to continue normal work. The nuncio 'worries the life out of us [bishops] with questionnaires'; new priests arrived in China and were sent to a language school in besieged Peking, although the superior general asked Cleary if he could accommodate them in an emergency; the archbishop of Nanchang continued negotiations for handing over part of his diocese to the Columbans. Patrick Brennan, the superior of the Columbans in China, advised the superior general 'that young priests should be sent to other Regions' because of the alarming reports from

36. Patrick Cleary to Jeremiah Dennehy, 26 Dec. 1947 (CFCA, China Correspondence: 402B).

north China, yet when he made a formal visitation of Nancheng in May 1948, getting to almost all parishes and finding the men in good spirits, 'the conversation always turned to convert work and their instruction'. Cleary knew that the line of the Yangtze would not hold out under any severe pressure, and there is a rather resigned tone in his comments on the report for the year ending 30 June 1948:

> There have been no evident signs of communist propaganda in the district. So far, the communist armies have not succeeded in gaining a foothold in South China, yet, while the issue in the North is still in the balance, we cannot see very far into the future. Will you kindly get all the prayers you can that, if it is the Lord's will, we may be spared an invasion.

He saw the 'steady improvement in attendance at Sunday Mass' as 'our best hope for the permanence of our work', but noted that:

> Several of our priests have, in season and out of season, preached the importance of the Rosary. Some of them, in tepid missions, have gone so far as to go round to the homes at night to share in the family rosary, and the results have been very remarkable. Wherever the Fatima Devotion of the First Saturdays has been introduced the response is very gratifying. Here in Nancheng it is not uncommon to have 300 for communion on a First Saturday.

The 'Fatima Devotion', according to José Galamba de Oliveira, Bishop of Leiria in Portugal, was requested by Our Lady in an apparition to three children in Fatima in 1917, but was made public, by Galamba, only in September 1939. It involved confession, communion, five decades of the rosary, and meditation on the mysteries of the rosary, on the first Saturday of the month.[37] The visionaries called her 'the Lady of the Rosary', and said that she wanted the faithful to pray the rosary every day. Part of the message of Fatima, quoted frequently in *The Far East*, would have appealed to Columbans threatened by communist armies, the promise that:

> The Holy Father will consecrate Russia to me and she shall be converted and a period of peace will be granted to the world.

Missionaries encouraged the people to say the rosary for the conversion of communists, but were also inculcating an exercise which the people could continue even if all the priests were expelled or in prison. Despite the threats,

---

37. Finbar Ryan, *Our Lady of Fatima* (Dublin, 1948), pp 178-179.

Brennan, the superior in China, continued to write to Ireland in 1948 about normal matters such as getting a new boiler for the superior's house in Shanghai, giving men time to study the language, and floods in Hanyang, before turning to politics in August 1948:

> The situation in China is about the same. Today the Nationalists are winning, tomorrow, the Reds claim a victory. Inflation is beyond this world. The realistic quotation for the $US is 13 million. Fortunately the government is printing notes of a higher denomination, otherwise you have to carry a suitcase full of paper to buy a newspaper.[38]

The Columbans held a general chapter in June 1947, the first since 1931, and elected a new superior general, Jeremiah Dennehy (1904-1951), who worked in Nancheng before World War II. He visited China and, in a talk to the priests in Kiangsi on 23 November 1948, when the Huai-Hai campaign was being fought just north of Nanking, ultimately allowing the communists to reach the Yangtze and southern China, gave challenging instructions:

> The Catholic Church does not retreat. In Kienchang we represent the church. For health reasons I am withdrawing two men. Every man present here has volunteered to stay. As your Superior General, I now ask you to stay at your posts no matter what happens. I hope and pray there will be no loss of life.[39]

Riberi, the papal internuncio, told Dennehy that, in the event of a communist victory, the Pope wanted sisters to remain at their posts, caring for the sick, the elderly and orphans, in the hope that they might be allowed to continue, and perhaps break down the hostility of the communists. Priests should remain in their parishes, even if their work was restricted. 'We must not run away.' Cleary was strengthened by Dennehy's message from the internuncio:

> You have taken a great weight off my mind. In spite of everything the decision to hold the priests and sisters had begun to weigh upon me; but the Internuncio's assurance that it is the will of the Holy Father makes a great difference as I feel on safe ground now.

Yet Dennehy, and other church leaders, recognised that a communist victory was imminent, and that missionaries would be expelled from China. The society received invitations from bishops in Japan, the Philippines,

---

38. Patrick Brennan to Michael O'Dwyer, 18 Aug. 1948 (CFCA, China Correspondence: 417B).
39. Luke O'Reilly, 'Red flows the tide' in *The Far East* (Australian ed.), (Oct. 1962), p. 11.

India, Fiji, and South Africa, and Dennehy told his council that 'the Society would need new mission fields in the immediate future'.

Communist victory, 1949
Communist armies crossed the Yangtze on 21 April 1949, and reached Nancheng on 10 May. Nationalist forces withdrew without a fight, and casualties were negligible. Cleary, in a letter posted in Hong Kong, was surprised at the good behaviour of the invading troops:

> The Communist forces went straight to the Government Office and did not come near the church. There has been no official visitation or examination, and no attempt to interfere with ourselves or our work … Discipline in the city was excellent and there was a manifest desire to create a good impression in the minds of the people.

The bishop asked O'Dwyer to notify the friends of the priests and sisters that all were well, but commented that 'of course you will want to be particularly careful now about what the *F. E.* (*Far East*) prints'. He complained about a 'fulmination' by Richard Cushing, Archbishop of Boston, in the April issue of the American *Far East*. Cushing wrote:

> Today the Kingdom of God on earth is under attack in China, and Catholic Christians will be among the first victims of a Red-Fascist victory over free China … you have a special right to ask me … to lift my voice against the rape of China by Red Fascism and the abandonment of China by free nations.

Cushing wanted the American government to help the nationalist government of China to defeat the communists, but Cleary believed that such protests put the missionaries in jeopardy. He wrote to Dennehy in April 1950, so angry that he wished he had some asbestos paper, because a Catholic newspaper published a report, emanating from the Columban headquarters in America, allegedly quoting Cleary's criticisms of events in China. 'I did not write a single sentence of it.' His reaction shows clearly that the Columbans in Nancheng lived in a 'somewhat nerve-racking' state after the communist takeover. While the army remained only a week, a new mandarin caused some anxiety. But the most immediate problem for the missionaries was lack of money. 'The liberation took place so suddenly that … we found ourselves with about 60 silver dollars on hands.' Fortunately they had a good stock of rice, and were able to earn a little from the sale of medicines, but by the end of July 1949 could no longer pay teachers. Mass, even a public Mass on

Sunday, continued and, in a letter to Dennehy, posted to Fergus Murphy in Shanghai to be given to a passenger on a visiting ship, Cleary could report:

> So far there has been no interference with us though as there was but little work during the summer months this is no indication as to whether catechetical work will be possible in the autumn in the country places ... The teachers had to attend an indoctrination class 'to reform their minds' during the summer.

There was no censorship of the mails in the summer of 1949, but priests wrote sensitive remarks in Latin, and Cleary suggested to Mark Kelly, in Hong Kong, that he use Irish. By December 1949 postal deliveries were returning to normal, although airmail service would have to wait until Britain recognised the new government in China. Cleary was obviously aware of the censor in a letter to Dennehy on 6 December, carefully using terms like 'liberation', saying that officials were 'almost ascetics and some of them are men of deep and sincere convictions', and stating that the Columbans were determined 'to observe the laws and regulations to the letter'. According to him all parishes were open, as was the hospital and some schools, and priests could move about freely. Edward MacElroy, the newly-appointed superior in Shanghai, used a simple code in January 1950, to give Dennehy an account of Columban affairs in China. In one paragraph he wrote:

> J. Pigott and all his men are fine. He has the good news that one of his new kirks makes an excellent granary ... You remember your old friend Dr H. Bennett. In a letter from Tom Fisher of Belfast he tells me that Hughie has got to give up his old-fashioned methods at last. The handbooks he used – Genicot and Tanq. – are much too antiquated ... His next-door neighbour Pat sees a lot of Bobby Peel these days.

Translated, the message was that one of Jeremiah Pigott's churches had been taken over by the authorities and was now a granary; Hugh Bennett had been accused of being reactionary; and the police had visited Pat Scully several times. Cleary told Dennehy that he had omitted some items, with a view to the censor, in a letter to Cardinal Pietro Fumasoni-Biondi, a commentary on his annual report for 1948-1949. 'Incidentally I may remark that I refused to supply C. F. Biondi with the answer to half of his questions.' However, he felt free to report to the cardinal, without any use of code:

> Since the liberation there has been no general improvement, and little headway is being made in the propagation of the faith. There have

been no noticeable perversions, and on the whole, the numbers that frequent the sacraments have not seriously declined.[40]

Schools were open, Cleary reported, on the understanding that religion was not taught. His most serious complaint was that churches and residences were subject to taxation, the cathedral complex alone being assessed at twelve hundred American dollars. Writing to Dennehy about the same amount he used a word, 'mileagusdaceud', which must really have challenged the censor, being rather tortured Irish for 'a thousand, two hundred'. He saw the increased taxation, together with anti-religious propaganda, as the government's plan for driving out foreign missionaries:

> We expect that this pressure [of taxes] will be kept up …We have an intensification of the propaganda against religion too and it may well happen that our Catholics will cease to practise even if there is not formal apostasy. We do not anticipate any direct persecution … it will be enough if we are left without a following and are ourselves impoverished.[41]

Cleary was increasingly worried about the priests, and especially the sisters. He suggested that the superior general should write to the men encouraging patience, and that he discuss 'a line of policy' with the mother general of the Columban Sisters. Fergus Murphy, superior in China until November 1949, reached San Francisco in May 1950, and wrote a long report to Dennehy. He revealed some of the pressures about which Cleary could not speak. While none of the missionaries had, as yet, had to face a people's court, one was accused of rape. The girl gave the bishop a written statement saying that the accusation was made under duress and was false. A sister, when another girl asked if she should join a communist society, inquired if she had permission from her parents. The sister had to make a public apology – parents' permission was no longer necessary. All foreigners had to fill up lengthy questionnaires as part of the process of acquiring a residence certificate. They were then subjected to cross-examination on their answers, and a mistake meant getting no certificate and having no legal existence. Without the certificate they could not even apply for an exit visa. Missionaries could do only a little work. Where Cleary had written that the schools were open Murphy revealed that the Columbans were forced to open them, and had no control over them, 'only the privilege of paying the bills'. Murphy stated:

---

40. Patrick Cleary to Pietro Fumasoni-Biondi, 5 Mar. 1950 (CFCA, China Correspondence: 430B).
41. Patrick Cleary to Jeremiah Dennehy, 21 May 1950 (CFCA, China Correspondence: 433A).

In Kiangsi the men are still in their parishes. In the southern part they can get around a certain amount with police passes. In the northern part ... they are pretty well confined to their compounds. Fr Luke O'Reilly was early accused of association with bandits as he failed to report their presence. It took a month of questioning by the police in Nancheng – followed by the inevitable written apology – to get out of that one.[42]

One of the greatest difficulties for all foreign missionaries was the lack of factual information about the government's plans for the churches or, indeed, about events elsewhere that could affect its thinking. Cleary had no radio, and when the Korean war began, on 25 June 1950, he had 'to depend on the meagre accounts given by the *North China Daily News*', a single line about the Columbans in Korea, 'Among the foreigners who are still in Seoul are ... some Columban Fathers.'[43] Chinese 'volunteers' were sent to fight in Korea on 19 October 1950, and in November Dennehy wrote to Cleary with the news that at least four Columbans had been killed, among them Patrick Brennan, who had been superior in China until October 1948.

The Chinese National Catholic Church
Several Protestant leaders met Premier Zhou Enlai in May 1950, issuing a 'Christian Manifesto', approved by Zhou, a document which prepared for the coming into being of independent Chinese churches.[44] Cleary told Dennehy that Zhou was reported as saying that:

> ... there is no desire to crush Christianity in the country, but the aim is the formation of an indigenous, self-supporting church. New missionaries will not be allowed into the country – unless possibly as doctors, technicians, or agricultural experts; those at present in the country will not be expelled provided they observe the law.

The first recorded alarm from a Columban about a similar move towards an independent Roman Catholic Church came in a letter from Edward McManus, in Omaha, Nebraska, to Dennehy in January 1951:

> A bunch of native priests in Sechuan [Szechwan] have issued a manifesto proclaiming a Chinese National Catholic Church. So far no comment from their bishop.

---

42. Fergus Murphy to Jeremiah Dennehy, 28 May 1950 (CFCA, China Correspondence: 434).
43. Patrick Cleary to Jeremiah Dennehy, 21 July 1950 (CFCA, China Correspondence: 436A).
44. John Tong, 'The Church from 1949 to 1990' in Edmond Tang and Jean-Paul Wiest (eds), *The Catholic church in modern China* (New York, 1993), p. 9.

The Szechwan manifesto, said to have been issued by a group of Catholics under the leadership of a Chinese priest, Wang Liangzuo, on 30 November 1950, recounted the history of the unequal treaties and other injustices imposed on China over the previous one hundred years, and alleged that religion had been used as a weapon of imperialism. Wang and his companions pledged:

> Henceforth we shall cut off all contact and connection with imperialists; we shall bring about the Triple Autonomy programme of the Catholic Church of China. The Triple Autonomy programme includes autonomy in administration, autonomy in finance, and autonomy in mission personnel.[45]

Priests and lay people in Nanchang, the capital of Kiangsi, signed a manifesto, which contained nothing opposed to Catholic doctrine, and with the consent of the archbishop, Zhou Jishi. Cleary, ever worried about the small group of Chinese priests and seminarians in his diocese, permitted them to sign the Nanchang manifesto:

> … but on their posters here they quoted a statement from me: The church condemns imperialism and fosters patriotism, and those who use the church in the interests of imperialism do wrong; it is the aim of the church to make the church in China self-supporting, with a sufficient number of priests subject to native bishops, as soon as possible, and I have been labouring for that object for the last twenty years.[46]

Pius XII appealed to the Chinese hierarchy and people to maintain unity with the Holy See. In an apostolic letter, *'Cupimus imprimis'* of 18 January 1952, he declared that Roman Catholics loved their country and obey the government. But the church calls all nations so:

> … it is wrong to ask it to break the unity with which its Divine Founder wished it to be marked, and separate churches having been set up in each nation, to withdraw these from this Apostolic See where Peter, the Vicar of Jesus Christ, and his successors live even to the end of time.

The Pope looked forward to the day when the church in China would reach such maturity that it would not need the help of foreign missionaries, but noted that the indigenous clergy was as yet unequal to that task. He

---

45. Luke O'Reilly, 'Red flows the tide' in *The Far East* (Australian ed.), xlvi (Sept. 1964), p. 15.
46. Patrick Cleary to Inigo Maximilian Koenig, 6 Feb. 1951 (CFCA, China Correspondence: 445C).

encouraged all Chinese Catholics to remain united, even if that meant false accusations and persecution.

Harassment by the authorities
Communist authorities in Nancheng began to orchestrate attacks on Columbans at the end of December 1950, accusing one of illegally storing the property of a landlord, another of assisting a suicide, a third of usury and cruelty to Chinese. Similar charges, for breaches of civil law, were made against almost all the priests and sisters, not attacks on religion as such. Foreign priests in Nanfeng were forbidden to do any work. 'A good Chinese priest who has signed the "three independence" might come to replace them.' In January 1951 a distressed Cleary wrote to Edward MacElroy, the superior in Shanghai, querying the wisdom, and even the morality, of the instruction of Antonio Riberi, the papal internuncio, ordering that 'All missionary personnel must remain at their post no matter what happens and even if it entails loss of life.' He objected, asking what missionaries should do if the government expelled them, or if they were approaching the limit of endurance. In a coded letter to Ireland, Cleary complained about the situation of his priests:

> Most of them are suffering from peeler trouble and have to rest all the time ... a change of air may become desirable or even necessary for most of them.

Cleary meant that the priests were being constantly harassed by the Communist authorities, that they were not allowed to do any work, and that perhaps some of them should leave China. Dennehy replied: 'Whatever you decide has my full approbation. I do think that sickness and danger of nervous breakdown is sufficient cause for a holiday'.[47] Four priests and all five Columban Sisters were expelled from China in March 1951. Three others, foreigners accused of various crimes, were placed in the custody of the bishop, while Lucas Teng was lodged in prison.[48] Those who remained in their parishes were under a form of house arrest, confined to part of their residences, or even an outhouse. Cleary advised two of them to study or do cross-word puzzles. By June 1951:

> Apart from Con O'Connell and Pat Gately, who are still in their residence but cannot be of the least help to their Catholics, all the men are in Nancheng ... There is no hope whatsoever that they will be

---

47. Jeremiah Dennehy to Patrick Cleary, 12 Feb. 1951 (CFCA, China Correspondence: 445D).
48. Patrick Cleary to Jeremiah Dennehy, 22 Feb. 1951 (CFCA, China Correspondence: 445E).

allowed to return to their Missions; and there is not work enough for the whole body here [in the city] ... Our church attendance had dropped miserably ... our Catholics, as you know, are not cast in the heroic mould.

Despite Cleary's pessimistic assessment of the Chinese Catholics, many of them were remarkably faithful, hiking in from the surrounding parishes for major feasts, in defiance of the threats of the authorities. When the commissar in the parish of Kiutu, an 'old christianity', demanded that the parishioners sign a document saying that the Catholic Church was the tool of imperialism, and renouncing their allegiance to the church and the Pope:

... the Yu tribe held a meeting ... The hard core of last ditch Catholics – and there were many of them – attended. At the meeting all present decided that they would never sign the document or renounce their faith.

Catholics attending Mass in Nancheng Cathedral on Christmas Day 1951 gave an even more striking demonstration of their obstinate faith. In the middle of December 1951 Cleary excommunicated three leaders of the autonomous church movement. A rumour circulated that the three planned to retaliate by seizing the cathedral pulpit during the bishop's Mass on Christmas Day. Cleary proposed that if they did so, '...we'll get the people to sing the Rosary and drown down the eloquence of our "guest speakers".' Undeterred by the presence of many communist officials, police, soldiers, and members of the patriotic church movement, the people did so. Luke O'Reilly, by then one of only two foreigners remaining with Cleary in Nancheng, recorded:

At the Communion, the Patriotic Church group took down the names of the 291 people who received Holy Communion that morning.[49]

The Three-Autonomy Reform Committee of Nancheng was formed in January 1952, and sent a greeting for Chinese New Year to all Catholics, appealing to their love of China, asking those 'who think that reform is apostasy ... to join the side of the people', and urging all to break away 'from the control of imperialist elements and their running-dogs in the church'. Those 'imperialist elements and their running-dogs', Cleary, two Irish priests both called O'Reilly, and two Chinese priests, James Yang and John Chang, were summoned to a meeting on 8 February 1952, at which they were accused of many crimes. Cleary recalled:

---

49. O'Reilly, *The laughter and the weeping*, pp 129-134.

For about two hours these accusers, beginning and ending with Mr Kuo (chairman of the reform committee), poured forth a tirade on the five of us, individually and collectively, as well as on most of the priests who have worked here for the last twenty years. They did not spare even Father Ellis, and the Sisters came in for their share of abuse. Father Yang and myself, however, were the arch-criminals ...[50]

The five accused priests were then brought through a crowd of high school students, who threw mud or spat on them, to a court, where the Irish were sentenced to house arrest and the Chinese to prison. There they remained for almost an entire year. Paul Yu, a Vincentian priest on loan from Nanchang, carried on the work of the parish 'in a modest way'. He and the three foreigners lived on less than forty-five American dollars a month. Four Chinese students, who had been studying theology under Cleary, James Yang, and the two Irish priests, wished to continue, despite all the dangers. Cleary ordained Joseph Peng a priest on 6 August 1952. A few weeks later he gave the younger seminarians minor orders, and was able to arrange for them to continue their studies in the seminary in Shanghai. Cleary was brought before a People's Court again on 14 December 1952, and sentenced to be expelled from China. Next morning he was escorted to the bus station for the five day journey to Hong Kong.[51] Luke and Seamus O'Reilly were expelled on 15 January 1953, the last Columbans to leave Nancheng.

The fate of the Chinese priests, 1953-1997

Of the five Chinese priests from the diocese of Nancheng, three were in prison, one under house arrest, and only the newly-ordained Joseph Peng free to conduct even a restricted ministry. Paul Yu, the Vincentian, worked in the cathedral while Cleary was still there but seems to have been under house arrest in his brother's house shortly afterwards. The three seminarians sent to Shanghai were ordained in 1957. All of these men remained in union with the Pope and suffered accordingly. Philip Chou (Plate 4.9) died, apparently of starvation, while under house arrest, in 1969 or 1970.[52] Four died in prison, but dates and details of their deaths are unobtainable. James Yang, vicar general of Nancheng, was released from prison in 1979, and wrote a lengthy, confidential, report to Edward MacElroy, the Columban representative in Hong Kong. He died on 28 November 1988. Before his death he smuggled a message to two visiting Columbans, Seamus O'Reilly and Thomas Murphy:

50. Report of Patrick Cleary, 10 Feb. 1952 (CFCA, China Correspondence: 466B).
51. John McNamara, *Bishop Cleary's expulsion*, Dec. 1952 (CFCA, China Correspondence: 466B).
52. James Yang to Edward MacElroy, Confidential report, 1980 (CFCA, CN A-5).

> Please inform the Holy Father that for over 30 years I have been united in one faith and one heart with him, and that despite having spent more than 30 years in jail and labour camps, I have never retreated from this faith. Moreover, the vast majority of the Catholics in the diocese are of the same faith and have never accepted the conditions of the government-sponsored church ...[53]

Joseph Wu taught English in the Fuzhou Teachers' College, Fukien, in 1979 and 1980, but was fired because he refused to join 'the Chinese Patriotic Church'.[54] While there he ministered to the Catholics in Fuzhou:

> We had a grand time on Easter here in Fuzhou. Three priests said Masses ... in a certain family. The hall and the courtyard were crowded. No less than two hundred Catholics attended each Mass. For many of them, it was the first time to attend Masses, to make confession, to receive Holy Communion, since twenty odd years or even since Liberation.

Wu managed to get a job in the Nanchang Teachers' College, but in 1981 he became ill and died. Two priests, trained by Columbans, Thomas Yu and Peter Xie Yunsheng, were in active ministry in 1997.

Conclusions

Columbans in Nancheng in 1928 inherited a church structure from their Vincentian predecessors. It comprised parishes, schools, a seminary and an orphanage. Each parish had a central church and residence, and a ring of rural mission stations, some of them 'old christianities' where the faith had endured for three hundred years. The aim of the Society of St Columban was:

> ... to preach the gospel according to the doctrine of the Holy Roman Church to the Chinese people ... to work for the conversion of the unevangelised; to provide both primary and higher education for those converted; to attend to their spiritual needs; to set up an indigenous clergy capable of ruling their fellow-countrymen.

In general the new missionaries found the existing structure a suitable means to that end, and they simply added more priests, built more churches and parishes, and recruited more catechists. Cleary doubted the cost-effectiveness of the orphanage, given the missionaries' goal of conversions. But the priests worked doggedly through a very disturbed period, repeatedly repair-

---

53. James Yang to Seamus O'Reilly and Thomas Murphy, 31 Oct. 1988 (CFCA, CN A-5).
54. Joseph Wu to Edward MacElroy, 20 Aug. 1980 (CFCA, CN A-5).

ing buildings, and seeking out Christians who had fallen away through fear. Cleary produced a catechism in the local dialect, hoping to shorten the period of instruction for catechumens. Columban Sisters joined the mission in 1935, running a school, the orphanage, and a dispensary. The fruits of the seminary were long in coming, with ordinations in 1939, 1942, and then not until 1952. War diverted the diocese to humanitarian care of the sick and wounded and hungry, although this was seen as a distraction from the principal work of conversion. Conflict led also to more intense formation of Christians, in the Japanese war by catechesis and retreats, and during the approach of the communist armies by the Legion of Mary and the rosary. One result of so much effort and sacrifice was a small, but heroic, Chinese clergy. It is clear that many lay Christians still have an enduring faith, but it is impossible to estimate how many.

The Columbans in Kiangsi involved lay people, catechists, teachers, and sisters, in the mission, yet it was only in the final years, with the coming of the Legion of Mary, that they expanded the role of the laity. This is not surprising, given that Pope Pius XI defined Catholic Action as 'the participation and collaboration of the laity with the apostolate of the hierarchy'. Yet the plenary council of China in 1924, while insisting that it was the duty of missionaries to evangelise 'pagans' themselves, argued that 'the missionary should exhort and move his Christians to bring their relatives and friends to him'.[55]

Nowhere in the sources is there any indication that the missionaries in Nancheng questioned the prevailing Roman Catholic attitude to other churches or faiths, as shown in the destruction of ancestral tablets and the humiliation of the Taoist priest. In this they were blinded by the theology taught in the seminary, and by the oath against Chinese Rites. An even more serious consequence of western theology was the training given to catechumens and seminarians. Catechisms followed the pattern of the *Catechism of Pius X*, using concepts that were foreign to China. The formation of students for the priesthood, imposing Latin, and the philosophy and theology of the West, resulted in a small number of ordinations, and produced men divorced from the culture of their own country.

Yet the Columbans laboured mightily, using a very difficult language, enduring great poverty and hunger, and showing tremendous courage and resilience in times of banditry and war. They revealed the love of God to countless sick and refugees. And their work lives on in a small church that has been tempered by persecution.

---

55. *Primum Concilium Sinense Anno 1924* (Shanghai, 1941), p. 272.

CHAPTER FIVE

Mission in Huchow 1946-1953

The third Columban mission in China, opened in 1946, comprised the civil prefecture of Huchow, in the archdiocese of Hangchow, Chekiang province (Figure 2.1, p. 39). Much of Chekiang is mountainous, but there is flat, rice land, laced by canals, north of Hangchow. Huchow, the most northerly prefecture of the province, has an area of 7,770 sq. km, evenly divided, with mountains in the west, plains in the east, and Taihu lake to the north. Temperatures range from 2°C in January to 32° in July. The population of the prefecture, in 1946, was two million, including about 3,500 Roman Catholics.[1] Their main livelihoods were fishing, farming and production of silk.

Place	Status	Period	Missionaries
Macao	Diocese	1575-1690	Portuguese
Nanking	Diocese	1690-1696	
Tché-kiang	Vicariate	1696-1790	Spanish Dominicans
Fo-kien, Tché-kiang et Kiang-si	Vicariate	1790-1838	
Tché-kiang et Kiang-si	Vicariate	1838-1846	French Vincentians
Tché-kiang	Vicariate	1846-1910	
Tché-kiang Occidental	Vicariate	1910-1946	
Hangtchow	Archdiocese	1946 –	

Sources : O. Werner, *Atlas des Missions Catholiques* (Fribourg, 1886), Table II, J.M. Planchet, *Les Missions de Chine et du Japon* (Pékin, 1933), p. 417, Jean Charbonnier, *The Catholic church in China* (Singapore, 1997), p. 482.

Figure 5.1 *Ecclesiastical history of the archdiocese of Hangchow, 1575-1946.* The figure uses the French names found in the sources for the period before the arrival of the Columbans in 1946.

Chekiang became a vicariate of the Roman Catholic church in 1696

---

1. 'A new mission field', *The Far East*, xxix (July 1946), p. 73.

(Figure 5.1) when it was separated from the diocese of Nanking. But missionaries were few during the persecutions of the eighteenth century, and from 1790 the province was administered from Fukien. In 1865 there were only 3,098 Catholics, served by three Chinese priests and six foreigners, French Vincentians, in the entire province. The vicariate was divided in two, east and west, in 1910. By 1926 the church had grown to 77,968, with seventy-three Chinese priests and thirty-three foreigners, and a third vicariate, of Taichow, wholly staffed by Chinese Vincentians, could be set up.

Negotiations for Huchow, 1934-45
The vicar apostolic of Hangchow, Paul-Albert Faveau, needed more priests. Edward Galvin worked in the vicariate from 1912 to 1916, and in 1934 Faveau wrote to him. Galvin passed on the message to Michael O'Dwyer:

> I had a letter ... from Bishop Faveau, saying he was proposing to you to take over the district of Huchow and asking me as an old friend and former priest of his to second his proposal.

Faveau's formal proposal was discussed by O'Dwyer and his council on 15 January 1935. However, the Columbans had taken on a new mission in Korea in 1933 and were considering a second there. The council was also conducting a protracted negotiation with Paul Dumond, vicar apostolic of Nanchang who, in January 1932, offered the society part of his vicariate. That proposal was blocked by Propaganda which planned to give Nanchang, eventually, to Chinese priests. The decision of Propaganda was made in July 1933, but apparently did not come to the attention of the papal delegate in China, Mario Zanin, until May 1935. When Faveau's invitation to Huchow reached Ireland in early 1935 O'Dwyer was planning for new missions in Korea and in Nanchang, and asked Faveau 'to postpone the offer for a year or so'.[2] There were further delays. The papal delegate, Zanin, planned to give Huchow to the Canadian Scarboro missionaries, who staffed the nearby prefecture of Chuchow (Lishui), and he was angry when he found that Faveau had offered the district to the Columbans:

> Hereupon the Delegate wrote him [Faveau] a pretty severe letter, telling him that it was Rome, and not the bishops, who had the right to divide existing vicariates.

Zanin changed his mind and, on 18 September 1935, called on William McGoldrick, the Columban superior in Shanghai, 'and definitely offered us

---

2. Michael O'Dwyer to Patrick Cleary, 15 Jan. 1935 (CFCA, China Correspondence: 305B).

the district of Huchow ... subject to the approval of Propaganda'. O'Dwyer made a formal petition to Propaganda, through the Columban procurator general in Rome, Michael Boyle, in October 1935. The reply of the Congregation, offering the district, and asking O'Dwyer 'to present three names for the selection of the future Prefect Apostolic' was sent to Ireland only in April 1937. However, the Sino-Japanese war began on 7 July 1937, and the Pacific war on 7 December 1941, making travel to China impossible. It was only on 18 December 1945 that McGoldrick could inform O'Dwyer:

> The Apostolic Delegate notified me last week that the mission of Huchow is now open to us; and today I have a letter from Msgr Deymier ... to the same effect. Msgr Deymier writes, 'I would be happy if your Society would provide a staff of men to undertake the care of the mission.'

O'Dwyer picked recently ordained men for the new Columban mission. The only seasoned missionary, its leader, was Jeremiah Pigott (1892-1976). He served as a chaplain in the British army in the First World War, and in the Royal Air Force in the Second. On joining the Columbans in 1922 he was assigned to Hanyang in 1923, becoming vicar general of the vicariate, and then pro-director. After an arduous, four-month voyage from Europe he arrived in Shanghai on 24 September 1946, to receive a message from Jean-Joseph Deymier, newly installed Archbishop of Hangchow (Plate 5.1) and successor to Faveau, asking that he, and the other Columbans, 'leave for Huchow at the very earliest opportunity'. Pigott found an area that had suffered terribly in the years of war since the Japanese occupied it in 1938. There were several fine churches, built by Faveau and two Scottish priests, Andrew McArdle and John Conway, in the eastern part of the district, but the city of Anchi and several towns in the west, and the churches, had been destroyed. Pigott noted:

> I have seen much destruction serving as a chaplain in two world wars, but nothing ever quite so pathetic as ruined Anjay [Anchi] in the gathering dusk of that February night. The church is razed to the ground – literally not a brick, not a trace of material remains.[3]

Deymier, the archbishop, left five Chinese priests in the district until the Columbans had mastered enough of the language to carry out their duties. On a visit to Huchow in November 1946 the archbishop had:

---

3. Jeremiah Pigott, *Huchow report, 1947* (CFCA, CN A-1: 90).

> ... one very delicate conference with [Pigott and] the Chinese priests concerning their status – this really meaning what regulation would obtain as to their Mass stipends.

McGoldrick warned O'Dwyer, as early as December 1945, that there would be difficulties about Mass offerings. The Chinese priests knew that priests in Columban missions received such offerings from America, and these could be considerably more than the 'support' given to priests in Hangchow. The papal delegate recommended that the Columbans in Huchow give the Chinese priests there the same 'support' as in the rest of the vicariate. 'It would stir up discontent among the Chinese clergy if it becomes known that priests under our jurisdiction receive so much more than others.' During the conference with Deymier and the Chinese priests in 1946 Pigott found that the discussion didn't seem to be leading anywhere. Finally he turned to the archbishop and asked:

> ... would his Grace allow these priests (this in English) 20 stipends like our priests (the bone of contention all the time was that they were being forced to work on unequal terms with brother priests) every month, provided they, like our priests, put their stipends into the work. His Grace said he would and we fixed it then and there.[4]

Pigott began to assign Columbans to parishes as assistants to the Chinese priests in January 1947. Some found unusual Christian communities. In Nanzin (Plate 5.2) the five hundred church members were drawn almost exclusively from fisher families 'who live from birth to death on their fishing boats':

> When one of these fisherfolk grows seriously ill they do not send for the priest. Instead, they sail directly for the church.

Most priests writing in *The Far East* detailed the destructive effects of ten years of war, with buildings destroyed and congregations decimated. Malachy Murphy and his catechist visited the eight christianities of Tehtsing parish, and described two as typical of the rest. Kantsen back in 1937 was

> ... a flourishing Christianity of four hundred Catholics, with two priests, a beautiful church, residence and school. At present, after the war years, the Catholics number one hundred and forty, the church and residence are completely destroyed, and the school in such disrepair as to be little better than a stable.

---

4. Jeremiah Pigott to Michael O'Dwyer, 6 Jan. 1947 (CFCA, China Correspondence: 388).

Murphy called on all the remaining Christians and found that a majority, 'through ignorance, fear of the devil, and the influence of paganism all around, were secretly practising superstition ...' In the village of Fukang he discovered only three Catholics. All the missionaries began training their people, and building residences and churches, before they could think of evangelising the 'pagans'. Pigott opened a central catechumenate, for children, in Huchow, and appealed for urgent financial help. The catechumenate was designed to remedy one of the worst effects of the war years, the lack of Christian education of children:

> What we feel most, however, is the fact that the children, who in those years have grown into boyhood and girlhood, have perforce grown up in complete ignorance of Catholic doctrine and in many cases have not even been baptised.[5]

A selection from the annual statistics for the district reveals, and conceals, much of the history of the short life of the Columban mission in Huchow (Table 5.1). Columban priests were limited to three parishes in the first year while they studied the language. In 1947-1948 more parishes were opened. Pigott rotated the foreign priests, giving them a few months as assistants to Chinese pastors before they took charge of parishes themselves.

	1946-47	1947-48	1948-49	1949-50	1950-51
Catholics	2,837	2,940	3,034	3,269	3,310
Adult Baptisms	26	76	114	169	171
Catechumens	288	623	940	1,206	1,271
Annual Confessions	1,011	1,169	1,266	1,547	1,654
Easter Communions	972	1,151	1,253	1,534	1,639
Priests	17	17	16	15	15
Sisters	6	5	6	9	
Catechists	5	11	12	33	28
Parishes	3	8	8	9	10
Parish Schools	4	5	1		
Primary Schools	1	1	1		
Childrenn under instruction	55	36	5		

Source: Huchow annual reports (CFCA, CN A-4).
Table 5.1 *Church growth in the Huchow district, 1946-51*. Growth was limited by the communist advances and the financial difficulties of the mission.

Missionary methods

Chinese sisters ran the central catechumenate, for children, in Huchow, and a school in Sinkadhay. Pigott hoped that the catechumenate, and the single

---
5. Jeremiah Pigott to Jeremiah Dennehy, June 1947 (CFCA, CN A-4).

registered primary school would sow the seeds of an educated Catholic laity. The statistics seem to suggest that schools were closed after The People's Liberation Army entered Huchow on the night of 27 April 1949, but as late as December 1949 Pigott told Dennehy that 'one of our registered schools has ceased to function but the remaining two are doing well considering'. Christian instruction of adults fell to the priests and to a rapidly growing team of catechists. The detailed reports recorded numbers of churches, chapels, christianities, of sermons preached by priests and catechists, and of sacraments. Two dispensaries treated the sick, and treatments were carefully listed. But church growth was modest. Some men looked for new approaches. Oliver Whyte arrived in China in 1948 and was assigned as assistant in Nanzin where he began the first praesidium of the Legion of Mary in the district. Three other praesidia followed, in Huchow city, Songlin and Sinkadhay.[6] Members of a legion praesidium undertake apostolic work, especially visitation of hospitals, prisons, hostels for down-and-outs, and private homes. Whyte asked the Nanzin legionaries to visit lax Christians, and to instruct house-bound catechumens. All the members of his praesidium were illiterate, except one lady who had to act as both president and secretary. Perhaps the greatest fruit of the Legion was the effect on the members themselves. Through involvement in the apostolate of the church, study of the Legion handbook, the discipline of a weekly meeting, and prayer, they became so committed that most could resist all communist pressure and indoctrination.

Communist interference

The first hint of interference by the communist authorities appeared in October 1949 when Fergus Murphy, the superior in Shanghai, wrote to Dennehy that 'J. P[igott] is having some trouble about some land attached to one of the schools'. Murphy's successor, Edward MacElroy, in coded language reported in January 1950, 'The Pigotts are as usual. They too got a touch of that bally 'flu but it is much milder.' Yet Pigott himself could state in March 1950 that although priests needed passes to move around, even within their parishes, the central catechumenate and the two registered primary schools were doing well. However, when the papal internuncio, Antonio Riberi, suggested that either MacElroy or Pigott apply to Archbishop Deymier to have Huchow set up as a separate prefecture, Pigott replied that:

> ... in the event of a further big upheaval whether it would be wise to be cut off from Hangchow is a question I just not dare to answer.

---

6. Jeremiah Pigott to Jeremiah Dennehy, 19 Aug. 1950 (CFCA, China Correspondence: 436).

Hangchow has Chinese priests to carry on in the event of extern priests having to leave, we would have none.[7]

The Congregation for the Propagation of the Faith pressed ahead with the plan to set up a prefecture in Huchow, and requested Dennehy to submit three names for the selection of a prefect. Dennehy asked MacElroy to 'get the men in Huchow to send me on individually three names, Dignus, Dignior, Dignissimus ... I don't know whether it is possible or not.' By January 1951 the situation of the church in Huchow had deteriorated, as the communist officials began to 'borrow' church premises and confiscate church lands. The government decreed that no financial help could come from 'imperialist countries'. Several of the parishes in Huchow could not support even one priest without foreign aid, and Pigott had to tell some priests to apply for exit visas.[8] A campaign of newspaper attacks began in June 1951, with bitter articles on the 'imperialists' in the church. Chief of these was the papal internuncio, Riberi, but the Legion of Mary was also mentioned. Riberi was expelled on 4 September 1951. Two days later Aedan McGrath, whom Riberi had appointed in 1948 to organise the Legion throughout China, was arrested. The Chinese government officially suppressed the Legion on 7 October 1951.[9] John C. Casey remembered how:

> The next day the secret police, dressed in black uniforms or in mufti, arrived ... From now on the destruction of the Legion of Mary was the immediate target ... Beating them, roping them and taking them half way to gaol were common methods used in the attempt to break them down ... This went on for over six months ... Yet not one of them broke down ... and in the end the Communists had to admit that they were beaten.

Four priests, Casey, Owen O'Kane, Patrick Reilly and Patrick Ronan, together with several members of the Legion of Mary, were arrested in June 1952. The priests were confined to prison, and subjected to many interrogations. For the next seventeen months Casey bore dysentery and beri-beri, supported by going through the prayers of the Mass each day and by meditating on hymns.[10] In another cell his companion, Patrick Reilly, was allowed to buy grapes because of illness, but used the juice and steamed bread to say

---

7. Edward MacElroy to Jeremiah Dennehy, 3 Apr. 1950 (CFCA, China Correspondence: 432).
8. Joseph Kennedy in Edward Kelly, *The Columban mission in Huzhou*, undated (CFCA, CN A-4, p. 12).
9. John Casey, 'A new phase' in *The Far East*, xxxviii (Feb. 1955), p. 4.
10. John Casey, 'Winter, 1952-1953' in *The Far East*, xxxviii (Mar. 1955), p. 8.

Mass. The four were expelled 'eternally' from China on 28 November 1953. Pigott and the other foreign priests had been deported already in 1952. Aedan McGrath was released on 2 May 1954. Edward MacElroy, based in Shanghai as superior of the Columban region of China, and the last Columban to be expelled, reached Hong Kong on 15 May 1954. Extant records are silent about the fate of most of the Chinese legionaries who were imprisoned along with the Columbans.

Pigott had to make what provision he could for the future of the church in Huchow. When the four Columbans were arrested in June 1952, recognising that eventually all foreign priests would be expelled, he distributed the three Chinese priests strategically:

> Father Yang was sent from Huchow to join Father Mick Healy in Nanzin (Nanxun) … Father Tsu was brought down from Siaofeng to look after the Huchow Catholics … Father Bao in Songlin would be in position to care for the Catholics of Senkateu as well as his own flock …[11]

Father Tsu Feng Chin came under intense pressure to bring charges against the Columbans. 'They even offered to make him Bishop of Huchow.' John Tsu Feng Chin became Bishop of Hangchow 1988-1997.[12] Edward Kelly, a Columban, secretly brought him a cross and bishop's ring from the Pope, a symbol of communion with Rome. Tsu said quietly, '*Deo gratias.*' Anthony Bao Ren Dao died in 1983, and Joseph Yang Yi Gen in 1988. Michael Healy, pastor in Nanzin in 1949, returned there in October 1990 and was recognised and welcomed by two of the Chinese sisters, Cecilia and Barbara Shen, then in their eighties.

Conclusions

The small group of Columbans in Huchow, 1946-1953, trained no students for the priesthood, and their ministry in the district might seem to have been fruitless. But their most striking achievement was the formation, in a very short time – Casey's praesidium existed for only two years – of several remarkable praesidia of the Legion of Mary. The communists searched for members of the Legion who would make accusations against McGrath or the other priests, and found none. When Oliver Whyte returned to Nanzin fifty years later he found a healthy church, and one faithful parishioner was the lady who had been the president of the praesidium.

---

11. Joseph Kennedy, in Edward Kelly, *The Columban mission in Huzhou*, undated (CFCA, CN A-4, p. 13).
12. Jean Charbonnier, *Guide to the Catholic Church in China, 2004* (Singapore, 2004), p. 629.

CHAPTER SIX

Mission in the Philippines 1929-1953

The Philippines was a peculiar choice in 1929 for the first undertaking of the Columbans outside China. It was not 'in the missions', a term in Roman Catholic canon law referring to territories that came under the jurisdiction of the Congregation for the Propagation of the Faith, commonly called Propaganda or Propaganda Fide. Nor did it fit the definition of missions used by a missiologist like Joseph Schmidlin, who stated that 'Missions … are among non-Christians.' Its inhabitants were already Christian. A state census in 1903 recorded a total population of 7,635,000, of whom almost 7,000,000 were at least nominally Roman Catholic.[1] The Holy See placed it under the jurisdiction of the Consistorial Congregation, not of Propaganda Fide. As a missionary society the Columbans were 'directly dependent on the Sacred Congregation of the Propagation of the Faith', which intended them 'for apostolic work among infidel peoples'.[2] Yet Michael O'Doherty, Archbishop of Manila (1916-1949), needed priests and pleaded with Michael O'Dwyer, the Columban superior general, to help.

Behind O'Doherty's request for priests to staff his diocese was a complex history: the Spanish conquest of the Philippines in 1565 and the conversion of most of its people to Roman Catholicism; the rebellion of the Filipinos (1896-98) giving rise to a Philippine Independent church; and the government of the country from 1898 by the United States of America which opened the door for Protestant churches. Church affairs were further complicated by the variety of nationalities among the foreign missionaries, first Spanish, followed by American, Dutch, Irish and others, each group bringing its own experience and attitudes. The Columbans included newly ordained priests, whose knowledge of missionary methods was gleaned from reading *The Far East*, others with some years' pastoral experience in parishes in Ireland or Australia, and veterans of the China mission, who knew first hand how to deal with people who were not Christian. But in the Philippines instead of seeking converts they saw their task as protecting their flocks from

---

1. Quoted in Samuel Hugh Moffett, *A history of Christianity in Asia* (2 vols, New York, 2005), ii, p. 556.
2. Congregation for the Propagation of the Faith to Michael Logue, 13 June 1917 in *AAS*, ix (1917), p. 395.

'Protestant missionaries and proselytising agents of all kinds'. They selected methods, some already familiar like the structure of centre and mission stations, others demanding creativity, especially for the religious formation of the thousands of students in Manila. The Japanese war (1941-45) devastated the country and the mission less than a dozen years after the arrival of the first Columbans. Recovery was a huge task, especially since the Philippines was not classed as a missionary country, which restricted the amount of money coming from the church elsewhere. Yet even that limited financial assistance made the missionaries rich in the eyes of Filipinos. Columbans worked in widely different situations, and came in contact with members of other churches and of tribal and Muslim communities. Their reaction, as missionaries, will be of interest.

Physical features
Stretching from the fifth to the twenty-first parallels north of the Equator, the archipelago of the Philippines comprises 7,100 islands, of which about 1,000 are populated (See Figure 6.1). Eleven islands make up 94 percent of the landmass of the country, and two of these – Luzon and Mindanao – measure 105,000 and 95,000 square kilometres respectively. All the islands are prone to earthquakes, being situated where two tectonic plates, the Eurasian and the Philippine, collide. The largely mountainous terrain creates narrow coastal plains and interior valleys where most of the population is concentrated. A tropical marine climate, with the northeast monsoon from December to February and the southwest monsoon from May to October, gives a mean annual temperature of 27°C. Frequent typhoons ravage the central and northern islands. The majority of the people are of Malay stock and speak some seventy languages and dialects, of which the most important are Tagalog and Visayan.

Spanish rule
Christianity was introduced to the Philippines by the Spaniards. Ferdinand Magellan reached the island of Leyte in 1521, and claimed it in the name of King Charles V, but permanent conquest began only after the expedition of Miguel López de Legazpi in 1565. The Muslims of the southern islands of Mindanao and Sulu maintained their independence during the entire Spanish regime. A revolution in 1896-1898 effectively ended Spanish rule,[3] but the last year of the revolution coincided with the Spanish-American war.

---

3. Pedro S. de Achútegui and Miguel A. Bernad, *Religious revolution in the Philippines* (Manila, 1961), p. 27.

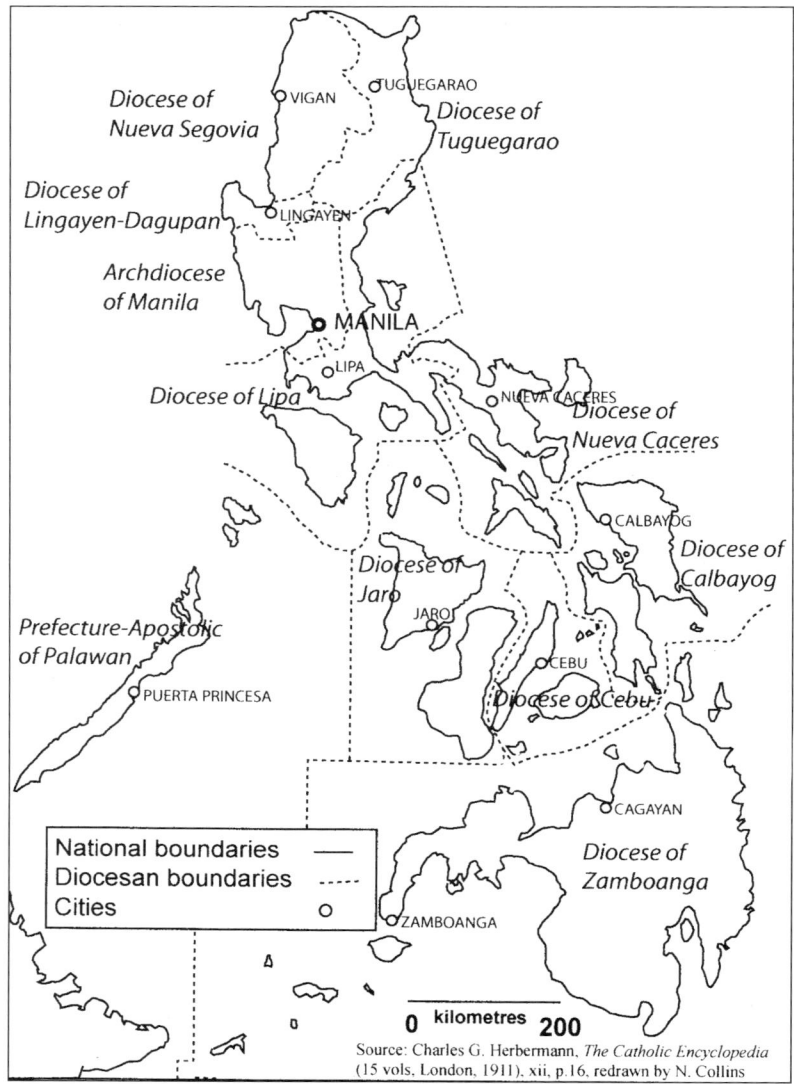

Figure 6.1 *Roman Catholic dioceses of the Philippines when the first Columbans arrived in 1929.* Manila was created in 1579, Nueva Caceres, Cebu and Nueva Segovia in 1595, Jaro in 1865, Calbayog, Lipa, Tugeugarao, Zamboanga and the apostolic prefecture of Palawan in 1910, Lingayen-Dagupan in 1928.

This resulted in the Treaty of Paris, concluded on 10 December 1898, which gave the Philippines to the United States. The Filipino congress and army resisted the Americans. Open warfare broke out in February 1899, and even after the defeat of the main Filipino forces, guerrilla units continued the struggle until the last two generals surrendered in 1902. By an act of the congress of the US, the Cooper Act of 1902, the Philippines became an American colony. Rule from Washington, interrupted by Japanese occupation (1941-1945), ended in 1946 when the Republic of the Philippines became a sovereign state.

Five religious orders, commonly referred to as 'the friars', and some secular priests evangelised the Philippines in the sixteenth and early seventeenth centuries. All were of Spanish birth. First to arrive were the Augustinians in 1565, followed by Franciscans (1577), Jesuits (1581), Dominicans (1587), and Augustinian Recollects (1606). In the space of about fifty years these missionaries converted most of the people on the coasts and plains to Roman Catholicism, but they had less success with the animist tribes in the mountain jungles, and none with the Muslims. The practice of the Spanish missionaries was to keep control of positions of greatest power in the Filipino church. Local diocesan priests received only poor training, a policy which promised the most serious long-term consequences. By 1870, three hundred years after the conquest, only 181 parishes from a total of 792 were entrusted to Filipino clergy, and those parishes were mainly small rural churches. This discrimination led to polarisation between Spanish friars and Filipino priests, and contributed to the revolution (1896-98), during which about forty friars were killed. Many others were forced to leave the country. In 1896 Spanish priests numbered 1,104, while in 1903 only 246 remained, working mostly in education.[4] Filipino clergy were too few and many parishes were without a priest.

Concurrent with the revolution against Spanish rule, a Filipino priest, Gregorio Aglipay (1860-1940), led a campaign to free the church in the Philippines from Spanish dominance. The country was divided into five dioceses, ruled by Spanish bishops. Aglipay rejected their authority, and wanted the Pope to appoint Filipinos in their place. Instead, in 1903 Rome introduced four American bishops. Two years later the first Filipino bishop, Jorge Barlin, was chosen for the diocese of Nueva Caceres. A nationalistic journalist, Isabelo de los Reyes, launched a movement for complete separation from Rome, and in September 1902 persuaded Aglipay to become the first bishop

---

4. Moffett, *A history of Christianity in Asia,* ii, p. 559.

of the Philippine Independent church, commonly called Aglipayan. It is estimated that about 100 of the 825 Filipino priests[5] and a quarter of the 7,000,000 lay people left the Roman Catholic Church and joined the new body. Many of the faithful saw little difference between this independent, Catholic Church led exclusively by Filipinos and the Roman Catholic one.

American protectorate

The change from Spanish sovereignty to American rule created problems for the Roman Catholic Church in the Philippines. Previously the clergy had been supported by the *patronato* of the Spanish crown. Now they depended on the generosity of their parishioners. In a very short time the Philippines experienced a new cultural colonisation, with the introduction of English, of American ways of government, and American law. Two changes affected every town and parish immediately, the separation of church and state, and the establishing of public schools. More than 1,000 American teachers, known as 'Thomasites', from the *SS Thomas* which brought the first of them to the country, fanned out across the archipelago to open non-denominational primary schools. Under American rule, Roman Catholicism no longer had a privileged place, and missionaries from the Presbyterian, Methodist, Episcopalian, Baptist, Congregationalist, United Brethren, and Seventh-day Adventist churches arrived to bring the Protestant faith to the Philippines. In a land where 91% of the people belonged to either the Roman Catholic or the Philippine Independent (Catholic) churches, 'the Protestant temptation to proselyte Filipino Catholics'[6] guaranteed future confrontation.

Pope Leo XIII attempted to meet the difficulties facing the church in the Philippines: shortage of priests; tensions between local and foreign clergy; and the religious instruction of children. In an apostolic constitution, '*Quae mari sinico*', issued on 17 September 1902, he recognised the ending of the Spanish royal *patronato*. He instituted four new dioceses, although these were not erected until 1910. The most significant and urgent need was to build seminaries and increase the numbers of local clergy. These were to be gradually given greater responsibilities, so that eventually they might take over parishes from the religious orders. Twice the Pope returned to the need for 'concord' between secular and religious priests. Bishops were charged to care for the religious education of students attending public schools. Finally, he invoked St Paul in a call for reverence for the civil government. The death of

---

5. Achútegui and Bernad, *Religious revolution in the Philippines*, p. 227.
6. Moffett, *A history of Christianity in Asia*, ii, p. 562.

Leo XIII in 1903 delayed the erection of the four new dioceses. Two Filipino bishops and one American were appointed in 1910, and an Irishman, Michael O'Doherty, became Bishop of Zamboanga in 1911.[7] In 1916 he was transferred to Manila as archbishop. A tenth diocese was added in 1928, with a Filipino as bishop (Figure 6.1).

Invitation to the Columbans

Despite the efforts of O'Doherty, Manila, like all the dioceses of the Philippines, was chronically short of priests. The archbishop searched for money to provide scholarships for poor students who wished to attend the diocesan seminary. Yet figures from 1920 to 1926 show only six ordinations of new priests each year, not nearly enough to fill the gap left by the exodus of Spanish priests during and after the Philippine revolution of 1896-98. In August 1928 O'Doherty wrote to the superior general of the Columbans, Michael O'Dwyer, describing the calamitous state of his archdiocese, and arguing that it was a suitable field for missionaries:

> I make no exaggeration when I say that right now 500 priests are needed in the Diocese of Manila alone. Can you conceive one parish in the very city of Manila with a population of 60,000 people, all baptised or supposed to be, and only one young, native priest to attend them ... And I have 50 parishes without any priest.[8]

O'Doherty offered the Columbans the parish of Malate, then staffed by Irish Redemptorists who wished to return to their more usual work of preaching short 'revivalist' missions in parishes anywhere in the Philippines. His invitation raised some difficulties for O'Dwyer. According to their constitutions the primary duty of Columbans was the evangelisation of the Chinese people. A mission in the Philippines would require the permission of the Holy See and, perhaps, a change in the constitutions. To complicate the matter further, the society had previously refused invitations from Propaganda to open missions in Siam (Thailand) and in India. The invitation to Siam arrived while Blowick was superior, in March 1924, and the unanimous decision of his council was to accept it. However the general congress in June of that year discussed the dire financial state of the society, in light of which the new administration voted, on 23 March 1925, to ask Propaganda to release it from the Siam undertaking because the bursar 'reports that the Society could not, without [financial] disaster, send a mis-

---

7. *Sacra Congregatio Consistorialis 'Provisio ecclesiarum'* in *AAS*, iii (Rome, 1911), p. 347.
8. Michael J. O'Doherty to Michael O'Dwyer, 6 Aug. 1928 (CFCA, RP A-1: 2).

sion to Siam'.⁹ A mission in India was considered in January 1928. The council recalled that in 1917 the Archbishop of Dublin, William Walsh, objected to the erection of the society, on the grounds that it was recruiting priests and collecting funds for a mission in China, while Walsh expected that the men would be sent to Japan instead.

> It was felt that the undertaking of such a mission [would] not be viewed with favour in Ireland and the same dangers that threatened the early life of the Society might ensue.¹⁰

The council refused the Indian invitation in February, making it embarrassing for O'Dwyer to propose, in September, to send priests to the Philippines. Instead he suggested that O'Doherty should write to Propaganda, saying that the Columbans were anxious to have a 'procure', or general business office, in Manila, and asking permission for them to take a parish there. The archbishop did so, and in February 1929 Jeremiah Dennehy, a Columban studying in Rome, could report that the archbishop's letter had reached Cardinal William Van Rossum, the prefect of Propaganda, and that the congregation would write to O'Dwyer inquiring whether the Columbans were willing to take the parish in Manila. In an interesting rider Dennehy went on to say: 'Mgr Pecorari told me to tell you not to show any enthusiasm in the reply.' Cesare Pecorari, an official in Propaganda, was advising his Columban friend how to play a rather diplomatic game with his own superior, Archbishop Francesco Marchetti Selvaggiani, secretary of Propaganda. Marchetti Selvaggiani was not fooled. Pecorari quoted him as saying, 'Oh, they will consent without doubt. He is an Irish bishop.' Writing in the name of the prefect of Propaganda, Van Rossum, Marchetti Selvaggiani sent Blowick a tart letter in March 1929, quoting the reasons given by the society for refusing the mission in India, and asking how the situation had changed. Blowick responded by claiming that the invitation to Manila did not involve a new mission, only a 'procure' and a refuge for priests whose health was unequal to the stresses of China.¹¹ Rome gave the necessary permission on 26 April 1929. Meanwhile O'Dwyer, recognising that a mission in Manila was a significant change for the Maynooth Mission to China, consulted other Columbans. He pointed out the merit of the work itself, the value of having

---

9. Council of directors, minutes of meetings 1917-1925, 23 Mar. 1925 (Columban central house, Dublin).
10. Minutes, superior general's council 1925-1937, 13 Jan 1928 (Columban central house, Dublin).
11. John Blowick to Propaganda, 9 Apr. 1929 (CFCA, RP A-1:23).

a 'procure' there to serve the missions in China, and suggested that the parish could be a refuge for priests who had to leave China for a time. Articles in *The Far East* explained the new undertaking in terms that were guaranteed to resonate with the Irish support base: 'Faith of ancient Catholic nation imperilled.'[12] Even before receiving official notification of the permission, O'Dwyer sent telegrams ordering Patrick Kelly (Plate 6.1) and Michael Cuddigan to Manila. They arrived at the end of May 1929, and began to study Spanish and Tagalog. One Redemptorist remained, temporarily, as parish priest, giving Kelly and Cuddigan time to learn the ways of Malate, but within a month the Columbans were saying Mass in Latin, hearing confessions in Spanish, and acting as chaplains to several schools where English was mandatory. They had to wait longer for some fluency in Tagalog before they could preach or even talk to the poor.

Manila and Lingayen
The Columban mission in the Philippines was limited to the single parish of Malate, as authorised by Propaganda, for the four years 1929-1933. However, Michael O'Dwyer instructed Kelly to keep separate accounts for parish and society funds, because 'there is the possibility of a future mission in the Philippines, which will need funds very badly'.

A general congress of the society, held in June 1931, proposed that the regions of the society be canonically erected according to the constitutions, the 'Region of America' to include the Philippines. Another proposal of the congress read:

> We also recommend reasonable expansion of the work of the Society in the Philippine Islands, with the permission of the Sacred Congregation of Propaganda.[13]

O'Dwyer and his council carried out the formal erection in April 1932, setting up four regions (Appendix 5), Ireland, America, Australia, and China. There were three pro-regions, Hanyang and Kienchang in the region of China, and the Philippines in the region of America. Michael O'Doherty, the Archbishop of Manila, was instrumental in initiating the proposed expansion of the mission. Garry Cogan, the third Columban to arrive in Manila, went to the rural parish of Binangonan (Figure 6.2, p. 196), where only Tagalog was spoken, so that he could learn the language. The archbishop made him parish priest on 21 October 1931. Two years later there were eight Columbans

---
12. Editorial, 'The call of the Philippines' in *The Far East*, xii (June 1929), p. 123.
13. Recommendations of the recent congress, June 1931 (CFCA, CA F-3).

in the Philippines. Theory caught up with practice in 1934 when Archbishop William Piani, the apostolic delegate in Manila, reported to Rome that many Chinese and Japanese lived in the islands, before asking permission for the Columbans to send more priests to help both 'Christians and pagans who live in the Philippines'.[14] In mentioning Chinese and Japanese the delegate was referring back to the documents establishing the primary aim of the society, that of evangelising the Chinese people. Yet he clearly wanted missionaries who would serve people of all races. Propaganda responded 'with joy' and 'willingly granted the faculty of sending missionaries'. As additional priests arrived parishes were taken over in Manila and in Lingayen-Dagupan.

Parish work in Malate included a heavy schedule of Masses, confessions on Saturday from 6.00 am until evening, a sermon on Sunday evening over the 'wireless', and school retreats. Other activities, introduced by the Spaniards, were new to the Columbans: the fiestas or feast-days of the patron saint of a locality, involving Masses and a procession of the saint's statue around the town; a pre-Christmas novena of dawn Masses; and the dramatic celebration of Holy Week, with a twin climax of the separation of the dead Christ from his sorrowing mother on Good Friday, and their joyful meeting in the early hours of Easter Sunday. Many of the rich traditional rituals were controlled and carried out by lay people. John Henaghan, assigned to Malate after the general congress of 1931,[15] penned a shocked letter to O'Dwyer, detailing the defects he saw in the Filipino church. He complained that the people didn't want priests, and were content with their fiestas; that their devotion involved burning candles to statues, while they seemed to know nothing about the Eucharist; and that many saw no difference between the Roman Catholic and the Aglipayan (Philippine Independent Catholic) churches. A young priest coming to the Philippines, he wrote, would be in danger of great discouragement because Catholics frequently got married civilly or in Protestant churches. That meant that, in the eyes of the church, they were not married and were living in sin. Yet they didn't confess the sin and still came to the eucharist. Such problems could be solved by a good, Catholic elementary education, but 'the product of the public school is just a godless, vain, fickle, unreliable specimen of humanity'. Henaghan delighted in the parochial school in Malate, run by two Missionary Canonesses of Saint Augustine from Belgium (Plate 6.2). He hoped for similar Catholic schools in every parish, preferably managed by nuns.[16]

---

14. Carolus Salotti to the Moderator General, 27 Feb. 1934 (CFCA, RP A-1:31).
15. 'The call of the Missions', *The Far East*, xiv (Aug. 1931), p. 187.
16. John Henaghan to Michael O'Dwyer, 15 Apr. 1932 (CFCA, RP A-4:3b).

The second parish staffed by Columbans, Binangonan, was typical of the country places outside Manila. Situated some twenty-five kilometres south-east of the capital, on a peninsula jutting into a lake, Laguna de Bay, it comprised a town of 10,000 inhabitants, and a ring of fifteen villages with another 10,000 people. Some of the villages were on an island in the lake. Mass was celebrated in most villages just once a year, at the fiesta of the local saint. Religious ignorance and apathy was so great that despite a series of sermons on the duty of annual communion – a standard measure for the success of a parish – only sixteen men and a hundred women received the sacrament at Easter 1932. The parish school drained the priest's funds, but he kept it going as a means of evangelisation.

One of the first considerations when taking on a new parish in the Philippines was its financial situation. O'Doherty, in his invitation for the Columbans to go to Malate, assured O'Dwyer that 'it would secure your men a decent living from the beginning'. However, the first superior, Patrick Kelly, found it necessary to accept the chaplaincy at San Scholastica's college, at £90 a year, to eke out support for three priests. Looking ahead, Kelly and his council recommended that the society gradually accept a line of parishes adjacent to Binangonan. However, they foresaw two problems. Several of those parishes were unlikely to become self-supporting, and:

> It is well to note in passing that there is a strong undercurrent of hostility especially among the native clergy against foreign priests securing good parishes.[17]

Kelly submitted a very modest budget request, totalling $689.75, to O'Dwyer at the end of 1933, and in the covering letter mentioned that Malate had several times to subsidise Cogan, in Binangonan:

> As you are aware, in our four and a half years here, we have received no financial assistance from the Society except about £80 in donations designated for the Philippines. All of this has long since been spent in medical expenses and in sending Fr Cuddigan [who collapsed with tuberculosis in 1930] to Australia.

O'Dwyer approved the budget, yet emphasised that the society was going through hard financial times due to the Great Depression of 1929. Cogan, he said, should be able to raise enough to support himself. Bishops in the Philippines wanted priests, but were also short of money. O'Doherty, as Archbishop of Manila, owned a bank, the Philippine Trust Company, which

---

17. Report of the council of the pro-region of the Philippines, 31 Jan. 1933 (CFCA, RP A-4:4).

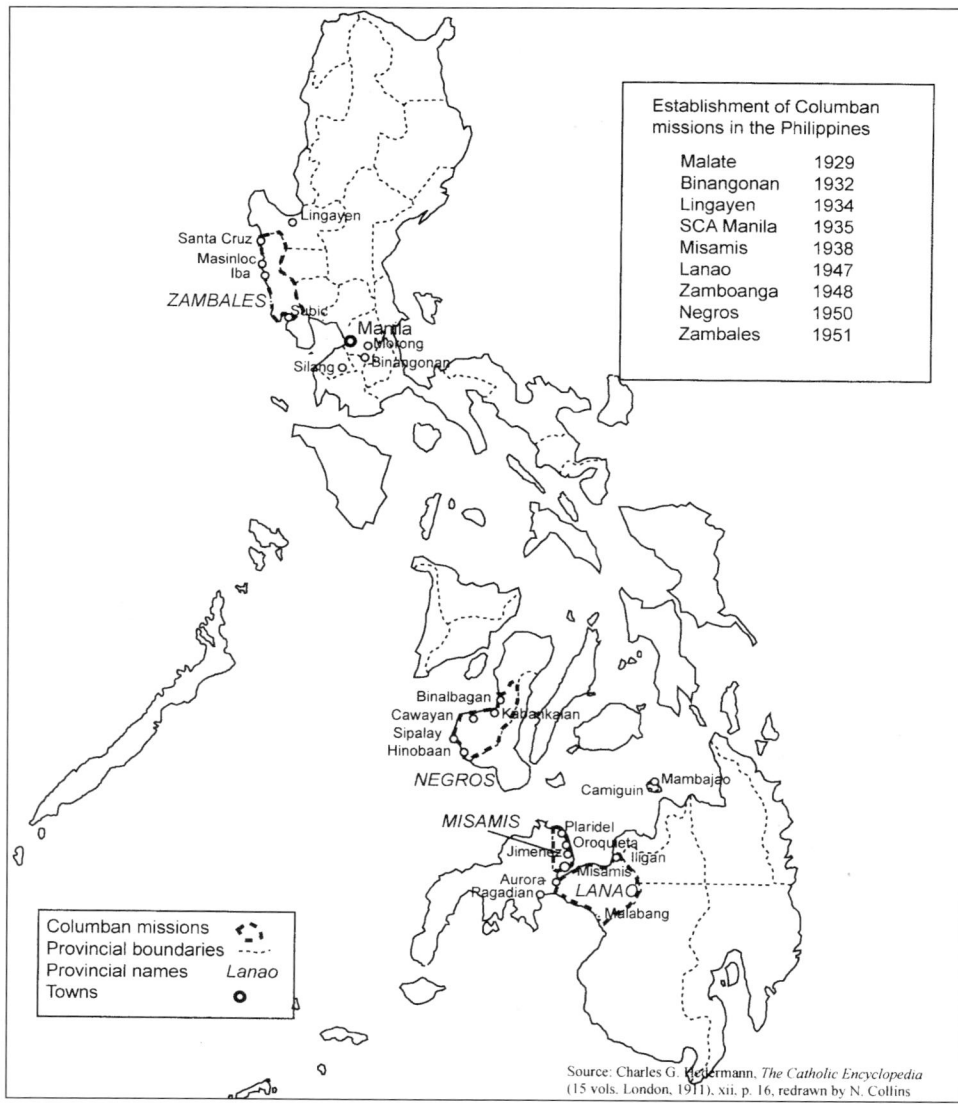

Figure 6.2 *Columban missions in the Philippines 1929-1954*. The Society of St Columban was entrusted with individual parishes like Malate and Binangonan, special ministries such as Student Catholic Action in Manila, and with large districts, beginning with Misamis Occidental.

was in trouble, and consequently he was unable to help poor parishes.[18] Yet O'Dwyer regarded many pastoral expenses as the responsibility of the archbishop, and felt that it would be unfair to the society and to 'the missions' – the vicariates in China – if he were to divert large sums to the Philippines.

Catechesis
Religious instruction of students attending public schools was a major concern for the leaders of the Roman Catholic Church in the Philippines. The public schools were set up by William Howard Taft, governor of the Philippines, in 1901.[19] Taft believed in the United States' non-denominational school system, but attempted to adapt it to the educational beliefs of Filipino Roman Catholics. In a letter to his brother Charles in January 1901 Taft explained:

> We are just now in the midst of the discussion of the School Bill. In it we have attempted to adopt the plan of Archbishop Ireland in Fairbault, Minn., in which it is permitted to send a minister or teacher of religion to the school house, before the regular hours, to teach such pupils as desired to be taught as expressed by their parents in writing.

Pope Leo XIII instructed the five Roman Catholic bishops of the Philippines that it was their duty 'to strive with all their might that the minds of the youths being educated in public schools should not lack religious knowledge'. Despite his clear command the bishops, all Spaniards, opposed the School Bill. Used to a Roman Catholic monopoly in education under the Spanish crown, they demanded Catholic schools, where only Catholic religious instruction would be given, and only Catholic teachers employed. American bishops, who replaced them in 1904, came from a long tradition of Catholic parochial schools, and followed the same policy, boycotting the public system. A national synod of the church in 1907 decreed that schools for boys and girls should be set up in every parish.[20] The code of canon law of 1917 obliged bishops in particular to found Catholic elementary and middle schools as well as national or regional universities. Michael O'Doherty, Archbishop of Manila, recognising that the canon was impractical for a poor country like the Philippines, and coming from Ireland where a system of state-funded, *de facto* Catholic, national schools was in place, wished to begin

---

18. Martin J. Noone, *The Columbans in the Philippines 1929-1950* (Manila, 1998), p. 28.
19. Edward J. McCarthy, 'An unwritten chapter' in *The Far East* (US ed.), xxxiii (Sept. 1950), pp 14-16.
20. Martin J. Noone, *Michael O'Doherty, Archbishop of Manila* (Manila, 1988), p. 58.

instruction in the public schools. But he faced intense opposition from the clergy and the apostolic delegate, William Piani. However, after a visit to Rome in 1931 O'Doherty felt strong enough to propose Catholic Action including, 'first, the teaching of catechism, particularly to the young attending schools where religious instruction is not given'. His initiative was so successful that in the archdiocese of Manila in 1933 catechists taught 128,450 pupils. Most of those, 108,381 in all, were in public schools, and attended classes given by Catholic Action groups.

O'Doherty's plan was adopted by all the other bishops. One of them, Cesar Maria Guerrero, Bishop of Lingayen-Dagupan, appealed to O'Dwyer in 1933. The cathedral parish was only one of several vacancies in his diocese, and he asked for a Columban as pastor:

> In this city are the State High Schools. Lingayen must have an English speaking priest to work among the students.[21]

Lingayen was 200 kilometres north of Manila, and the language there, Pangasinan, was very different from Tagalog. The distance would cut off a priest assigned there from his brother Columbans in Malate, and the language difference would make normal rotation of parishes difficult. Yet the situation was so critical that a young Columban, Samuel Sheehan, was sent. Apart from being pastor for 25,000 Catholics in the city and in twenty surrounding villages, he was expected to care for 2,000 state high school students, ranging from fourteen to twenty-two years of age, and the pupils in twenty-five public, elementary schools. Some of the teachers were American Protestants. The bishop suspected them of proselytising and requested an English-speaking priest to counteract their influence. Sheehan trained volunteer catechists, and became so heavily involved in the work with students that Kelly, the superior, sent a second Columban, Michael Donoher, to help with the parish. When the bishop gave Sheehan responsibility for all the public schools in the diocese, James McDevitt took over his work in the high school. By 1939 Sheehan was able to organise a two-week course for sixty volunteer catechists from twenty parishes. Help came when the new Bishop of Lingayen-Dagupan, Mariano A. Madriaga, invited the Columban sisters to open schools in Lingayen and in the town of Malasiqui early in 1939 (Plate 6.3). Within months the sisters could report that in Malasiqui:

> Our kindergarten pupils now number thirty and the school will grow as we gradually build up the grades. Three of us go to the neighbour-

---

21. Cesar Maria Guerrero to Michael O'Dwyer, 27 June 1933 (CFCA, RP A-4:7b).

ing Academy [high school] every Tuesday and Thursday to give religious instruction to the pupils ... Every Monday, Tuesday and Thursday we teach Christian Doctrine in the public elementary school. Over one thousand children are attending this school, and we have eleven catechists to help us.[22]

But the public high school in Lingayen remained a problem. Even though the education act of 1901 allowed the teaching of religion in schools for half an hour three times a week, it was difficult to find catechists to teach, and officials could be obstructive. McDevitt described some of the problems in 1938:

> In the Provincial High School, situated here in Lingayen, there are 3,350 students, ranging from twelve to nineteen years of age. They come from every town and village in an area as large as the province of Ulster. In the school there are seventy-two teachers. It is obvious that I cannot find catechists to teach Christian Doctrine to these students.[23]

McDevitt was forced to do most of the work himself, giving two or three lectures daily in the high school. But the time given, by 'a Protestant Masonic school superintendent', was 11.50 am. Morning classes ran from 7.00 to 11.45, when students were released to go home for lunch. Few were prepared to stay for religious instruction. As an alternative McDevitt 'tramped the streets, with a blackboard strapped on his back', and held classes in the students' boarding-houses nightly from 5.30 to 9.00 p.m. Average weekly attendance at catechetical classes in the school was 175, and in the evening classes 300. His unremitting work bore fruit, changing the attitudes of the principal and teachers in the school. As a result seven priests heard confessions from 6.00 am until 7.30 pm on Saturday, 16 March 1940, and a thousand students from the public high school received Holy Communion in the cathedral in Lingayen the following day, Palm Sunday. He had reached one third of the student body.

However, while religious instruction of pupils in public elementary schools was increasing in Manila and in provincial centres like Lingayen, students in public high schools, colleges and universities in the capital were neglected until Edward J. McCarthy arrived in 1935. One of the founding fathers of the Columbans, McCarthy was superior of the American region

---

22. 'Letter from a sister of St. Columban in the Philippines', *The Far East*, xxii (Dec. 1939), p. 275.
23. James McDevitt, 'The tragedy of the Philippines' in *The Far East*, xxii (Jan. 1939), pp 6-8.

when it went into serious debt due, at least partly, to the Wall Street Crash. O'Dwyer asked him to resign, and transferred him to the Philippines. Already forty-five years old when he reached Manila McCarthy found Tagalog too great a challenge. Instead he responded to complaints made by parents in Malate parish about the anti-Catholic teaching of some of the lecturers in the University of the Philippines. Since the university was non-sectarian he could not teach religion there. Instead he enrolled as a student of anthropology, made friends with other students, and soon had enough people to form a scholastic philosophy club, 'Catholic Action' being too challenging a name. He trained the members of the club to meet the attacks of the anti-Catholic lecturers, and created a storm in the media in January 1936 when 'Fr Ned in one of his lectures at the Scholastic Club made some references to some of the teachings at the State University.' One lecturer, Nathan Roy, from Calcutta, had a stock syllogism which ran, 'All who eat human flesh are cannibals. Catholics eat the flesh of Christ. Therefore Catholics are cannibals'.[24] McCarthy made a detailed report to the archbishop in 1938, describing the pastoral problem and the efforts of Students' Catholic Action to answer it, before begging for a house in the centre of the university area for a Newman Club.

Of the 53,015 students attending colleges and universities in Manila, 20,065 were in Catholic institutions and 32,950 in secular or non-sectarian ones. McCarthy guessed that 90% were baptised Roman Catholics, and that not more than 40% of the men were receiving the sacraments. Catholic Action groups (Plate 6.4) organised classes, student Masses, and sermons in English, which had replaced Spanish as the common language of the country. Yet he estimated that such efforts reached only 8,000 students, and:

> ... even assuming that many of them go to other Masses, there must still remain a vast number who do not go to Mass at all and scarcely ever hear a sermon of instruction even on Sundays.[25]

McCarthy went on to point out the dangers from communist and other subversive and immoral propaganda, and the proselytising efforts of some Protestant groups. To meet the need he proposed that the archdiocese build a Newman Club to train students who would be Catholic Action leaders among their fellow students. The archbishop was unable to respond to his request. Yet Catholic Action made a significant impact, and in 1939 the newspaper of the archdiocese, *The Philippines Commonweal*, reported on a Youth

---

24. Noone, *The Columbans in the Philippines 1929-1950*, p. 62.
25. Edward J. McCarthy to Michael J. O'Doherty, 12 Dec. 1938 (CFCA, RP A-4:19).

Eucharistic Week. Churches were crowded for sermons and solemn adoration of the Blessed Sacrament, and a final procession, in the heart of Manila, involved 15,000 young men and women, led by Major General Basilio J. Valdez, Chief of Staff of the Philippine Army. But McCarthy was in poor health, due to overwork, and doctors insisted that he have an immediate change and a prolonged rest. John Henaghan, superior in Manila since 1938, sent him to Australia in April 1939. He was replaced by Thomas Connolly before the Pacific war put an end to all forms of Catholic Action until 1947.

Mindanao

An American bishop, James Hayes, offered the Columbans a large section of his diocese on the southern island of Mindanao in 1938.[26] Hayes, a member of the Jesuit order, became bishop of the diocese of Cagayan when it was created on 20 January 1933. His territory, previously part of the huge diocese of Zamboanga, included six provinces and several substantial islands, stretching along the northern coast of Mindanao (Figure 6.3). The bulk of the population were settlers from the central islands, who brought with them various dialects of the Visayan language. An editorial in *The Far East* described the bishop's task:

> He has 450,000 Filipino Catholics and 175,000 non-Catholics, including Mohammedans, pagans and followers of various Christian sects.[27]

Hayes proposed to give the Columbans the province of Misamis Occidental to which Spanish missionaries had first brought Christianity. The Spanish government assigned all of western Mindanao to the Jesuits in 1622, and they established mission stations, one of them at Misamis. When the order was suppressed in 1773, Augustinian Recollects assumed responsibility for the whole island. In Misamis Occidental they set up seven parishes between 1776 and the revolution of 1898 (Table 6.1), when they were forced to withdraw.

Two Spanish Recollects, Cipriano Chocarro and Pedro Jimenez, returned to the parish of Jimenez in September 1901, followed by Jose Abad in November. The Recollects found that many communities had joined the Philippine Independent Church. In the town of Misamis only about a dozen families remained Catholic.[28] Members of the Aglipayan church persecuted

---

26. Minutes, superior general's council 1937-1952, 14 June 1938 (Columban central house, Dublin).
27. 'Enter new field in Philippines', *The Far East* (US ed.), xxii (Jan. 1939), p. 7.
28. Achútegui and Bernad, *Religious revolution in the Philippines*, p. 215.

Misamis	1776-1898
Jimenez (Palilan)	1886-1898
Plaridel (Langaran)	1886-1898
Oroquieta	1886-1898
Aloran	1893-1898
Clarin (Loculan)	1893-1898
Tudela	1893-1898

Source: Martin Noone, *The Columbans in the Philippines*, p. 111.
Table 6.1 *Parishes founded by Spanish missionaries, Augustinian Recollects, in Misamis Occidental, 1776-1898.*

the priests, raising uproar during their sermons, and disrupting ceremonies. The Augustinians bore the hatred, as well as isolation and poverty until, in 1919, the last of them withdrew, leaving the province in the hands of a single Spanish Jesuit, Gabriel Font. Two more Jesuits, Americans, arrived in 1925. Others followed, and by 1938 the Bishop of Cagayan could report that there were six priests in six towns. There were also five parochial schools, two in the care of the Franciscan Sisters of Mary.[29]

Ten Columbans were assigned to Misamis in the autumn of 1938 (Plate 6.5).[30] Peter Fallon, leader of the group, was a veteran in China since 1923 before transferring to Manila. His companions, an American, an Australian, and seven Irish, were newly ordained. Hayes, the bishop, placed half in parishes on the island of Cebu to learn Visayan while David Daly, the Jesuit pastor of Misamis, escorted the others to Mindanao. Eight months later, at the end of July 1939, the Jesuits handed over complete control to the young Columbans. John Henaghan, the Columban superior in Manila, visited the province and sent O'Dwyer a glowing report about 'the wonderful possibilities of the place' and 'a friendly type of people [who] greet you with a smile', unlike those in the parishes around Manila. He also commented on some of the problems the society could expect: financial support for the parochial schools; Roman Catholics who were baptised but unevangelised; and the people who 'fell away' to join the Philippine Independent church. Parochial schools were the preferred means for the religious instruction of the young in the diocese of Cagayan. It was staffed by Jesuits from the New York province, where every parish had such a school. The bishop even put a ban on teaching religion in public schools, apparently expecting all Catholics to attend parish schools.[31] But many of these were not self-supporting and the Jesuits

29. Noone, *The Columbans in the Philippines 1929-1950*, p. 97.
30. Michael O'Dwyer to Samuel Sheehan, 23 June 1938 (CFCA, RP A-4:16).
31. John Henaghan to Michael O'Dwyer, 11 July 1939 (CFCA, RP A-4:26).

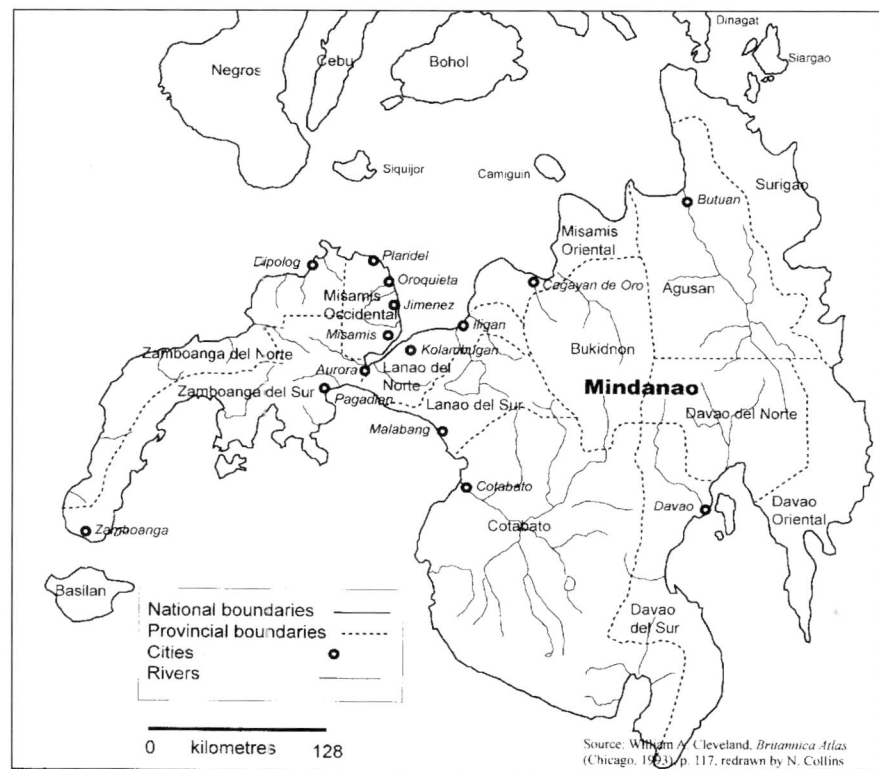

Figure 6.3 *Mindanao 1938, at the first arrival of the Columban Fathers in Misamis Occidental.* The diocese of Cagayan included the civil provinces of Surigao, Agusan, Misamis Oriental, Bukidnon, Lanao del Norte and Misamis Occidental. Columbans began staffing the parishes of Misamis in 1938, Lanao del Norte in 1947, Zamboanga de Sur in 1948, Lanao del Sur in 1949, and Camiguin Island in 1952.

kept them going with donations from America. When such gifts dried up in 1939 Hayes, the bishop, was tempted to close uneconomic schools, and instead to train and pay full-time catechists to teach in the public schools and to go into the villages to prepare the children for the sacraments. On more mature reflection he kept both options going. In 1941, on his instructions, the Columban Sisters set up a school in the parish of Misamis, while two veteran missionaries conducted a course for 200 volunteer catechists from all over the province.

Columbans in Misamis consistently regarded the religious instruction of children as a greater priority than the evangelisation of the adults, yet spent the greater part of their time attempting to reach grown-ups. Of a total population of 700,000 more than half, 400,000 were nominally Catholic.[32] Most of the remainder were members of the Philippine Independent Church. John Henaghan summarised the huge challenge facing the missionaries:

> Most of the people in Misamis are baptised – but that is all. There are many who fell away into Aglipayanism thro' lack of Catholic priest – till a few years ago there was only one Spanish priest doing the whole district on horseback. There is about 100 miles of coastline with a new road along the sea – it is a coconut plantation area – and the hills rise up 6 or 7 miles inland.[33]

Typically, Henaghan was hopeful, quoting incidents like a Mass said in a *barrio* by one of the new arrivals, a man still ignorant of Visayan: 'Over forty people came and said they wanted to become Catholics again.' But a priest needed food, shelter, a parish church, *barrio* chapels, and soon economics became the dominant theme in Henaghan's letters. The Jesuits were very generous, leaving 'everything, furniture, beds, books, some old cars', to the Columbans. However, according to parish records they recorded large donations from America as parochial income. Without that help from abroad many parishes could not support a priest. Church income was divided: 50% for maintenance of the priest, 46% for upkeep of the church and the work of the parish, and 4% for the bishop. To ease the crisis Hayes allowed the Columbans to use the church's share for the upkeep of the priest. Even then Henaghan reported:

> By close examination of all the parochial revenues, we find that nine priests can be supported by the parish funds, while five other priests require partial support [from the society].

32. Patrick Cronin, 'A Philippine province' in *The Far East*, xxx (Jan. 1947), p. 2.
33. John Henaghan to Michael O'Dwyer, 8 Mar. 1939 (CFCA, RP A-4:23).

The Columbans in Misamis, increased to fourteen in 1939, and working in eleven parishes, appealed, in letters to O'Dwyer and in articles in *The Far East*, for essentials that ranged from priests' houses and repair of parish churches to *barrio* chapels. Vincent McFadden, in the parish of Oroquieta, estimated that of a total population of 21,000 roughly 11,000 belonged to the Philippine Independent Church. Apart from a few Protestants most of the others were Roman Catholic. But:

> I soon learned that these Catholics could be divided into two classes: 80% Catholic merely by baptism, with scarcely any knowledge of religion or even the simplest prayer; a small number, chiefly townsfolk, who were ordinarily good Catholics, knowing their religion fairly well, coming to Mass and receiving the sacraments frequently.[34]

McFadden was assisted by Franciscan sisters who ran the parochial school and, temporarily, by another Columban, Martin Noone, who took charge of the religious education of the children in the public schools. That enabled him to concentrate on work in the community. He asked for funds for his chief concern, the parish church, which was falling to pieces:

> One can imagine the effect this dilapidated shack has on the minds of the people, especially the young, who contrast it with the modern and comfortable Evangelical church across the way and with the beautiful schools and government buildings which dot the parish.

Two other Columbans, in the parish of Tangub, also regarded the religious instruction of the children as their most important duty, and were able to provide catechists for eight of eleven public schools. But 'doing the *barrios*' was a major part of their work:

> The most thickly settled *barrios* were chosen and arrangements made for Mass to be said there once a month on a fixed day ... To the smaller *barrios* the priest went once every three months. To the rest, Mass was given only on the occasion of the *barrio* fiesta and perhaps one other time during the year.[35]

'Doing the *barrios*' involved more than Mass and a sermon. Even a newly-arrived priest could learn enough basic phrases to be able to hear confessions. Baptisms were conducted in Latin. There might also be some sick calls, often involving long hikes, or journeys on horseback. On the occasion of a fiesta

---

34. Vincent McFadden, 'An old record' in *The Far East* (US ed.), xxiv (May 1941), p. 17.
35. William F. Hennessey, 'My freshman year' in *The Far East* (US ed.), xxiv (Mar. 1941), p. 5.

there were weddings and a noisy procession for the patron saint of the village. In the central town in each parish a major problem was the apathy of the men. Francis Chapman, pastor of Misamis parish, started the Society of the Holy Name, a male confraternity dedicated to reverence for the names of God and of Jesus, and the suppression of blasphemy and perjury. He wanted to encourage the Roman Catholic men to attend Mass and the sacraments. Later he suggested that the members of the confraternity run for office, with the result that the town council, previously controlled by Aglipayans, became solidly Roman Catholic.[36]

World War II, September 1939
The outbreak of war in Europe in September 1939 made life more difficult for everyone in the Philippines, including the Columbans:

> The people here are beginning to feel the effect of the war and there is much poverty in the provinces – much speculation as to what the future may bring ... I have not had a letter from Ireland for months but I suppose all's well.[37]

Travel between Ireland and Asia became impossible for newly-ordained priests or men wishing to return from holiday. Yet the work continued, and there were even plans for expansion. Henaghan heard rumours in June 1941 that the society might be invited to staff a new district in Mindanao. In November he reported that Hayes, the Bishop of Cagayan, had asked him if the Columbans could send priests – from America, the bishop suggested – to some unspecified parishes adjacent to Misamis Occidental. The only reference to the world situation in Henaghan's long, four-page letter was the single sentence, 'We are all well here thank God and still hoping that the peace will not be broken by war in the Orient.' O'Dwyer replied on 8 December 1941:

> I see in today's paper that war has broken out between the United States and Japan. This, I think, will make travelling difficult for some time in the Pacific; but whenever circumstances permit, the Council is in favour of accepting the proposal of Bishop Hayes.

Henaghan sent a telegram, received in Ireland on 20 December 1941, saying, 'Sisters priests all well greetings Rev John Henaghan'.[38] After that there was silence.

---

36. Interview by author with Francis Chapman, Cagayan de Oro, Philippines (5 Jan. 2001).
37. John Henaghan to Michael O'Dwyer, 12 Sept. 1940 (CFCA, RP A-4:27a).
38. John Henaghan to Michael O'Dwyer, 20 Dec. 1941 (CFCA, RP A-4:29a).

Leaders of church and state made preparations for the war in the Pacific between Japan and the US. American and Filipino forces installed artillery at Lingayen, one of the likely invasion points. Hayes, the Bishop of Cagayan, instructed his priests that in the event of an invasion they should remain in their parishes, but he advised them to place all church records with a dependable family in a safe house some miles inland. Yet the Japanese attack on Pearl Harbor on 7 December 1941, and on airfields in the Philippines, seems to have caught everyone by surprise. Patrick Cronin heard the news from excited parishioners as he came from the church after Mass on the feast of the Immaculate Conception, 8 December. The Japanese landed at many points around the coast of Luzon, and to avoid encirclement McArthur, the American commander, withdrew his forces, both American and Filipino, to the Bataan peninsula, and the island-fortress of Corregidor. Fighting continued until the surrender of Bataan on 9 April 1942, and of Corregidor on 6 May. Lingayen was occupied on 1 January 1942, Manila the following day, Binangonan and the Columban parishes near the city four days later. It was only after the fall of Bataan that the Japanese had forces to take over the southern islands, reaching Misamis Occidental in May.

Japanese officers reacted in different ways to the presence of foreign priests and sisters. Irish Columbans were neutrals in the war, but those from Australia, New Zealand or the US were 'enemy aliens'. When Dermot Feeney brought the passports of the four Columbans in Lingayen to the garrison headquarters to obtain necessary passes an officer explained that Thomas R. Dwyer, from New Zealand, would have to go to an internment camp. Feeney asked the interpreter, a Japanese man born in the Philippines, 'Are you Japanese or Filipino?' 'Japanese, of course!' 'But you were born in the Philippines.' 'True. But my father and mother are Japanese.' 'It's the same with Fr Dwyer. He was born in New Zealand, but his father and mother are Irish.' Dwyer received a pass.[39] The Columbans in Mindanao were ordered to report to the Japanese headquarters, but Francis Chapman, Australian, William Hennessey, American, and some of the Irish decided not to obey.[40] Six who complied ran into difficulties. An interpreter confused 'Irlanda' with Holland, an enemy of the German-Japanese Axis, and the only available map showed Ireland in the bright red colour of British possessions. For ten, tense days the six were confined to the home economics department of a school beside the army headquarters, before being released. Only one Columban,

---

39. Noone, *The Columbans in the Philippines*, p. 150.
40. William Hennessey to Michael O'Dwyer, 28 Dec. 1944 (CFCA, RP Misc:3).

Vincent P. McFadden, born in Colorado, but raised in Ireland from the age of twelve, was interned.

One of the first effects of the war for Columbans in the Philippines was isolation. Japanese bombers sank most of the inter-island ferries, and the only motorised transport on the roads belonged to occupation forces. For the duration of the conflict the missionaries in Lingayen, the archdiocese of Manila, and in Misamis were cut off from each other. Only a few, clandestine, short-wave radios brought news other than Japanese propaganda. Schools were closed, and often used as barracks by the military. Yet priests could continue some of their work. Guerrillas captured the towns of Misamis and Oroquieta in September 1942. For the next ten months, until June 1943, there were no Japanese in the province, and life was almost normal. The guerrilla leaders made contact with McArthur in Australia, and submarines began to arrive, bringing arms and radios, and also Mass wine and wheat flour, for communion wafers, for the priests. When the Japanese returned people and priests withdrew to the hills. For the rest of the war the occupation forces were largely confined to the towns, and the Filipinos remained in the hills. The Columbans lived with the people, depended on them for food and shelter, and endured the same dangers. Later they would remember how the experience of those years broke down all barriers. By using mountain trails the missionaries were able to travel around the *barrios*, saying Mass, instructing some of the children, performing baptisms and marriages, and attending the sick and dying. American officers often visited them, bringing news, cigarettes, and even clothes.

Deaths

The Columbans in Luzon (Figure 6.2) remained in their *conventos* and were able to celebrate the sacraments, although the pastors of Binangonan and the neighbouring town of Cardona, both from New Zealand, were forbidden to perform marriages. A guerrilla movement placed the missionaries in jeopardy by coming to their houses at night asking for rice and news. To refuse was to incur the wrath of the guerrillas, but to give could bring retribution from the Japanese. In July 1943 the Japanese seized Frank Douglas in the parish of Pililla. They seemed to believe that he was privy to knowledge about the guerrillas in the district. Witnesses reported:

> That night Father was taken to a nearby parish named Paete and was locked up in the Baptistery. Here the investigation and the torture continued for three days and three nights.[41]

---

41. Gerald Cogan to Michael O'Dwyer, 24 May 1945 (CFCA, RP Misc: 24).

Douglas was beaten savagely and given the 'water cure' where the victim's stomach is forcibly filled with water. Then a board is placed across the abdomen and pressure exerted on it to expel the water. For those three days and nights Douglas was tied by one hand to a pillar in the church, unable to lie down. A Filipino guerrilla, Frank Quesada, one of many men imprisoned in the same church, told how the priest prayed the rosary in Tagalog, and heard his, Quesada's, confession. On the evening of 27 July 1945 Japanese soldiers took Douglas, threw him, covered in blood, into a truck and drove him away. His fate remains unknown.[42]

John Lalor turned the Malate school into the Remedios Hospital, funded by members of the Catholic Women's League and staffed by volunteer doctors and young men and women from the area. The first patients in the middle of 1942 were wounded and sick Filipino prisoners-of-war just released by the Japanese. By the end of the year most had recovered enough to be discharged. Their places were taken by sick American prisoners from the internment camp in Santo Tomas university.[43] Patrick Kelly became chaplain for the internees in the university itself, offering Mass in the open air. Both Lalor and Kelly, together with many of the volunteers in the hospital, were involved in getting food and medicines to the American prisoners. In a letter to the commanding officer of US forces in the Philippines an American prisoner-of-war listed many people, Filipino and foreign, who helped the internees, and claimed that:

> The Catholic Priests of Malate who died did great work. Fr Kelly aiding escaped prisoners in Manila, contact between internees and their families. Fr Lalor who first opened the smuggling to Park Ave Elementary School, aid Bilibid [prison] POWs also. Fr Monaghan, who asked for old clothes, shoes and money for POW. Fr Henagohan [*sic*] who also did good work.[44]

The Japanese arrested Kelly, Lalor and Monaghan for these activities on Christmas Eve 1944, and brought them to the military police headquarters at Fort Santiago, Manila, where they were brutally beaten and questioned for four days. After their release they would not talk about their ordeal. When

---

42. Nicomedes Rosal, Information regarding case of Fr Douglas, 25 July 1945 (CFCA, RP Misc: 27).
43. Pedro Picornell, 'Remedios hospital', undated (unpublished MS in CFCA, Dalgan Park, RP Misc, pp 18-25).
44. Thomas O'Brien to George F. Moore (undated), cited in George F. Moore to Joseph Monaghan, 25 Aug. 1947 (CFCA, RP Misc:31).

In the Walled City:	
Augustinians:	14
Franciscans:	10
Recollects:	6
Capuchins:	6
Missionaries of the Sacred Heart:	1
Vincentians:	1
Secular priests:	2
In other city districts:	
Jesuits:	3
Vincentians:	14
Columbans:	5
Capuchins:	3
Secular priests:	1
De la Salle Brothers:	16

Source: Pietro Fumasoni-Biondi to Michael O'Dwyer, 30 May 1945 (CFCA, RP Misc:26).
Table 6.2 *Priests and brothers killed by Japanese in Manila, February 1945.* Many of the churches and colleges in the centre of Manila were staffed by members of religious orders, which explains why only a few secular priests were killed.

American bombing of Manila started on 21 September 1944, the hospital treated those wounded in air raids. US troops returned to the Philippines in October 1944, entering Manila on 3 February 1945. A terrible battle ensued, and much of the city was destroyed in a fierce artillery duel. Thousands of civilians died, many of them from 'friendly fire'. An untold number perished in an appalling massacre. During the last days of January and early February Japanese forces divided the city into zones, rounded up the men, and killed them. Priests and religious, most of them Spaniards, Germans and Irish, were among the dead. The superior of the Dominican order sent Pietro Fumasoni-Biondi, the prefect of Propaganda Fide, a list of priests and brothers killed in the walled city of Manila, Intramuros, and in the suburbs (Table 6.2).

Russell Brines, Associated Press correspondent, reported on many of the atrocities. He interviewed Francis J. Cosgrave, a Redemptorist, the only survivor of seventy people bayoneted in De La Salle College and recorded that:

> Nearly half the victims were women and children, many of them babies who died while reaching for the protection of their parents' hands. Some had been bayoneted repeatedly. Ten of the victims are believed to be American priests. Others included fourteen German and Irish Brothers of the Christian Schools.[45]

45. Russell Brines, 'Father Cosgrave describes De La Salle College massacre' in *Letter from America* (Office of War Information of the United States, Dublin, 2 Mar. 1945) (CFCA, RP Misc:12).

Four Columbans, Patrick Kelly, John Henaghan, Joseph Monaghan, and Peter Fallon, and all the laymen in the Malate church, were taken away on 10 February 1945. Their bodies were never found. John Lalor was in the Remedios Hospital and escaped the round-up. Three days later he was resting with some of the hospital staff when an American shell hit the wall beside them killing all except one.[46]

The first news of the tragedy reached Ireland in a long telegram from Timothy Connolly in America to Michael O'Dwyer. O'Dwyer broke the news to the families of the men in the Philippines before releasing the telegram to the media. Published in the *Irish Independent* ten days later[47] it sparked off a controversy between the American minister to Ireland, accusing the Japanese of burning the priests alive, and the Japanese consul-general. Connolly's telegram stated:

> Father Lalor buried in Manila by Father McFadden. Father Douglas almost certain killed a year ago body not found. Malate church and rectory destroyed. Fathers Henaghan, Kelly, Fallon, Monaghan, Cogan, Connolly, Donoher, O'Reilly not contacted yet and first four rumoured killed. No definite news of these or last four. All others safe.[48]

Rebuilding

Surviving Columbans in the Philippines began the task of rebuilding in February 1945, even though hostilities continued until the Japanese surrender on 2 September. O'Doherty, the Archbishop of Manila, insisted that the society continue to staff the parishes assigned to it. Gerald Cogan, temporary superior in place of the dead John Henaghan, had difficulty in finding enough men. Six had been killed, others interned in the final months of the year, and all were in need of rest and medical treatment. Cogan's task was Herculean. He took charge, alone, of the parish of Malate, where the church was reduced to a shell and the *convento* totally destroyed. For church services and his dwelling he used part of the school, and with volunteers he began clearing the rubble and searching for materials for building repairs. In his capacity as superior his responsibilities ranged from getting entry permits for new or returning priests, to visiting the men in Misamis, to sorting out the wills of the dead Columbans. The council in Ireland promptly assigned eight

---

46. Gerald Cogan, 'Last days in Malate' in *The Far East*, xxviii (Aug. 1945), p. 59.
47. *Irish Independent*, 31 Mar. 1945.
48. Timothy Connolly to Michael O'Dwyer, 21 Mar. 1945 (CFCA, RP Misc:13).

priests from the US to Mindanao, and appointed Samuel Sheehan as superior in the Philippines. Sheehan, in Ireland when war broke out in the Pacific, became a chaplain in the British Army 1943-1945. After many delays he reached Manila, via America, on 8 June 1945, and was horrified by what he saw:

> Manila is a terrible shambles. I thought I had seen the extremes of war devastation in London, but it is as nothing compared to Manila. Those who had come home had warned me to expect the worst, but it is necessary to see it to realise the state it is in. In all this district of Manila there are just a handful of houses standing. The people are still living here in anything and everything under the most appalling conditions.

Sheehan was impatient to get Malate church 'in suitable condition for the bare administration of the sacraments', partly because of the wonderful devotion of the people towards the dead priests. An Irish tenor, Hubert Valentine, serving in the American army, joined members of the parish to help Cogan raise almost $20,000, and priests who had been Kelly's classmates in St Patrick's College, Maynooth, sent £302 for a memorial to him.

Dermot Feeney's church, the cathedral in Lingayen (Plate 6.6), was totally destroyed in the bombardment that preceded the American landing there in January 1945. In three days 62,000 shells were poured into the city. Feeney had no money to rebuild. 'Financially we are on the rocks.' American servicemen helped the priests build a temporary chapel, using discarded crates that had held aircraft parts for the floor and walls. Parishioners added a roof of nipa palm. The same materials provided a convent for the Columban sisters who returned from their wartime refuge in Malasiqui. Inside, the walls betrayed their origin, being stamped, 'Handle With Care', or 'This Side Up'.

In 1946 religious instruction of the young, neglected for all the years of conflict since 1941, was the most pressing need. Columbans, despite consistent obstruction from freemasons in the department of education,[49] used the twin methods of parish schools and catechists in the public schools. Peace came early to Misamis Occidental when the Japanese withdrew in December 1944. The priests returned from the hills to their churches and *conventos*. Most found that while all furniture had been burned there was little serious damage to buildings, which left them free to begin reorganising instruction. In Jimenez:

---

49. Interview by author with Malachy Toner, St Columban's, Dalgan Park, Navan, Co Meath (23 Oct. 2006).

We threw ourselves into the work enthusiastically. People brought us any scraps of paper they could find and we collected pencils from ... the US soldiers. Teachers volunteered their services and time. We went to work finding rooms, equipment, furniture of any kind ... a kindergarten grew into an elementary school, then a High School and by the time I returned from my vacation in 1949 we had some 1,200 students.

The Columban Sisters in Misamis, after three years in a series of ten different hideouts in the mountains, and on a tiny island, discovered that their convent had been the headquarters of the Japanese, who burned all their furniture to heat the officers' baths. When they were allowed back in March 1945 the sisters recovered books and school equipment hidden before the occupation. By August they taught 500 students in the elementary school, and had re-opened the high school (Plate 6.7).[50] In Manila James McDevitt resurrected Student Catholic Action, recruiting catechists from the Roman Catholic colleges and universities to instruct the city's public primary school children. The number receiving religious instruction rose from 7,000 in 1947 to 100,000 in 1953. His successor, Malachy Toner, with four priest assistants, tackled the needs of students in the large, non-confessional, private universities in 1951. Active membership of Student Catholic Action grew from 1,000 in 1947 to 18,026 in 1953. They provided religious instruction for more than half the students in non-denominational schools.[51]

Young American Columbans began to arrive in Manila in the second half of 1946, travelling in the Spartan accommodation of troopships. Those assigned to Mindanao endured even more arduous voyages, the first being lucky to find a berth on a hatch cover under an awning. All were rushed straight into parishes, with no period of language study, and only a short apprenticeship with an older Columban before the veteran went home to recover from the stresses and deprivations of war. The directory of the society for 1946 lists thirty-nine priests for the pro-region of the Philippines. Seventeen of the names are in parentheses, indicating that the men were home, 'temporarily absent from their missions'. Timothy Connolly, superior of the American region of the society, made an official visitation of the Philippines in 1948, and reported while it was absolutely necessary to send the older Columbans home and replace them with newcomers, there were problems:

---

50. Francis De Sales Hogan, 'Mindanao madre' in *The Far East* (US ed.), xxix (Sept. 1946), p. 7.
51. 'Among Manila's students', *The Far East*, xxxvii (June, 1954), pp 8-9.

These were young men without the language and, what is more serious, without an understanding of the people. This latter lack was aggravated by the fact that most of them had parish experience at home and started off with the idea that a P.I. [Philippine] parish could be run like a home parish.

Connolly listed another difficulty, the huge task of reconstruction and development facing young and inexperienced priests. To aggravate the headache there were no society funds for building, practically no parish funds, and nothing from the bishop. Priests were forced to appeal to friends at home. The poverty of the government added to the plight of the neophyte missionaries. It could not provide enough 'grade' schools and:

> The net result is that education has become a commodity for which people will make great sacrifices. This became evident to businessmen intent on making money on private schools ... It also provided an opening for Protestant funds ... Our priests felt they had to counteract these influences if they were to save the faith of the young people.

There was bitterness among the young Columbans. who questioned the policy of the society which helped men in China to build churches and schools, but denied similar aid to those in the Philippines. Connolly passed on, with approval, a proposal that the society make loans of about $5,000 for school building. As a school became viable it could repay the loan. Another cause for grumbling was that the society gave no help towards the cost of transporting catechists to the public schools. In Connolly's opinion:

> If the Society could provide some subsidy for catechetical work, this would take precedence over anything else except maintenance [of the priest]. This subsidy, of course, could not be repaid.

The complaints of the young Columbans about finances highlighted the peculiar status of the pro-region of the Philippines. As a '*pro-regio extra Missiones*' it did not receive the same financial support as the vicariates in China. Such problems should be brought to a general chapter of the society. However, the pro-region of the Philippines was not represented at the chapter of 1947. Superiors of pro-regions '*in missionibus*' were *ex officio* members of the chapter. But the Philippines was not in 'the missions'. Similarly the Columbans in each pro-region '*in missionibus*' elected a delegate to represent them. Columbans in the Philippines could be elected, but only as members of the American region. None were chosen. As a result there was no-one at the chapter to present their arguments. The report of the chapter made no mention of subsidies for churches, houses or schools. Sheehan complained to the new superior general, Jeremiah Dennehy:

> I am disappointed that the Acts of the Chapter makes no mention of the financial policy of the Society in regard to the P. I. [Philippines] although I take it for granted that the matter was discussed. It has been a major 'headache' here as I have been stalled again and again by the reply 'wait until the matter comes up at the Chapter'.[52]

Dennehy replied that the chapter had decided to make the Philippines a region, subject to the approval of Rome. As a region it would submit a budget, and it would be treated equally with the 'home regions', Ireland, USA and Australia. It became a region in February 1948. Even then the matter of building subsidies still festered, although Dennehy assured Sheehan that any reasonable budget for the Philippines would receive favourable consideration.[53] Sheehan, at Dennehy's suggestion, circularised the priests in 1949 asking for specific requests. They responded listing rectories, chapels, schools, refrigerators and many other items. There is no record of how much assistance the society gave. When Dennehy died in December 1951 his successor was Timothy Connolly who, as superior of the American region when it included the Philippines, had argued for loans for building and some help with catechists. Not surprisingly, budgets for the region of the Philippines after Connolly's election in 1951 included subsidies for parishes, and specifically for schools, houses, churches, jeeps, and transportation for catechists. With limited income the society could give only partial assistance, which meant that priests still had to find much of the money from their parish or from friends abroad. Yet by 1953 every parish in Misamis Occidental had a high school, with some of their graduates going on to the seminary. In the town of Misamis the Columban Sisters ran a complete school, with kindergarten, grade, high, and college departments. Similar projects in the whole Philippine region in 1954 received grants totalling 133,740 pesos, or $66,870.

New ventures 1947-52
Further Columban expansion in the Philippines became necessary in 1948 because of the communist advances in China. Jeremiah Dennehy was planning ahead and wrote to Samuel Sheehan:

> In case the political situation in China gets too difficult we should be looking out for some other place in the P.I. [Philippines]. Hanyang has

---

52. Samuel Sheehan to Jeremiah Dennehy, 22 Aug. 1947 (CFCA, RP A-4:37c).
53. Jeremiah Dennehy to Samuel Sheehan, 12 Sept. 1947, (CFCA, RP A-4:37d).

been overrun with Reds but, thank God, all the men escaped. Keep your eyes and ears open for some sort of decent place. I did not intend to take any more districts till about 1950, but if the priests will not be wanted in China we must find some place for all the young men coming on.[54]

Several Filipino bishops, observing the annual arrival of young Columbans and the return of older men from vacation, and no doubt aware of events in China, seem to have anticipated Dennehy's dilemma, and in 1947 invited the society to staff other parishes. Mariano A. Madriaga, Bishop of Lingayen, offered the parishes of Labrador and Sual. In Mindanao James Hayes, of Cagayan, needed to replace the Jesuits in Lanao del Norte, and the island of Camiguin. The only land corridor from Misamis Occidental to Lanao ran through the diocese of Zamboanga, and when Aloysius del Rosario, Bishop of Zamboanga, proposed that he entrust the Columbans with Aurora (Figure 6.3, p. 203) and two other parishes, Dennehy readily agreed. Between August 1947 and November 1949 Columbans moved into several huge parishes in Lanao del Norte, Lanao del Sur and Zamboanga del Sur. Four went to Camiguin in February 1952. The Holy See showed its approval of the development of the mission in Misamis Occidental and Lanao by combining them into a new prelature in January 1951,[55] with a Columban, Patrick Cronin, as bishop.

Entry into Lanao and Zamboanga brought the Columbans into contact with Muslims for the first time. Islam arrived in the Philippines, from Malaysia and Indonesia, in the fourteenth century and spread as far as Manila. After the Spanish conquest Muslims were forced to retreat from many of the islands. However, they remained in control of most of Mindanao and the Sulu archipelago until the Americans subdued them finally in 1915. Three different Muslim tribal groups occupied the areas to be served by the Columbans in 1947-1949, Maranaos and Iranuns in Lanao, and Maguindanaos in Zamboanga del Sur.[56] Christian settlers from the islands to the north were flooding into all three provinces in such numbers that the priests seem to have had little time to get to know their Muslim neighbours. Instead they drew their information from observation at a distance or from American servicemen and Filipino Christians. Typically they used words like 'Moro' or 'Mohammedan', terms that were offensive to Muslims, and wondered how to bring them into the Roman Catholic Church. Thomas Brennan, pastor of Dansalan (Plate 6.8),

---

54. Jeremiah Dennehy to Samuel Sheehan, 24 Jan. 1948 (CFCA, RP A-4:40a).
55. Pius XII, *'Supremum nobis divinitus'* in *AAS*, xviii (Rome, 1951), pp 353-5.
56. Peter Gordon Gowing, *Mandate in Moroland* (Quezon City, 1983), p. 6.

where there were 2,800 Christians and 17,000 Muslims, was 'convinced that it will take a miracle to convert them to Christianity'. Further south, in the town of Malabang, Thomas Holohan opened a school in 1954 and reported that:

> I am very fortunate that the local Moros, even several in authority, welcome my efforts to open a Catholic school. Most of the students will, of course, be Catholics, but I expect more than 20 Moro children to enroll.[57]

The editor of *The Far East* added, 'He is hopeful, however, that the school, under the patronage of Our Lady of Peace, will help numerous Mohammedans to see the light.' Apart from this limited contact with Muslims through the schools, Columbans concentrated on building and on the usual services to their Christian parishioners.

Negros
Archbishop Egidio Vagnozzi, the apostolic delegate, initiated the next expansion of the Columban mission in the Philippines. Samuel Sheehan, the superior of the society in Manila, sent an urgent letter to Jeremiah Dennehy in January 1950:

> The Delegate called me in today … The Diocese of Bacolod … is in a scandalous position for want of priests and something has to be done. He is going to force the Bishop to give up two vicariates … and wants us to take them. It would mean an immediate TEN priests this year, with another TEN or more to follow … So, would you please send me a cable as soon as possible stating if we can accept the Delegate's offer …

Dennehy cabled immediately accepting the proposal. The diocese of Bacolod (Figure 6.2, p. 196) comprised the islands of Negros and Siquijor. It was staffed by Filipino secular priests and Spanish Augustinian Recollects. Spanish and Filipino Vincentian Fathers ran a diocesan seminary. Although he needed priests the bishop, Casimiro Lladoc, was unwilling to accept more foreigners, fearing that they would look down on the Filipino clergy.[58] He resisted until the apostolic delegate threatened to report the matter to the Consistorial Congregation.

Negros is about 240 kilometres long and 80 wide. A mountain range, dominated by Canlaon volcano, divided it into two sections, east and west.

---

57. Thomas Holohan, 'A Catholic school in a Mohammedan town' *TFE* xxxvii (Aug. 1954), p. 9.
58. James McCaslin, *The Columbans in the Philippines* (4 vols, Manila 2000), iv, p. xvii.

The island was famous for sugar, exporting it to Spain, Britain and America. Away from the sugar-growing plains the main crops were coconuts, corn and rice. Between 1850 and 1893 sugar production grew from 3,000 piculs to 1,800,000, and the population from 30,000 to 320,606. When the Columbans arrived in 1950 immigration from neighbouring islands had boosted the inhabitants to 1,500,000.[59] Of these a minority, the elite, owned vast estates and sugar centrals (mills), while a worker was 'a wage or debt slave who owned, quite literally, nothing more than his clothes and cooking utensils'.[60] The majority spoke Ilongo, a dialect of Visayan, similar to the Cebuano used in Misamis. Spanish was common among the landowners and, as elsewhere, English in schools. Sheehan recognised:

> There is one snag and that is that the whole area is owned completely by *hacienderos* (ranchers). However, realising that the church is a bulwark for them against communism, they are very willing to help financially. When matters are fixed up I, or whoever is appointed Superior down there, will try to see them individually.[61]

Ten Columbans took over a rather remote block of parishes in the centre and south-west of Negros. Edward Allen noted that the modern highway did not reach them. Instead they had a dirt road. In some parishes they found good churches and houses. Other churches, such as the one in Isabela and most of the village chapels, were destroyed in the war. Allen described the ruins in Isabela:

> Most of the four walls are still standing, but the roof and the furnishings are gone ... In fine weather Mass is still said there on Sundays and holydays, but the Mass must be said early before the sun gets too hot.

The church in Ilog was 'almost a complete ruin', and the house 'a small *nipa* house barely habitable for a priest' (Plate 6.9), while in Cawayan the house and church had been almost completely demolished by a recent typhoon. There were no parish schools. Only Frank Chapman, the leader, was an experienced missionary, a member of the first batch in Mindanao. Most of the others were ordained in 1946-1948. They faced the tasks of reconstruction, and of bringing the gospel and sacraments to the people. Spurring them to greater efforts was the presence of Protestant missionaries. Gerald Cogan in Manila noted tartly:

---

59. Edward Allen, 'Discovering Negros island' in *The Far East* (US ed.), xxxiii (Dec. 1950), p. 10.
60. Alfred W. McCoy, 'A queen dies' in Alfred W. McCoy and Eduardo C. de Jesus, *Philippine social history* (Manila, 1982), p. 325.
61. Samuel Sheehan to Jeremiah Dennehy, 30 Apr. 1950 (CFCA, RP A-4:50b).

Because of the lack of priests, the Protestants have had a great time down there, especially after liberation, perverting all they could with their 6 million dollars which they collected in their post-war drive. They have nice little churches and clinics all over the place, and their missionaries eat well.[62]

Protestant churches present in Negros included Methodists, Baptists, and Seventh Day Adventists. Their greatest success was in the town of Ilog where the Baptists had a high school, with an enrolment of about 300. Timothy Connolly recorded in 1953 that, of the total population of 3,600 in the town, 2,200 were 'non-Catholic'.[63] In their work of evangelising, Protestant missionaries distributed good, cheap, yet well-printed bibles in the local dialect. Some discouraged the fiestas celebrated in honour of the patron saint of a village and conducted frequent revival meetings.

For the Columbans a source of hope was the Legion of Mary, the Roman Catholic organisation of lay people dedicated to apostolic work. The first praesidium in the area was established in Kabankalan in 1947, and by the time the Columbans came in 1950 there were seventeen praesidia in five parishes. The principal work of the legionaries was:

> ... to teach the young and to visit homes instructing the ignorant, assisting the sick, and inviting all to participate more fully in the life of the church.

Only sixty of the 12,000 Roman Catholics in the parish of Magallon attended Mass when Michael Cullen arrived in 1951. Through the activities of the Legion, that number increased to 400 four years later.[64] Apostolic work in the Legion increased the faith of the legionaries themselves, and eight members of a boys' praesidium in Isabela parish entered the seminary. Six girls from the same parish entered convents.[65] Columbans also invested in parish schools, following the practice already established by the society elsewhere in the Philippines. In some cases they were able to buy existing establishments. By 1954 the Columban team had grown to twenty-seven, and the *Status animarum* for 1955 listed fifteen parishes, two chaplaincies attached to sugar centrals, and one linked to a school. Twelve parishes had schools with a total enrolment of 2,855.

Visiting Columbans regularly commented on the injustice of the *hacienda*

---

62. Gerald Cogan to Joseph Whelan, 16 Aug. 1950 (CFCA, RP A-4:53b).
63. Timothy Connolly, Visitation of the region of the Philippines 1953 (CFCA, RP A-7, p. 61).
64. Michael Cullen, 'A parish reborn' in *The Far East*, xl (Sept. 1957), p. 15.
65. Bernard Smyth, 'Treasure island' in *The Far East*, xxxviii (Apr. 1955), p. 2.

system in Negros. The priests assigned there seem to have been too engrossed in finding ways to reach the thousands of members of their parishes to write much about the social question. But several of them mentioned the problem to Timothy Connolly, on his tour of visitation in 1953. In Kabankalan, the southern limit of the sugar cane industry, he learned that income from copra, the dried meat of the coconut, was less than that from sugar, but that it was better distributed throughout the year. For sugar workers:

> There is extreme poverty and misery for all that part of the year in which the crop is not being harvested, as it is impossible to get them to save the money they make during the harvest season.... Under the sugarcane economy great wealth is also concentrated in the hands of a few people who often tend to flaunt and abuse it.

The plight of seasonal workers who came from neighbouring islands during the busy seasons was even worse, since they were paid only for the days when they worked. Bernard Smyth also noted the wide social chasm between the *haciendero* class and the labourers. He met Mrs Jesus Nolan who visited the shacks of the workers and thought that, 'Perhaps it is to people like her that we can most hopefully look for a solution of the social problems of Negros.'[66] Priests were limited in what they could do to tackle the problem. In their houses and parochial schools they employed working students, young people from poor families, who were given free tuition. Many helped promising students to continue through college. A large number of the Filipino clergy and religious owed their education to this system.

Filipino social problems struck Columbans in Lingayen in a more savage way in November 1950. Sheehan sent Dennehy a hurried note:

> I got a telegram from Dermot [Feeney] on Tuesday afternoon saying 'Labrador raided. Flynn taken', so I drove up there immediately. Facts are few. The Huks raided Labrador on Monday night, burnt a few houses, killed a few people and escaped back to the mountains ... the Commander ... told Tommy they would have to take him with them but that he would not be harmed.

Thomas Flynn was killed. Remains found in a burned-out house may have been his. The Huks who captured him were members of the *Hukbó ng Bayan Laban so Hapón*, the People's Army to Fight the Japanese. Founded by the joint communist and socialist parties of the Philippines in 1942 in central and southern Luzon, the Huks were one of the guerrilla groups fighting the

---

66. Bernard Smyth, 'Treasure island' in *The Far East*, xxxviii (Apr. 1955), p. 2.

Japanese, and when the Americans returned they found them in control in a number of provinces. Several Huks won seats in the Philippine congress in 1946, but were unseated. They returned to the hills and attempted to organise a communist revolution. By 1950 they had expanded into the provinces of Pangasinan and Zambales, and were operating in the outskirts of Manila. Normally they did not threaten priests other than ones accused of working against them. The death of Thomas Flynn remains a mystery.

Zambales

Egidio Vagnozzi, the papal delegate, approached Samuel Sheehan confidentially in February 1951 asking if the Columbans could staff the province of Zambales (Figure 6.2, p. 196), beginning immediately with six parishes including the town of San Marcelino.[67] Two months earlier the Huks raided Aglao, a village of San Marcelino, on the grounds that some of the people were government informers. Women and children were among the dead. Sheehan was aware that the Huks were in the area but 'a serious drive is already under way to drive them from the province', and he had no hesitation in recommending that the society accept the delegate's invitation. Zambales is a poor province on the west coast of Luzon, and practically cut off from the rest of the island by a mighty range of mountains. It stretches 120 kilometres from north to south, and is never more than 40 kilometres wide. Three distinct language groups occupy the coastal strip, Tagalog, Ilocano and Zambal. In 1951 the Aeta, the earliest inhabitants of the area, lived in the mountains. The agricultural base of the province produced coconuts, rice and corn, but the major employer was the huge American naval base at Subic Bay.

Spanish Augustinian Recollects brought the faith to the province, beginning in 1607, and the church flourished until the revolution of 1898 when the Spaniards were driven out. For more than a quarter of a century there were only two Roman Catholic diocesan priests, and one of them joined the Philippine Independent Church. So did many of the people. Michael O'Doherty, Archbishop of Manila, invited the Society of the Divine Word (SVD), a Roman Catholic missionary congregation founded in Holland, to staff the area in 1928. But the SVD lost more than 800 priests, brothers and students worldwide in the Second World War, and by 1950 was so heavily committed to education in many parts of the Philippines that it had to withdraw five men from Zambales. The SVD provincial asked the papal delegate

---

67. Samuel Sheehan to Jeremiah Dennehy, 7 Feb. 1951 (CFCA, RP A-4:61).

to assign another congregation to the province, and Vagnozzi invited the Columbans. There were fourteen parishes, eleven belonging to the diocese of San Fernando and three to Lingayen-Dagupan. Vagnozzi planned to combine these and create a new prelature. About forty per cent of the people were Roman Catholic, the rest Aglipayan, or members of the *Iglesia ni Cristo*,[68] or of various Protestant churches 'who made great inroads into the once flourishing Aglipayan or Independent Church'. On a preliminary visit to the province Gerald Cogan and another priest looked for the Roman Catholic church in the town of Subic. They found three churches, one Aglipayan, one Methodist, and one *Iglesia ni Cristo*. When they asked a local for the Roman Catholic church he directed them to the cemetery. The only Catholics in Subic were dead ones.

The first task for the Columbans arriving in Zambales in May 1951, many of them fresh from the seminary, was to learn whichever of the three languages was dominant in their parish, as well as the local customs. Building came next, replacing or repairing old *conventos* and churches, and setting up schools. Connolly, the superior general, recorded some of the dilemmas discussed with him on his visitation in 1953. In the town of San Narciso an existing school was for sale, encumbered with a large debt. But the town was seventy per cent Aglipayan, and it was doubtful if it could support a Catholic school. 'On the other hand, Aglipayans can be converted only when young.' By 1955 there were thriving schools in six parishes, but not in San Narciso. Three Columban sisters managed the elementary and high school in Olongapo.[69] The other approach to religious instruction of the young, through catechists and members of the Legion of Mary (Plate 6.10), reached a greater number, 13,190 as opposed to 1,614 in parochial schools. To encourage adults, especially men, to attend Mass and the sacraments the Legion was invaluable, and also the Society of the Holy Name. Gerald Cogan reported that 'the Holy Name Society has already increased the men's communions enormously'. The Aeta were neglected by the Columbans, even when those mountain people were driven down to the towns by military activity against the Huks. There was too much to do in ministering to the Roman Catholics in their parishes. By 1955 the mission was so well established that Zambales became the Roman Catholic prefecture of Iba, named for the capital of the

---

68. The *Iglesia ni Cristo* was founded by Felix Y. Manalo in Manila in 1914. It claims that the original church of Christ was corrupted in the first century, and restored through Manalo. It is intensely anti-Catholic.
69. 'Valiant women', *The Far East*, xxxvii (July, 1954), p. 12.

province, on 18 October.[70] Henry Byrne, Columban superior in Mindanao, was named as bishop.

Conclusions

Growth, from three to one hundred and thirty-eight priests between 1929 and 1954 is what is most striking about the first twenty-five years of the Columban mission in the Philippines. What began with seemingly grudging approval from the Vatican for a 'procure' and a single parish in Manila spread into seven dioceses. A special jubilee edition of *The Far East* in 1954 could boast that Columbans staffed sixty-six parishes, with a total population of over 1,000,000. The priests came into a church where the majority were baptised but ignorant of their faith, where priests were few, where state-run education did not include religious instruction, and where a breakaway Catholic Church and a host of other denominations were trying to convert the nominal Roman Catholics. In their first quarter century the Columbans succeeded in staffing parishes, bringing many adults to the practice of their faith, and establishing schools and various forms of Catholic Action that enabled them to provide at least basic religious instruction for more than half of the students in their care. Some of the lay people who worked with them entered seminaries and religious congregations, or grew to be leaders in many fields.

Adaptability and constancy are two contrasting themes running through the development. Columbans in the Philippines, society superiors in Ireland, apostolic delegates and officials in the Vatican were open to some change and new ideas, yet the men in the field had the same aims and methods in widely different situations, and the officials were slow to alter legal structures that obstructed the work. The Columbans were flexible in their readiness to be assigned in very different places, to huge, rural parishes, to difficult posts in Muslim areas, or to tackle religious formation of the immense number of students in Manila. Some lived in danger, others in great poverty. They learned different languages and new customs. Circumstances, such as the need to replace men worn down by war, frequently meant that newcomers had to pick up the language even as they began work in a parish. Priests and sisters were so few that they involved the laity, in traditional roles such as catechists and teachers, and in more recent organisations like the Legion of Mary. Yet their goal everywhere was the same, to revive a church whose members were mostly nominal Catholics, ignorant of their faith and indifferent to the Mass or the sacraments. The means they chose were practically the same in each Columban area. Their first priority was the religious instruction of youth.

---

70. Pius XII, '*Venisse Christum*' in *AAS*, xxii (Rome, 1955), pp 708-710.

Canon law enjoined the building of parochial schools. Columbans in the Philippines tried to do that but, realising that parishes in a poor country could never provide places for all its sons and daughters, they recruited volunteer catechists for the public schools. To reach adults they travelled around the *barrios* of their parishes, preaching and bringing the sacraments. But they also depended on the laity, in organisations like the Holy Name Society and the Legion of Mary. A huge amount of their time went into building, of houses, churches, and schools, and searching for the money for all these activities.

Both Rome and the leaders of the society were flexible enough to send missionaries, intended for China and 'pagan' countries, to answer the urgent needs of a church that was *extra missiones*. Invitations came from bishops and from the apostolic delegate. However the canonical distinction between missions and established churches seems to have governed their thinking, especially in the matter of financial support of the work in the Philippines. The society eventually took practical steps to ease the problem, but the legal structures were not changed to match reality.

Priests in every area of the Philippines struggled to find money for their work. The majority of people were poor. Traditionally support for the church came from the Spanish *patronato*, not from the parishioners. For many years after the revolution of 1898 there were few priests, and Roman Catholic practice was limited to traditional devotions like the procession of a patron saint. A generation grew up who knew nothing about Mass and the sacraments, or about supporting a priest to provide them. In the earliest Columban undertakings, in Manila, Lingayen and Misamis Occidental, the bishop promised that the parishes were self-supporting but they were not. Had society superiors been aware of the true situation perhaps they would not have sent men to the Philippines at all.

Columbans were aware of the unjust division between rich and poor in the country. While their primary interest in schools was as vehicles of religious instruction, they also invested in education to help poor students to gain employment. But their thinking on alleviating the situation seems to have been limited to assisting individuals rather than changing society. People saw them as wealthy, and the planters in Negros counted them as allies against communism, yet there is no indication that the missionaries asked if their affluence and power, relative to the poor around them, could be a counter-sign to the gospel.[71] Despite being aware of how the deaths of

---

71. Jonathan J. Bonk, *Mi$$ion$ and money* (New York, 1991), p. 79.

the Malate priests, and the life in the mountains of the men in Misamis, had given Christian witness to the people and changed their attitudes, no Columban seems to have asked how the experience might modify their lifestyle. No-one questioned the huge investment in building churches and schools, or the infusion of money from abroad. For them, and for the leaders of the church, the priority was religious instruction. Baptism and the eucharist were of divine institution, to be received with faith. Such faith had to be instructed and nurtured. With so few priests the only means for instruction were parochial schools and, in the public schools, catechists. In addition the Columbans felt that they had to attempt to reach out to all who had been baptised in the church.

The task of serving the spiritual needs of those already baptised Roman Catholic left the Columbans hardly any time to consider what to do about those outside. Men living close to the Aeta or Muslims showed little interest in their life and beliefs, partly because they were so busy, but also due, no doubt, to the prejudices they brought with them to the Philippines, and the attitudes they picked up from their parishioners. Columbans, and all Roman Catholics in the Philippines, experienced opposition from some Protestants, Aglipayans, the *Iglesia ni Cristo*, and freemasons, and taught their leaders how to counter their criticism. They saw communists, too, as opponents. Their hope was that they could convert all of these eventually by means of the schools. In their estimation they were not proselytising, since those in Protestant or Aglipayan churches had been poached from the Roman Catholic tradition.

Columbans were conscious of the Roman Catholic men who remained aloof, and that their catechetical programmes were not reaching all the students. Yet they were proud of their martyrs, and of what they achieved. They had a dream, dim in times of discouragement, of a Filipino church, with an educated laity, local clergy and religious orders, which would one day send its own missionaries to the rest of Asia.

CHAPTER SEVEN

Mission in Korea 1933-54

In terms of modern missionary history, the introduction of Roman Catholicism to Korea was unusual. The gospel was first brought there, not by foreign priests, but by a Korean layman. In 1784 Yi Sung-hun (1756-1801) accompanied his father on a diplomatic mission to Peking. Scholars in Korea knew of the Jesuit Matteo Ricci's *True principles of Catholicism* in the early seventeenth century. One such scholar, Yi Pyok, asked Yi Sung-hun to contact the foreign priests in China and bring back more information about their religion. Yi was baptised and given the name Peter. He was also presented with Catholic books. On his return to Korea he baptised others who threw themselves so enthusiastically into the study and practice of their new-found faith that within a few months they reported a thousand followers asking for baptism. Not being fully informed about Roman Catholicism, they chose leaders and 'ordained' them as priests, commissioning them to say Mass and administer the sacraments, until further study of the books from Peking led them to recognise that such democratic practices were not in accord with Roman Catholic procedure.

The Korean church appeared to have begun with many of the ingredients necessary to guarantee success: an enthusiastic lay indigenous community; leaders from the high and educated class; and many converts. Why, after such a promising start, did the Roman Catholic church in Korea need to invite Columban missionaries a century and a half later in 1933? To answer that it will be necessary to explore the politics of isolation of Korea, nicknamed 'the hermit kingdom' in the West, and the series of French missionary expeditions interspersed with persecution. Korea was part of the Japanese Empire from 1910, and Japanese policies designed to subjugate the country to the Japanese system: the introduction of three and a half million colonists from the southern islands of Japan; the imposition of Japanese language and names; schools tailored 'to educate Koreans to perform menial tasks for Japanese bureaucrats and technicians'; and constant surveillance of foreigners, all affected the work of missionaries. The first Columbans to go there were led by veterans of the Chinese mission (founded 1920), men with a dozen years of experience of the methods used in Hanyang. It will be interesting to ask how they adapted to a new language and situation. They endured the Pacific (1941-45) and Korean

(1950-53) wars. Seven members of the society were killed. Work was disrupted, buildings destroyed. There were years of tension before and during each war. Money was a constant problem since the Columban society was in difficulties due to the world recession following on the Wall Street Crash of 1929, and the currency in Korea collapsed after the defeat of Japan. Korean priests, sisters, catechists and teachers laboured with them. A key question will be how the Columbans related to the local church, and their efforts at helping that church reach self-sufficiency.

Physical features

The Korean peninsula runs 970 kilometres from north to south, jutting out from the northern provinces of China (Figure 7.1). At the top, where it touches the Asian mainland, it is 320 kilometres wide, but further south narrows to about 200, giving a total area of 236,784 square kilometres. A ridge of high mountains, the Taebaek range, runs down the east coast, and from it extend several other ranges oriented in a north-east to south-west direction. Habitable land is confined to small river valleys and narrow coastal plains. There are about 3,500 islands. The climate is affected by the Asian continent, with hot summers and cold winters. In July the average temperature is 25°C, while in January it drops to -5°C in Seoul and 2°C in Pusan. Korea, in 1929, had a total population of 20,164,973, of which 104,422 were Roman Catholic.[1] Apart from a Chinese minority of about 20,000, almost all the inhabitants were Korean, and spoke the Korean language.

Missionaries in Korea 1795-1933

Choson, or Korea, suffered a devastating Japanese invasion in the sixteenth century, conquest by the Manchus in the seventeenth, and Western intrusions in the nineteenth. The Yi dynasty (1390-1910) responded by attempting to exclude all foreign trade and ideas, apart from those brought back by bi-annual embassies to China. A year after the introduction of Roman Catholicism in 1784 the king, Chongjo (1776-1800), proscribed the faith and attempted to suppress it. But a Chinese priest, Chou Wen-mo, entered Korea secretly in 1795, revived the fortunes of the new religion, and before long there were about 4,000 converts. Chongjo died in 1800 and under his successor, Sunjo (1800-1834), there was a persecution in 1801 in which prominent Korean Catholics were put to death or sent into exile. The Roman Catholic Congregation for the Propagation of the Faith (Propaganda) entrusted the

---

1. J. M. Planchet, *Les missions de Chine et du Japon* (Pékin, 1933), pp 581-598.

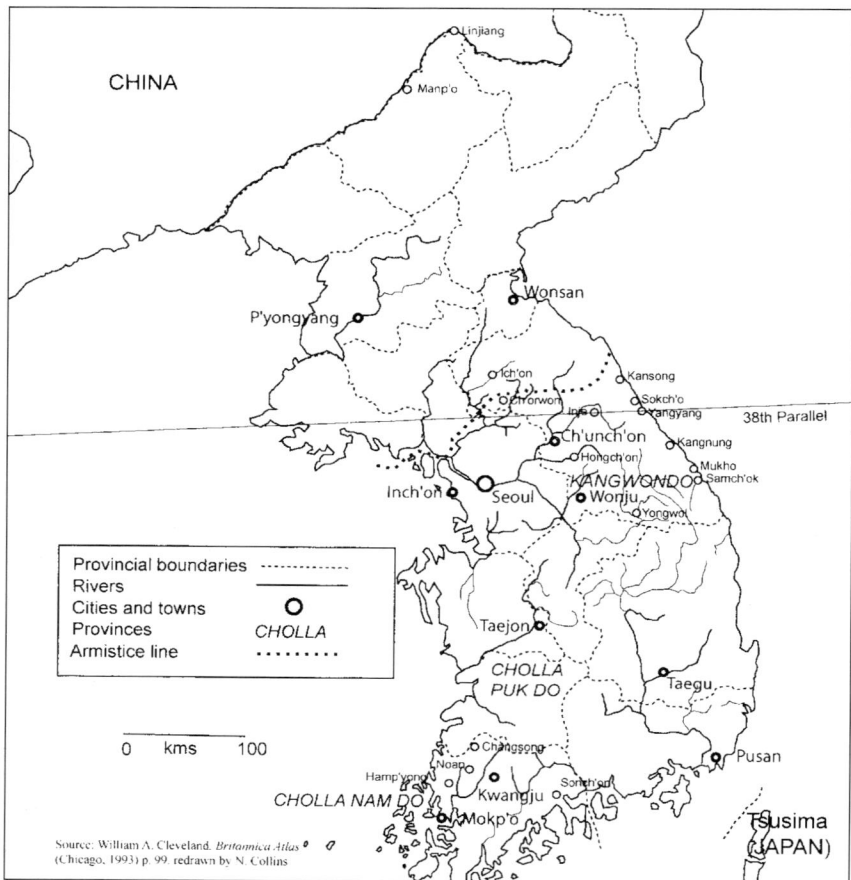

Figure 7.1 *Korean Peninsula*. Columban missionaries were assigned to Cholla Nam Do in 1933 and to Kangwondo in 1938. With the defeat of Japan in 1945 the country was divided at the 38th parallel, leaving three parishes of Kangwondo in the Russian-controlled north. After the Korean war (1949-53) an armistice line marked the boundary between North and South Korea.

apostolic vicariate of Korea to the *Société des Missions-Étrangères* in 1831. Pierre-Philibert Maubant, a priest of the society, entered the country in 1836 and was joined by two others in the following year. All three, together with many Korean converts, were executed in 1839. The first Korean priest, Kim Tae-gon, trained in Macao, secretly returned to Korea but was martyred in 1846. Under a new king, Ch'olchong (1849-1863), the anti-Catholic policy was relaxed. Twelve French priests arrived, and the number of converts rose to 20,000. Nine of the priests were executed in the next wave of persecution in 1866. One, Félix-Clair Ridel, escaped to China where he invited the admiral of the French Asiatic squadron to take punitive action against Korea. In one of a series of attacks a French detachment pillaged the administrative centre of Kanghwa island, gateway to the Han river and Seoul, but Korean forces repulsed the invaders and the ships withdrew. America, in 1871, and Japan, in 1876, attempted to force Korea to open its ports to trade. To block the Japanese, China persuaded the Korean government in 1882 to conclude treaties of commerce with the US, France, and other western nations. Twelve years later, in 1894, Japanese troops invaded, and the Sino-Japanese War of 1894-95 was fought on Korean soil. It was the beginning of the end for the Yi dynasty. Japan steadily took over the Korean peninsula and, in 1910, reduced it to a colony. It exploited the agricultural and mineral wealth of the nation and imposed a unification policy compelling Koreans, in 1938, to visit Shinto shrines and, in 1940, to adopt Japanese names.

Protestant missionaries were quick to avail of the treaties of commerce signed between Korea and western powers in 1882 which allowed foreigners to reside in treaty ports. But, as was the case of the Roman Catholic Yi Sung-hun in 1784, the first Protestant evangelist was a Korean layman, Suh Sang-Yun. He entered the country from China in 1883, bringing copies of the gospel of Luke, and formed a house church. In the following year an American Presbyterian missionary, Dr Horace N. Allen, arrived. By saving the life of a nephew of the queen, who had been attacked by assassins, he got permission to set up a royal hospital. Methodist missionaries opened a school for boys and, a huge innovation in a male-dominated Confucian society, one for girls. Church growth was slow, and by 1894 the Presbyterians could report only fifty-two communicants. Missionaries began to venture outside the treaty ports. Samuel A. Moffett (1864-1939) made frequent attempts to found a mission in P'yongyang, and just as frequently was driven out. The great land battle of the Sino-Japanese war (1894) was fought in P'yongyang, destroying the city, and Moffett's house. But on his next visit the people, non-Christians joining the Christians, welcomed him. By October 1895 he reported seventy-three baptised communicants. The Presbyterian mission in Korea adopted the advice of a veteran China missionary, John L. Nevius, in 1890. Nevius urged them to set up structures in which Koreans, from the beginning, would be able to evangelise and exercise government, and build churches in a local style from their own resources. But even though Presbyterians aimed at the ideal proposed by Nevius they made a 'limited and judicious use of foreign money – only so much as not to endanger progress towards self-support'. Soongsil academy, founded in P'yongyang in 1897 became, in 1908, Korea's first degree-granting college, and the Presbyterian theological seminary, also in P'yongyang, graduated its first class of seven in

1907. Initially the mission was governed by foreigners, but in 1901 three Korean elders and six evangelists joined the Presbyterian council. These inclusive methods seem to have been among the reasons for the rapid growth of the Protestant churches. By 1910 there were 73,517 Roman Catholics in Korea, and 167,352 Protestants.[2]

The Roman Catholic mission in Korea was under the jurisdiction of the vicariate of Peking from 1784 until in 1831 Propaganda created the apostolic vicariate of Korea. This was divided into the vicariates of Seoul and Taegu in 1911, both staffed by French members of the *Société des Missions-Étrangères* and a growing number of Korean secular priests. German Benedictines arrived in 1920 and were given a new vicariate, of Wonsan. An apostolic prefecture, of P'yongyang, was set up in 1927, and entrusted to the Catholic Foreign Mission Society of America.[3] By 1932 there were eighty-nine foreign priests, and seventy-two Koreans in the country. Sisters, French, Korean, German and American, ran dispensaries, orphanages and schools. There were a few salaried catechists and many voluntary ones. Earlier converts, in the eighteenth century, came from the upper, *yangban*, classes. Persecution brought a gradual decline in their numbers, and from the end of the nineteenth century the majority of church members were peasants, craftsmen and even day labourers, with an increasing number of women. Most were concentrated in Seoul and nearby areas, and Catholicism was largely a faith for urban dwellers.

Invitations to Columbans 1933-38

Columbans were offered two districts in Korea, the provinces of Cholla Nam Do in 1933 and Kangwondo in 1934 (Figure 7.1). The process followed in the invitation to Cholla Nam Do was simple. Florian Demange, vicar apostolic of Taegu, and a member of the *Société des Missions-Étrangères* wished to divide his vicariate and asked Propaganda to entrust part of it to another missionary institute. Pietro Fumasoni-Biondi, the prefect of Propaganda, forwarded the invitation to Michael O'Dwyer in Ireland.[4] O'Dwyer and his council accepted the invitation unanimously, even though Korea was not in China, the country for which the Columbans were founded. He followed a recommendation of a general chapter of the society in 1931:

> As a future policy in regard to new missions we recommend that, while retaining Constitution N. 3 that China be the *finis praecipuus*

---

2. Samuel Hugh Moffett, *A history of Christianity in Asia* (2 vols, New York, 2005), p. 545.
3. J. M. Planchet, *Les missions de Chine et du Japon* (Pékin, 1933), pp 594-598.
4. Pietro Fumasoni-Biondi to Michael O'Dwyer, 6 June 1933 (CFCA, KOR A-1:1).

[primary end] of the Society, the Superior General and Council may accept any mission offered by the Holy See in pagan countries, and may if they think it advisable petition for such missions.

O'Dwyer reminded Propaganda of the financial difficulties of the society. 'We are not in debt; but … we are struggling along.' He suggested that Rome should 'be benevolent in helping the new Mission as regards material means'. More immediately he asked for all the information that Propaganda possessed about the new territory, especially the number of priests that would be required.

The first suggestion of the possibility of a second Korean mission for the Columbans came in May 1934 during an after-supper conversation between Adrien-Joseph Larribeau, vicar apostolic of Seoul, and Owen MacPolin, Columban superior in Cholla Nam Do. A few days later MacPolin wrote to Larribeau reminding him that:

> I was speaking to you about the need which the Society of St. Columban had for new territory for its increasing number of priests and you remarked that you thought 'we could get more territory in Korea'.

Larribeau made no reply to MacPolin's letter, but in January 1935 he raised the matter again, telling MacPolin that in November 1933 he had proposed to Propaganda to divide his vicariate. MacPolin immediately reported both incidents to O'Dwyer in Ireland, enclosing a map and relevant statistics of Kangwondo. O'Dwyer replied, informing MacPolin that he would not write to Propaganda as there was a possibility of a new mission in China, which would absorb all the resources of the society. A few months later, when the China prospect came to nothing, O'Dwyer instructed Michael Boyle, Columban procurator in Rome, to approach Propaganda concerning Kangwondo. Boyle met Carolus Salotti, the secretary of Propaganda, who told him that the apostolic delegate to Japan, Paul Marella, would shortly send a report about Kangwondo, and that the Columbans must wait for that report before making any petition. The correspondence dragged on for another two and a half years, the society superiors not knowing whom to blame for the delay. Previously, in January 1935, MacPolin had heard that if the superior of the *Société des Missions-Étrangères* in Paris, Jean-Baptiste-Marie Budes de Guébriant, was 'not keen on the division [of Kangwondo from Seoul] Propaganda might not be inclined to move'. A year later, according to MacPolin, Demange, vicar apostolic in Taegu, and like Larribeau a member of Société des Missions-Étrangères, mentioned that:

He hasn't much confidence in Mgr Larribeau's business capacities. He even said you couldn't be sure whether 'that man' wrote when he said he would: he is always behind in his work and putting things off.

O'Dwyer heard from Rome that 'what is holding up the question of a Mission in Seoul is the fact that the Apostolic Delegate in Japan has not sent any report to Rome about it'. When Propaganda, in June 1938, finally invited the Columbans to take over the province of Kangwondo, Pietro Fumasoni-Biondi acknowledged the letters submitted by Boyle in August and October 1935, but stated baldly that matters could not be pressed forward '*variis de causis*'.

Cholla Nam Do and Kangwondo
The two provinces offered to the Columbans were very different. Cholla Nam Do in the fertile south-west corner of Korea included many islands, one of them, semi-tropical Cheju, lying eighty-five kilometres from the mainland. Measuring 13,887.37 square kilometres, the province, in 1933, had a total population of 2,332,000, of whom only 2,048 were Roman Catholic. By 1938, when Owen MacPolin submitted the first Columban report to Rome, the population was 2,457,786, of whom 4,356 were Roman Catholic, and 16,777 Protestant.[5] Kangwondo province was almost twice as large as Cholla Nam Do, with a total of 26,265 square kilometres, dominated by the Diamond mountains which ran down the east coast and rose in places to more than 1,700 metres. Winters were intensely cold, with deep snow from December to March or April. The population, in the state census of 1937, was 1,529,071, and in 1940 there were 10,444 Roman Catholics and an estimated 7,000 Protestants.[6]

Cholla Nam Do in 1933 was 'almost totally pagan' according to Florian Demange, the vicar apostolic of Taegu. Demange wished to separate the two provinces of Cholla from his vicariate, and to entrust them to Korean priests. Propaganda, however, judged that Cholla Nam Do could not support local priests, with no access to funds from abroad, and directed that the northern province, Cholla Puk Do, be given to Koreans and Cholla Nam Do to a foreign missionary society. There were four priests, all Korean, in Cholla Nam Do in 1934. The central parish in Mokp'o (Plate 7.1), founded in 1899, had a fine, foreign-style church and residence. Most of the other missions were opened around 1923, with very simple Korean-style chapels and houses.

---

5. Owen MacPolin, *Prospectus status missionis*, 3 Aug. 1938 (CFCA, KOR A-4).
6. Owen MacPolin, *Prospectus status missionis*, 25 July 1940 (CFCA, KOR A-4).

Vocations to the priesthood were few in the province, with only two ordained priests and five students who were just beginning to study Latin.[7] Kangwondo was 'better developed [than Cholla Nam Do] in the ecclesiastical line', wrote Thomas Quinlan in 1938. Larribeau, the vicar apostolic of Seoul, described how Roman Catholicism came to the province about a hundred years earlier:

> For many Christians, fleeing persecution, left everything in their home region and sought refuge in the mountains of Kogendo [Kangwondo]. There they procured food for themselves, some by farming new fields in the mountains, others, indeed the majority, by practising the art of potters.

Larribeau had twelve Korean priests in the province, assigned to eleven central mission stations. By agreement with the Columbans three of these priests would stay in the new mission, and seventy-four year old Augustine Cheng wished to remain also. There were churches 'properly so called' and adequate residences in five stations, but only 'provisional' chapels and houses in the others. Quinlan reported that there were twenty students from the province studying for the priesthood in the seminary and explained that 'Being "old Catholics" here vocations are more plentiful than in the south [Cholla Nam Do]'.[8]

Ten Columbans, led by Owen MacPolin (Plate 7.2) and destined for Cholla Nam Do, began to study Korean in the seminary of Taegu in October 1933 before moving out to live with Korean pastors in April 1934. Two were dispatched to Tokyo to learn Japanese, to enable them to serve Japanese Roman Catholics in Korea and to deal with the colonial authorities. By February 1935 three members of the society were in charge of parishes. The mission developed slowly until it was erected as the apostolic prefecture of Kwoshu (Kwangju) on 13 April 1937, with Owen MacPolin as prefect.[9] Propaganda used a very different process in Kangwondo. Thomas Quinlan and Patrick Brennan were transferred from Cholla Nam Do to Ch'unch'on, capital of Kangwondo, in September 1938, with Quinlan as superior. Eight months later, in May 1939, Larribeau, the vicar apostolic, gave Quinlan news that surprised him:

> The gist of it was that Kogendo (Kangwondo) has been erected into a

---

7. Owen MacPolin to Michael O'Dwyer, 21 Oct. 1935 (CFCA, KOR A-4:9c).
8. Thomas Quinlan to Michael O'Dwyer, 10 Apr. 1940 (CFCA, KOR A-4C:3b).
9. Pietro Fumasoni-Biondi to Michael O'Dwyer, 19 Apr. 1937 (CFCA, KOR A-1b:35).

Prefecture with Syunsen (Ch'unch'on) as centre, and Monsignor MacPolin is its Apostolic Administrator.

O'Dwyer described the arrangement where MacPolin in Cholla Nam Do would be simultaneously the administrator of Kangwondo pending the appointment of a prefect apostolic as 'extraordinary'. Priests in Korea regarded it as a 'wallop' from Propaganda to Larribeau for his tardy responses during the process of dividing the vicariate (1935-38). Quinlan, as superior, found it more difficult to deal with an administrator far down in Cholla Nam Do rather than with a vicar just three hours away in Seoul. A second anomaly was that at the time when the new prefecture was erected he was superior of just two Columbans, and of twelve Korean priests, most of whom belonged to the vicariate of Seoul. Rome's solution was to make Quinlan prefect on 22 November 1940.[10]

Missionary methods

The missionary methods which Columbans inherited from the French pioneers in Korea in 1933 involved primary stations where a priest resided, and a corona of secondary stations which he visited at regular intervals. Quinlan had eighteen secondary stations in Ch'unch'on, and in mountainous terrain a full circuit of the parish took more than a month. By 1938 each parish in the Kwangju prefecture had at least two salaried catechists, as the culture demanded strict separation of the sexes. Male catechists were paid more than female ones. Ch'unch'on prefecture, in 1941, had only eleven paid catechists, one for each parish. These were supplemented by 143 'resident' catechists, unpaid volunteers living in their own villages. Harold Henry, in Kwangju, described the work of Kim Matthew, a paid catechist:

> … he started night classes in catechism for the pagan youngsters of the town. During the day he visited their parents. When anyone was sick, Matthew would be there and if the person was dying, he instructed him and baptised him. After death, he would roll up his sleeves and prepare the body for the coffin and would be on hand to help out the afflicted family in any way possible.[11]

Catechumens, those receiving religious instruction, had to live as Roman Catholics for at least six months, after which they were given a rigorous examination on the 156 questions in the catechism and what the answers

---

10. *Sacra Congregatio de Propaganda Fide*, 'Nominationes' in *AAS*, vii (Rome, 1940), p. 557.
11. Harold Henry, 'My faithful staff' in *The Far East* (US ed.), xxvi (Jan. 1943), p. 15.

meant. They were also expected to memorise, and understand 'the twelve prayers', including the Lord's prayer, the Hail Mary, acts of faith, hope, charity, and contrition, and the ten commandments. If their grasp of doctrine was deemed inadequate baptism would be postponed until they reached the required grade.

The standard of education in Korea was very low when the Columbans arrived in 1933, and 'the number of middle and elementary schools were too few to meet the needs of the Korean people'.[12] Japan laid stress on the teaching of Japanese and on vocational education since it wanted a work force with the skills necessary for war industries. Missionary groups, especially Protestant ones, attempted to meet the need for education. Several Columban parishes ran elementary schools, and in Kangwondo one of these was managed by three Korean Sisters of St Paul de Chartres. One priest, Thomas Neligan, opened a school in 1936, with forty-one pupils and two teachers, he being one of them. In the second year there was such a press of would-be students that he instituted an entrance examination, instructing the two examiners to limit the total student body to 100. A year later the school had 156 children on the rolls. He described them:

> Not all our pupils ... are Catholics. As is to be expected in a ... new mission, the majority are pagans. But in the school these children have an opportunity to learn ... about the church and naturally they are drawn towards it. Through these pagan children ... we are able to establish contact with many pagan families who would otherwise stand aloof from us ... In this way old prejudices are gradually being broken down and we hope the ground is being prepared for a number of conversions ...[13]

Parishes also had 'doctrinal schools' such as the one in Mokp'o, Cholla Nam Do, in 1937 (Plate 7.3). Church growth was slow in the Roman Catholic prefecture of Kwangju in the years between the first entry of the Columbans into parishes there in 1934 and the beginning of the war in the Pacific at the end of 1941. The annual reports sent by MacPolin to Propaganda show that around five hundred adults entered the church each year (Table 7.1).

---

12. Ki-baik Lee, *A new history of Korea*, trans. Edward W. Wagner (Cambridge, Mass., 1984), p. 368.
13. Thomas Neligan, 'They like our school' in *The Far East* (US ed.), xxii (Nov. 1939), pp 4-5.

	1936-37	1937-38	1938-39	1939-40	1940-41	1945-46
Catholics	3,843	4,356	4,852	5,346	5,773	5,652
Baptisms: Adults		399	515	497	505	
Children of Catholics		185	206	173	164	
In Danger of Death		357	510	235	549	
Catechumens		712	1,206	871	824	
Annual Communions		2,490	2,553	2,850	3,284	
Devotional Communions		54,782	75,308	80,438	90,822	
Marriages, Catholic		49	32	27	48	
Marriages, Mixed		13	12	5	16	
School pupils: Boys		558	607	770	558	
School pupils: Girls		356	431	509	173	
Catechists, Male		12	18	15	13	
Catechists, Female		14	16	20	20	
Priests		21	20	19	19	

Source: Annual Reports, Prefecture of Kwangju (CFCA, KOR A-4(SR)).
Table 7.1 *Church growth in the prefecture of Kwangju, 1936-46.* The economic recession that affected the whole world meant that the Columbans had little money for church building in Korea.

There are only two reports from the prefecture of Ch'unch'on, in 1940 and 1941, and they show an even more discouraging picture. There were 201 and 276 adult baptisms in the prefecture in those two years, and the total number of Roman Catholics actually dropped.[14] Columbans in Korea, aware that their confrères in China were recording much higher numbers of adult baptisms, regarded the flow of converts as very low. They were hampered by lack of money. In his letter to Propaganda in 1933 accepting Cholla Nam Do, O'Dwyer mentioned that the society was 'struggling financially'. MacPolin listed his most urgent needs as 'maintenance' – the money for food and board for his priests – running expenses, and property. The small houses and chapels built by Korean priests needed to be extended as parishes grew, and land could be bought more cheaply by those Koreans before the foreign priests arrived. Edmond Lane, bursar general of the society, in a minute to the superior general, gave his opinion 'that only those sites that are necessary should be purchased and that no money should be allocated to Korea for some time for erection of foreign style buildings'. Quinlan complained in 1939 that the men in Kangwondo were in financial difficulties having received just enough funds for their personal maintenance:

> They try to raise a bit by letters for the work but if they have to spend that buying a bed and a table and chair they lack zeal in their appeals and are inclined to go for scalps [of superiors].

14. Thomas Quinlan, Reports for the prefecture of Syunsen, 30 June 1940 and 1941 (CFCA, KOR A-4(SR)).

Even the books, vestments, chalices, and other equipment necessary for the celebration of the sacraments would be in short supply in Kangwondo when Columbans replaced the Korean priests, as the Koreans would bring them with them. Quinlan suggested that the young priests coming from Ireland should acquire such things from the Society for Apostolic Work in Belfast and Dublin. He also requested money for buying land in towns where there were big 'christianities' but no priest. A railway was under construction in the area and land prices would soar. The society would save money if it could buy immediately, even though Quinlan would be unable to build until government restrictions linked to 'the trouble in China' (the Sino-Japanese war) were lifted. He asked for £1000. An apologetic O'Dwyer could send only £500. By 1940 Quinlan's priests could not pay their salaried catechists a living wage. He deplored the result:

> The priests here are very unhappy about the instruction allowance. Msgr. [MacPolin] has allowed only twenty-five yen for each parish, and that is supposed to pay a man who will be a catechist and priest's teacher.... The cost of living has soared here so much that twenty-five yen won't support a servant. The result is that all progress has stopped here, and the priests are getting discouraged.[15]

Columbans cited other reasons for their slow progress including the traditional anti-foreign attitude of Koreans and, even more, the activities of the Japanese police. Catholics were held in suspicion, and discouraged from contact with the priest. Police followed the missionaries on their visits to mission stations. A priest had to submit a copy of his itinerary to the police station in the central town and to the subsidiary stations anywhere he planned to stay the night. The sacrament of confession, where the penitent spoke in total confidentiality to the priest, had to be celebrated at times when the policeman was off duty. Local police stations were normally staffed by three men, a Japanese officer in charge, and two Korean subordinates. Some were reasonable men. One Columban, Francis Gallagher, described a constable: 'He was honest. He was straight. He knew what justice was. Oh, he did his work, but you respected him.' The willingness of the Columbans to endure poverty and police harassment impressed some Koreans:

> A fellow came up to me one time and stopped me on the road and asked me into his house and gave me tea and told me he appreciated men like us coming from so far, having suffered so much and stayed.

---

15. Thomas Quinlan to Michael O'Dwyer, 7 Sept. 1940 (CFCA, KOR A-4C:4e).

World War II

Missionary work by foreigners in Korea halted completely on 7 December 1941 at the outbreak of war in the Pacific. Columbans in both Kwangju and Ch'unch'on were arrested by the police and placed, usually, in the local jail, where they were subjected to days of interrogation. Church records, documents and letters were confiscated, laboriously translated, and then provided material for endless questions.[16] Harold Henry recorded how the children from the Catholic parish school in Naju, despite their fear of the Japanese police, would bring food to him:

> Sometimes when the youngsters were allowed to pass the food to us they would say, 'Father, as we have no priest at the church, we can't go to confession. Can we go now?' So they went to confession, passing in the food very slowly so as to have more time. Sometimes a policeman would be sitting no more than four feet away.[17]

All foreign priests in Ch'unch'on were interned in January 1942 (Plate 7.4) in what was formerly the home of a Methodist missionary. Larribeau, the vicar apostolic in Seoul, sent four Korean priests to help care for the parishes. Columbans in Kwangju were lodged in the central Columban mission in Mokp'o. On 11 March 1942 the Japanese recognised the neutrality of the Irish Free State and most of the Irish priests in Kwangju were able to return to their parishes, but with so many restrictions that they could do very little pastoral work. Nine months later they were interned again. American, Australian and New Zealand Columbans were repatriated, leaving Korea on 1 June 1942. All thirty-five priests and twenty sisters of the Catholic Missionary Society of America (Maryknoll) were expelled at the same time, and just three Korean priests remained to care for the 22,000 Roman Catholics in the prefecture of P'yongyang. Three Irish Columbans were stationed on the island of Cheju where there were many military installations. The Japanese detected radio signals coming from the island, giving military intelligence to the American forces. They suspected the three foreigners, charged them with being spies, and sentenced them to terms in prison. One of the three, Patrick Dawson, remained incarcerated until the Japanese surrender in 1945.[18] The spy, captured and executed a few weeks before the end of the war, was Japanese. Most of the priests who were interned suffered from malaria and dysentery. Fearing epidemics, the Japanese authorities in

---

16. Patrick Monaghan, 'Watch the birdie' in *The Far East* (US ed.), xxix (Sept. 1946), p. 21.
17. Harold Henry, 'Loyal to the last!' in *The Far East* (US ed.), xxv (Dec. 1942), p. 5.
18. Patrick Dawson, 'Three years in a Korean jail' in *The Far East*, xxix (May, 1946), pp 50-51.

Ch'unch'on transferred the priests to several parishes. To keep sane some missionaries adopted a disciplined routine:

> So we got up at a certain time, we had our meditation, said Mass, thanksgiving, the little breakfast we had we used to take it. Then we'd go for a bit of a walk and then we'd come back and we'd study. We studied Korean and we'd study … a [Korean] Christian Doctrine book. We used to study that. And … there was a Korean translation of the gospels just out and we went through that. And … Pat Deery and I in Hongch'on we studied a lot of Korean and I must say Pat became very good at it.

In the last months of the war, those in Kwangju were moved to the remoter town of Hongch'on, in Kangwondo. When one of them, Henry Gillen, fell seriously ill with dysentery it was impossible to get the necessary medicine in time and he died on 6 August 1945.[19] An atomic bomb was dropped on the Japanese city of Hiroshima that same day, and the Japanese government began the process of surrender on 10 August.

Peace and turmoil 1945-47

Korean nationalists expected that their country would become 'free and independent' in 1945 after the Pacific war. Instead, Russian troops crossed the frontier on 9 August and, by agreement with the US, occupied the land as far south as the thirty-eighth parallel (Figure 7.1). Three parishes of the prefecture of Ch'unch'on were in the Russian zone. The Korean pastors, Timothy Li and Damasus Paik together with Maurus Kim, a Benedictine on loan from the vicariate of Wonsan, continued work until they were executed in 1950.[20] American forces landed at Inch'on on 8 September 1945, and gradually spread throughout the southern half of the peninsula. The US military authorities refused to recognise any of the more than fifty political parties that were hurriedly formed and opted to conduct the administration themselves. Neither the State Department in Washington nor the Americans in Korea knew much about the country. Missionaries like the Columbans were able to help as interpreters, and occasionally with advice, but they had to be sensitive. Harold Henry observed:

> The Koreans, naturally, resent the presence of the army, so we are careful not to pay too much attention to the military.[21]

---
19. Joseph O'Brien, 'Interned in Korea' in *The Far East*, xxix (Aug. 1946), p. 91.
20. Thomas Stewart, 'History of the diocese of Chuncheon', Sept. 1988 (Unpublished ms in CFCA, Dalgan Park, Navan, KOR A-5).
21. Harold Henry, 'Return to Korea' in *The Far East* (US ed.), xxxi (Mar. 1948), p. 10.

Refugees struggled down from the Russian zone, totaling more than 800,000 by the end of 1947. Brian Geraghty, pastor of Kangnung, just south of the thirty-eighth parallel, assisted many of them. Among the refugees were thousands of Japanese, 'worn out, hungry and almost naked'. Columban James Doyle, a fluent Japanese speaker, obtained supplies of food, clothing and medicine from the US military government. The country was ill-prepared for the flood of refugees from the north, and another million from China and Japan. During the fighting all production had been geared to the war effort. Peace brought dislocation. Furthermore, the Japanese authorities put billions of yen into circulation in the weeks between the surrender and the American landings, bringing on severe inflation. Rice bought on the black market early in 1946 cost eight times the legal price, and many starved. Priests observed people 'digging for grasses and roots' and 'eating and cooking bark'.[22] By early 1947 American Catholic Relief Services and voluntary groups, including a committee of wives of US soldiers in Mokp'o, were distributing food and clothing to refugees.

The Roman Catholic Congregation for the Propagation of the Faith had a pragmatic approach to restoring the hierarchy in Korea in 1945. Under pressure from the Japanese authorities in 1942 foreign church leaders submitted their resignations to the Holy See,[23] and were replaced by Japanese or Koreans. After the Pacific war the Vatican left the two vicariates in the hands of Korean bishops, confirming Paul M. Ro in Seoul, and installing John B. Choe in Taegu in 1949. Two prefectures lay in the Russian sector, Wonsan and P'yongyang. Bonifacio Sauer, the German abbot of Wonsan, died in prison in August 1949. The Korean vicar apostolic of P'yongyang, Francis Hong, was imprisoned in 1949. There were three vicariates in the south. Bartholomew Kim became prefect of Chonju, Cholla Puk Do, in 1947. MacPolin and Quinlan resumed leadership in Kwangju and Ch'unch'on in 1945 as apostolic administrators. However, in 1948, due to ill-health and depression, MacPolin resigned again. Propaganda appointed Patrick T. Brennan as prefect apostolic in Kwangju, and re-appointed Quinlan as prefect in Ch'unch'on on 12 Nov. 1948. The Vatican recognised Korean independence on 17 July 1947 by appointing Patrick J. Byrne, a member of the Catholic Foreign Mission Society of America, as the first apostolic visitor to Korea, with the powers of an apostolic delegate. Byrne was ordained a bishop in 1949, and promoted to become apostolic delegate.[24]

---

22. An N.C.W.C. report, 'Famine is menancing Korea' in *The Far East* (US ed.), xxix (Oct. 1946), p. 19.
23. Edward Fischer, *Light in the far east* (New York, 1976), p. 64.
24. *Sacra Congregatio de Propaganda Fide, 'Provisio ecclesiarum'* in *AAS*, xvi (Rome, 1949), p. 468.

Columbans in Korea returned to work in 1945. Statistics for catechumens and adult baptisms in Kwangju show that growth between 1946 and 1948 was even slower than before the Pacific war. Then in 1948-49 the numbers were almost doubled. The increase seems to be linked with the arrival of new priests and the employment of paid catechists (Table 7.2).

	1946-47	1947-48	1948-49	1949-50	1950-51
Catholics	6,140	6,374	6,978	7,830	8,059
Baptisms: Adults	338	310	507	761	740
Children of Catholics	258	246	282	278	263
In Danger of Death	332	477	447	382	721
Catechumens	552	597	1,186	2,262	1,849
Deaths	82	85	90	162	302
Annual Communions	2,803	2,984	3,348	3,819	4,364
School pupils: Boys	119	191	240	356	127
School pupils: Girls	163	188	226	395	120
Catechists, Male	3	3		61	60
Catechists, Female	7	8		37	36
Priests	11	13	20	29	29

Source: Annual Reports, Prefecture of Kwangju (CFCA, KOR A-4(SR)).
Table 7.2 *Church growth, prefecture of Kwangju, 1946-51*. The statistics suggest that the great surge in numbers of Catholics was directly linked to the increased number of catechists and priests.

The economic situation in Korea from 1945 until 1948 was so bad that the government restricted immigration, which meant that missionary societies like the Columbans were unable to send new missionaries. Yet the men who had endured the war badly needed home leave. Kwangju was left with five foreign and six Korean priests. Harold Henry reported, 'It is very difficult getting other than US nationals into this country unless they have been out here before'.[25] In Ch'unch'on the number of Roman Catholics, 11,166 in 1941, dropped dramatically after the Pacific war, to 10,849 in June 1946, and 7,997 a year later (Table 7.3). Possibly the latter figure did not include the 3,000 members of the three parishes in North Korea, since normal contact with them became impossible. Catechists in Ch'unch'on were described as 'resident' in the 1945-46 report. The only qualifying adjective in that of 1947-48 is that ninety were men and four women. There is no indication that any received a salary to enable them to give full-time service to their parish.

---

25. Harold Henry to Jeremiah Dennehy, 29 Nov. 1947 (CFCA, KOR A-4:22).

	1945-46	1946-47	1947-48	1948-49
Catholics	10,849	7,997	9,299	9,697
Baptisms: Adults	72		92	243
Children of Catholics	553		471	455
In Danger of Death	331		288	400
Catechumens	177		197	344
Annual Communions	5,543		5,252	5,765
Pupils: Boys	378		156	167
Pupils: Girls	394		67	86
Catechists: salaried				
Catechists: Voluntary	79		94	
Priests	13	13	16	18
Population	1,700,000		1,700,000	

Source: Annual Reports, Prefecture of Ch'unch'on (CFCA, KOR A-4(SR)). Table 7.3 *Church growth, prefecture of Ch'unch'on 1945-49*. The prefecture lost three parishes, cut off in the communist north in 1945. There was some growth, but it was very slow.

Political turmoil in South Korea (1945-50) must have affected church growth, but Columbans rarely mentioned it as an obstacle. Korean nationalists wanted independence, and when the foreign ministers of the US, Great Britain, and the Soviet Union agreed in December 1945 to place Korea under four-power trusteeship (US, Britain, China, and Soviet Union) for five years there was public outrage from all parties, expressed in demonstrations and strikes.[26] In May 1946 police found evidence of large-scale currency counterfeiting at a printing press used by the Korean communist party. The American authorities ordered the arrest of the party leaders, whereupon the communists went underground. Harold Henry reported to Propaganda in 1948 that the intellectual class 'was tempted not only by materialism and bolshevism but also by atheism and indifferentism, while the lower class was oppressed by economic destitution'. A year later, in 1949, Henry announced an increase in those taking religious instruction and the return of many 'fallen-aways', where 'formerly some stayed away from the church because they were afraid to declare themselves anti-communists by joining'.

The most disturbed area in the prefecture of Kwangju and in all South Korea (1947-1949) was the island of Cheju. Henry informed Propaganda:

> In the island of Cheju, within the boundaries of this prefecture, communists have been causing great disturbance for six months already. They, around 3,000 in number, fight with modern weapons and threaten the inhabitants with death if they help the guardians of public

---

26. Lee, *A new history of Korea*, p. 376.

security or plant crops, in order to overthrow the administration of the island.

According to Henry, many on Cheju who were not left-wing sided with the communists because of the abuses of the Korean police and military. The communists, in their attacks on towns, did not threaten foreign priests, but 'none of the indigenous clergy remains on the island as it seems too dangerous for them'. Communist forces held the mountainous centre of the island, making frequent raids on coastal villages and towns. Austin Sweeney, a Columban in Cheju city, recorded that:

> A majority of Cheju's population is suffering from starvation. In some areas the people are living on a single sweet potato a day. The farmers are abandoning the inland farms and moving to the large towns along the coast.[27]

Help for the homeless victims of the war in Cheju came from relief agencies and from the American army. The Korean government estimated that 15,000 people were killed and 90,000 made homeless. After nearly three bitter years the communists were defeated, the last two leaders of the guerrillas being 'killed while resisting capture [and] hung on crosses in the main square of the city'. With peace came an increase in the number of converts. Thomas D. Ryan, in Sugwipo, the second parish on Cheju, announced:

> In one catechism class we have over 300. For the whole island we have around 800 under instruction. Of course, not all will be baptised; still the majority probably will, please God. We had fifty-one baptisms at Christmas and with the baptisms at Pentecost our total for the year ending in June is almost 300.[28]

Building 1948-50

The arrival of new priests beginning in 1948, and access to funds from abroad enabled the Columbans in Korea to build more churches for their growing flocks. Quinlan, in Ch'unch'on, did not wait until he had sufficient money or building materials before buying a plot for a cathedral early in 1947. He found 'a river of granite stone' close to the thirty-eighth parallel. Korean workers, using equipment loaned by the American army, leveled the site and cut the granite into blocks. Servicemen from the military government group of the United States army, Catholic and Protestant, contributed to a fund to

---

27. Austin Sweeney, 'Columbans in the news' in *The Far East* (US ed.), xxxii (June, 1949), p. 21.
28. Thomas D. Ryan, 'Columbans in the news' in *The Far East* (US ed.), xxxiii (Sept. 1950), p. 12.

enable Quinlan to order building materials through the Columbans in Omaha, Nebraska. Patrick Brennan, prefect apostolic in Kwangju, appealed to American donors for funds for his ambitious dreams as 1950 began:

> Our present plans center around twelve key spots in the mission. We would like to erect a building in each place which would be a combination rectory-and-church. According to our estimates we would need $3,000 for each building. This figure does not include the cost of the land. At the present time, we are trying to purchase the sites for these combinations …[29]

Brennan could announce, in 1950, 'a big increase in spiritual returns over last year and former years'. In Ch'unch'on new parishes were opened in 1948 and 1949, and 1950 'began with an increase in conversions and smooth progress in the building of the cathedral'. The superior general of the Columbans, Jeremiah Dennehy, erected Korea as a region of the society on 1 February 1949, with Brian Geraghty as director. Kwangju and Ch'unch'on became pro-regions.

Yet simultaneously with the promising signs of conversions and building work, letters between Korea and Ireland contained warnings that the American army would withdraw from the peninsula and that the communists would take over. As early as February 1947, still in America after being deported by the Japanese in 1942, Harold Henry told Michael O'Dwyer, 'It is rumoured that the US army will pull out of Korea in a year and let the Russians have the whole country.' The United Nations general assembly, on 14 November 1947, approved an American proposal for an election in Korea, followed by independence and the withdrawal of all foreign troops. Russia refused to allow the UN electoral commission access to the north, and the election, on 10 May 1948, was limited to South Korea. On 20 July 1948 the national assembly chose Syngman Rhee as president of the Republic of Korea. Geraghty, the Columban superior in Korea, wrote to Dennehy, the superior general, that 'several of the fathers have asked me what our policy would be in the event of US moving out and the danger of the Reds taking over here'. Dennehy, having lived in China from 1929 to 1941 where two of his companions died at the hands of communists, and others were held for ransom or brutally beaten, replied:

> As regards the policy to be pursued in case of a Red drive southward, it is hard to state any hard and fast rules at this distance. Things have

---

29. Patrick Brennan, 'New year, new plan' in *The Far East* (US ed.), xxxiii (Jan. 1950), pp 8-9.

generally to be decided on the spot in accordance with the trend of events. It is certain that no good can be accomplished by allowing the priests to fall into the hands of the Reds. My advice for the present, therefore, would be to work as long as it is possible, but not to get caught by communists.[30]

Members of the Catholic Foreign Mission Society of America, the Maryknoll missioners, in Korea had 'orders from their headquarters to pull out with the army if it leaves'. American troops began to withdraw from Korea and by June 1949 only a five-hundred-man military training group remained. The Russians had already pulled back to their own border, leaving the North Korean army 'a large arsenal of tanks, artillery and military aircraft'. America denied the southern forces 'armour and heavy artillery'.[31] There were frequent skirmishes along the north-south border.

Korean war 1950-3
Columbans in Korea in 1950 were so inured to the duels along the thirty-eighth parallel that they paid no attention to the artillery barrage when the North Korean army invaded on 25 June 1950. American troops, under the banner of the United Nations, were rushed in from Japan on 4 July. But these were from an army of occupation, lightly armed like the South Koreans. In the months that followed fighting raged the length and breadth of Korea, the North Koreans first pushing the United Nations forces to a small enclave in the south-east corner around Pusan and Taegu, then, on the arrival of American reinforcements and the UN landing at Inch'on on 15 September 1950, retreating northwards. South Korean units reached the Yalu river, the border between Korea and China, on 25 October 1950, but on the same day Chinese 'volunteers' entered the war. The UN armies retreated and fighting gradually fell into a stalemate near the thirty-eighth parallel.

Ch'unch'on prefecture, the Columban mission right on the border between north and south Korea, was occupied by the North Korean army in the opening days of the war, the provincial capital falling on the 27 June 1950.[32] Although Quinlan expected that 'this may be final for all of us' and that some of the priests could lose their lives, several Columbans decided to stay with their people. What followed was described bluntly in a Latin report to Rome in June 1951 (Table 7.4).

---

30. Jeremiah Dennehy to Brian Geraghty, 28 May 1948 (CFCA, KOR A-4c:7a).
31. Max Hastings, *The Korean war* (London, 1987), p. 34.
32. Thomas Quinlan, 'Arrest in Korea' in *The Far East*, xxxvi (July, 1953), p. 3.

Prospectus Status Missionis, Choon Chun, 1 July 1950 – 30 June 1951	
Name of Ordinary:	Thomas Quinlan
Postal Address:	He was captured by Communists in the month of July 1950, we do not know if he is alive or dead.
Priests:	Two Irish were killed.
	Two Irish were captured.
	One Australian was captured.
	Seven Irish, one New Zealander, and three Koreans remain.
Sisters:	Three Korean Sisters of St. Paul de Chartres.
Catechists:	On account of the war they cannot work.
Population – Total:	Unknown on account of the war.
Catholic:	5,000 (approx.)
Schools:	In time of war the schools have ceased.
Changes in the number of Catholics:	Many fled and about a thousand are dead from disease.
Spiritual Fruits:	Almost all Christians fled the prefecture at least for a time, and those who returned have almost all received paschal Confession and Communion.
Submitted (place and date):	Seoul, 23 July 1951.
Signature:	Hubert Hayward Pro-prefect.
(Seal of the prefecture)	Lost in the invasion

Source: Spiritual Returns of the Prefecture of Ch'unch'on, trans. N. Collins (CFCA, KOR A-4 (SR)).

Table 7.4 *Annual report of the prefecture of Ch'unch'on, 30 June 1951*. The report, in Latin, gives a starker picture of a prefecture devastated by war than any detailed account could have portrayed.[33]

Quinlan, the ecclesiastical superior or 'ordinary', Francis Canavan and Philip Crosbie, priests from Ireland and Australia, were captured by the North Koreans. Canavan died of pneumonia on 6 December 1950. Crosbie and Quinlan were presumed dead until their names appeared on a list of prisoners released by the Russians in February 1952.[34] Three other priests were shot, Anthony Collier on 27 June, James Maginn on 4 July, and Patrick Reilly (Plate 7.6) on 29 August. Hubert Hayward, pro-prefect of Ch'unch'on, in his

---

33. See Appendix 7, p. xxx.
34. 'Editorial', *The Far East*, xxxv (Apr. 1952), p. 1.

report to the Vatican, did not know of the death of Maginn and recorded him as captured. Only a few Korean Roman Catholics fled in the first invasion from the north, but their experience of communist occupation was so bitter that when the province, retaken by the United Nations forces, was captured again, this time by the Chinese, just after Christmas 1950, they joined thousands fleeing across the snow-covered mountains. Columbans in Seoul and Kwangju in June 1950 prepared for the North Korean invasion. Brian Geraghty, the regional superior, ordered five recent arrivals to join the party of American nationals who were being flown from Kimpo airport, Seoul, to Japan. He called on the apostolic delegate, Patrick J. Byrne, who decided that 'the Pope's representative should remain to give what support he could to the Korean bishops and their people'. Geraghty joined the mass of refugees streaming south, crossing the bridge over the Han river just hours before it was blown up by the retreating South Korean army, and reached Mokp'o. On 16 July an American vice-consul informed the Columbans there that the US forces did not intend to hold the south-west, the prefecture of Kwangju, which was sure to fall to the communists. Most of the priests retreated to Pusan, some in a convoy of jeeps, others on an American minesweeper. Patrick Brennan, the prefect, Thomas Cusack, the parish priest, and John O'Brien, his assistant, decided to remain in Mokp'o,[35] and four Korean priests stayed in other parishes.[36] In a letter to his mother Cusack wrote, 'Mother, if I were to leave my people, I would never have a sound night's sleep again.' When she read the letter she said, 'Had I been there with him, I would have told him the same thing.' Brennan, Cusack, and O'Brien were arrested by the North Koreans on 24 July 1950 and taken to Taejon prison with captured American soldiers.[37] Before the North Koreans retreated from Taejon on 24 September they massacred their prisoners. It is thought that the three priests were among them but their bodies were not identified. During the occupation of Kwangju prefecture by the North Koreans local Christians were among those singled out as anti-communist. Two seminarians, Gregory Tjen and Peter Ko, were beaten to death in September 1950.

The three Columbans, Quinlan, Canavan and Crosbie, taken prisoner in July 1950 in Ch'unch'on, were interned in a school outside P'yongyang in a group of seventy-four foreign civilians.[38] Their companions included French priests of the *Société des Missions-Étrangères*, French and Belgian sisters

---

35. Fischer, *Light in the Far East*, p. 98.
36. Harold Henry to Pietro Fumasoni-Biondi, 30 June 1951 (CFCA, KOR A-4(SR)).
37. Alexander G. Makarounis, 'I met them in jail' in *The Far East*, xxxiv (Sept. 1951), p. 10.
38. Philip Crosbie, *Three winters cold* (Dublin 1955), pp 64-5.

belonging to the orders of St Paul de Chartres and Carmel, American Maryknoll Fathers Patrick Byrne, the apostolic delegate, and his secretary, William Booth. Captured British missionaries included Cecil Cooper, head of the Anglican church in Korea, one of his priests, Charles Hunt, and a nun, Mary Clare Witty. Herbert A. Lord of the Salvation Army was another Briton. His courage and mastery of the Korean language made him the chosen spokesperson of the group in several tense confrontations with their captors. The staff of the Methodist mission and hospital in Kaesong included Americans and an Austrian doctor. Others captives were diplomats, mining engineers, journalists, the manager of the Chosen hotel in Seoul who was a Swiss, and Turkish and Russian families with young children. Many of the prisoners were old and sick. Paul Villemot MEP, was eighty-two years old, and the St Paul de Chartres sister, Béatrix Edouard, seventy-six. Thérèse Bastin, a Belgian Carmelite, was so ill she had to be carried and Marie-Madelaine Marquier, another Carmelite, was blind. When the North Koreans retreated in September 1950 the prisoners, together with more than 700 captive American servicemen, were taken by train to a series of camps around Manp'o on the Yalu river (See Figure 7.1). On 31 October 1950 a Korean major, given the bitter nickname, 'the tiger' by the American POWs, took command and drove them, soldiers and civilians, on a series of forced marches. The more able-bodied captives helped the weak, but the trek led them up and down a snow-covered mountain pass. On the first two nights they slept in the open, and on the second morning ten of the American POWs were dead from exposure. Béatrix Edouard collapsed and guards compelled her companion to leave her. Soldiers began to drop out and were shot, and the missionaries realised that Eduoard had shared the same fate. Mary Clare Witty, the Anglican nun, died in her sleep on the 6 November. The 'death march' ended at Linjiang on 8 November 1950. It had cost the POWs ninety-six dead. Of the civilians, only the two sisters and one of the Russian women died on the way, but fourteen others succumbed soon after to the effects of the march, the cold, the poor food, compounded by dysentery and pneumonia. Five members of the *Société des Missions-Étrangères* perished including the brothers, Antoine (76) and Julien Gombert (74). Patrick Byrne, the apostolic delegate, already suffering from beri-beri, contracted pneumonia and died on 25 November 1950. Quinlan used his own monsignor's soutane in which to bury him, hoping that the metal buttons would 'afterwards help us to identify his remains'.[39] The Belgian Carmelites, Mechtilde Devriese and Thérèse Bastin, followed on the 18 and 30 November.

---

39. Thomas Quinlan, 'The long captivity' in *The Far East*, xxxvi (Aug. 1953), p. 12.

Conditions improved for the surviving prisoners with the arrival of a more humane camp commandant on 2 February 1951. The change may have been due to the success of the communist armies in driving the UN forces away from the Chinese border. For the next two years the captives, and their guards, were often hungry, and some prisoners died, but the dominant theme in the accounts given by survivors was uncertainty, with constant rumours about imminent release. For Quinlan the journey to freedom (Plate 7.7) began on 20 March 1953. Crosbie followed in May.

A time of growth 1951-4

Columban missionaries who escaped to the area around Pusan, where they acted as chaplains to the UN forces, or to Japan returned to devastated prefectures. The war that lasted from 25 June 1950 to an armistice signed at P'anmunjom on 27 July 1953 killed or scattered their converts and demolished churches and houses. Yet the priests discovered that the Korean clergy and Catholics remained faithful.[40] In Kwangju two Korean priests were imprisoned by the North Korean army. Paul Kim was held for fifty-five days before he managed to escape. Lucius Chang, incarcerated for fifty days, shared half his daily handful of rice with a fellow prisoner, and his example, it was reported, led the man to become a Christian. When the communists retreated, local Catholics broke down the door of the jail and released the prisoners minutes before a charge of dynamite destroyed the building. Brian Geraghty, the Columban superior, reached the town of Kangnong, in the prefecture of Ch'unch'on, where he had founded an orphanage. All twenty-two orphans were safe, protected by a young Korean nurse during the months of occupation. One war correspondent encountered a party of Koreans, men, women and children, trudging south. Through an interpreter he learned that:

> ... they were peasants from a town near the 38th parallel. They had been converted by the Columban Fathers and they had elected to abandon the little they owned in the world and brave a walk of some 300 miles rather than renounce their faith.[41]

The correspondent concluded that they were not 'rice Christians', people who joined the church merely for food or some other material advantage. Columbans found 'their refugee Catholics in Chonju, Taejon, Pusan and

---
40. Brian Geraghty, 'War-stricken Korean missions' in *The Far East*, xxxiv (Feb. 1951), p. 3.
41. Hal Clancy, 'The equipment that worked', in *The Far East* (US ed.), xxxiv (Mar. 1951), pp 4-5.

even on islands off the coast'. A family of three, Joseph, Veronica, and their daughter Mary, fled from Mokp'o to the island of Huk San, and soon had thirty catechumens preparing for baptism.[42] The first presence of the Roman Catholic Church in many towns and villages can be traced to the arrival of such refugees.

Encouraged by the faith and strength of their flocks Columbans began to repair the damage caused by the Korean war. A chart of the statistics for church membership from 1936 to 1955, very fragmentary in the case of Ch'unch'on (Figure 7.2), provides a summary of the history of both prefectures.

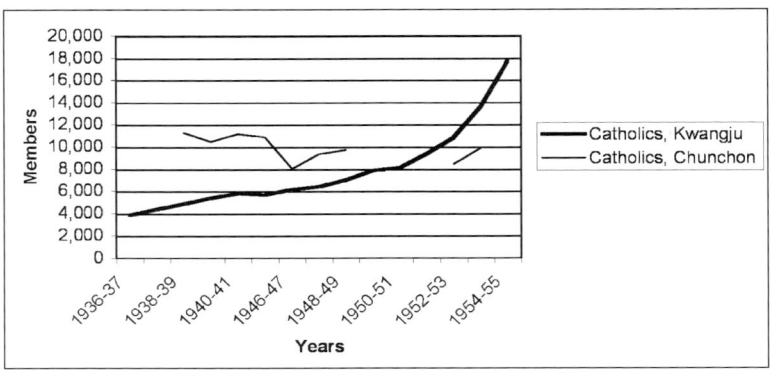

Source: Annual reports, Prefectures of Kwangju and Chunchon (CFCA, KOR A-4).
Figure 7.2. *Roman Catholics in Kwangju and Ch'unch'on, 1936-55*. Fragmentary reports from Ch'unch'on show a steady decline with a small recovery in 1953, while those from Kwangju indicate steady and then spectacular growth.

Before the Pacific war (1941-45) there were more Roman Catholics in Ch'unch'on than in Kwangju, but while the line for church members in Kwangju climbs steadily year by year, that for Ch'unch'on has a sharp dip in 1945 indicating the loss of 3,000 Catholics stranded in North Korea, and a complete break from 1950 to 1954 which surely illustrates the greater savagery of the war in the vicinity of the thirty-eight parallel. Yet in 1954 even Ch'unch'on was growing.

Kwangju, in the extreme south of Korea, was occupied only once by the communists, from July to September 1950. By October or November most priests had returned to their parishes. Harold Henry, pro-prefect in place of the dead Patrick Brennan, and two other Columbans were back in Mokp'o. Wartime restrictions interfered with the celebration of the feast of Christmas:

> For the first time since the Christmas after Pearl Harbor …we were

---

42. Thomas Moran, 'The road to the isles' in *The Far East* (US ed.), xxxv (Sept. 1952), p. 3.

unable to offer Midnight Mass. But the curfew was lifted at 6.30 Christmas morning and every Mass was packed. As there was not sufficient room in the church, the people had to gather at the windows for Benediction after the last Mass. Our churches are crowded for daily Mass and the Rosary, and we have many under instruction.

Henry wrote a letter to Propaganda, to accompany his report for the year ending in June 1951, and explaining that the statistics for the number of Catholics was 'not accurate as records were lost in several parishes during the Red occupation, but every effort was made to be as accurate as possible'. More priests returned but as the UN forces went further north guerrillas attacked towns and villages in Kwangju, making it impossible to station priests in two parishes. Three central churches and five mission chapels had been destroyed in the war, and 'every church and rectory was looted completely'. Canon law prevented Henry, as only deputy for the prefect Brennan, from making any 'innovations'. Yet he believed that such innovations were urgently needed. In April 1952 he wrote to Michael O'Dwyer:

> The sufferings and destruction in Korea are always stressed but hardly a word about the opportunities which were never better; but we are missing the boat. If we want to get in on the ground floor we should have men available now.

The political scene was so threatening that the leaders of the Roman Catholic Church in Korea, at a meeting in March 1952, discussed what priests should do in the event of a third world war, and affirmed the policy that the pastor should remain with his flock. Yet Henry, like the apostolic delegate, Max de Furstenberg, was opposed to a 'policy of waiting to see what will happen'. Instead he had plans to establish new parishes, and the delegate told him 'to blaze away'. Their optimism was justified and statistics for subsequent years show steady growth in the prefecture. The annual totals of Catholics, of adult baptisms, of catechumens, and of Easter communions climbed consistently. To deal with the flood of converts the number of ministers also grew, from eleven catechists and thirteen priests in 1948 (Table 7.2, p. 241), to one hundred and twenty-nine respectively in 1951 (Table 7.5).

Numbers of children in church-run primary schools were small and Henry complained:

> ... we are having great difficulty in getting the children of school age properly instructed, whether they are Catholic or catechumens. These children are made to attend the Public Schools from early morning

until dusk; they are then too tired and hungry to come to doctrine classes.[43]

	1950-51	1951-52	1952-53	1953-54	1954-55
Catholics	8,059	9,362	10,796	13,575	17,676
Baptisms: Adults	740	1,073	1,292		3,438
Children of Catholics	263	386	339		683
In Danger of Death	721	663	1,721		604
Catechumens	1,849		2,222		6,335
Deaths	302	155			122
Annual Communions	4,364	5,178	6,848		9,772
School pupils: Boys	127				304
School pupils: Girls	120				314
Catechists, Male	60		62		37
Catechists, Female	36		38		54
Priests	29		22		32

Source: Annual Reports, Prefecture of Kwangju (CFCA, KOR A-4(SR)).
Table 7.5 *Church growth, prefecture of Kwangju, 1950-5.* The Catholic population of the prefecture more than doubled in five years. Many of the new Christians were from the educated classes.

Many of the adults seeking baptism in Kwangju after 1952 were from the professional classes, doctors, teachers and civil officials, who formerly 'were ashamed to enter the church'. These, according to Henry, were attracted because 'the prestige of the church was never greater'. The figure of 1,721 for people baptised in danger of death in 1952-53 is anomalous, 900 of them having been baptised by one sister working with condemned guerrillas in a prison camp. Henry learned on 3 December 1954 that Rome had appointed him to be prefect of Kwangju, removing all canonical restrictions on his ambitious plans for the future of the church there.[44]

The northern prefecture of Ch'unch'on was part of the battlefield for the entire war, the provincial capital being 'taken four times by the communists and re-taken four times by UN forces' before the frontline was stabilised some forty-five kilometres to the north in June 1951. Columbans returned in August 1951 and set up temporary churches. They celebrated Christmas 1951 in twelve parishes with reduced congregations ranging from 100 to 500 people. Building 'materials were absolutely impossible to get, except from the armed forces. Labour was required to help the people to get on their feet'. Roman Catholics in the US forces helped with 'scrapped' materials, and the priests employed local workers to replace churches and residences. People began to trickle back and 'the sight of the church cross reminded (the Roman

---
43. Harold Henry to Pietro Fumasoni-Biondi, 30 June 1951 (CFCA, KOR A-4(SR)).
44. Fischer, *Light in the far east*, p. 117.

Catholics among them) of the past and gave them hope for the future'. Some returned to land beyond the thirty-eighth parallel, places ruled by communists until the UN armies pushed them further north. A new parish was established in Sokch'o to serve them. Timothy Connolly, superior general of the Columbans, visited the prefecture in 1953 and described both the devastation and the recovery:

> Before the Korean war Chunchon had fifteen parish plants. Six of these, including the cathedral, were completely demolished, and nine were cruelly damaged. Of these, three are still in ruins, ten have been rebuilt, two are rebuilding and three new parishes have been opened…

Priests in Ch'unch'on were almost overwhelmed by the huge number of people wishing to enter the church beginning in 1952. Total numbers of adult baptisms, rarely more than 250 in the years before the Korean war, rose to 436 in 1952-3, and 757 in 1953-54. Even more spectacular was the increase in catechumens, from around 340 before the war to 1,273 in 1952-3, and 2,566 the following year. Some appear to have been seeking answers to the horrors experienced during the Korean war. Thomas Quinlan told how:

> … the intelligentsia as well as the plain people are turning towards the church … Families of prominent Koreans whom the communists took north as prisoners in 1950 and who are still missing held a meeting in Seoul some months ago. They agreed that they should have some religion. They chose Catholicism.[45]

Other converts to Roman Catholicism, poor and hungry because of the war, may have asked for baptism to gain access to the relief goods, the rice and clothing, which agencies like the American National Catholic Welfare Conference channeled through missionaries in 1953. When life improved after the war many Catholics lapsed, but significant numbers persevered.[46] Columbans in Korea and their church officials supervised religious practice carefully, using a system inherited from their French predecessors in which the priest had a *status animarum*, record, for each family. Every individual in the family, whether Catholic or not, had a line on the record, listing baptism, confirmation, and other sacraments. At Easter time the people paid their annual dues to the catechist. Then they were examined by the priest on the catechism, and at the same time he checked if they had incurred any 'imped-

---

45. Thomas Quinlan, 'An interview with Mgr T. Quinlan' in *The Far East* (US ed.), xxxviii (Oct. 1955), p. 5.
46. Interview by author with Michael O'Loughlin, Dalgan Park (22 Nov. 2006).

iment', e.g. by getting married outside the church. Should they fail in any of these matters they were not allowed to make their Easter confession and communion. Those who passed were given a *pyo*, a ticket, which they surrendered to the priest when they actually received the sacraments, and were duly credited in the family *status animarum*. Many Columbans disliked the system as introducing undue pressure on people to receive the sacraments. In the words of Pius XII, '*Dieu ne force personne à accepter la grace sacramentelle*'.[47] But Koreans liked it, and Korean priests enforced it strictly. A statistic with perhaps more significance for the future of the prefecture was that the number of priests had grown from eighteen in 1949 to twenty-three in 1954, and of that number thirteen were Koreans. Ten young men from the prefecture were in the seminary in Seoul, four of them approaching ordination to the priesthood.

Thomas Quinlan returned to Korea in 1954 in the dual role of prefect in Ch'unch'on and regent of the apostolic delegation in Seoul, temporarily taking the place of a papal delegate.[48] He found that 'A great movement into the church, and to other Christian churches as well, was now in full swing all over the country'.[49] *The Far East* ended the year 1954 with an upbeat account of the growing number of conversions and of the tiny number of priests and sisters. It appealed for more missionaries and announced the good news that the Jesuits were about to open a university in Seoul and the Columban Sisters a hospital in Mokp'o.

Conclusions
Columbans in Korea aimed to set up the local church on the model laid down by canon law, and reviewed in annual reports to Rome. Their overall methods derived from that model in creating quasi-parishes, building churches, preaching, catechising, and celebrating the sacraments, but the system of central stations and out-stations was inherited from their predecessors of the *Société des Missions-Étrangères*. Catechists were key personnel, both those employed full-time in instructing converts, and the majority who led the local services in their own communities. Adequate instruction and understanding of the faith was a high Columban priority. There were more vocations to the priesthood in Ch'unch'on than in Kwangju, coming from the 'old Catholic' families who had taken refuge in the remote mountains, but Columbans in both prefectures sought young men who wished to become

---

47. Pius XII, *Allocutio V* in AAS, xxiv (Rome, 1957), p. 1030.
48. James Buckley, 'Return to Korea' in *The Far East*, xxxvii (Aug. 1954), p. 6.
49. Thomas Stewart, 'History of the diocese of Chuncheon', Sept 1988 (Unpublished ms in CFCA, KOR A-5).

priests, and supported them in the seminary in Seoul. Sisters were few but greatly desired.

Protestant missionaries had hospitals and schools as ways of reaching out to people of other faiths, but the Columbans arrived during the Japanese occupation of Korea, when the government controlled education. In the circumstances, Roman Catholic schools were small and appear to have attracted few converts. During the periods of starvation after the Japanese and Korean wars some people were thought to have become catechumens to obtain relief goods. Others turned to Catholicism seeking an answer to questions aroused by the chaos of war. Some Roman Catholic refugees, fleeing to villages where there was no church, gathered people for prayer and instruction and Columbans built on their example by encouraging each Catholic to try to convert one neighbour each year.

The earliest Protestant missionaries arrived in Korea in 1883, a century after the first Roman Catholic was baptised, yet by 1910 Korean Protestants out-numbered Roman Catholics two to one. This calls the methods of the Roman model into question, and even asks if numbers were a valid way of measuring success. Annual reports to Rome, articles in *The Far East*, and the stories of the priests suggest that an increase in numbers of converts, catechists, and local ordinations was the criterion. Yet while Roman Catholic missionaries regarded such statistics as important they also aimed at creating a particular kind of church, faithful to the Pope and to 'the gospel according to the doctrine of the Holy Roman Church'. They put huge efforts into forming well-instructed Christians, encouraging communities to contribute what they could in building churches, and inspiring young Koreans to become priests and sisters. Instruction of converts and the philosophical and theological training given to Korean students for the priesthood were full of European concepts and values. Perhaps Roman Catholic missionaries could have married the gospel to Asian values and ideas. But Columbans in general, and the members of the *Société des Missions-Étrangères* and the Catholic Foreign Missionary Society of America, were of a pastoral rather than an academic bent. Their aim in language study was usually to learn enough to be able to deal with the people in their parishes. They were not equipped, nor did they have time, to study Confucius or the Buddha, or to integrate that with the teaching of Jesus. To build churches and employ catechists Columbans had to appeal to supporters abroad for funds. Presbyterians hoped to produce a self-evangelising, self-governing and self-supporting church. So did the Columbans, although they expected that the period of gestation would be longer than that envisaged by their reformed brethren.

Persecution of Roman Catholics, and other Christians, happened repeatedly in Korea. It would appear to have come from the desire of rulers, Korean, Japanese, or communist, to eliminate all who thought differently from the dominant culture rather than from disapproval of specific beliefs or practices. A second reason was the suspicion that the missionaries, and their converts, were spies for western powers. While Harold Henry was aware that foreign priests should distance themselves from the US forces, he and his companions were prepared to use army materials and equipment for building churches. Koreans surely saw them as having a special relationship with the occupying power. The treatment of their prisoners by the North Koreans in 1950 seemed particularly cruel, and some of the captors were brutal, yet usually the guards shared the same poor food and accommodations as the captives.

Many missionaries, like Quinlan, believed that the shepherd should stay with his flock, but others were beginning to query the value of such sacrifice, at least as a general principle. Dennehy, the Columban superior general, urged that 'no good can be accomplished by allowing the priests to fall into the hands of the Reds', and many priests acted on his advice. The American Maryknoll fathers fled and lived to work in other missions, while the Benedictine monks, German and Korean, were captured in 1950 and died in prison. Yet the example of Roman Catholics, lay and cleric, led many to the faith.

The European or Roman model of church and of mission guided Columbans in Korea even though government control of schools or the procrastination of a bishop like Larribeau of Seoul might create obstacles. Each time war destroyed their achievements they started again, building, instructing, providing the sacraments. Like Robert Bruce's spider, they eventually succeeded, and the growth of the church since the Korean war is their monument.

CHAPTER EIGHT

Mission in Burma 1936-1954

The Congregation for the Propagation of the Faith invited the Columbans to open a mission in the remote north of Myanmar, then called Burma, in 1936.[1] This chapter will examine the geographical and political context of the new undertaking, and the work of earlier missionaries in the country. All the first Columbans to go to Burma were young, with no experience of foreign mission. Even their leader, Patrick Usher, was only thirty-seven years old, and from his ordination in 1923 had been bursar in the Columban mission college in Ireland. It will be necessary to ask how much they learned from their predecessors, priests of the *Société des Missions-Étrangères*. Foreigners in Burma faced many challenges, of climate, language, culture, food, and accommodation. Usher and his companions were further tested by the remoteness of northern Burma, and a population scattered in tiny villages over a very mountainous terrain. The Columban mission in Burma falls into three convenient stages: the period under British rule, from 1936-42, and after the world war from 1945-7; the Japanese occupation, 1942-5, and the time of adjustment to the government of the independent 'Union of Burma', 1948-54. Some of the people in the new mission were Buddhists. Earlier missionaries found that these were not easily evangelised, while the majority in the northern hills, animist Kachins, were more open to the gospel. The American Baptist church, established in the area assigned to the Columbans since 1877, competed with the Columbans for converts especially through education.

Burma
Burma stretches more than 2,000 kilometres from the eastern Himalayas south to the Indian Ocean and on to the Isthmus of Kra, with a total land area of 678,500 sq. km. The country is surrounded on three sides by mountain ranges covered by thick jungle which have, historically, provided natural barriers to invaders, and preserved the Buddhist culture of the majority when it was overwhelmed by Hinduism in India (Figure 8.1). Four great rivers flow south into the Bay of Bengal, the Irrawaddy and its tributary the Chindwin,

---

1. Michael Boyle to Michael O'Dwyer, 2 Dec. 1935 (CFCA, BUR A-1).

Figure 8.1 *Burma*. Paris Foreign Missionaries staffed two vicariates in Burma based in Rangoon and Mandalay. In 1936 at the invitation of Albert Falière, vicar apostolic of Northern Burma, Columbans accepted a new mission in the Kachin Hills. Propaganda added Mogok and the Naga Hills to the mission in 1951.

the Sittang and the Salween. Central Myanmar has thickly wooded valleys dotted with low hills and plains producing rice and millet. There are three seasons: hot from mid-February to May, when temperatures soar to more than 40°C; rainy from June to late September; and cold from October to January. According to the government census Burma had a total population of 16,800,000 in 1941. There were at least ten major ethnic groups and a hundred sub-tribes, with the Burmans making up nearly two thirds of the population. Others included the Shan, Karen, Karenni, Rakhine, Mon, Kachin and Chin, who lived mostly in the hills that encircle central Burma. Chinese and Indian merchants controlled much of the economy including the vital rice trade. The Burmans, Shans and Rakhines were Buddhists while the hill tribes were animists, worshipping spirits or *nats*. Kachins lived thinly scattered over the rugged mountains – about 500,000 in the north of Burma and 2,000,000 in China – the terrain presenting special problems for government officials and Christian missionaries.

Archaeological evidence suggests that Burma has been inhabited since at least 2500 BC, with a series of Mongolian tribes moving down from western China. The Burmans arrived in the eighth or ninth century and have dominated the country since then. Three dynasties controlled much of the territory, the first established by Anawrahta in 1044, and the third conquered by the British in a series of wars between 1824 and 1885. Britain governed from 1885 until the 'Union of Burma' became independent on 4 January 1948, apart from the years of Japanese occupation, that is 1942-5. The majority of the Burmese did not accept British rule, forcing the colonial power to deploy military and police forces largely composed of Indians and members of the minority hill tribes. Much of the colonial civil service was Anglo-Indian.

British administrators, in a policy introduced in 1866 to encourage education, were prepared to fund the schools attached to Buddhist monasteries provided they accepted some modification of the curriculum and teaching methods, and introduced subjects such as arithmetic and geography. Most monasteries refused to co-operate and the colonial government turned to mission schools. While government schools were introduced in the 1870s the authorities continued to favour the mission schools, and to give them substantial grants. Both Baptist and Roman Catholic missionaries saw such schools as important tools for evangelisation.

Christianity in Burma
Christian beliefs may have arrived in Burma in the middle ages, brought by the Karen from China. Certainly some of the ideas of the Karen – about

God, an eternal being, sovereign master and rewarder, creator of all things visible and invisible; about Ada and Y-ou, the first parents tempted by the devil; about the deluge; and about heaven and hell – are so close to the biblical doctrines that they seem to have come from a Jewish or Christian source, probably the Nestorian Christians who flourished in China from the seventh to the twelfth centuries. The first Roman Catholics to have bases in Burma were the Portuguese. In 1519 Anthony Correa entered into an official trade agreement with the lord of the port of Martaban. Twenty-six years later a parish priest or 'vicar of the town' resided in Pegu. But Portuguese missionaries found the Burmese resistant to their preaching and their ministry was limited to Portuguese and other Christians in the ports and to captives, Portuguese, Indian, and those of mixed race, settled by the Burmese crown in villages around Mandalay.

Rome attempted a more organised evangelisation of Burma from 1741 entrusting the mission to a succession of religious orders (Figure 8.2). Each of these in turn looked for openings to bring the gospel to the Buddhist majority, producing catechisms and other books in Burmese, but found converts only among the Karen people in Bassein.

Portuguese missionaries 1535-1741
Clerics Regular of St Paul (Milan) 1741-1832
Congregation of Pious Schools (Italy) 1831-40
Oblates of Mary the Virgin (Sardinia) 1840-56
Société des Missions-Étrangères (Paris) 1856-1966
Columban Fathers (Ireland and Australia) 1936-79

Source: Edward J. McCarthy, 'The history of the Catholic church in Burma' (CFCA, BUR A-5, pp 36-86).

Figure 8.2 *Missionaries in Burma prior to the Columbans, 1535-1936.* The first Roman Catholic missionary to work in the Kachin hills, Louis Biet, went there in 1872.

The energetic French missionary, Paul Ambroise Bigandet (1813-94), carried on a life-long study of Buddhism, writing many books including *The life or legend of Gaudama, the Buddha of the Burmese* (Rangoon, 1858), an apologetic work 'exposing the religious system of Buddhism as it is, explaining its doctrines and practices as correctly as has been in his power ... [to] undermine the foundations of a false creed'. But like his predecessors Bigandet found the Burmese Buddhists unconvertible. To counteract the 'cage of memorised Buddhist formulas which were neither understood nor questioned' he worked to improve the standards in parish schools. Observing that in these also 'the children ... sang out by rote the lessons of the day without understanding, then or later, a single word', he introduced the De La Salle brothers and several congregations of sisters who used a different method. The schools would also produce catechists and teachers and lead, hopefully, to the formation of indigenous priests and sisters. At his request Propaganda entrusted the east of the country to the Milan-based Pontifical Institute for Foreign Missions in 1867, and set up separate vicariates in lower and upper Burma in 1870. By 1887 the Roman Catholic population of the vicariate of Lower Burma had grown from 2,000 to 18,000, the increase being mostly among the Karen. Bigandet's successors in lower Burma focused their evangelisation on the Karen and on Tamils and Anglo-Indians, descendants of immigrants from India. Roman Catholic Karens numbered 38,355 in 1933, and were served by thirteen European priests and thirty-three from their own tribe. The first Tamil priest was ordained in 1932.

Protestant missionaries, the American Baptists Adoniram Judson (1788-1850) and his wife Ann, reached Rangoon in 1813. William Carey (1761-1834), Baptist missionary in India, regarded 'the preaching of the gospel by every possible method, and the support of the preaching by the distribution of the bible in the languages of the country' as keys to missionary advance. Judson followed the same priorities. He searched for points of access to preach to the Buddhist community, and after four years built a *zayat*, a bamboo and thatch reception shelter, near his home, as a meeting place for Burmese men. Most of his visitors, he thought, came out of curiosity, but in June 1819 one, Maung Nau, was baptised. Judson's literary work included the writing of a Burmese grammar and a task that would take twenty-four years, the translation of the bible. A doctor, Jonathan Price, joined the mission in 1821. Both men were imprisoned and tortured during the first Anglo-Burmese war (1824-6). However, the war ended in a peace treaty ceding the provinces of Arakan and Tenasserim to Britain. Judson immediately began preaching in Tenasserim and soon had a thriving church with converts chiefly from the animist tribes. He ransomed a debt-slave, Ko Tha Byu, a Karen thief and murderer, in 1827. In the following year Ko accompanied George and Sarah Boardman to initiate a successful mission among the Karen. By 1856 there were forty-two Karen churches with over two thousand members, thirty-nine Karen preachers, and thirty-six village schools. Baptist missionaries, an American, Josiah N. Cushing, and a Karen, Thra Saw Pe, first arrived in Bhamo in 1877. Saw Pe, an ordained minister, gathered the first converts. Others missionaries followed but illness and death took a heavy toll until William H. Roberts came in 1879. Although he was no linguist, Roberts completed the first tentative translation of the gospel of Matthew into Kachin. In 1950, the first Columban superior in Bhamo, Patrick Usher, reported to Rome:

> But for a long time Protestant missionaries, enjoying the favour of the authorities, opened primary schools everywhere, and even higher schools. They especially tried to educate the sons of the chiefs, with the result that now almost all the chiefs belong to the Baptist sect or at least favour it.[2]

The Baptist mission in Burma in 1813 had an impact on the parent church in America. Luther Rice, the Judsons' companion on the voyage to India, returned home for medical reasons and to raise support for them. In the polity of the Baptist church each congregation is independent. Rice motivated the creation in 1814 of the General Missionary Convention of the Baptist Denomination in the United States, renamed in 1972 the American Baptist Board of International Ministries with its headquarters in Valley Forge, Pennsylvania. The Myanmar Baptist Convention has been independent since 1965, but the American Baptist churches still support missions to Burmese refugees in Thailand.

Roman Catholic missionaries in the vicariate of Northern Burma between 1870 and 1885 had little opportunity for evangelisation among the Buddhists or the animist hill tribes. While the king, Mindon Min, allowed them to minister to the traditionally Catholic villages northwest of Mandalay he placed obstacles in the way of missionary work elsewhere. After the British capture of Mandalay in 1885 two priests, Pelletier and Herr, worked among the Buddhists. Pelletier was in charge of a Roman Catholic orphanage and founded a village for those orphans who had reached marriageable age. Then, knowing that it would be almost impossible to convert and form Roman Catholics in a Buddhist village, Pelletier opened his settlement to all who wished to become Catholics. Word went around that good land was available and soon people from Buddhist villages joined. Inevitably the offer of free land attracted 'lazy people, gamblers and ne'er-do-wells', but the missionaries attempted to test applicants by rigorous instruction and examination. The main Roman Catholic missionary effort, however, was centred on Bhamo, on the Chinese and Burmans of the town and the Kachins and Shans of its district.

Bhamo

Bhamo, 1,600 kilometres from the mouth of the Irrawady, is only 110 metres

---

2. Patrick Usher, *Relatio quinquennialis 1950* (CFCA, BUR A-4(ES)).

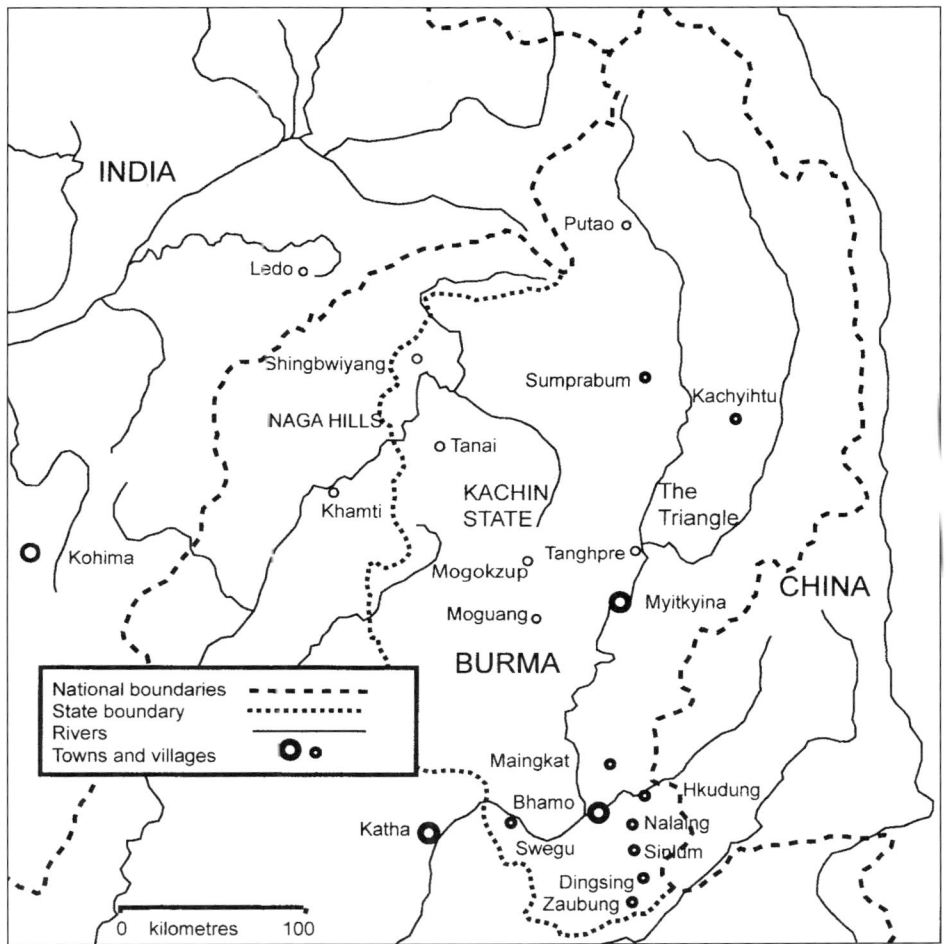

Figure 8.3 *The Prefecture of Bhamo*. Propaganda entrusted the districts of Bhamo, Myitkyina and Katha to the Columbans in 1936. At first most priests were concentrated in villages within an eighty-kilometre radius of Bhamo, with two in Myitkyina. In 1939 they were invited to staff the 'Triangle', establishing a station in Kachyihtu. Further stations were erected north-west of Myitkyina after World War II. Bhamo and Myitkyina became the Kachin State in 1946.

above sea-level, yet the Kachin village of Hkudung (Figure 8.3), thirty-five kilometres into the hills, is almost a thousand metres higher. The broad central Burma plains narrow steadily until they disappear a little above Myitkyina. Most of the land is mountainous and the highest peak, Hkakabo Razi, at 5,881 metres, forms the southern tip of the Himalayas. Total land area of the Kachin state measures 87,809 sq. km. The population in 1943 was estimated to be 750,000, of whom two thirds were Burman-Shans, living in the plains, and the rest mainly Kachins, in the hills.[3] The plains people were predominantly Buddhist and the majority of the Kachins animist.

Louis Biet, the first Roman Catholic missionary to live in Bhamo, arrived in 1872 and while his own small bamboo house was under construction he stayed with the British Resident, Captain Cooke. The progress of the Roman Catholic mission was hindered by sickness and death among the missionaries. Bhamo was notorious for cerebral malaria. A second obstacle was the reluctance of the Kachins to give up their spirit-worship.

Two priests, Cadoux and Faure, got very close to the people, but their efforts at conversion were blocked by the social structure of the Kachin village:

> If any household received Baptism they could not participate in the public spirit ceremonies of their village, and … every bit of subsequent accidental misfortune would be attributed to the anger of the spirits at their abstention. Nobody dared to flout public opinion at his own very real peril, and past that point … the missionaries could not get.

Cadoux attempted to solve the problem of spirit worship by founding a village to which only those who abjured the practice would be admitted. In 1892, twenty years after the arrival of Biet, Cadoux baptised the first converts, thirty-three persons. A few months later he succumbed to malaria. Others of his companions attempted to evangelise the Shans, the Chins, and the Chinese in the towns. Charles Gilhodes (Plate 8.1) opened a mission in the village of Hkudung in 1902, attracting the children with 'bon-bons' and learning the language from them. Gilhodes founded the first Catholic school in the hills in 1907, run by lay teachers until sisters from the Franciscan Missionaries of Mary took over the education of the girls and the general management of the school in 1923. A Roman Catholic central school was opened by Allard in Bhamo in 1919. The influenza epidemic of 1918 killed five missionaries in Bhamo leaving the bishop of northern Burma, Eugene Charles Foulquier, short of manpower. With no replacements coming from France, and all the priests advancing in years, Foulquier's successor, Albert Falière, in 1935 asked Propaganda 'to relieve him of the care of a portion of his vicariate and to set up this portion as an independent mission'.[4]

---

3. Edward J. McCarthy, 'The history of the Catholic church in Burma', ed. Patrick Usher (1941, MS in CFCA, BUR A-5), p. 158.
4. Pietro Fumasoni-Biondi to Michael O'Dwyer, 20 Feb. 1936 (CFCA, BUR A-1).

A Columban mission in Burma
The unnamed official responsible for India in the Congregation for the Propagation of the Faith discussed the possibility of a Columban mission in Burma with Michael Boyle, procurator of the society in Rome, on 2 December 1935. Boyle immediately informed Michael O'Dwyer, the Columban superior general, that Pietro Fumasoni-Biondi, prefect of Propaganda, 'would like very much that we should take the portion of the Vicariate mentioned', and said that 'as the territory borders China, there is no reason why our Society should not go there'. Falière was offering 'the districts of Bhamo and Myitkyim [Myitkyina] and the greater part of the district of Katna [Katha]', and estimated the land area to be 58,174 sq. km, with a population of 508,476. The vicar provided a religious breakdown of the inhabitants (Table 8.1):

	Buddhists	Animists	Protestants	Catholics
Bhamo	65,584	39,970	7,600	3,147
Myitkyina	79,197	70,242	4,300	108
Katha	200 529	12,000	25	43

Source: Notes of Michael Boyle, 2 Dec. 1935 (CFCA, BUR A-1).
Table 8.1 *Population statistics by faith for the Kachin state, 1931.* In Katha the majority were Buddhists and converts were very few.

Boyle warned that the statistics for the new mission did not include the Hukaung valley 'which is still little known, and of which the government census [of 1931] does not give any data'. There were nine Roman Catholic stations in the Bhamo district. Churches had been built at each, also one at Katha and one at Myitkyina, and there were twenty village chapels. The Franciscan Missionaries of Mary had two convents in the area, with European and local sisters running orphanage-school-dispensary combinations in Bhamo and Hkudung. Finances of the mission were limited to the income from a few fields serving the upkeep of one orphanage, and the salaries paid by the colonial government to the teachers in seven Roman Catholic schools. O'Dwyer responded that his council 'is prepared to do all in its power to accede to the wishes of the Cardinal Prefect'.[5]

Eight Columbans, led by Patrick Usher, arrived in Rangoon in the autumn of 1936 to begin a mission in Bhamo. Usher found that:

> The population of the district may be divided into four sections, the foreign community, the Burmans proper, the Shan-Chinese, and the

---
5. Michael O'Dwyer to Michael Boyle, 10 Dec. 1935 (CFCA, BUR A-1).

Kachins. Among the first are the small but important Anglo-Indian and Tamil sections, who have long been pillars of the church in Burma. The second, the Burmans proper, including the almost indistinguishable Shan-Burmans, belong to the Buddhist religion. Among them, for the present, progress is difficult.[6]

Falière, the bishop, gave Usher an introductory tour of the main stations around Bhamo before the new arrivals settled to language study, two to learn Burmese, three Shan and three Kachin. Some priests had to acquire several languages. After two years, according to Usher, 'McAlindon speaks Burmese like a native and needs only a little practice to be equally good at Kachin.' Eleven French and Burmese priests who had previously worked in the area remained until the Columbans were ready to take over their duties. Early in October 1937 Usher assigned his men as assistants with the veteran missionaries in established stations, almost all within eighty kilometres of the town of Bhamo, and in November could report to O'Dwyer that:

> The 'Shans' are five or six weeks at work with great results. I have planned, with everybody's approval, for Fr McAlindon to occupy Myitkyina in January with a companion or two.

'Great results' meant catching up on the backlog of tasks such as persuading lapsed Catholics to return to the practice of the faith or regularising invalid marriages rather than any strictly missionary outreach to people of other faiths. Another urgent task was to build 'a wooden combination of chapel, school and residence' in the station at Maingkat, to give the priests there 'a reasonable chance of surviving the rains'. The district of Myitkyina was practically 'untouched' in terms of Roman Catholic missionary outreach[7] and Usher sent Denis McAlindon to establish a Columban presence there and to explore the possibilities for mission in the hills further north.

Schools and competition
Usher planned to 'spread out into the great area which still remains unevangelised', especially in the Kachin hills beyond Myitkyina, to set up mission stations and, above all, schools, believing that:

> The Kachin is very fond of education, as it opens out possibilities beyond those of the hard life of the hills. Schools are the great means of evangelisation. Owing to the sparseness of the population they

---
6. Patrick Usher, 'Our mission in northern Burma' in *The Far East*, xx (Sept. 1937), p. 198.
7. Patrick Usher to Michael O'Dwyer, 25 Nov. 1936 (CFCA, BUR A-4:2b).

must be boarding-schools; otherwise none but the few children of one village could attend and even those would hardly come regularly.[8]

Schools were a priority for the British colonial authorities. Imperial policy 'that the empire should be run at the minimum cost to the domestic taxpayer' led administrators to employ Christian missions 'to service the structure of colonial rule by the provision of medicine and supremely of education'. The government of Burma invited Usher and other representatives of the Roman Catholic Church to a four-day meeting in Bhamo to discuss a 'regeneration scheme' for the Kachins. Proposals included 'more schools and the people themselves to support them'. But when Denis McAlindon called on the deputy commissioner, Maguire, in Myitkyina 'he was told that the Kachin country up here is reserved for the Baptist Mission'.[9] In discussion with Usher, Maguire's superior, Commissioner R. MacDougall, explained:

> ... that there would be no question of hindering our religious activities; government is interested in cutting out waste of civilising influence, e.g. rival schools in the same village. He is getting a map with existing schools marked, to study the situation.

However, in a meeting with Falière, the bishop, the commissioner 'registered alarm at this invasion of twenty or thirty Irishmen ... and expressed fear at what these inexperienced lads might do'. One member of the staff of the governor of Burma said that 'the only concern of the authorities was to avoid friction with the Baptists' and proposed that Roman Catholics and Baptists work in different zones. Such a comity agreement, 'dividing the area into noncompetitive geographical zones' allotted to different churches, was acceptable to many Protestant denominations in India and China, but not to Roman Catholics. Falière offered a compromise, pointing out that the government could in practice effect a zoning scheme for state-aided schools, and agreeing that the Columbans would not target places where the Baptists were already established, but insisting that 'if people anywhere wished to enter the church we could not ... exclude them'.

As noted by Usher from the outset, boarding schools were essential in the Kachin state because villages tended to be too small to support a school in each. Village size was limited by the slash-and-burn agriculture of the Kachins. In January the village chief and his council decided which piece of land should be cultivated that year. Shrubs and trees were cut, allowed to dry,

---

8. Patrick Usher, 'Our mission in northern Burma' in *The Far East*, xx (Sept. 1937), p. 200.
9. Patrick Usher to Michael O'Dwyer, 27 Feb. 1938 (CFCA, BUR A-4:5).

then burned, and the ash fertilised the new rice crop. After harvest the plot lay fallow for ten years while the jungle regenerated. This system meant that a large tract of land, enough for ten such plots, was needed to support even a few families, and the average size of a village was about twenty houses with five persons to a house. Usher observed that:

> Level spots to build on are none too plentiful and the Kachin does not like to be crammed up against his neighbour. So you have a ledge with three or four houses on it, a blank while you work your way down a dizzy slope, next a shelf with a single house, then around a knob of a hill to a few more, and so on.

Selecting a site for a mission station in northern Burma involved choosing a village that would be central to several others, and negotiating with the chief and village elders for a plot of several acres, large enough for church, residence, school, playgrounds, and a garden which would provide much of the food for the priest, teachers and boarders.

The Triangle

The Columban mission in Burma expanded into the Kachin hills in 1939 in response to an unexpected invitation from Sir Walter Booth-Gravely, 'counsellor' to the governor of Burma, and 'the man who has the last say in hills matters'.[10] When the bishop, Falière, withdrew the members of the *Société des Missions-Étrangères* in the course of 1938 Usher had four elderly priests, two French and two Burmese, and fourteen Columbans, all except one still in their twenties, to staff a territory more than two thirds the size of Ireland. He assigned most of them to Hkudung, Sinlum, Nalaing and Maingkat and other stations in the civil district of Bhamo (Figure 8.3, p. 263), and expected to place others in several 'promising' areas in the same district. There were just two priests in Myitkyina. Booth-Gravely's offer was for:

> … the part of the Myitkyina district known as the Triangle on the understanding that we should make our special effort there for the present and that no other missionaries would be allowed to interfere with us there. In every other place we are free to attend to our Catholics, to send them catechists and, if necessary, to open schools for them …

Usher felt it necessary to explain the opening of the new mission in the Triangle to readers of *The Far East* since it was 'one hundred and fifty miles

---

10. Patrick Usher to Michael O'Dwyer, 25 Jan. 1939 (CFCA, BUR A-4(ES):2a).

away from any existing station'. He mentioned that the site was a good centre of population, that the people were friendly, and that it was only thirty-eight miles, 'two easy days' from Sumprabum where there was a hospital, but omitted any reference to the invitation from Booth-Gravely, the representative of the British government. Despite improved relations between Britain and Ireland and the signing of the Anglo-Irish Trade Agreement of 1938, Usher judged rightly that Columban supporters in Ireland would not approve of his co-operating with the colonial authorities. His meetings with government officials helped to overcome their suspicions of young Irishmen to the extent that in April 1940 he was promised another tract similar to the Triangle and told that 'we are not only welcome all over our whole territory but considered necessary by the government'. Indeed:

> One of the ablest officials, a non-Catholic, dins it into everybody that the one hope of saving the degenerating Kachin race is the Catholic Church because the priests go and live their people's lives.

Two Columbans, the accomplished linguist Denis McAlindon and James Stuart, destined to become a legendary figure, explored the Triangle early in 1939. The area took its name from being shaped by two rivers, the Mali and the N'mai, which started nearly a hundred kilometres apart near the foothills of the Himalayas and tended towards each other during a two hundred kilometre journey south until they joined to form the Irrawaddy.

A mountainous jungle tract, the Triangle was brought under civil government only in 1927, with government centres at Htingnan and Kachyihtu. Usher reported that the population, 64,337 in 1939, had fallen drastically and was in crisis:

> When we start in the Triangle in November, please God, the proposition will be to assist at re-colonisation and to try to save the remnants of a people rapidly dying out (60% or 70% gone in twenty years, inbred, rotten with bodily and mental disease).[11]

A second Columban reconnaissance by Stuart and James Doody in December 1939 attributed the shrinkage in population to emigration, 'to stories of El Dorado down south'. Stuart and Doody returned to the Triangle in January 1940 and explored for three months, finding the people friendly but 'no chiefs specially enthusiastic in forcing building-sites on them'. The colonial authorities in Burma ruled the Triangle indirectly, leaving the traditional leaders in place, but installing an over-chief for a group of villages. La Doi,

---

11. Patrick Usher to Michael O'Dwyer, 14 Apr. 1939, CFCA (BUR A-4(ES):5).

taung-ok or over-chief of the southern Triangle, invited the Columbans to make Kachyihtu their central station, and negotiated with the village elders for a five-acre site. Usher accompanied Stuart and John Dunlea, Usher riding a bicycle and the others on ponies, to Kachyihtu in October 1940. In good weather they covered twelve to fifteen miles a day and reached Sumprabum, but:

> After Sumprabum our luck deserted us. A two-days' rainfall kept us indoors and the Irrawaddy [Mali] rose by 20 ft. ... holding us up for 3 days in a Kachin village ... In all, the 38-mile journey consumed 8 days.[12]

After inspecting the site of the new mission Usher returned to Myitkyina where he developed a high fever and thought it was malaria. Up in Kachyihtu Stuart and Dunlea also were sick. Stuart recovered quickly but Dunlea grew steadily worse. La Doi found men to carry the young priest to the hospital in Sumprabum where typhoid was diagnosed. Counting backwards for the incubation period of ten to fourteen days the doctor concluded that all three priests had caught typhoid from the water or food in the Kachin village where they were storm-steaded. Dunlea grew steadily weaker and died on 16 November 1940.

Apostolic Prefecture, 1939
The mission in the Kachin state was developing, albeit slowly. In 1938 Usher had twenty young Columbans in Bhamo and Falière requested Rome to set up a separate mission. Pius XI erected the apostolic prefecture of Bhamo on 15 January 1939, with Usher as prefect.[13] Each priest was responsible for a huge 'quasi-parish', with a central station and as many as thirty-eight villages. Riding ponies, the priest and a catechist made regular circuits of the outlying stations, instructing the people, celebrating the sacraments, and treating 'sore eyes, dirty wounds, skin diseases, fevers and colds'.[14] The multiplicity of tiny villages scattered over a large, mountainous area created special problems for adequate evangelisation:

> I hardly ever go out to a village but some families call on me to throw out their *nats* or household gods. Thus the number of people seeking instruction in the Faith is increasing all the time. But while the ceremony of casting out the *nats* is a simple affair, the problem of instructing our would-be Christians is another matter.[15]

---
12. Patrick Usher to Michael O'Dwyer, 4 Dec. 1940 (CFCA, BUR A-4(ES):8).
13. Pius XI, '*Birmaniae Septemtrionalis*' in *AAS*, vi (Rome, 1939), pp 161-2.
14. 'Life in Burma', *The Far East*, xxiii (Aug. 1940), p. 151.
15. William Kehoe, 'In the Burman hills' in *TFE*, xxiv (June 1941), p. 98.

The progress of the mission in Bhamo and the difficulty in providing adequate instruction for those wishing to enter the church are clear in a chart detailing church growth (Figure 8.4). While the number of Roman Catholics increased each year the statistics for catechumens, for those seeking instruction and baptism, constantly outstripped the totals for adult baptisms. Part of the discrepancy can be explained by the conversion of whole families, since the children would not be among those instructed. Yet clearly the missionaries needed more priests and catechists. Children would be instructed in parish boarding schools which multiplied from eleven in 1936, to twenty-eight in 1940, and fifty-three in 1954.

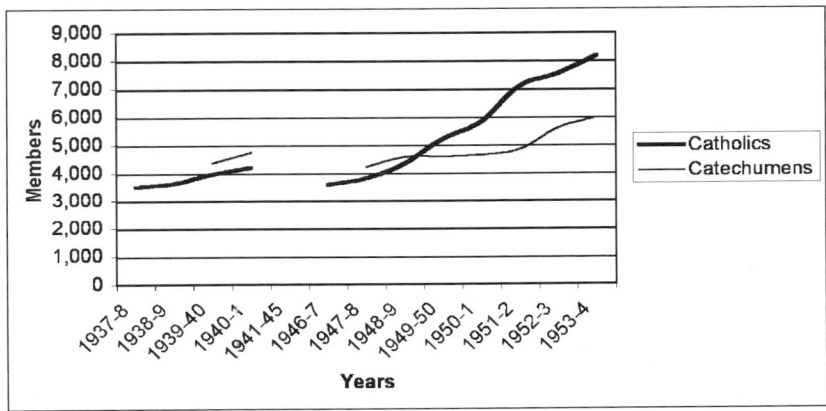

Source: Annual reports of the Columban Fathers (CFCA, BUR A-4).
Figure 8.4 *Church growth, prefecture of Bhamo, 1937-54.* The total number of Catholics increased steadily each year, apart from the period of World War II when the missionaries were interned. Limited personnel and funds meant that many who asked for baptism could not be instructed or baptised.

A school for catechists opened in Bhamo in 1939, giving a three-year course to men – men only, due to the rugged terrain – who would teach the adults. Usher had no illusions when he observed that:

> Numbers are growing steadily, but the standard of instruction and of personal religious life remain low. However, they die well and the generation now passing through the schools should know more. It will be four or five years before we shall have Kachin catechists who know anything about what they are supposed to teach.[16]

Progress in Bhamo was so slow, with twenty priests in stations in a corner of the vast territory, and just two in Myitkyina and another pair in the

---

16. Patrick Usher to Michael O'Dwyer, 17 Jan. 1940 (CFCA, BUR A-4(ES):6c).

Triangle, that Usher asked Michael O'Dwyer in April 1940 how he viewed the mission. 'Could a better use be made of the big number of men and the money?' The Kachin hills seemed to be just the sort of mission rejected by Edward Galvin in China in 1918 as 'very thinly populated ... mountainous ... damp, malarial and unhealthy'. The entire population of the Kachin state 'would fit into three or four Chinese towns'.

Instruction, whether by catechist or in school, or in the sermons of the priest, had to deal with the spirit-worship of the people. Belief in spirits, the *nats*, was so endemic in all the peoples of Burma that even the dominant Buddhist faith incorporated it. *Nats* influenced all aspects of human life:

> There is a *nat* which presides over health and a *nat* which presides over disease, one for good and one for bad harvests, and so on. Observers declare that the people have no love or respect for these *nats*; they regard them simply as beings who must be propitiated in order that they may not give vent to their spite by inflicting misfortunes of various kinds.[17]

Each village in Burma had its own shaman who could divine which spirits needed to be propitiated. Appeasing the *nats* involved the sacrifice of a buffalo, ox or fowl. A succession of misfortunes quickly destroyed a family's livestock. Converts frequently voiced such sentiments as, 'We are tired of the *nats*. They do not help us. We wish to do away with their altars and burn them.' When a family wished to become catechumens there was a ceremony which involved destroying all symbols of the *nats* in their home, yet for many Burmese belief in the spirits continued to influence every aspect of their lives.[18]

Nationalism

References to politics, both national and international, began to appear in the correspondence of Columbans in Burma in 1937. The Burmese as a whole never accepted British rule, the exception being the minority peoples, many of whom regarded the British as protectors from their ancient Burman enemies. University students and Buddhist monks were actively anti-British and in 1936 Ko Aung San, a leading nationalist and editor of the student magazine, was expelled from university for refusing to reveal the identity of the author of an inflammatory article. Usher announced the arrival, at an awkward moment, of the second group of Columban missionaries in 1937 and added:

---

17. 'The Kachins of upper Burma', *The Far East*, xxiii (May, 1940), p. 88.
18. Khoo Thwe, *From the land of green ghosts*, pp 20-43.

But when they came to Rangoon they found sore trouble, the B[ishop, Frederick Provost, MEP] practically driven out by his native clergy led by Donohue and others.[19]

Patrick O'Donohue, born in Madras, son of an Irish father and Indian mother, worked as a doctor with the Columbans in China 1921-25 before becoming a priest in the vicariate of South Burma in 1934. It seems more than likely that the conflict between the French bishop of Rangoon and the Burmese priests was inspired by nationalism. The unrest reached Bhamo in 1939:

> There is a great deal of trouble in Buddhist Burma with school-strikes of a political kind. So far, thank God, ours here is not affected; the spot of bother in other schools in the town a couple of weeks ago petered out, but there is a new more organised outbreak today.

World War II

Trouble of a more serious nature threatened the mission in northern Burma in 1937 when the Sino-Japanese war erupted across the border in China. Apart from wishing that 'this war will pass over without harming the priests and sisters in Hanyang', Usher hardly mentioned it until, in 1941, he complained that the price of rice had doubled 'owing to the war in China'. War in Europe in 1939 added new problems, preventing new priests from sailing from Ireland, and delaying mail and money. When Italian missionaries in the prefecture of Kentung, eastern Burma (Figure 8.1, p. 258), were arrested by the British in June 1941 Usher sent several Columbans to take their place. Japanese forces invaded Burma from Siam (Thailand) on 15 January 1942, and reached Bhamo on 3 May.[20] Most of the Columbans, by then twenty-six in number, were in their parishes around Bhamo, James Cloonan pastor up in Myitkyina, and Stuart and McAlindon in the Triangle. The visiting Edward J. McCarthy was in the hill town of Maymyo near Mandalay, recuperating from illness, William Kehoe and Michael Kelly in Kentung, Thomas Rillstone helping in Lashio, Daniel Cooney in Toungoo, and Jeremiah Kelleher a chaplain in the army. Before the war Kelleher ran a school for catechists in Bhamo and spent his evenings in a military barracks instructing Kachin soldiers in catechism. At the outbreak of hostilities the Kachin troops were ordered south, and Kelleher accompanied them. Seeing that his charges

---

19. Patrick Usher to Michael O'Dwyer, 17 Nov. 1937 (CFCA, BUR A-4:4).
20. Patrick Usher, 'After three years' in *The Far East*, xxviii (June, 1945), p. 41.

were being scattered through other units and being used mostly in garrison duty he moved to the Inniskilling Fusiliers 'who lived in constant danger in active fighting'. During the long retreat Kelleher was:

> ... cut off while attending a dying soldier ... had heat-stroke and lay down to die. An officer of the tank corps missed him and immediately went back for him, blasting his way in and out through a forward post.[21]

When the British troops withdrew into India Kelleher preferred to stay in Burma and reached Myitkyina. There he was arrested together with Cloonan and interned in Rangoon. Kelly and Kehoe, cut off in Kentung, attempted to return to Bhamo through the mountains but were forced to trek into China, where they waited out the rainy season at a mission station staffed by French priests, and arrived at Kunming in May 1943, a year after leaving Burma.[22] From there they were flown to India. Rillstone, in Lashio, 'made a pact with myself that if the people remained, I too would stay'. When the population of the town fled he joined a convoy on the Burma road and reached Bhamo.

Usher and the priests in Bhamo prepared for the Japanese occupation by hiding important documents and church furniture in safe places. Japanese forces occupied the mission house on 4 May 1942, interning the priests in the local gaol. Franciscan sisters, four French and nine Burmese, were also imprisoned but the Burmese were released after a few days. Over the next weeks missionaries from the hill stations were also arrested. On occasion Japanese soldiers acted more humanely than their Burmese collaborators:

> Father [Kevin] Flatley was brought down from the hills under arrest by the chief native Baptist pastor and handed over to the Japanese on a charge of harbouring British officers. To the poor pastor's chagrin, a military policeman cut away the ropes that had sunk in the priest's wrists and gave him tea and a cigarette, then took him to join the rest of us.

The Japanese in Bhamo allowed their captives to say Mass, exercise, and even play games. Friends supplied food and 'our Catholics braved every danger to bring us presents'. An Italian priest, Perego, and a Japanese captain, Bando, helped where they could until the prisoners were released on 18 June. Meanwhile 'in response to representations made by the Vatican' to the gov-

---

21. Patrick Usher, 'Through the war years in Burma' in *The Far East*, xxviii (Nov. 1945), p. 82.
22. 'Two priests complete hike from Burma into China', *The Far East* (US ed.), xxvi (Oct. 1943), p. 1.

ernment of Japan, orders came from Tokyo in October 1942 that the missionaries were to be protected. The reaction of the authorities in Burma was to intern the Columbans in Mandalay where they were joined by Edward J. McCarthy and Daniel Cooney. Accommodated in 'a good house' under guard, and later in a ward of St John's Leper Asylum, the priests were given freedom to move around the town. They gardened, baked bread, made shoes, and studied languages. Usher re-wrote the history of the Catholic Church in Burma from materials collected by Edward J. McCarthy before the war, McCarthy being too ill to write it himself. Lawrence Hickey compiled a Kachin dictionary. Nearly a hundred nuns were interned in the same asylum, and two of them taught Bernard Way to read music and play the organ. He also prepared two Kachin catechisms, one for adults and one for children. Falière, the Bishop of Mandalay, whose cathedral was burned down during the invasion and his personal possessions destroyed, shared all he had left with the Columbans. American bombers began to attack Mandalay and when one bomb fell close to the asylum:

> Somehow the news got to Bhamo and to Major Brown of the American Air Force. This good officer, with the help of a former American Baptist missionary, Captain Cummings, got in touch with all pilots, told them our whereabouts and ordered them to keep well clear of our refuge.[23]

House arrest for the Columbans in northern Burma ended in 1945. From February they could hear the boom of guns and when a British unit dug in at the corner of the asylum grounds on 15 March the priests and the patients were in the middle of a battle.

> Next morning, while the priests were saying Mass, a random Japanese shell burst right above them. Father [Thomas] Murphy fell in his vestments mortally wounded. Seven others were injured.

An American ambulance unit evacuated most of the missionaries to safety while Usher and Lawrence McMahon remained with Falière and some sisters to care for the lepers until relieved by two local priests, on St Patrick's Day.

Two Columbans in the Bhamo prefecture remained free all during the Second World War. James Stuart and Denis McAlindon were assigned to Kachyihtu in the Triangle. During the British retreat from Burma in 1942 a Colonel Stevenson wrote to Stuart asking him to take care of some refugee children stranded in Sumprabum. There were twenty-five children from the

---

23. Patrick Usher, 'Through the war years in Burma' in *The Far East*, xxviii (Nov. 1945), p. 84.

Bishop Strange Home, an Anglican institution in Rangoon, together with seventeen adults who had seven children of their own. McAlindon was looking after Burmese refugees in a camp in the north of the Triangle. A Japanese unit which entered Sumprabum on 19 July 1942 proposed sending Stuart under guard to Rangoon. The Kachins protested vigorously. After three years they had come to regard the priests as their spiritual fathers and, in many ways, temporal protectors. Stuart was allowed to stay. A Japanese lieutenant, a Christian who had attended a Baptist Sunday school, provided him with several bags of rice for the refugees and even loaned him his revolver to shoot pigs. When the Japanese withdrew from the area they left Stuart behind. He and McAlindon gathered porters and elephants and, on 2 October 1942, after the monsoon, set out to escort the refugees to Fort Hertz (Putao), near the Himalayas, from where they were flown to India. The two missionaries returned to Burma where, according to Thomas Murphy in *The Far East*, the Kachins in Kachyihtu greeted them with the declaration:

> We want no other missionaries than those of your church. We believe in you, and your religion must be true.[24]

McAlindon remained in Kachyihtu while Stuart was constantly on the move 'wandering throughout the northern portion of the prefecture'. He caught the attention of war correspondents for his exploits in helping to rescue downed aircrew and escorting further refugees to safety (Plate 8.2). At Christmas 1944 he was in a jungle clearing outside Myitkyina, 'a dashing figure ... in paratrooper boots, GI suntans, a neckerchief of yellow parachute cloth, and an Aussie hat', saying Mass for American soldiers.[25] When peace returned he was awarded an OBE and the American Legion of Merit.

Difficulties of reconstruction

Usher and the other Columbans released from internment in Mandalay in March 1945 were unable to return to Bhamo immediately. Four were given seats on an aeroplane in April and on arrival:

> ... we received something of a shock. The Bhamo of old had ceased to be. Not a house was standing; everywhere there were trenches, shell-holes, bomb-craters.[26]

Bhamo was captured by Chinese troops on 15 December 1944 after twenty-

---

24. Thomas Murphy, 'Two priests in northern Burma' in *The Far East*, xxviii (Jan. 1945), p. 1.
25. Edward Fischer, *The chancy war* (New York, 1991), p. 167.
26. Thomas McEvoy, 'Burma letter' in *The Far East*, xxviii (Sept. 1945), p. 69.

eight days of intense fighting. Artillery and the American Tenth Air Force completely destroyed Bhamo, Katha and Myitkyina while smaller places like Maingkat, Hpunpien and Zaubung were burned to the ground. Mission stations in the hills, away from the battlefronts, were less affected. From devastated Bhamo Thomas McEvoy visited his former parish near the Chinese border:

> You may judge our surprise then when we found that, except for a number of things that had been looted, everything was more or less the same. In Panghkak my teacher and his wife remained to look after the school and the chapel, and I must say they did their work wonderfully well and saved most of the property for us.

McEvoy was even more delighted when he found 'that in most places not only was there no decrease in the number of Catholics, there was actually an increase'. Even while he was delayed in Mandalay Usher was optimistically making plans. The Ledo road opened places hitherto inaccessible in the north of the prefecture and Stuart had made many friends up there. Blocking tactics by the Baptist church 'will [not] carry weight any longer'. He warned O'Dwyer that 'we shall apply to you for a dozen priests' and he would invite the Columban sisters to start a foundation in the prefecture.[27] On his return to Bhamo in May 1945 Usher moved quickly and in June had McEvoy and John Howe on their way to open new stations in Sumprabum and Tanghpre, while Stuart opened the Hukaung valley from a centre in Mogokzup (Figure 8.3, p. 263). Other Columbans began to rebuild, using bamboo, the only material available, and by early 1946 had sixteen central stations and many schools in some kind of working order.

The war in Burma took its toll of buildings but above all of the missionaries themselves. An American air force colonel, Roland H. Cipolla, described them as 'nothing more than skin and bones and in many cases disease-ridden'.[28] Some priests were so gravely ill that they were evacuated to hospital in Bangalore, India. Others suffered from nervous disorders, among them Usher who wanted to resign as prefect apostolic:

> I am sorry to say that something is breaking down in me and I feel unable to continue in my present position. Wretched phobias are taking hold. To make any decision or to look ahead, to interview anyone or meet a difficulty is an agony and getting worse.[29]

---

27. Patrick Usher to Michael O'Dwyer, 4 May 1945 (CFCA, BUR A-4(ES):14a).
28. Roland H. Cipolla, 'I won't/can't forget' in *The Far East*, xliv (Nov. 1961), p. 14.
29. Patrick Usher to Michael O'Dwyer, 29 Oct. 1945 (CFCA, BUR A-4(ES):16).

O'Dwyer advised him not to resign, at least for the moment, but to come to Ireland for a rest. He, O'Dwyer, had already assigned twelve young priests to Bhamo and on 26 October 1945 asked permission from the office of the high commissioner for Burma for them to enter the country. They would replace sick and dead missionaries and those in need of vacation. But an official in the colonial government, Stevenson, was blocking their passage. A frustrated Usher wrote, in April 1946, to Sir Gilbert Laithwaite at the Burma Office in London asking for clarification. The reply cited the policy of the government of Burma: 'Replacements for missionaries who have left Burma may be admitted provided there is nothing against them personally.' However, 'the Government of Burma still desire to be consulted in advance of individual cases'.[30] Permission was granted. The twelve new priests arrived in September 1946 and settled down to language study.

Mission schools remained a high priority for the Columbans in Burma after World War II. In the immediate aftermath of the conflict:

> Greatest difficulties are lack of books, slates and equipment generally, the old trouble of shortage of qualified teachers, and temporary absence of rice for boarders. In spite of all we must try to establish ourselves in a few more strategic points around Bhamo and in whole areas up north.

Perplexed by the shortage of teachers for Roman Catholic schools, and particularly ones qualified to teach English, Usher asked O'Dwyer if priests coming to Burma might somehow 'get a primary teacher's certificate without doing the course', or if the mission college in Ireland could be recognised as a branch of St Patrick's College, Maynooth, to enable it to grant BA degrees.[31] He invited the Columban Sisters to open a school in Myitkyina in 1948.[32] A proposal to bring Irish Christian Brothers failed because the brothers had not enough men.

The colonial government in Burma, which had been paying the salaries of teachers in most mission schools, issued a directive in December 1945 terminating such aid. It was a terrible blow for the struggling mission in Bhamo:

> In our area the scheme is to have a couple of big Government highschools (all Baptist teachers actually). These will be fed by primary schools. Probably the Baptists will turn their primary schools into

---

30. A. Dibdin to Patrick Usher, B/P & G. 1570/46 (CFCA, BUR A-4(ES):17b).
31. Patrick Usher to Michael O'Dwyer, 13 Aug. 1945 (CFCA, BUR A-4(ES):14d).
32. Sister Columcille McCormack, 'And now Burma' in *The Far East* (US ed.), xxxi (July, 1948), p. 20.

Govt. schools (they can be sure of having Baptist teachers in them, so it will not hurt them), and at all points we shall be left out in the cold.[33]

Usher's immediate reaction to the loss of government funding of mission schools was to propose an independent Roman Catholic system, totally supported by the church, and of such a standard as to be able to compete with the government's schools. He estimated that his scheme would cost the society 131,000 rupees, or about £10,000, annually. O'Dwyer put the matter to his council in January 1946 and replied that, 'while I am not in a position to guarantee an annual sum totaling £10,000, I wish to assure you that the Society will back you each year as far as ever it can'. Government policy remained unclear for some months until, in March 1947, Usher went to the head of the education department and found 'the schools policy most satisfactory'. The mission could either keep its schools, and if they came up to the required standard they would be recognised, or it could make its schools state schools. In October 1947, with independence for Burma imminent, he accepted that:

> When political changes will be completed next year our principal schools with be State schools … There is no avoiding this, and anyhow the cost of independent schools would be prohibitive. Catechism can be taught daily in these State schools if we can arrange it. We can have small doctrine schools for younger children …[34]

Independence for Burma
Burma was in turmoil in the years immediately after the world war, with strikes organised by nationalists. Usher, returning from Ireland in March 1947, travelled from Rangoon to Mandalay by train:

> The trip to Mandalay was tiring. There had been two trains derailed and shot-up, with heavy loss of life, so that travel now is by day only, and the journey took thirty-six hours instead of the normal fourteen.

Elections for a constituent assembly were held in April 1947 with Aung San's Anti-Fascist People's Freedom League winning an overwhelming majority. But on 19 July he and six aides were assassinated by gunmen sent by U Saw, a leader of the opposition.[35] The country became independent at midnight on 4 January 1948. Almost immediately several groups rebelled: com-

---

33. Patrick Usher to Michael O'Dwyer, 6 Dec. 1948 (CFCA, BUR A-4(ES):17).
34. Patrick Usher to Jeremiah Dennehy, 4 Oct. 1947 (CFCA, BUR A-4(ES):22a).
35. Aung San Suu Kyi, *Freedom from fear and other writings* (London, 1991), pp 33-5.

munists, Aung San's veterans, and Karens who wanted an autonomous state. Since the Kachins remained loyal to the central government the Bhamo prefecture was peaceful although Columbans suffered from high prices and disruption of the mails. The Columban superior general, Jeremiah Dennehy, proposed coming on visitation in 1949 and Usher warned him:

> At the present time ... there is no great difficulty in reaching Bhamo by the weekly plane from Rangoon. There is no road, rail or river transport. I can see no sign of any improvement in the near future. The drift is towards chaos.... It is pretty hard to get around our parishes now, there being no buses nor petrol.

A priest of the *Société des Missions-Étrangères*, Perrin, was killed near Bassein in March 1950, 'no details received'. However three months later Usher could announce great improvement in the political situation. Land communication was restored between Rangoon and Mandalay, reducing prices a little. Many of the Karen rebels were Baptists which made the government suspicious of other Christians too. One of the outstanding Baptist missionaries in upper Burma was Dr Gordon Seagrave, a lieutenant colonel in the US Army. He was put on trial in 1950:

> The case of Dr Seagrave, Baptist medical missionary at Namhkam, now being tried for assisting rebels, has done a lot of harm, even though it is recognised that the Catholic slate is clean.[36]

An indication of Usher's sensitivity to the weak position of Christians of all denominations in the new Burma, governed by the Buddhist majority, was his reaction in July 1950 to a speech of Prime Minister U Nu praising the Roman Catholic Church. Forwarding a report of the speech from the *New Times of Burma* to Dennehy, he suggested that it be given to the Catholic press in Ireland and Britain. Dennehy rightly thought that the papers would regard the speech as insincere.

Government policy on foreign religious missions
The new government of Burma published a policy concerning foreign religious missions in May 1948, and Usher (Plate 8.3) realised immediately that it posed a serious threat to the future of the Roman Catholic Church and especially of the Columban prefecture in Bhamo. A memorandum outlining the policy quoted the constitution of the Union of Burma guaranteeing freedom of conscience and religion before stating that:

---
36. Patrick Usher to Jeremiah Dennehy, 30 Nov. 1950 (CFCA, BUR A-4(ES):29).

... the Government of Burma ... cannot ignore the political disadvantages of any tendency towards a greater division of religious beliefs among the citizens of the Union.[37]

Burma was in chaos, with Karens and others of the multitude of tribal groups in rebellion, demanding autonomy or even independence. An even greater threat was that local communists might receive support from the forces of Mao Tse-tung who were sweeping to power across the Chinese border. Understandably the government wanted to avoid further divisions. In pursuit of that policy it did 'not desire an extension beyond the present scope of the activities of Foreign Missions in Burma'. Foreign missionaries already working in the country could remain. If they went abroad for a short period of rest and recuperation they could return. But applications for permits for new personnel would be treated like those from any foreigner, meaning that:

... the application will be refused unless exceptional circumstances can be established, e.g. that the Foreign Missionary is required for work for which a Burma citizen of the same religious faith cannot be found.

For a prefecture entrusted with an area more than two thirds the size of Ireland, composed largely of rugged mountains, and with a staff of thirty priests, all foreigners, the government's policy sounded extremely ominous. The memorandum was careful to state that the new regulations applied to all faiths, and would cover Buddhist missions from abroad. Usher's interpretation was that the embattled government did not wish 'to give the Communists any ground for raising the cry that Buddhism is in danger, and non-Catholic missionaries have behaved badly in the Karen business.'[38] In the ten years following on publication of the new policy in 1948 Usher's representative in Rangoon, James Fisher, proffered repeated petitions and arguments in government offices, and was granted permits for just two priests. Dennehy appointed John Walsh, Patrick Conneally and four others to Burma in August 1950, and forwarded their names to Fisher.[39] By 17 October 1951 the other four had been refused entry and 'there is no sign of visas for the two priests (Walsh and Conneally) yet'. The two men finally reached Burma in 1952.

Falière, Bishop in Mandalay, suffered from a lack of men similar to that in Bhamo. Consequently, in 1947 he offered to transfer substantial sections

---

37. Policy of the Union government in regard to foreign religious missions in Burma, 18 May 1948 (CFCA, BUR A-4:13).
38. Patrick Usher to Jeremiah Dennehy, 24 Aug. 1950 (CFCA, BUR A-4(ES):28y).
39. Jeremiah Dennehy to Patrick Usher, 6 Sept. 1950 (CFCA, BUR A-4(ES):28z).

of his vicariate, the Mogok subdivision and the Naga Hill tracts, to the prefecture of Bhamo (Figure 8.1, p. 258).[40] Usher, prior to Burmese independence and the memorandum limiting entry of foreign missionaries, recommended enthusiastically that the Columbans accept the offer. Mogok, a centre for ruby mining, 'from a missionary point of view … is hopeless':

> The point about Mogok is that it is a healthy hill-station with some of the trappings of civilisation – roads, shops, running water and fairly good housing – which would make a badly-needed holiday place for our priests, or at least a good place in which to recuperate after illness or strain.

Among the attractions drawing Usher to Mogok were a school run by the Good Shepherd sisters and a road, 'motorable in the dry season', linking the town to Bhamo. The Naga hills straddled the Burmese-Indian border to the west of Bhamo, and the Burmese portion was nearer to the Columban prefecture than to Mandalay. Usher had 'no hope that they will be missionised for a good many years', but was willing to accept them. He visited Mogok in April 1948 and, in 'ravings'[41] due to a fever, proposed dividing Bhamo into the new prefectures of Myitkyina and Mogok, supporting 'the whole mission by entering the ruby trade'. A startled Dennehy responded by reminding him that only Rome could set up a new prefecture, and disapproving of any dealings in rubies. Falière sent his proposal for transfer of Mogok and the Naga hills to Rome. But the immigration policy of 1948 limiting the entry of new missionaries, and the departure of four Columbans due to ill-health, forced Usher to ask Dennehy if he could halt the process. It was too late for second thoughts. On 14 June 1951 Propaganda decreed that Mogok and the territory inhabited by the Nagas be separated from Mandalay and attached to Bhamo.[42] At Falière's insistence two Columbans, Daniel Treanor and James Feighery, had already begun caring for Mogok on 6 January.

Catechists and finances

The Roman Catholic mission in Bhamo needed increased numbers of catechists (Plate 8.4) and teachers in 1947, especially as many priests were sent home to recuperate after the world war. Their salaries placed a huge financial burden on the prefecture even though they were working for very little.

---

40. Patrick Usher to Jeremiah Dennehy, 28 Dec. 1947 (CFCA, BUR A-4(ES):24).
41. Patrick Usher to Jeremiah Dennehy, 3 June 1948 (CFCA, BUR A-4(ES): 28).
42. *Sacra Congregatio de Propaganda Fide, 'Decretum de finium mutatione'* in *AAS*, xviii (Rome, 1951), p. 809.

Immediately after the world war rice sold at sixteen times the pre-war figure and the priests were 'dressed in pieces of American army clothing, there being no clothes or cloth to be had'. Even when some normality returned, the cost of living was four times that before the war. Usher illustrated his predicament in 1948:

> Only yesterday a catechist to whom we were paying 40 rupees per month took a job behind a counter at 165 rupees per month. The fact is that no one can possibly live on 40 and we cannot pay more unless by retreating and cutting down numbers.[43]

Frustrated by the insoluble financial difficulties of a poor, remote mission he regularly lashed out at Columban superiors, the Pontifical Society for the Propagation of the Faith, and the whole process by which the prefecture was created. He suggested that the Society of St Columban, in accepting new missions, 'should make a fight against being assigned the tail-ends of territories'. When the society was young and unknown it had to take such places, but in future negotiations it should insist on getting a reasonable share of the property of the vicariate or 'a stiff sum in lieu of same'. In the allocation of money by the Society for the Propagation of the Faith, he protested, there were anomalies.[44] His prefecture received $7,000 in 1948, the same as the prefecture of Akyab, staffed by American La Salette Fathers, even though Akyab had 'only 14 priests and few stations' while he had to support thirty-two missionaries, sixteen primary stations, and thirty-seven secondary. Kentung prefecture, with nineteen Italian priests and 'exactly the same kind of country as ours', received $11,000. Even Dennehy, the Columban superior general, did not escape bitter criticism when he deducted £1,000 from the 1948 budget for Bhamo. While Usher acknowledged gratefully that the society 'has been plenty decent to us', he pointed out that it had not given any money for reconstruction, and claimed that the needs of Bhamo were greater than those of other Columban missions:

> ... we were battered flat and looted bare, without a trousers, a cup, a plate, a pot, a lamp, a book, a thing. As for undestroyed buildings of wood, you know what happens them in the tropics if they are 4 years unoccupied and neglected.[45]

---

43. Patrick Usher to Jeremiah Dennehy, 8 Mar. 1948 (CFCA, BUR A-4(ES):24f).
44. Patrick Usher to Jeremiah Dennehy, 30 Aug. 1949 (CFCA, BUR A-4(ES):28j).
45. Patrick Usher to Jeremiah Dennehy, 8 Apr. 1948 (CFCA, BUR A-4(ES):26).

Such an outburst would be followed by an apology. Despite its straitened circumstances the prefecture increased the number of catechists from thirty in 1947 to fifty-four in 1954. Yet the apostolic delegate, Martin Lucas, on a visit to Bhamo in 1955 spoke 'of getting funds for a half-dozen high-grade catechists for us to ease the strain on the priests'.

Emphasis on catechetical instruction in Bhamo in the years after World War II gave rise to the danger that religion would be seen as purely cerebral, a matter of answering the questions of the catechist or priest. To develop the affective and missionary aspects of Christian practice, the Columbans introduced the Confraternity of the Sacred Heart, the family rosary, and the Legion of Mary in 1950. The confraternity, using a symbol of the heart of Christ burning with love for people and pierced by a lance for their sins, encouraged personal and family devotion to him. Most Roman Catholic houses had pictures of the Sacred Heart and of the Virgin Mary (Plate 8.5) as well as a crucifix. Parents, by having their family pray the rosary together, influenced the faith of their children. Members of the legion strengthened their own Christian life and reached out as apostles to others. The missionaries hoped that these practices would make catechumens 'more anxious to participate in the full Catholic life and ... therefore be more eager for instruction', and that in a 'truly Catholic home ... children may grow up in goodness and innocence, among whom, here and there, a vocation (to the priesthood or religious life) may arise'.

Sisters

Several communities of sisters, members of the Franciscan Missionaries of Mary, carried out valuable work in the Bhamo mission. Invited to Mandalay from France in 1897 the congregation took over an orphanage, school and dispensary in Hkudung, near Bhamo, in 1923. There was already a novitiate in Bhamo when the first Columbans arrived in 1936 and a total of twenty-five sisters in the mission. Usher judged that:

> The sisters seem almost as necessary as the priests for work among girls and infants. These Franciscans seem particularly suitable, because they run their convents with a few European and several native sisters.[46]

A visitor to Hkudung in 1953 found 'four Kachin sisters, two Spaniards, one Burmese, one Austrian, and one English', the Austrian being 'a daughter of a German Field Marshal in the first world war'. Some of the Burmese sisters were descendants of the Christian captives settled in villages around

---

46. Patrick Usher to Michael O'Dwyer, 25 Nov. 1936 (CFCA, BUR A-4:2b).

Mandalay in the sixteenth century. Four sisters moved to Nalaing, a town in a Shan area, in 1938 where they opened a school and dispensary. All the foreign sisters were interned in 1942, but after the war re-opened the dispensary despite a critical shortage of medicines. However, their parish priest, James Foley, on a visit to an American supply base at Shingbwiyang in the Hukaung Valley, met an army doctor who gave him a large consignment of 'surplus army drugs'. Of particular value for Nalaing were ampoules of vitamin B-1, used to treat beriberi. The Shans preferred their rice highly polished, a process which removed the vitamin B, making them prone to beriberi. Within a short time the dispensary at Nalaing was attracting people 'from distances of up to eighty kilometres, and in some cases from further away' and treating 25,000 patients annually.[47]

Five Missionary Sisters of St Columban arrived in Rangoon on 6 June 1947, and flew to Myitkyina in a British army plane. Two other sisters joined them, from China and the Philippines. Despite the best efforts of the Columban fathers to prepare a convent the sisters were discouraged with the small structure, the first storey of brick, the upper of bamboo covered with plaster, and the roof of thatch. To add to their discomfort they arrived just at the beginning of the rainy season which Columcille McCormack judged to be worse than those she had experienced in China or the Philippines. The sisters couldn't get their clothes dried and their white habits were being destroyed with mildew. Their new school constructed of bamboo and thatch opened on 1 July with over 120 pupils, Burmans, Indians, Anglo-Indians, Tamils, Chinese, and some Kachins:

> Each sister and a lay teacher teach two grades. Sister takes one class for the subjects that are taught through the medium of English while the teacher takes the other for the subjects in Burmese. At the end of the period they change classes.[48]

After school three sisters studied Kachin and the others Burmese to enable them to deal with the local people. The priests in the mission stations were 'most anxious for us to open dispensaries and schools in these places' (Plate 8.6). But the government's policy restricting the immigration of foreign missionaries put an end to that plan. Two sisters had to return to Ireland because of ill-health and one, Celestine Kelly, died of cerebral malaria in 1954.[49]

---

47. Lawrence McMahon, 'The golden needle' in *The Far East*, xliii (Sept. 1960), p. 10.
48. Sister Gabriel O'Mahony, 'Cold in the sky' in *The Far East* (US ed.), xxxvii (Apr. 1954), p. 14.
49. Fischer, *Mission in Burma*, p. 135.

Printing

The Columban mission in Bhamo acquired a small printing press in 1950, and quickly saw it as a way to compensate for the shortage of priests. Members of the *Société des Missions-Étrangères* left the Columbans a legacy of Roman Catholic literature including a life of Christ, a catechism, and a combined prayer book and hymnal. The two catechisms written by Bernard Way during internment in Mandalay were printed in Calcutta. Neither printers nor proofreaders understood Kachin and errors were many. A new, larger catechism in Kachin was produced on the hand-operated press in Bhamo. But Way, stationed in the parish of Tanghpre, with thirty-five villages scattered over a mountainous area measuring 110 kilometres by 70, needed to contact his flock regularly:

> I dream of a newspaper that they can read in their homes and aloud to the others on Sunday. You see, nowadays even in the hills, there is always someone who knows how to read Kachin. The hill schools teach Kachin up to the fourth grade … so someone in the village can read the message on Sundays.

Way began producing a monthly magazine, the *Jinghpaw Kasa* (Kachin Messenger), at first using a typewriter and mimeographing machine before acquiring a tiny press.[50] Readers of *The Far East* donated funds for more sophisticated equipment until Way employed educated Kachins to translate the bible and began printing it book by book. In this the Columbans were learning from the American Baptist missionaries who, in the nineteenth century, attempted to produce Kachin literature using the Burmese alphabet. But they found it difficult to express the correct pronunciation of some words. Instead Dr Ola Hanson used the Roman alphabet to compile a Kachin-English dictionary before providing a Kachin hymnal and bible. His translation of the bible was accepted by the government in 1895, and Columban priests used it, in a covert manner, because of its beautiful use of the Kachin language and to improve their preaching and catechesis.[51]

Kachin priests and bishop

A missionary enterprise is incomplete as long as it depends on foreign leadership. The superiors of the Franciscan sisters in Bhamo in 1953 were still French and German, but they were training young Kachin women to take

---

50. Bernard Way, 'Kachin Messenger' in *The Far East* (US ed.), xl (May, 1957), p. 13.
51. Interview by author with Owen O'Leary of St Columban's, Navan, Co Meath (1 Mar. 2007).

their place. Finding men who could be ordained as priests was a slower process, but in 1952 Usher reported:

> The most important beginning made during the year was the opening of a preparatory seminary at Mogok … The first batch of candidates are six in number, all of them from among the best Catholic families we have. A small house suffices for them at present, and a priest and lay-teacher take care of their instruction.[52]

The boys selected for the school in Mogok (Plate 8.7) came from the families of teachers and catechists. Most Kachin children 'were allowed to grow up with practically no supervision whatsoever' but those educated in Mogok were 'accustomed to a measure of obedience and discipline'. After a year spent mainly in improving their Burmese and English, the boys went to the minor seminary at Maymyo in the diocese of Mandalay. One of that first group, Paul Grawng, on completion of his studies in Maymyo in 1958 entered the major seminary in Rangoon for a further seven years. He was the first Kachin Roman Catholic priest when he was ordained in 1965. In 1976 he was appointed Bishop of Myitkyina.[53] Among those present at his installation were the ten remaining Columbans and ten young Kachin priests. As more local priests were ordained to take their place the aging Columbans withdrew from Burma, the last three leaving in 1979. Paul Grawng became Archbishop of Mandalay in 2003.

Conclusions

The Columbans in Burma followed the Roman model of mission in their aims and in the means used to achieve them. Their goal was to create a diocese complete with a local bishop and priests, who could bring the word of God and the sacraments to their own people, and their dream was that all would become Roman Catholics. To reach that objective they set up central stations, each with its ring of secondary stations. All centred on the priest, assisted by catechists, teachers, and sisters.

Much of the resources of the mission was spent in catechetical instruction. The colonial government encouraged mission schools; a strong Baptist mission had long been using education to seek converts; and the people were scattered in small villages over a large mountainous region, all leading the Columbans to place a huge emphasis on schools. Training of catechists was a

---

52. Patrick Usher, Annual returns for the year ended 30 June 1952 (CFCA, BUR A-4(ES):30).
53. Interview with Paul Grawng, 23 Sept. 1991 (CFCA, Oral History Archive).

priority of equal importance. And the shortage of personnel led priests to supplement live instruction with the printed word.

Sisters, like catechists and teachers, were auxiliaries of the priest, 'almost as necessary' as him for certain tasks. There was no recognition that the sisters might have their own missionary role, even though the dispensary in Nalaing attracted thousands of every creed from all over northern Burma.

Both the Baptist and the Roman Catholic missions aimed at converting the Burmese, even the members of other Christian churches. Buddhists were notoriously difficult to change, and it was thought that animists like the Kachins would be an easier target. Today 36.4% of the people of the Kachin state are Christian, a figure which vindicates that judgement.[54] But anecdotal evidence suggests that many have strong Christian faith together with beliefs in *nats* who can cause sickness or a poor harvest, just as the Irish in the later nineteenth century, Christian for hundreds of years, used holy water and the sign of the cross to protect cows from the 'Little People'. Columbans learned to respect the Buddhists, but did not reflect on the deeper meaning of their loyalty to their own faith.

The Baptist mission in northern Burma reached Bhamo in 1878 and was well entrenched by the time the Columbans arrived. It aroused the envy and emulation of Roman Catholic missionaries. Some Baptists, in positions of power in local or national government, used their dominance to obstruct Columban schools or even immigration permits for new priests. Usually Usher merely hints at such interference, hesitating to speak ill of others, and sometimes balancing news of harm done by a Baptist with the account of the good action of another. But ecumenism between Roman Catholics and Protestants was still in the future.

Lack of resources was a constant theme in Columban correspondence. There were too few priests, not enough trained catechists and teachers, and money was always in short supply. One positive result was that there was no material advantage in becoming a Roman Catholic, and when tested by the Japanese occupation the converts remained faithful.

The emphasis on schools eventually produced a group of boys who were suitable for seminary training, and before they left Burma in 1979 the last surviving Columbans saw, not a completely Roman Catholic Kachin state, but a local church equipped with its own bishop, priests, sisters, and catechists, and largely able to support itself.

---

54. 'Kachin State' at Kachin State, Northern Myanmar (http://www.katchinstate.com) (13 Feb. 2006).

Conclusion

The founders of the Columban Fathers envisaged, in 1916, an Irish vicariate in China, with a mission college in Ireland training priests for the vicariate, and a society binding the two together and enlisting the support of Irish Roman Catholics everywhere. Priests of the society would labour to convert the Chinese, and to set up a strong, indigenous Roman Catholic Church, led eventually by Chinese bishops and staffed by Chinese priests, brothers and nuns. Inspiring all, founders, volunteers, and supporters, was a hunger for the eternal salvation of the people of China, often presented in negative terms as a picture of millions seen as rotting in sin and despair in this life and damned forever in the next.

Indigenous church

The concern of missionaries of all denominations to establish indigenous churches, each with its own native leaders, is self-evident. From the constitutions of the Roman Catholic *Société des Missions-Étrangéres*, founded in 1658, to the Congregationalist Rufus Anderson, senior secretary of the American Board of Commissioners for Foreign Missions (1832-66), missionary thinkers appealed to the experience of the primitive church in arguing for 'a native ministry' to lead indigenous churches. Edward J. Galvin and John Blowick were also guided by the bible, as summarised in the Great Commission in Matthew 28:19, to 'make disciples of all nations, baptise them ... teach them'. But their image of a highly structured, institutional church owed more to their experience of their home dioceses, and to the textbooks studied in the seminary than to the house churches of the New Testament. In verbalising their plans, they borrowed from the constitutions of the *Société des Missions-Étrangéres*, and from the instructions which Propaganda gave to the first vicars apostolic of that society in 1659. Local clergy were so essential if the Roman Catholic faith was to take root that Propaganda permitted the ordination of Chinese priests who did not understand Latin, provided they could read 'the canon of the Mass and the formulae of the sacraments'. Yet two and a half centuries later, in 1919, Benedict XV complained that in countries, like China, where the church had been established for centuries, there was no indigenous clergy except of a lower class.

The early Columbans seem to have accepted the 'gradualist' approach of other European missionaries, in which a church must have a substantial number of members before it could produce its own ministers. 'Old Christianities', villages in China and Korea that had been Roman Catholic for several generations, were seen as the most likely source of vocations to the priesthood. Most converts came from the poorer classes, where the majority were practically illiterate. Suitable candidates for the priesthood were few and needed lengthy education. A preparatory seminary was opened in Burma in 1952 and the boys selected were from the families of teachers and catechists where they had experienced obedience and discipline. Presbyterian missionaries in Korea in 1903 organised theological training for local pastors on 'a three-months-a year schedule for five years, with assigned reading and practical ministerial experience for the other nine months' and ordained the first class of seven in 1907. But Roman Catholic seminarians, in Asia as elsewhere, had a much longer struggle with Latin, scholastic philosophy, theology and canon law. Two students who entered the junior seminary in Hanyang in 1928 were ordained in Rome in 1942. For fourteen years they experienced a training programme like that proposed by Rufus Anderson a century earlier, where they would be 'boarded in the mission, be kept separate from heathenism, under Christian superintendence night and day'.[1] The programme of studies was so long, and so alienating, that an Irish bishop in the Philippines in 1965, having listened to the first sermon of a young Filipino priest trained in a similar regime, advised him that he needed to re-learn his own language. Textbooks in Latin, the liturgy in Latin, church meetings conducted in English or French, all conspired to prevent an Asian priest from reaching the level of linguistic and other competences where he could lead a vicariate in which some of his priests were Europeans. Yet, despite such a long, European-style training programme, and the disruption caused by the society's financial problems and by wars, the Columbans left the nucleus of a local clergy in each mission.

The Roman model
Propaganda developed, as the means for creating an indigenous church, a complete system of prefectures and vicariates, each divided into mission stations, equipped with churches, schools and clinics, and served by priests, sisters, teachers and catechists. This 'Roman paradigm' for mission was the fruit of long experience, and a valuable guide for new missionaries. The methods

---

1. Wilbert R. Shenk, 'The origins and evolution of the three-selfs in relation to China' in the *International Bulletin of Missionary Research*, xiv (New Haven, Jan. 1990), p. 29.

were sanctioned by the leaders of the church; the emphasis on categories and tangible, measurable results was reinforced by the detailed forms for the annual and quinquennial reports which the superior of each mission had to submit to Propaganda. However, this approach was open to the criticism levelled by Roland Allen in 1912 at the methods used by Protestant missionaries, of being exotic, dependent, and of looking remarkably the same in very different cultures.[2] While Galvin's insistence on more intensive methods, with more priests, sisters, catechists and parish schools providing better religious instruction became a characteristic of Columbans in all missions, they generally followed the 'Roman' model. Whether in Confucian-Buddhist countries like China and Korea, the predominantly Roman Catholic Philippines, or in the animist hill country of Burma, they used not only the same bible and sacraments but everywhere expressed their doctrines in similar concepts, and organised their missions along very similar lines. In common with all Christians, Roman Catholic missionaries believed that the bible was the word of God. They accepted that Christ instituted all seven sacraments. The divine origins of bible and sacraments made them sacrosanct, but the Greek concepts of theology, and church structures such as dioceses and vicariates were human inventions which could be replaced in dialogue with the ideas and cultures of Asia. Only occasionally did Columbans, individually or in groups, question parts of the 'Roman' programme, as the priests in Hanyang did in 1927 in doubting the value of schools for converting the Chinese. Innovations, such as the introduction of the Legion of Mary in 1937, were rare. The use of Latin in the liturgy was symbolic of the exotic, European nature of the Roman model, which made easier the work of the foreigner missionary but created barriers for the Asian people.

Relations with Rome
The Congregation for the Propagation of the Faith, commonly called Propaganda, was:

> in charge of missions for the preaching of the Gospel and Catholic doctrine, stations and changes the necessary ministers, and has the power to deal with, do, and pursue to the end everything necessary or opportune for this purpose.

But, even though seminary textbooks described the church as 'a monarchical society', Roman officials could not behave in a purely dictatorial man-

---

2. Roland Allen, *Missionary methods: St. Paul's or ours?* (London, 1930), quoted in Shenk, ibid., p. 30.

ner. In canon law it belonged 'exclusively to the supreme ecclesiastical authority', the Pope and his curia, to erect or divide vicariates. Yet this study has shown that the initiative for such division might come from a nuncio, the bishop of the parent vicariate, or the superior of a missionary society. The process of division involved consultation with the cardinals of Propaganda, the nuncio, the vicar apostolic, and the heads of the religious orders concerned. Bishops in the missions, especially those belonging to long-established religious orders, were often reluctant to lose part of their territory, and had power to delay and obstruct the wishes of Rome. Anglican missionary societies in India in 1903 showed similar possessiveness towards mission fields they had long occupied.

The Vatican exercised its authority in many ways. Encyclical letters and directives from the Pope were the most authoritative, yet missionaries sometimes judged, in matters such as the promotion of indigenous priests, that the instructions were not relevant to the situation in the field. Plenary councils, convened by the bishops of several ecclesiastical provinces, and convoked by the Pope, applied canon law and papal directives to the local situation. Papal nuncios encouraged and corrected missionary leaders. The most systematic form of direction was the series of questions drafted by Propaganda in 1877 and updated in 1922 for the reports demanded by canon law from vicars and prefects apostolic. Within the parameters set by the 'Roman' model, Columbans in each mission in Asia consistently searched for the most effective ways of doing mission. Just as George Sherwood Eddy, an American Congregationalist in India, used 'lasting conversions' as a measure of his success, Roman Catholics discriminated among the statistics sent annually to Rome, judging some to be better indicators of growth than others. Adult baptisms were regarded as more significant than those of children or of people in danger of death; and the number of '*inconfessi*', those who failed to confess their sins at least once a year, was a warning that some converts were not yet fully committed. But the most reliable evidence for the success of a mission, the members who remained faithful in time of persecution, could never be recorded in statistical form.

Religious instruction
Missionaries, whether Roman Catholic or Protestant, placed great emphasis on preaching and instruction. But where Protestants hastened to translate the bible into the local language, Roman Catholics made instruction in the catechism the first priority. In catechesis, memorisation seems to have been regarded as more important than comprehension, even in the missionaries'

home church. The catechism covered doctrines, moral living, worship and prayer, and it was expected that there would be a sort of dialectic among these four in the gradual conversion of the new Catholic. Ideally the convert lived in a Catholic village; a catechist continued weekly instruction, led a service, and monitored the lives of his flock; religious symbols had places of honour in the little churches and individual homes, whether texts from the emperor K'ang-hsi in China or pictures of the Sacred Heart and Our Lady in the Philippines and Burma; and the priest visited regularly, checking on progress and bringing the sacraments. Parish schools and adult catechumenates were the most common vehicles of instruction. In Korea, with a secular public school system, there was a parish-based catechetical programme with very strict testing, and in the colleges and universities in the Philippines members of Student Catholic Action attempted to meet the need.

Women
The special needs of women in rural China were made obvious to Galvin by his experience in Hangchow in 1914 and in Hanyang in 1921. Women were generally housebound and illiterate, making it difficult for them to attend religious instruction in a mission station and self-study impossible. In times of famine a father might sell his daughter into prostitution. Yet it was widely recognised that a well-instructed Christian wife and mother had a powerful influence on the whole family. Columbans, especially in China, the Philippines and Burma, needed religious sisters to educate women and to manage parish schools. The Sisters of Loretto at the Foot of the Cross from America joined the mission in Hanyang in 1923; Blowick and Frances Moloney in Ireland founded the Missionary Sisters of St Columban in 1922; and Galvin set up a Chinese congregation, the Sisters of St Mary, in 1939. Sisters from many congregations played vital roles in each mission opened by the Columbans in Asia, running schools and clinics, instructing converts, visiting the sick, helping refugees, and baptising those in danger of death. Inevitably, as men of their time, the priests in 1920, and later, were paternalistic in their dealings with sisters. Blowick made key decisions about the founding of the Columban Sisters without even consulting Frances Moloney, and the priests in China considered that 'the sisters do not require any very special training or qualifications beyond an ordinary National School education'. That surely indicated that they were expected to be subservient to the pastor. While sisters were consulted, generally but not always, about their work or their safety, important decisions were regularly made by the male leaders of the mission, or by British or American consuls. The American

Loretto sisters, according to Galvin, were 'inclined to think for themselves' but even they on occasion had to resort to female wiles to get their way. Sent to Shanghai as refugees in 1927, but wishing to return to Hanyang for the ordination of Galvin as bishop, the Loretto sisters used their tears to change the heart of Celso Costantini, the apostolic delegate. They reached Hanyang in time. Yet, like the majority of Protestant women missionaries, they seem to have accepted the 'subsidiary roles' which have 'historically been left to women'.[3]

Relations with Protestants
Like Roman Catholic missionaries everywhere prior to Vatican II, Columbans in Asia were trained to see Protestants as competitors. The founders in 1919-1920 used the large number of Protestant schools in China as an argument to persuade Propaganda to grant the society a mission in Hupeh. Editorials in *The Far East* described the resources, in personnel and money, available to Protestant missionaries to encourage similar generosity among Roman Catholics. However, in China and Korea, where Christians of all denominations were a tiny minority, there was little contact or friction between the churches. While he explored the civil prefecture of Anlu in 1921, Galvin admired the work of Wesleyan Methodists, Mr and Dr Rowley, and valued their advice. Prejudices surfaced when missionaries of different churches entered into competition as happened when the Irish Christian Brothers in Hanyang in 1923 explored the possibility of opening a college in Changsha, Hunan province, because 'we knew that it was one of the most important Protestant strongholds in China'. Where members of one church were in positions of civil power, and were seen to abuse that power to obstruct the work of another denomination, there was great anger. Protestant officials in the educational departments in the Philippines and Burma were accused of hindering Roman Catholic religious instruction or even the opening of Catholic schools. But in times of danger, missionaries from different churches offered sanctuary to each other. Respect grew in situations which allowed for mutual acquaintance, especially when working together to help refugees such as the victims of the great flood of central China in 1931 or those fleeing from the Sino-Japanese war in 1937. Men and women thrown together in suffering on a death march in northern Korea in 1950 learned to admire the human and Christian qualities of those of other churches.

---

3. Rose Uchem, 'Gender inequality as an enduring obstacle to mission' in *Sedos Bulletin 2006*, xxxviii (Rome, Sept/Oct. 2006), p. 270.

Relations with the colonial powers
Columbans appear to have experienced a similar change of attitude in their relations with the colonial powers in Asia 1920-50. The first group to arrive in Hanyang in 1920 wished to distance themselves from British officials knowing how Chinese resented colonial control of their ports and trade. Most, those from Ireland, were consciously nationalist in outlook. But their passports were British and to buy property the mission, reluctantly, had to accept the help of the British consul in Hankow. During times of conflict, especially World War II, the Irish missionaries asserted that they were neutrals. However, when two priests, Patrick Laffan and James Linehan, were taken prisoner by communists and in danger of death in Hanyang in 1930, Galvin accepted the help of W. Russell Brown, the British consul in Hankow, who arranged that *HMS Mantis*, a gunboat of the Royal Navy, carry Galvin and a ransom to rescue the two captives. In the afterglow of their liberation relations between missionaries and seamen improved to the extent that Henry Howden, captain of *HMS Mantis*, sent a dispatch to his admiral, 'The church drank the navy under the table.' Columbans in Nancheng and in Burma assisted allied soldiers and airmen during World War II. Thomas Quinlan in Korea in 1948 did not hesitate to accept assistance from the American army in building a cathedral. Priests served as chaplains in the allied forces during World War II and the Korean war. Even if the missionaries had kept their distance absolutely from colonial officials and soldiers inevitably the people of Asia would have seen them all as Western 'foreign devils'. The penalty for the identification of Christians with the western powers occupying many places in China was the hatred shown in events from the Boxer uprising of 1900 to the communist victory in 1949.

Attitudes to Asian cultures and religions
With very few exceptions, missionaries in Asia in the early twentieth century shared 'the trite negative ideas that still remained prevalent in the West about the worth or lack of worth of the other religious traditions'. Protestant missionaries regarded the cultures they encountered as 'in no sense religiously neutral – rather they were under the control of the Evil One'.[4] Roman Catholic bishops, all foreigners, meeting in the first Chinese plenary council in 1924, used conflicting language in their instructions on dealing with Confucianism, Buddhism and Taoism. Missionaries should refute and condemn such 'idolatrous worship and superstitions', but avoid 'useless disput-

---

4. Brian Stanley, *The Bible and the flag, Protestant missions and British imperialism in the nineteenth and twentieth centuries* (Leicester, 1990), p. 161.

ations', and follow the prudent norm of St Paul, 'to do the truth in love'. Columbans tended to be ultramontane in their obedience to the Pope, Benedict XV, who described other religions as 'the cruel slavery of demons'. Their narrow missiological education contained little cultural input beyond Irish nationalist traditions. Most were over-worked, with little time, inclination, or opportunity to follow the example of the Vincentian priest, Vincent Lebbe, who in 1911 began to engage with the Chinese classics and enter discussions with educated Chinese people. Instead they appear to have employed enthusiastically the common missionary practice of tearing down Chinese tablets honouring 'Buddha or the shades of their ancestors', or replacing the 'idol' of a Taoist priest. For Columbans in China in 1924 the words 'pagan' and 'heathen' and the name of Buddha were linked with terms such as 'diabolical' and 'darkness'. A quarter of a century later in Burma a seasoned missionary described the worship of *nats* as devil worship. Columbans used the same language to describe communism in China in 1952, calling it 'diabolical' and stating that 'Satan's objective [was] atheistic communism'. Churches had yet to discover that a person 'does not possess the truth in a perfect and total way but can walk together with others towards that goal'.[5]

Buddhists, Muslims, and Hindus rarely became Christian. Missionaries found that most converts came from the poorer, less educated classes in China, the untouchable and low-caste groups in India and minority tribes such as the Karens and Kachins in Burma. Buddhists, for example, convinced of the truth of their own faith, and despising Christianity as a foreign religion, were supported by the communal celebrations of their village, and even by the memory of their ancestors. Catholics spoke of the conversion of a Buddhist as almost miraculous. The entry of someone from the mandarin class was just as rare. A French Jesuit, A. Gaspement, trying to explain why, in 1931 after 300 years of preaching, China had not been converted claimed that 'An immense weight lies on the understanding of our Chinese', a weight rooted in original sin, and the sins of pride and attachment to the good things of the earth.[6] Columbans, like other missionaries, used education and medicine to reach those of other faiths. Parish schools taught religious doctrine to children and through them reached the parents, with the result that whole families became Roman Catholic. People approached the church with

---

5. Secretariat for non-Christians, 'The attitude of the church towards the followers of other religions: reflections and orientations on dialogue and mission' in the *IBMR*, ix (Ventnor, NJ, Oct. 1985), p. 189.
6. A. Gaspement, in *Les Missions Catholiques* (Jan/Feb. 1931), quoted in Jean Comby, *How to understand the history of Christian mission* (London, 1996), p. 152.

a variety of motives, many of them quite worldly such as protection by association with the foreign missionary, or the hope of financial assistance in time of famine. Priests used the catechumenate, a period of instruction and of Christian living under the eye of a village catechist, to help those preparing for baptism to become convinced believers. Aware that isolated Catholics would find it difficult to resist the pressures of a 'pagan' environment, missionaries preferred that a whole family, or even a whole village, enter the church together. Communal ceremonies, the burning of the 'gods and ancestral tablets' to be replaced by Christian symbols, were used to strengthen the resolve of the new Roman Catholics. The attempt by missionaries to replace the previous Buddhist or Confucian milieu of the village with a Christian one shows that they were prepared to learn from the local culture. But they would have been startled by the statement of the Second Vatican Council that, 'The Catholic Church rejects nothing which is true and holy in these religions. She looks with sincere respect upon those ways of conduct and of life, those rules and teachings which … often reflect a ray of that Truth which enlightens all men'.[7]

An alternative model?
Many questions remain which go beyond the scope of historical investigation. Would the church have been better served by an Asian model of mission? Could students for the priesthood have been trained in a shorter, vernacular programme? Was it wise to scatter priests in isolated parishes or should they have lived together as Protestant missionaries did? Could the Roman Catholic Church have been more flexible in relation to the Three-Self movement in China or was the suffering of Chinese Catholics necessary to keep the value of unity with the Pope alive in the hierarchy in China? While the 'Roman paradigm' for church and mission was in some ways a helpful guide for missionaries it seems undeniable that it was also a straitjacket, stifling local initiatives. The Pope, Pius XI, in 1931 advised those in power in the state to respect the role of 'the various subsidiary organisations' in civil society.[8] Had the same principle operated within the Roman Catholic Church the council of bishops meeting in Shanghai in 1924 might have devised methods of evangelisation and for the formation of local priests more suited to the reality of China. That would have demanded that the council fathers, predominantly European, respect the advice given to the vicars apos-

---

7. '*Nostra aetate*' in Walter M. Abbott (ed.), *The documents of Vatican II* (6th printing, London, 1972), p. 662.
8. Pius XI, '*Quadragesimo anno*', in *AAS*, xxiii (Rome, 1931), p. 203.

tolic of *La Société des Missions-Étrangères* by Propaganda in 1659, not to import foreign customs to China.[9] Such a colossal transformation of cultural values would have necessitated years of slow, patient experimentation and reflection, similar to the work done by Matteo Ricci and the Jesuits in the sixteenth and seventeenth centuries, or the liturgical, biblical and patristic studies that prepared the way for Vatican II in the twentieth. The experience of Columbans, as outlined in this thesis, suggests that the control exercised by Propaganda and its agents was a major obstacle to such efforts and change.

Courage and faith
The most striking quality of the missionaries, male and female, in each territory assigned to the Columbans, was their courage. It must have been daunting, even in normal times, to leave home, to immerse oneself in the masses of an Asian country, to wrestle with a strange language and culture, and to undertake extremely arduous journeys and labours. Wars, prison, and bandits made the situation even worse. Between 1929 and 1950 seventeen Columbans were killed in China, the Philippines, Korea and Burma. Others were kidnapped by bandits, beaten by mobs, imprisoned or interned. Many had to flee for their lives, and all endured protracted danger and the most appalling fear. Yet their instinct was to remain with their flocks or, when ordered to go to a safer place, to return as soon as possible. Some, their nerves shattered by what they had suffered, asked to be re-assigned to less hazardous posts, although there were dangers in every Columban mission.

Priests and sisters were sustained by their faith, and sometimes by makeshift symbols. A priest in a Chinese gaol in 1953 offered Mass using steamed bread and juice squeezed from grapes. Missionary prisoners in Korea in 1950 shared a breviary – the prayer book used by priests, consisting of prayers, psalms, readings from the bible and the early church fathers – hidden by a French priest and a New Testament belonging to a Methodist missionary. Others prayed the rosary or sang hymns. The habitual practice of mental prayer, the celebration of Mass, visits to the Blessed Sacrament, the rosary, and the recitation of the canonical hours became so central to their lives that even when deprived of these devotions in prison they attempted to duplicate them.

The Missionary Society of St Columban set out to build up the indigenous church in China, and later in other Asian countries. In 2007 the church in China is alive but divided. Priests, sisters, and lay people in Hanyang and

---

9. *Sacra Congregatio de Propaganda Fide*, 'Hoc in primis' in *Collectanea S. Congregationis de Propaganda Fide* (2 vols, Rome, 1907), i, pp 42-3.

Nancheng who survived the trials of the Mao Tse-tung era have gathered young disciples. Many, old and young, seem keen to claim legitimacy through their links with Columbans who served there. Even in Huchow, where members of the society worked for just seven years, they are remembered with affection. Elsewhere in Asia there are vigorous churches ruled by local bishops and staffed mainly by local clergy in the areas that were predominantly or largely in the care of Columbans prior to 1954, including twelve dioceses in the Philippines, four in Korea, and two in Burma. Within those churches many attribute their faith to a Columban parish priest or university chaplain. Men and women who have reached high positions in their professions, in the church, the law, education, and government, remember with gratitude the Columban who founded their local school, or the sisters and other teachers who worked there. Despite the human limitations of its members and the calamities of the first half of the twentieth century, it is fair to state that the society made a huge contribution to the Roman Catholic Church in Asia.

Appendices

1. Approval of the Irish bishops for a mission house for China	301
2. Oath of aggregation	302
3. Glossary of Chinese and Korean names	303
4. Missions not accepted	305
5. Structures of the society	308
6. Significant dates	309
7. *Prospectus Status Missionis* of the prefecture of Ch'unch'on 1950-51	310

APPENDIX 1

Proposal to Establish a Mission House for the Training of Irish Priests as Missionaries for China [1]

The Cardinal, Archbishops and Bishops of Ireland, assembled in general meeting, have received with much satisfaction a memorial signed by representative priests from several parts of Ireland asking for the approval and blessing of the Bishops on the project of establishing a Mission House or College in Ireland for the training of Irish priests who are prepared to devote their lives to the propagation of the Catholic Faith in China.

The memorialists state a fact which is already widely known, that China presents a fruitful soil for the labours of the missionary priest.

A beginning has already been made with notable success by a few Irish priests who set out a few years ago as missionaries to China. Encouraged by this experience, a number of young, zealous Irish priests, the memorialists state, are ready and anxious to give themselves to this apostolic work, and only await the approval and encouragement of the Bishops. But a Mission House or College for the training of those priests in their special work is a first necessity.

The Bishops, having given careful consideration to this important memorial, joyfully approve and bless the project and earnestly commend to the generous help and support of the faithful the establishment of this Mission House for the training of Irish missionaries for China, who, in a spirit worthy of our missionary race, offer their lives for the propagation of the Faith in a pagan country.

    MICHAEL CARDINAL LOGUE, Chairman
    ROBERT, Bishop of Cloyne) Secretaries
    DENIS, Bishop of Ross   )

---

1. *Irish Times*, 11 Oct. 1916.

APPENDIX 2

The Formula of Oath for Final Aggregation

Ego ... plenam habens notitiam finis quem sibi proponit Societas Sancti Columbani pro Missionibus apud Sinenses, ipsius Constitutionibus me sponte subiicio, easque diligenter observare promitto. Spondeo et iuro quod in ista Societate perpetuo permanebo, et in ea sub Superiorum dependentia in officio missioneve quae mihi commissa fuerit laborem meum et operam impendam. Spondeo quoque et iuro quod in omnem regionem vel locum quo Superior generalis me miserit sine mora proficiscar; et quod iussis mandatisque a Superioribus secundum Constitutiones datis fideliter obediam. Sic me Deus adiuvet et haec Sancta Dei Evangelia.[2]

I ... having full knowledge of the purpose of the Society of St Columban for Missions to the Chinese, do voluntarily submit myself to its Constitutions, and I promise to observe them faithfully. I promise and swear that I will remain in the Society permanently, and in it under the authority of the Superiors I will serve in any office or mission committed to me. I also promise and swear that I will proceed without delay to any place where the Superior General may send me; and that I will obey faithfully any orders given me by the Superiors in accordance with the Constitutions. So help me God and these Holy Gospels.

---

2. *Constitutiones Societatis Sancti Columbani pro Missionibus apud Sinenses* (Dublin, 1932), no. 14.

APPENDIX 3

Chinese and Korean names

A variety of methods for the romanisation of Chinese names appears in the sources, a French system in documents from the Vatican or French missionaries and Wade-Giles (1859)[3] for English ones prior to 1958. In that year the government of the People's Republic of China approved the use of Pinyin. Since Columbans used the Wade-Giles this book does too.

Columban Usage	*Pinyin Romanisation*
Chang Tang Kow	Changnangkou
Chekiang	Zhejiang
Ch'ing	Qing
Chi Wu Tai	Qi Wu Tai
Fukien	Fujian
Hangchow	Hangzhou
Hankow	Hankou
Hengtsun	Hongcun
Huchow	Huzhou
Hupeh	Hubei
Hwang Kia Shan	Huang Jia Shan
K'ang-hsi	Kangxi
Kiangsi	Jiangxi
Kiukiang	Jiujiang
Kuomintang	Guomindang
Kwangchang	Guangchang
Kwangtung	Guangdong
Kweichow	Guizhou
Lichwan	Lichuan
Nanzin	Nanxun
Ningpo	Ningbo
Sientaocher	Xiantao
Shinti	Xin Di
Siaoshi	Xiaoshi
Sinkadhay	Shen-Jia-De
Songlin	Shuanglin
Sung-shih	Songshi
Szechwan	Sichuan
Tientsin	Tianjin
Yokow	Yuekou
Yuin Lung Ho	Yonglonghe

---

3. The Wade-Giles romanisation system for Chinese developed by Thomas Wade in 1867 was revised by Herbert Allen Giles in 1912. A new scheme, Hanyu Pinyin Fang'an, was introduced by the Chinese government in 1958. Benjamin Ao, 'History and prospect of Chinese romanization', available at CLIEJ (http://www.white-clouds.com/iclc/cliej/ cl4ao.htm). (21 Sept. 2007).

APPENDIX 3 *continued*

The sources for the history of the Columbans in Korea contain a variety of ways of romanising Korean names, e.g. the location of the first Columban mission was called *Province de Tjyen-la-to sud* by French missionaries, *Zenra Nan Do* by the Japanese colonial authorities, and *Cholla Nam Do* (Cholla South Province) in church documents beginning in 1948. Korean has more letters, both vowels and consonants, than the Latin alphabet. The McCune-Reischauer system[4] of transliteration, invented in 1937, is perhaps the most accurate method for representing that multiplicity, and is adopted in this book, except for quotations. Beginning in 1946 Columbans generally used simpler, less accurate, methods, writing 'Chunchon' or 'Choon chun' where the McCune-Reischauer system uses 'Ch'unch'on'.

Since documents concerning the Columban missions in Korea between 1933 and 1948 used the Japanese style this appendix gives the McCune-Reischauer and Japanese usages.

Korean Usage	*Japanese Usage*
Cholla Nam Do	Zenra Nan Do
Mokp'o	Moppo
Kangwondo	Kogendo
Ch'unch'on	Syunsen
Taegu	Taikyu
Naju	Rasyu
Hongch'on	Kosen
Seoul	Keijo

---

4. The McCune-Reischauer system was invented by two graduate students in 1937, 'McCune-Reischauer System' at McCune-Reischauer System (http://mccune-reischauer.org) (15 Nov. 2006).

APPENDIX 4

Missions not accepted

Kweichow, China, 1918
In 1918 Propaganda invited the Columbans to send priests to the vicariate of Kweichow.[5] The proposal triggered a vigorous correspondence among the scattered members of the society before John Blowick replied to Rome. Blowick argued that the main reason for founding the new mission was to combat English-speaking Protestants, and that there were few of these in Kweichow. Instead he asked for a territory in Hupeh.

Outer Mongolia, 1922
The Columban central council discussed a letter from Propaganda on 11 May 1922, proposing a new mission in 'Mongolia Exterior'.[6] While the councillors were in favour of accepting the proposal they begged for a delay, giving as reasons the need for personnel in Hanyang, the fact that only newly-ordained priests were available, and the drain on the finances of the society caused by building in China, Ireland and America, and by the cost of founding the Missionary Sisters of St Columban. When the matter was discussed again in 1924 the council refused the invitation since the society had agreed to go to Siam.

Siam (Thailand), 1924
Propaganda asked John Blowick in 1924 if the Columbans were willing to send priests to Siam. Among the arguments used by Rome were the great number of Chinese in Siam, the presence of Protestant missionaries, and the wide use of English in the kingdom.[7] Blowick and his council initially accepted the invitation. However, Owen MacPolin, the bursar of the society, reported that 'the society could not, without a disaster, send a mission to Siam'. Michael O'Dwyer, the newly-elected superior general, informed Propaganda that '*propter rationes oeconomicas*' he could not take up the offer.

India, 1927
In December 1927 Propaganda proposed that it entrust to the society a district in India 'where there were many places to which the proclamation of the gospel has not yet been brought'.[8] The superior general's council decided to refer the matter to the Irish bishops since a mission in India might be seen by the people as contrary to the purpose for which the society was founded, mission to the Chinese. Michael O'Dwyer attended the meeting of the standing committee of the bishops on 17 January 1927 and was advised that 'if Rome insisted we should go, but to press our difficulties'. O'Dwyer visited William van Rossum, the prefect of Propaganda, in February and explained why the society could not accept the invitation.

East Indies, 1927
Michael O'Dwyer, in his reply to Propaganda concerning a mission in India, referred to an invitation, from Propaganda, to open a mission in the East Indies. There is no record of any

---
5. Propaganda to Michael Logue, 26 Mar. 1918 (CFCA, CN A-1.1).
6. Propaganda to John Blowick, 4 May 1922 (CFCA, CA A-20).
7. Propaganda to John Blowick, 26 Feb. 1924 (CFCA, CA A-20).
8. Propaganda to Michael O'Dwyer 20 Dec. 1927 (CFCA, CA A-20).

discussion of the matter in the minutes of the superior general's council. However in the archives of the society there is a single, undated page, a draft, in which O'Dwyer acknowledged the invitation to the East Indies, dated 20 December 1927. In the style common to such communications he went on to say that the society was willing to accept the invitation before mentioning that there were difficulties which would demand a delay, at the very least.[9] The difficulties and the polite refusal of the offer would have been on the missing second page.

Malaya, 1929
Dr R. M. Connolly offered the Columbans an estate in Malaya in 1929, to be run as a school for Eurasians, Chinese and Tamils or as a sanatorium and novitiate for Chinese clergy. Michael O'Dwyer turned down the offer 'for want of men and money' and because the work was not in keeping with the aim and nature of the society.[10]

Nanchang, Kiangsi, 1932
Paul Dumond, vicar apostolic of Nanchang, approached Edward Galvin in 1932 proposing to give part of his vicariate to the Columbans.[11] Michael O'Dwyer agreed to accept. However, when the superior general of the Vincentians, the congregation staffing the vicariate, heard of the offer he opposed it. Mario Zanin, the apostolic delegate, re-opened the matter in 1934, only to find that his predecessor, Celso Costantini, had recommended that the territory be given to a Chinese bishop, and not to the Columbans. Since Costantini was the secretary of Propaganda Zanin let the idea drop. Zhou Jishi, Archbishop of Nanchang (1931-72), made a similar offer in 1948 but the communist victory ended the negotiations.

Mozambique, 1936
John Kyne, vice-rector of the Irish College in Rome, passed on a message from an official of the secretariate of state in March 1936, inviting the society to undertake a mission in Mozambique. Portugal, the colonial power, could not supply priests and was unwilling to accept men from other countries with colonial ambitions. Irish priests were ideal. The Columban superior general refused the offer, citing China as the principal field of the society, the new missions in Korea and Burma, and the financial limitations of the society.[12]

College for mission to Muslims, 1939
Eugene Tisserant, secretary of the Congregation for the Oriental Church, asked Michael O'Dwyer in 1939 to found a college to train missionaries to work among Muslims. Tisserant thought that Columbans had missions in Muslim countries. O'Dwyer responded that since the society had no contact with Muslims it could not undertake such a college.[13]

Calcutta, 1947
John Hannon, English assistant to the Jesuit superior general in Rome, wrote to Michael O'Dwyer in May 1947 offering the society a territory in the archdiocese of Calcutta. A general chapter of the society, meeting in June 1947, refused the invitation explaining that new missions in China and Japan would 'swallow up our men and resources for some time to come'.[14]

---

9. Michael O'Dwyer to Propaganda, undated draft (CFCA, CA A-20).
10. Michael O'Dwyer to John Blowick, 12 May 1929 (CFCA, CA A-20).
11. Owen MacPolin to Michael O'Dwyer, 18 Jan. 1932 (CFCA, CN A-1.108).
12. John Blowick, Talk to students, 1959 (CFCA, P.2).
13. Michael O'Dwyer to Eugene Tisserant, 15 May 1939 (CFCA, CA A-20).
14. John Blowick, Talk to students, 1959.

APPENDIX 5

Structures of the Society of St Columban, 1932-48

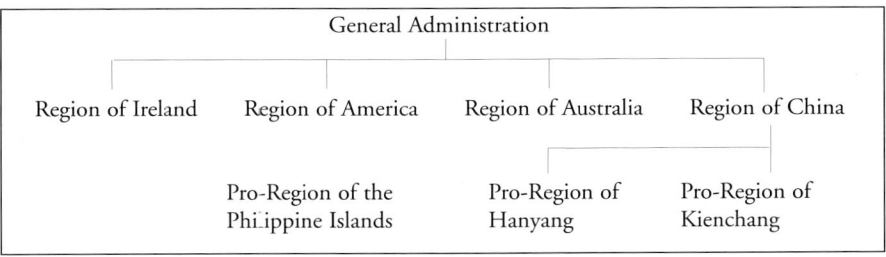

Structure of the society in 1932

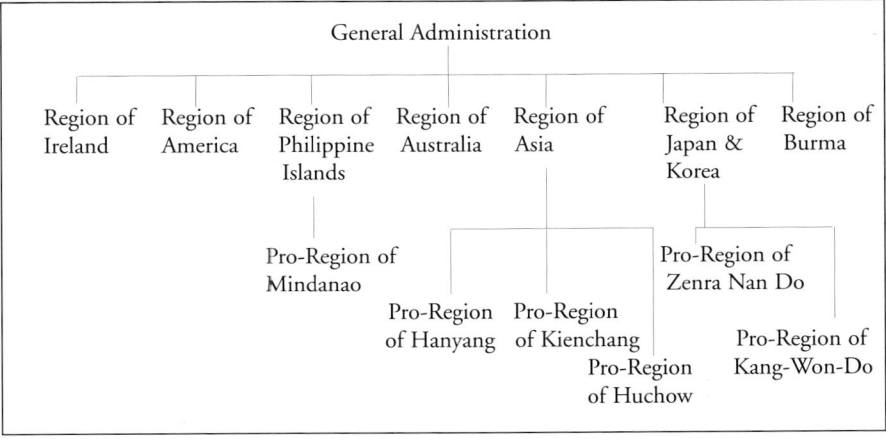

Structure of the society in 1947

Structure of the society in 1948

Source: Directories of the Society of St Columban, 1932, 1947, 1948 (Library, St Columban's, Dalgan Park, Navan).

APPENDIX 6

Key dates in the history of the Columban Fathers

10 October 1916	Approval by the Irish bishops for a mission college for China
1 January 1918	First publication of The Far East
29 January 1918	First students arrived in Dalgan Park, Shrule, Co. Galway
29 June 1918	Society canonically erected by the bishop of Galway
14 December 1918	Society canonically erected in the diocese of Omaha
8 June 1919	Congress of the society
6 January 1920	Edward Maguire and James Galvin arrived in Australia
26 June 1920	The first three Columbans arrived in Hankow
19 October 1923	First Loretto sisters arrived in Wuhan
8 June 1924	First general chapter of the society
29 September 1924	Missionary Sisters of St. Columban erected
5 June 1925	Constitutions approved by the Holy See
4 April 1928	First Columbans appointed to Nancheng
17 July 1929	Timothy Leonard killed in Nanfeng
26 April 1929	Propaganda gave permission for a 'procure' and parish in Manila
29 October 1933	First Columbans in Korea
20 October 1936	Patrick Usher and Bernard Way arrived in Burma
31 January 1937	First praesidium of the Legion of Mary set up in Hanyang
7 December 1941	Pearl Harbor
1 October 1949	Founding of the Peoples' Republic of China
25 June 1950	Korean war
15 May 1954	Edward MacElroy was the last Columban to be expelled from China

APPENDIX 7

Prospectus Status Missionis

A die I mensis Iulii anni 1950 usque ad diem XXX Iunii anni 1951

Nomen missionis: Choon Chun
Ordinarius:
    Nomen et cognomen: Thomas Quinlan
    Residentia habitualis: Choon Chun, Kangwondo, Corea.
    Inscriptio postalis: Captus erat a Communistis mense Julii 1950 viventem vel mortuum nescimus
Sacerdotes :   2 *Hiberni occisi sunt*
        2 *Hiberni capti sunt*
        1 *Americanus captus est*
        1 *Australiensis captus est*
        7 *Hiberni, 1 ex Nova Zealandia, et 3 Coreani manent*
Sorores :   3 *Coreani, Societatis de Sancti Pauli de Chartres*
Catechistae :   *Propter Bellum non laborare possunt*

De populatione :
    Num. totalis : Ignotum propter bellum
    Catholici indigenae: 5,000 (approx.)
De scholis : Tempore Belli Scholae cessaverunt
De mutationibus in numero Catholicorum :
    Multi fugerunt et circa mille propter morbum mortui sunt
De vita et fructibus spiritualibus :
    Christiani fere omnes fugerunt Praefecturam saltem pro tempore, cum opportunitas esset Sacramenta receperunt et rediti fere omnes paschalem Confessionem et Communionem receperunt.
Datum (locus, dies, mensis et annus) Seoul, 23 die Julii 1951
Signatura : Hubertus Hayward, Pro-Praefectus
(Sigilum Ordinariatus) In invasione perditum

---

15. Spiritual returns of the prefecture of Ch'unch'on (CFCA, KOR A-4 (SR)).

Bibliography

PRIMARY SOURCES

MANUSCRIPT SOURCES
Columban Central Archive, Dalgan Park
Anonymous Chinese priest to Edward Kelly, Dec. 1988 (CFCA, CN A-5).
Blowick, John, Diary, 1920-21 (CFCA, P.2).
Blowick, John, Longer notes (5 vols, c. 1923, CFCA, P.2).
Blowick, John, Shorter notes (c. 1921, CFCA, P.2).
Blowick Correspondence (1917-24, CFCA, G-1, CA A-1, CN A-5, P. 2).
Blowick Correspondence with Propaganda (1918-22, CFCA, CA A-17, CA F-1, CN A-1, CN A-5).
Blowick Correspondence with Propaganda (1929, CFCA, RP A-1).
Callanan, Thomas, 'Memoirs 1937-80', (1980, CFCA, RP Misc).
Cleary, Patrick, Correspondence (1932-52, CFCA, China Correspondence, CN A-1, CN A-4).
Cogan, Gerald, 'Recollections' (1954, CFCA, RP A-5).
Cogan, Gerald to Joseph Whelan, 16 Aug. 1950 (CFCA, RP A-4).
Columban Sisters' Correspondence (1918-30, CFCA, CA A-12).
Connolly, Timothy, Visitation of the Philippines 1953 (CFCA, RP A-7).
Costantini, Celso, Epistola ad Vicarios Apostolicos, 19 Mar. 1923 (CFCA, China Correspondence).
Demange, Florian, Circular No. 86, 13 Sept. 1933 (CFCA, KOR A-1).
Dennehy, Jeremiah, Correspondence (1947-51, CFCA, China Correspondence, RP A-4, KOR A-4).
Dennehy, Jeremiah to John Blowick, 8 Feb. 1929 (CFCA, RP A-1).
Dumond, Paul to Owen MacPolin, 13 May 1935 (CFCA, CN A-1).
Feeney, Dermot to Paul Waldron, 26 Jan. 1945 (CFCA, RP Misc).
Fraser, John Mary, 'Pillar of the kingdom, the memoirs of Monsignor John Mary Fraser, founder of Scarboro missions' in Scarboro Missions, lxxxiii (Jan/Feb. 2002).
Galvin Correspondence (1912-1920, CFCA, G-1, CN A-4, USA A-1).
Galvin Correspondence (1920-56, CFCA, CN A-1, CN A-4, CN A-5, CN A-8, CN A-12, China Correspondence).
Glennon, Thomas, Report on China visit (12 Jan. 1989, CFCA, CN A-5).
Halliden, William to Edward Cassidy, 20 Dec. 1988 (CFCA, CN A-5).
Henry, Harold, Correspondence (1947-52, KOR A-4).
Kelly, Edward, The Columban mission in Hu-zhou (undated, CFCA, CN A-4).
Larribeau, Adrien-Joseph to Propaganda, 30 Jul. 1938 (CFCA, KOR A-1).
Loretto Annals (1923, CFCA, CN A-5).

Loretto Correspondence (1921-25, CFCA, CA A-12, CN A-5).
MacPolin, Owen, Correspondence (1934-40, KOR A-1, KOR A-4).
McCarthy, Edward J, 'The history of the Catholic church in Burma', ed. Usher, Patrick (1941-5, CFCA, BUR A-5).
McNamara, John, 'Hanyang under the communist regime' (1950, CFCA, CN A-4).
Maguire, Edward to John Blowick (1920-1, CFCA, AUS A-4).
Manion, Patricia J, 'The China story' (2002, CFCA, CN A-5).
Mongey, Sister Michael, 'Reminiscences' (1964, CFCA, P.14).
Moore, George F. to Joseph Monaghan, 25 Aug. 1947 (CFCA, RP Misc).
O'Dwyer, Michael, Correspondence (1925-52, CFCA, CA A-1, CN A-1, CN A-5, CN A-12, China Correspondence, RP A-1, RP A-3, RP A-4, RP A-8, RP Misc, USA A-4, KOR A-1, KOR A-4, BUR A-1).
Picornell, Pedro, 'The Remedios hospital' (undated, CFCA, RP Misc).
Pigott, Jeremiah, Correspondence (1946-50, CFCA, China Correspondence).
Quinlan, Thomas, Correspondence (1938-54, CFCA, KOR A-4).
Recommendations of the general chapter of 1931 (CFCA, CA F-3).
Rogner, Clementia, 'Loretto under communism' (undated, CFCA, CN A-5).
Rosal, Nicomedes, Information regarding Fr Douglas, 25 Jul. 1945 (CFCA, RP Misc).
Smyth, Bernard T (ed.), 'Galvin and Galvin-related letters, 1912-27' (CFCA, P.1).
Stewart, Thos, 'History of the diocese of Chuncheon' (Sept. 1988, CFCA, KOR A-5).
Tierney, Cornelius to Edward J. McCarthy, 31 Oct. 1918, (CFCA, USA A-1).
Usher, Patrick, Correspondence (1936-55, CFCA BUR A-4).
Wu, Joseph to Teresita Yu, 12 May 1980 (CFCA, CN A-5).
Wu, Joseph to Edward McElroy, 20 Aug. 1980 (CFCA, CN A-5).
Yang, James to Edward McElroy, 1980 (CFCA, CN A-5).
Yang, James to Seamus O'Reilly and Thomas Murphy, 31 Oct. 1988 (CFCA, CN A-5).
Yu, Joseph to Michael O'Farrell, Dec. 2002 (CFCA, CN A-5).
Zhang, Peter to Edward McElroy, 3 June 1979 (CFCA, CN A-5).

Columban Archives, Donaghmede, Dublin
Council of directors, minutes of meetings, 1917-25.
Minutes, Superior general's council, 1925-37.
Minutes, Superior general's council, 1937-52.
Edward J. McCarthy correspondence with Joseph O'Leary (1916-17, P. 24).

Columban Archives, Omaha
McCarthy, Edward J, 'Life of Father Henaghan' (undated).
McCarthy, Edward J, 'Reminiscences' (1950).

Columban Archives, Manila
McCaslin, James, 'Columbans in Mindanao' (1990).

Dublin Diocesan Archives
Correspondence of John Blowick to William J. Walsh, 1916-9 (Walsh Papers, 385-6).

Archives of the Irish Bishops, Mullingar
   Minutes of the meetings of the Irish bishops, 1916-20.

Allen Library, Dublin
   Constitutions of the Brothers of Christian Schools of Ireland (Rome, 1923).

Legion of Mary Archives, Dublin
   McGrath, Aedan, 'The Legion in China' (1959).

Archives of the Good Shepherd Sisters, Cork
   Wason, Dorothy, 'Burma Good Shepherd Story' (1966).

The National Archives, Public Record Office, Kew
   Maynooth Mission to China, FO 371/3699 (1919-20).
   The Maynooth Mission to China August 1918-May 1919, FO 371/3699.
   Maynooth Mission, Summary, 22nd April, FO 371/5341 (1920).
   Thomas Quinlan to W. Russell Brown, 29 Apr. 1930, FO 371/14681.

Archives of the Congregation for the Propagation of the Faith, Rome
   Diomede Falconio to Gerolamo Gotti, 11 May 1911 (AP, Vol. 601, p. 184).
   Gerolamo Gotti to William Gibbons, 3 July 1911 (AP, Vol. 601, p. 202).
   Minutes of the meeting of the archbishops, USA, 27 Apr. 1911 (AP, Vol. 601, p. 191).
   Michael O'Riordan to Propaganda, 24 Dec. 1916 (AP, Vol. 601, p. 26).
   John Blowick to Propaganda, 5 June 1918 (AP, Vol. 601, p. 130).
   Pro-memoria of Gulielmus M. Van Rossum, 23 Mar. 1919 (AP, Vol. 643, p. 638).
   Propaganda to Graziano Gennaro, 27 June 1918 (AP, Vol. 601, p. 135).
   Propaganda to Cimino Serafino, 28 June 1918 (AP, Vol. 601, p. 137).
   Graziano Gennaro, 24 Sept. 1918 (AP, Vol. 601, p. 153).

Archive of the Pontifical Irish College, Rome
   James MacCaffrey to John Hagan, 23 July 1917 (APCI, HAG1/1917/61).

PRINTED PRIMARY SOURCES
Columban Printed Sources
Foundation and society
   Blowick, John, 'The Maynooth Mission to China' in *The Catholic Truth Annual* (Dublin, 1917).
   Cyprian, *St Cyprian, letters*, trs Donna, Rose Bernard (Washington, 1964).
   Constitutiones Societatis Sti Columbani pro Missionibus apud Sinenses (Rome, 1925).
   Constitutiones Societatis Sti Columbani pro Missionibus apud Sinenses (2nd ed., Rome, 1932).
   Constitutions of the Maynooth Mission to China (1918) (CFCA, CA F-3).
   Maynooth Mission to China, Constitutions (1919) (CFCA, CA F-3).
   Provisory constitutions and students' rules for the approval of the Irish bishops (1917) (CFCA, CA F-3).

Règlement de las Société des Missions-Étrangères (Rome, 1890).
Walker, G. S. M, *Sancti Columbani opera* (Dublin, 1970).

China
   Galvin, Edward, *Letters from an Irish missionary in China* (Dublin, 1916).
   Leahy, Timothy, *Beyond tomorrow* (Dublin, 1968).
   Lynch, Luke, *To the end of the road, travels of a Columban missionary* (Galway, 1996).
   O'Reilly, Luke, *Passing the torch* (Dublin, 1995).
   O'Reilly, Luke, *The laughter and the weeping* (Dublin, 1991).
   Planchet, J. M, *Les missions de Chine et du Japon* (Pékin, 1916, 1917, 1925, 1927, 1929, 1931, 1933).
   Primum concilium Sinense anno 1924 (Shanghai, 1941).
   Smyth, Bernard T. (ed.), *But not conquered* (Westminster, 1958).
   Tierney, Cornelius, *Part of the bargain*, ed. Bernard T. Smyth (Dublin, 1963).
   The official handbook of the Legion of Mary (Dublin, 1953).

Philippines
   McCarthy, Edward J, *Radio sermons, talks for students* (Manila, 1936).
   O'Brien, Niall (ed.), *Columban martyrs of Malate* (Manila, 1995).

Korea
   Crosbie, Philip, *Three winters cold* (Dublin, 1955).
   Herlihy, Francis, *Now welcome summer* (Melbourne, 1946).

Burma
   Rillstone, Thomas, *And behold we live, days of danger in wartime Burma* (Melbourne, 1946).

Magazines, Periodicals and Newspapers
   Annals of the Propagation of the Faith (Dublin, 1920-21).
   Catholic Truth Society Annual (Dublin, 1917).
   Columban Intercom (1988-2007, an in-house magazine, published in Dalgan Park).
   Frontier Evangelization (Seoul, Autumn 2005).
   Interchange (Santa Fe, 1999).
   International Bulletin of Missionary Research (1950-2006, published in Ventnor, NJ until 1987, and subsequently in New Haven, CT).
   Irish Ecclesiastical Record (Dublin, 1899-1968).
   Pagan Missions (1922-33, 1940-86, published in Dalgan Park, Navan).
   The Far East (1918-2007, published in Dalgan Park, Galway until July 1927, and in St Columban's, Navan, since then).
   The Far East (US ed.) (1918-2007, published in St Columban's, Omaha, Nebraska; renamed *Columban Fathers Missions* in 1967).
   The Far East (Australian ed.) (1920-2007, published in St Columban's, Melbourne).
   The Lamp, New York.
   Freeman's Journal.

Irish Catholic.
Irish Independent.
Irish Times.
Times, London.

Works of Reference

Abbott, Walter M. (ed.), *The documents of Vatican II* (6th printing, London, 1972).
Acta Apostolicae Sedis (Rome, 1916-1969).
Bettenson, Henry (ed.), *Documents of the Christian church* (2nd ed., Oxford, 1967).
Bouscaren, T. Lincoln and Ellis, Adam C, *Canon law, a text and commentary* (Milwaukee, 1963).
Catholic Conference of Korea, *Catholic Address Book* (Seoul 1995).
Catholic directory of the Philippines, 1976 (Manila, 1976).
Charbonnier, Jean, *Guide to the Catholic Church in China,* 1997 (Singapore, 1997).
Charbonnier, Jean, *Guide to the Catholic Church in China,* 2004 (Singapore, 2004).
Codex iuris canonici (Rome, 1919).
Collectanea S. Congregationis de Propaganda Fide (2 vols, Rome, 1907).
Denzinger, Henrico and Bannwart, Clemens, *Enchiridion symbolorum* (13th ed., Friburg, 1921).
Funk, Isaac K (ed.), *The new standard dictionary of the English language* (2 vols, London, 1914).
Gasparri, Petrus (ed.), *Codicis iuris canonici fontes* (9 vols, Rome, 1923).
Gramatica, Luigi, *Testo e atlante di geografica ecclesiastica e missionaria* (Bergamo, 1927).
Herbermann, Charles G (ed.), *The new Catholic encyclopedia* (15 vols, London, 1911).
McDonald, William J (ed.), *New Catholic encyclopedia* (15 vols, New York, 1967).
McHenry, Robert (ed.), *The new encyclopedia Britannica* (29 vols, Chicago, 1993).
Marthaler, Berard L (ed.), *New Catholic encyclopedia* (2nd ed., 15 vols, Washington, 2003).
Martini, Rafael de (ed.), *Iuris pontificii de Propaganda Fide* (2 vols, Rome, 1888).
Meagher, Paul Kevin (ed.), *Encyclopedic dictionary of religion* (3 vols, Washington, 1979).
Müller, Karl (ed.), *Dictionary of mission* (New York, 1997).
Smith, Jonathan Z (ed.), *The HarperCollins dictionary of religion* (Washington, 1995).
The Canon Law Society of Great Britain and Ireland, *The code of canon law* (London, 1983).
The Official 2006 Catholic Directory of Myanmar (Yangon, 2006).
Twitchett, Denis and Fairbank, John K (eds.), *The Cambridge history of China,* vols xii (Cambridge, 1983) and xiii (Cambridge, 1986).
Werner, O, *Atlas des missions Catholiques* (Fribourg, 1886).
Who's who in China (Shanghai, 1931).

Interviews and Talks
    Blowick, John, Talk to students, 1959 (Transcript in CFCA, P. 2).
    Blowick, John, Talk to students, 1968 (Transcript in CFCA, P. 2).
    Collins, Henry, transcript of interview (14 Feb. 1987, CFCA, P. 145).
    Fitzgerald, Daniel, Dalgan Park, Navan, interview (20 Feb. 2004).
    Fitzgerald, Daniel, Dalgan Park, Navan, interview (28 Sept. 2005).
    Fleming, Kevin, Blanchardstown, interview (28 Sept. 2006).
    Gallagher, Francis, recorded interview (1983, CFCA Oral history archive).
    Geraghty, Brian, interview (29 Apr. 1958, CFCA, KOR A-5).
    Grawng, Paul, recorded interview (23 Sept. 1991, CFCA, oral history archive).
    Healy, Michael, Dalgan Park, Navan, interview (12 Feb. 2006).
    Justyn, Justa and Rogner, Clementia, transcript of interview (CFCA, A-5).
    Li, Joseph, Kildare, interview (22 May 2006).
    McGrath, Aedan, transcript of interview (24 June 1993, CFCA).
    Maheu, Betty Ann and Sloboda, Michael, Hong Kong, interview (6 Apr. 2006).
    Mullany, Francis, Dalgan Park, Navan, interview (22 Nov. 2006).
    Troy, Daniel, Wuhan, China, interview (12 Sept. 2005).
    Yu, Teresita, Wicklow, interview (3 Dec. 2005).
    Yu, Thomas, Shanghai, interview (June 1990).
    Whyte, Oliver, Dalgan Park, Navan, interview (12 Feb. 2006).
    Zhang, Xiao Jin, Wuhan, China, interview (19 Apr. 2006).
    Zhao, Huai min, Nancheng, China, interview (8 Jan. 2006).
    Zhou Wen Bing, Brigid, interview (21 Apr. 2006).

SECONDARY SOURCES
General

    Amaladoss, Michael, *Mission today, reflections from an Ignatian perspective* (Gujarat, 1989).

    Billington Harper, Susan, *In the shadow of the Mahatma, Bishop V. S. Azariah and the travails of Christianity in British India* (Grand Rapids, 2000).

    Bosch, David J, *Transforming mission* (New York, 1991).

    Condon, Kevin, *The missionary college of All Hallows 1842-1891* (Dublin, 1986).

    Comby, Jean, *How to understand the history of Christian mission*, trs John Bowden (London, 1996).

    Corish, Patrick, *The Irish Catholic experience, a historical survey* (Dublin, 1985).

    Crowley, Patrick, *Those who journeyed with us 1918-2004* (Dublin, 2005).

    Dorr, Donal, *Mission in today's world* (Dublin, 2000).

    Douglas, Mary, *Natural symbols* (London, 1973).

    Dries, Angelyn, *The missionary movement in American Catholic history* (New York, 1998).

    Duster, Charles J., 'The canonical status of members of missionary societies of apostolic life of pontifical right' (D.C.L. thesis, University of St Thomas Aquinas, Rome, 1994).

Gaughan, J. Anthony, *Olivia Mary Taaffe, 1832-1918, Foundress of St Joseph's Young Priests' Society* (Dublin, 1995).

Guanipa, Carmen, 'Culture shock' at Amigos – Culture shock (http://edweb.sdsu.edu/people/CGuanipa/cultshok.htm) (27 Mar.2007).

'Gentiles' at Gentiles/Torah 101/Mechon Mamre (http://www.mechonmamre.org/jewfaq/gentiles.htm) (5 Mar. 2007).

Hogan, Edmund M., *The Irish missionary movement* (Dublin, 1990).

Kiggins, Thomas, *Maynooth mission to Africa, the story of St Patrick's, Kiltegan* (Dublin, 1991).

Knitter, Paul F., *No other name? A critical survey of Christian attitudes towards the world religions* (London, 1985).

Luzbetak, Louis J, *The church and cultures* (New York, 1988).

McDowell, W. H, *Historical research, a guide* (London, 2002).

McGlade, Joseph, *The missions: Africa and the Orient* (Dublin, 1967).

Moffett, Samuel Hugh, *A history of Christianity in Asia*, ii (2 vols, New York, 2005).

Neill, Stephen, *A history of Christian missions* (2nd ed., London, 1986).

O'Hanlon, W. A., 'Christian Brothers in China' in *Christian Brothers' Educational Record* (1975).

Ó Murchú, Pádraig, *Misean Mhaigh Nuad chun na Síne 1916-1963* (Dublin, 2003).

Preston, Margaret H, *Charitable words: philanthropy and the language of charity in nineteenth-century Dublin* (Westport CT, 2004).

Ryan, Finbar, *Our Lady of Fatima* (Dublin, 1948).

Schmidlin, Joseph, *Catholic mission history*, trs Matthias Braun (Techny, Ill., 1933).

Schmidlin, Joseph, *Catholic mission theory*, trs Matthias Braun (Techny, Ill., 1931).

Stanley, Brian, *The bible and the flag, Protestant missions and British imperialism in the nineteenth and twentieth centuries* (Leicester, 1990).

Tanquerey, Adolphus, *Synopsis theologiae dogmaticae* (3 vols, Tournai, 1935-8).

Tosh, John, *The pursuit of history* (London, 2002).

Thompson, Jack (ed.), *Into all the world, a history of the overseas work of the Presbyterian church in Ireland 1840-1990* (Belfast, 1990).

Uchem, Rose, 'Gender inequality as an enduring obstacle to mission' in *Sedos Bulletin 2006*, xxxviii (Rome, Sept/Oct. 2006).

Ward, Kevin and Stanley, Brian (eds.), *The Church Mission Society and world Christianity, 1799-1999* (Grand Rapids, 2000).

Wodarz, Donald M, 'Church growth: the missiology of Donald Anderson McGavran' (Unpublished D.Miss. dissertation, Gregorian University, Rome, 1979).

Foundation

Cairns, Barry, 'Some emphases to be made in the spiritual formation of Columban students preparing for cross-cultural mission' (Unpublished M. Theol. thesis, Jesuit School of Theology at Berkeley, 1977).

Greene, Kevin P, 'The Far East, mirror of the missions' (Unpublished M.A. thesis, Marquette University, Milwaukee, 1960).

Henaghan, John, *Pathways to God* (reprint, Pasay City, 1997).

Henaghan, John, *White martyrdom* (Manila, 1940).

Hoare, Francis X, 'The influence of the 'Crusade' symbol and the 'War' metaphor on motivation and attitudes in the Maynooth Mission to China, 1918-1929' (Unpublished M.Sc. in Social Anthropology essay, London School of Economics, 1989).

Lucey, Sheila, *Frances Moloney, co-founder of the Missionary Sisters of Saint Columban* (Dublin, 1999).

Smyth, Bernard T., *The Chinese batch, The Maynooth mission to China 1911-1920* (Dublin, 1994).

Mill Hill Missionaries' archives, 'St Joseph's Missionary Society', available at Mundus (http://www.mundus.ac.uk/cats/37/268.htm) (14 June 2004).

Morrissey, Thomas J, *William J. Walsh, Archbishop of Dublin, 1841-1921* (Dublin, 2000).

O'Neill, Clare, 'The Irish home front 1914-18' (Unpublished Ph.D. thesis, National University of Ireland, Maynooth, 2006).

Pearse, Pádhraic, *The story of a success*, ed. Desmond Ryan (Dublin, 1917).

Rossignol, Raymond, 'The Paris Foreign Missionaries', available at The Paris Foreign Mission Society (http://www.rc.net/malaysia/collegegeneral /MEP.htm) (9 July 2004).

Rue, Charles D, 'Journey to the margins: Columban mission, Australia 1920-2000' (Unpublished Ph.D. thesis, Australian Catholic University, Fitzroy, Australia, 2002).

China

Ao, Benjamin 'History and prospect of Chinese romanization' at CLIEJ (http://www.white-clouds.com/iclc/cliej/cl4ao.htm) (21 Sept. 2007).

Barrett, William E, *The red lacquered gate* (New York, 1967).

Bennett, Milton J, 'Towards ethnorelativsm: a developmental model of intercultural sensitivity' in Paige, Michael (ed.), *Education for the intercultural experience* (Yarmouth, Maine, 1993).

Berger, Peter L, *Modernisation and religion* (Dublin, 1981).

Breslin, Thomas A, *China, American Catholicism and the missionary* (Pennsylvania, 1980).

Cary-Elwes, Columba, *China and the cross* (London, 1957).

Chang, A. B. 'An independent, autonomous and self-administered church' in *Tripod*, xix (July 1999).

Chang, Jung and Halliday, Jon, *Mao, the unknown story* (London, 2005).

'Chinese archbishop of Fuzhou dies', at China Infodoc Service (china.infodoc@online.be) (5 Feb. 2007).

Clubb, O. Edmund, *20th century China* (New York, 1964).

Fenby, Jonathan, *Generalissimo Chiang Kai-shek* (London, 2003).

Fischer, Edward, *Maybe a second spring, the story of the missionary sisters of St Columban in China*, (New York, 1983).

Fleming, Peter, *One's company, a journey to China* (London, 1934).

Forristal, Desmond, *The bridge of Lo Wu* (Dublin, 1987).

Gittings, John, *The changing face of China, from Mao to market* (Oxford, 2005).

Hanson, Eric O., *Catholic politics in China and Korea* (New York, 1980).

Jaegher, Raymond de, *Father Lebbe: a modern apostle* (New York, 1950).

Kelley, Francis Clement, *The bishop jots it down* (New York, 1939).

Kelly, Edward T, 'San Tzu Ching, A translation and commentary' (Unpublished M.A. thesis, Seton Hall University, South Orange, 1962).

Kelly, Edward T, 'The anti-Christian persecution of 1616-1617 in Nanking' (Unpublished Graduate Studies dissertation, Columbia University, New York, 1971).

Lam, Anthony S. K., *The Catholic church in present-day China* (Hong Kong, 1997).

Latourette, Kenneth Scott, *A history of Christian missions in China* (London, 1929).

Leclercq, Jacques, *Thunder in the distance: The life of Pere Lebbe*, trs George Lamb (New York, 1958).

Lehane, Padraig, 'Catholic reaction to the declaration of the People's Republic of China (A case-study of the changing attitudes of Irish missionaries in China, 1916-1953)' (Unpublished M.A. thesis in history, NUI Dublin, 1985).

Li Li, 'Christian women's education in China in the nineteenth and early twentieth centuries' available at Salem State College (http://www.samford.edu/-lillyhumanrights/Li_Christian.pdf) (21 Mar. 2007).

Mac Caomhánaigh, Pádraig, *Kao Er Wen, beatha Éamainn Uí Ghealbháin, easpaig Hanyang, an tSín* (Baile Átha Cliath, 1965).

McCarthy, Eamonn and Walsh, Michael (eds), *From Navan to China, the story of a 'Chinese Irishman', Aedan W. McGrath SSC (1906-2000)* (Dublin, 2008)

McPartland, Peter, 'School legislation of the first plenary council of China' (Unpublished D.C.L. dissertation, Gregorian University, Rome, 1940).

Madsen, Richard, *China's Catholics, tragedy and hope in an emerging civil society* (Berkeley, 1998).

Manion, Patricia J, 'Sister Isobel Huang dies in China' in *Interchange* (Santa Fe, 1999).

Manion, Patricia Jean, *Venture into the unknown, Loretto in China 1923-98* (St Louis, 2006).

Myers, James T., *Enemies without guns, the Catholic church in China* (New York, 1991).

O'Hanlon, W.A., 'Christian Brothers in China,' in *Christian Brothers' Educational Record* (1975).

Payne, Robert, *Portrait of a revolutionary: Mao Tse-tung* (New York, 1950).

Pius XI, '*Rerum Ecclesiae*' at Papal Encyclicals online (http://www.papalencyclicals.net/pius11/p11REREC.HTM) (12 Jan. 2004).

Pius XII, '*Evangelii praecones*' available at Vatican: the Holy See (http://vatican.va/holy_father/pius_xii/encyclicals/documents/hf p_xii_enc_0206) (11 Oct. 2005).

Reilly, Robert T., *Christ's exile, Bishop Edward J. Galvin* (Dublin, 1958).

Rigney, Harold W., *Four years in a red hell* (Donamon Castle, 1958).

Schram, Stuart, *Mao Tse-tung* (London, 1966).

Sheridan, James E, *Chinese warlord, the career of Feng Yu-hsiang* (Stanford, 1966).

Spence, Jonathan D, *The search for modern China* (New York, 1999).

Sweeten, Alan Richard, *Christianity in rural China, conflict and accomodation in Jiangxi province 1860-1900* (Ann Arbor, 2001).

Tang, Edmond and Wiest, Jean-Paul (eds.), *The Catholic church in modern China* (New York, 1993).

'Travel China guide', available at China Travel Service (http://www.travelchinaguide.com/climate/ningbo.htm) (20 Dec. 2005).

Tripod staff, 'Estimated statistics for China's Catholic church (Oct. 2005)', available at Holy Spirit Study Centre (http://www.hsstudyc.org.hk) (23 Mar. 2006).

Tripod staff, 'Statistics for China's Catholic church (Nov. 2006)' in *Tripod*, xxvii (Hong Kong, Spring 2007).

Wardlaw Thompson, R., *Griffith John, the story of fifty years in China* (London, 1907).

Whyte, Bob, *Unfinished encounter, China and Christianity* (London, 1988).

Wiest, Jean-Paul, *Maryknoll in China* (New York, 1988).

Wright, Jane, *She left her heart in China, the story of Dr Sally Wolfe* (Groomsport, 1999).

Yan kejia, *Catholic Church in China* (Beijing, 2006).

Philippines

Agoncillo, Teodoro A., *A short history of the Philippines* (Manila, 1975).

Achútegui, Pedro S. de and Bernad, Miguel A., *Religious revolution in the Philippines* (Manila, 1961).

Bonk, Jonathan J, *Mi$$ion$ and money* (New York, 1991).

Brooks, Patricia, *With no regrets, the story of Francis Vernon Douglas* (Manila, 1998).

Fischer, Edward, *Mindanao mission, Archbishop Patrick Cronin's forty years in the Philippines* (New York, 1978).

Library of Congress Country Studies, available at (http://lcweb2.loc.goc/cgi-bin/query/r?frd/cstudy:@field/DOCID+ph0051) (6 Aug. 2006).

McCaslin, James, *The Columbans in the Philippines* (Zambales 1951-1990), ii (4 vols, Manila, 1998).

McCaslin, James, *The Columbans in the Philippines* (Luzon 1951-1990), iii (4 vols, Manila, 1999).

McCaslin, James, *The Columbans in the Philippines*, (Negros 1950-1990), iv (4 vols, Manila, 2000).

McCoy, Alfred W. and de Jesus, Eduardo C. (eds.), *Philippine social history* (Manila, 1982).

Noone, Martin, *Michael O'Doherty, Archbishop of Manila, his life and times* (Manila, 1989).

Noone, Martin, *The Columbans in the Philippines* 1929-1950, i (4 vols, Manila, 1998).

Noone, Martin, *The islands saw it, the discovery and conquest of the Philippines, 1521-1581* (Dublin, 1982).

O'Brien, Joseph F, 'The Philippines and the United States' (Unpublished Masters in Peace Studies paper, University of Bradford, 1981).

Taruc, Luis, *He who rides a tiger* (London, 1967).

Korea

Cahill, Joseph A., 'The effects of environmental transition on the missionary and on his message' (Unpublished D.Min. paper, Andover Newton Theological College, 1976).

Channel 4 history at (http://www.channel14.com/history/microsites/H/history/t-z/titfortat4.html) (16 Nov. 2006).

Deane, Philip, *Captive in Korea* (London, 1953).

Fischer, Edward, *Light in the Far East, Archbishop Harold Henry's forty-two years in Korea* (New York, 1976).

Hastings, Max, *The Korean war* (London, 1987).

Herlihy, Francis, *Swords and ploughshares, fifty years of mission in Korea* (Blackburn, 1983).

Hyde, Douglas, *One front across the world* (London, 1955).

Kelly, Jeremiah, *The splendid cause 1933-1983* (Seoul, 1984).

Lee, Ki-baik, *A new history of Korea*, trs Edward W. Wagner, (Harvard, 1984).

McCune-Reischauer System, available at McCune-Reischauer System (http://mccune-reishauer.org) (15 Nov. 2006).

Shin Ahn, 'Korea should be a Scotland of Japan, not an Ireland' (unpublished lecture, Yale-Edinburgh meeting, 8-10 July 2005).

'The Chinese Spring offensive' at Center for Military History (http://www.koreanwar.org/html/maps/map32_full.jpg) (27 Nov. 2006).

Winchester, Simon, *Korea, a walk through the land of miracles* (London, 1983).

Burma

'About the Kachin', available at Kachin News Group (http://www.kachinnews.com-KNG-Eng/About%20Us/About%KNG.htm) (10 Feb. 2007).

'Adoniram Judson: an intellectual evangelist', available at National Ministries (http://www.nationalministries.org) (5 Feb. 2007).

Aung San, Suu Kyi, *Freedom from fear and other writings* (London, 1991).

Binkley, Duane and Marcia, 'Situation along the Thai/Burma border' at Missionary Journal (http://www.internationalministries.org/journal.asp?journal ID=2035 &id=2) (5 Feb. 2007).

Carbery, Mary, *The farm by Lough Gur* (Cork, 1973).

Dawson, G. W, *The Bhamo district* (Original date not determined, reprint Rangoon, 1960).

Fischer, Edward, *Mission to Burma, the Columban Fathers' forty-three years in Kachin country* (New York, 1980).

Fischer, Edward, *The chancy war* (New York, 1991).

Harvey, G. E, *History of Burma* (New Delhi, 1925).

'Kachin state', available at Kachin State, Northern Myanmar (http://www.kachinstate.com) (13 Dec. 2006).

Khoo Thwe, Pascal, *From the land of green ghosts* (New York, 2002).

Lee, J. J., *Ireland 1912-1985, politics and society* (Cambridge, 1989).

'Myanmar Baptist Convention' available at Myanmar Baptist Convention (http://mbc1813.org/historical.htm) (5 Feb. 2007).

Palmer, Martin, *The Jesus sutras* (London, 2001).

Thompson, Julian, *War in Burma 1942-5* (London, 2002).

US Department of State, 'Burma', available at (http://www.state.gov/r/pa/ei/bgn/35910.htm) (4 Dec. 2006).

'Who we are' at American Baptist Churches (http://www.abc-usa.org/whoweare/default.aspx) (24 Feb. 2007).

Wilkinson, Peter J, 'A mission to Burmese Buddhists' (Unpublished D. Miss. dissertation, Gregorian University, Rome, 1970).

Index

Aglipay, Gregorio (Philippine Independent Church) 189-90, 201, 204, 222
Ancestral tablets; *see also* idols 35-6, 149-50
Animism 257, 288
Annals of the Propagation of the Faith 33, 56
Anti-foreign, *see also* treaties 20, 87, 107
Apostolic delegate, internuncio 30, 42, 88, 95, 112, 130, 164, 167, 173, 180, 194, 198, 217, 231, 247, 251, 254, 284
Association of the Holy Childhood 33, 118-9, 147
Attitudes to Asian culture and religions 27-8, 34-6, 149-50, 295-7
Attitudes to women 24-5, 30, 83, 85, 116-7, 128-9, 293-4
Aung San 272, 279
Australia 43, 48, 70-2, 103, 126, 207, 246
Bandits; *see also* communists 118, 128, 142, 171
Bhamo 262, 265, 270, 273, 276-7, 283, 284
Blowick, John 16, 22, 25, 32, 36-8, 47-50, 53-4, 58, 62, 75, 79, 83, 86, 102, 110, 115, 131, 191, 289, 293, 305
Brennan, Patrick 165, 233, 240, 247
Buddhism 22, 34, 38, 136, 150, 260, 265-6, 288
Building 96, 100, 140, 182, 211, 214, 224, 243, 269, 277
Burma 18, 21-2, 257-288, 296
Byrne, Henry 223
Byrne, Patrick J. 240, 247-8
Casey, John 184
Catechism 26, 30, 40-1, 96, 117, 148, 153, 155, 165, 169, 177, 197-201, 202-5, 213, 234, 275, 279, 286, 291, 292-3
Catechists 39, 91, 96-8, 118, 127, 213, 234, 237, 241, 251, 253, 270-1, 282-4
Catechumens, catechumenates 38, 98, 100, 109, 118, 120, 123, 141, 182, 234, 250, 251-3, 271-2, 284, 297
Chiang Kai-shek 117, 123, 144, 150

Chang, John 159, 174
Chapman, Francis 206, 207, 218
Chinese National Catholic Church (Three-Self Movement) 133, 171-6, 185
Cholla Nam Do *see also* Kwangju 228, 230-6
Chou, En-lai (Zhou Enlai) 145, 171
Chu, James 125, 130-3
Ch'unch'on 233-254, 309
Church growth 97, 100-1, 120-5, 141, 182, 223, 236, 241-2, 249, 252, 271, 292
Class 42-3, 96, 102, 119, 165, 252
Cleary, Patrick 83, 145-176
Clerc-Renaud, Jean-Louis 140
Cogan, Gerald M. (Garry) 193, 211, 222
Cohalan, Daniel 44, 45, 47
College, *see also* Dalgan Park 42, 45, 47, 50, 52-5, 59, 69, 72, 83
Colonialism, colonial policy 76-7, 87, 123, 265-9, 278, 293
Columbans killed 142, 144, 208-11, 220, 246-7, 275, Plate 7.5
Communists; *see also* bandits 108, 118, 122, 132-4, 142-4, 162-3, 168-176, 183-5, 220, 242-3, 244-9
Confucius 35-6, 38, 136
Congregation for the Propagation of the Faith, or Propaganda 49-50, 59, 75-80, 89, 91, 95-8, 117, 140, 180, 184, 186, 191-2, 230-2, 240, 265, 290-2, 298, 305-6
Congress, Chapter 63-6, 93, 136, 100, 193, 214, 230-1
Connolly, Timothy 211, 213, 215, 220, 253
Consistorial Congregation 186, 217
Constitutions 21-2, 57-67, 93, 97, 104, 110, 129, 191
Conversion 14, 25, 40, 59, 90, 93, 95, 112, 116, 121-6, 141, 149, 153, 165, 177, 186, 217, 223, 235, 251, 253, 257, 272, 290, 292-3, 296
Cronin, Patrick 207, 216
Crosbie, Philip 246-9

Cupimus imprimis 133, 172
Dalgan Park, *see also* college 52-5, 72, 81
Del Rosario, Aloysius 216
Demange, Florian 230-2
Dennehy, Jeremiah 167-8, 173, 215, 244, 256
Deymier, Jean-Joseph 180-3
Diocese 25, 57, 93,132, 164
Dumond, Paul 179
Easter duty, *inconfessi* 100-1
Ellis, Thomas 154, 157-8
Embroidery school 113-4
Evangelising 30, 59, 83, 86, 93, 95-6, 97-8, 100, 112, 118, 127, 163, 177, 195, 202, 204, 219, 229, 255, 259, 266, 270, 297
Falière, Albert 264-7, 275
Fallon, Peter 202, 211
Far East 55-6, 68, 71, 80-1
Faveau, Paul A. 51, 73
Fraser, John M. 33-4, 36, 38, 40, 45
Freeman's Journal 33
Freemason 199, 212, 225
Finances 43, 81-2, 97, 100-1, 106, 114, 130, 140, 155, 170, 172, 175, 182, 184, 195, 200, 212, 214, 218, 235-7, 243, 282-3, 305
Floods 113, 122
Franciscans 35, 73, 77-82, 88, 90, 93-4, 96, 105, 123, 130, 189, 210
Fumasoni-Biondi, Pietro 230, 232, 265
Galvin, Edward J. 14, 16, 17, 32, 38-45, 48-9, 56, 59, 62-8, 73-80, 86, 89, 91, 93-6, 103-9, 112-4, 116-122, 127-133, 140, 289, 291, 293, 295
Gennaro, Gratien 73-4, 77-81, 89, 92, 96
Grawng, Paul 287
Guerrero, Cesar Maria 198
Hangchow 178, 180, 185
Hankow 73-5, 79-82, 87, 95, 107, 130
Hanyang 74, 78, 80-2, 89-90, 95-6, 98-101, 105-6, 111, 115, 119-125, 126-7, 130-1, 133-4
Harty, Patrick 104-7
Hayes, James 201-7, 216
Henaghan, John 32, 45, 55-6, 194, 202, 204, 206, 211
Henry, Harold 238, 242, 250-2
Hospitals, dispensaries, *see also* doctors 60, 76, 93, 98, 117, 122, 128, 132, 151-2, 209, 254
Huchow 178-185

Huks 220-1
Idols 34, 40, 85, 149, 157, 296
Indigenous priesthood, hierarchy 14, 24, 33, 38, 40, 43, 58, 73, 120, 126-7, 129-34, 140, 157-9, 163, 171-5, 181, 185, 189, 215, 217, 220, 232-3, 238-241, 249, 286-7, 289-90
Intelligence reports 76-7
Irish Catholic 33, 44
Irish Christian Brothers 103-9
Irish Ecclesiastical Record 33-4, 36-8
Irish Independent 211
Irish hierarchy 44, 57
Irish Times 47
Ius commissionis 91
Japan 33, 51, 87, 107, 126, 206-11
Japanese 126, 132, 144, 151-5, 161-2, 167, 180, 226, 229, 233, 237-40, 273-6
Jesuits 35, 138, 160, 189, 201-2
Justyn, Justa 128-9
Kachin 264, 266-72, 275, 276, 284-5, 287
Kachyihtu 269-70, 275-6
Kangwondo or Kogendo 231-7
Kelly, Patrick 193, 195, 209, 211
Kiangsi 138, 140, 143-5, 148, 153, 161, 164
Kienchang; *see also* Nancheng 138, 140-1, 145, 152, 167
Korea 226-256
Kuomintang 102, 107-8, 117, 123, 145
Kwangju or Kwoshu 233-252
Lanao 216
Language of controversy 26-8, 34, 84-5, 136, 295-6
Language study 28, 75, 93, 153, 193, 198, 201, 221, 248, 255, 266, 286
Larribeau, Adrien-Joseph 231-4, 238
La Société des Missions-Étrangères 57-9
Laurenti, Camillus 50, 51, 57, 67, 78-80
Leahy, Timothy 123-5
Lebbe, Vincent 95
Legion of Mary 126, 133, 164, 183-4, 219, 222, 284, 291
Les missions de Chine et du Japon 89, 92
Lingayen 198-9, 207, 212, 220
Lladoc, Casimiro 217
Logue, Michael 44-5, 49-50, 59, 78
McAlindon, Denis 266, 269, 275-6
McCarthy, Edward J. 16, 22, 32, 36, 42, 61-4, 68, 69, 78, 199-201, 275
McDevitt, James 198-9, 213

McDonald, Mary Jane 114
MacElroy, Edward 169, 173, 175, 183-5
McGoldrick, William 163, 179-81
McGrath, Aedan 164, 184
MacPolin, Owen 231-7, 240
Madriaga, Mariano A. 198, 216
Malate 191, 193, 195, 200, 209-11
Manila 186-7, 191-4, 200, 207, 209-11, 212
Mao Tse-tung 127, 138, 142-4, 160
Maynooth Mission to China 45, 52, 59, 62, 65
Medical mission 19, 60, 83, 93, 98, 102, 114-7, 122, 151-2, 155, 209, 248, 265, 270, 285
Mill Hill Fathers 57
Mindanao 187, 210-6, 207, 216
Misamis Occidental 201-8, 212-3, 215
Mission:
    as soul-saving 34-8;
    as *plantatio ecclesiae* 39-40, 93, 97-8, 129, 163, 290;
    as a missionary society 45, 47, 49, 52, 68;
    as evangelisation 59, 93, 104, 116-8, 198-200, 205, 234, 270, 292, 301;
    as a territory 24, 75, 89, 91;
    as foreign mission 24, 59, 87
Mission, Theology of 34-5, 36-8, 39
Missionaries 24, 35, 76, 83, 88, 91, 93, 95, 122, 129, 138, 155, 161, 167, 189, 191, 219, 227, 229, 247
Missionary methods; *see also* schools, catechists 25-6, 43, 95-8, 109, 111, 112, 118, 121, 141, 146, 182, 186-7, 200, 234, 266, 284
Mokp'o 232, 238, 247, 254
Moloney, Frances (Mother Patrick) 18, 83, 86, 115
Mongey, Sister Michael 152, 161
Motive for mission 14, 34-8, 48, 55, 59, 93, 129, 157-158
Muslim 37, 53, 216-7
Myitkyina 265-6, 268, 277, 278, 287
Nancheng; *see also* Kienchang 141-2, 146, 148, 151, 152, 154-5, 157, 158-9, 163, 164, 168, 173-5
Nationalism 53, 55, 77, 107, 131, 133, 171, 239, 242, 272-3, 295
Negotiations with Rome 49-50, 72-81, 179-80, 191-3, 230-2, 265
Negros 217-20, 224
O'Doherty, Michael 186, 191-8

O'Donoghue, Alban104-9
O'Dwyer, Michael 83, 100, 106, 109, 114, 117, 140, 152, 179-80, 186, 191-3, 195, 200, 206, 211, 230-3, 237, 265, 278-9, 305-6
O'Leary, John 107-9, 112
O'Leary, Joseph 32, 35-6, 42, 44, 63, 74
O'Reilly, Luke 17, 171, 174-5
O'Riordan, Michael 48-9, 73
Old Christians 92, 127, 131, 135, 144, 148, 160, 174, 233
Orphanages 98, 118-9, 146-7, 167, 249, 262, 265, 284
Pecorari, Cesare 192
Persecution 127, 135, 170, 173, 184-5, 201, 208-11, 246, 249, 264, 265
Philippines 186-255
Pigott, Jeremiah 180-5
Policy to stay with people in time of danger 56, 108, 123, 167, 173, 244-5, 247, 274, 298
Pope 25, 72, 134, 167, 174, 185, 292, 297;
    Pius IX 34;
    Leo XIII 190, 197;
    Benedict XV 25, 43, 50, 59, 74, 129, 296;
    Pius XI 119, 152, 163, 177, 270, 297;
    Pius XII 132, 163, 172, 216, 254
Population 88, 138, 142, 148, 178, 186, 204, 227, 232, 257, 259, 269
Preaching 34, 39, 40, 53, 55, 58, 94-8, 118, 142, 157, 166, 183, 191, 193, 224, 254, 286
Prefecture, prefect 25, 72, 74, 80, 98, 114, 119, 138, 148, 152, 180, 183, 222, 233-6, 240, 250, 251, 270, 271, 281
Prejudice; *see also* language 26, 43, 132, 225, 235, 294
Prospectus status missionis 98
Protestant 26, 37, 56, 74-6, 79, 91, 106, 186, 198-200, 214, 218, 248, 277, 288, 294, 305
Quae mari sinico 190
Quinlan, Thomas 97, 109, 233-4, 237, 240, 245-9, 254
Redemptorists 191, 210
Refugees 113-4, 121-3, 126, 128, 145, 152, 155, 157, 240, 247, 249, 276
Region 67, 72, 168, 193, 214-5, 244, 307
Relief, *see also* refugees 122, 158, 240, 243, 253

Sacraments 22, 26, 37, 39, 41, 98, 100, 126, 143, 170, 200, 205, 212, 222, 238, 253, 270, 291
Schools 42, 60, 76, 91-6, 97, 100, 103-8, 111-3, 118, 132, 142, 147, 150, 170, 182, 190, 194, 197-9, 202, 213-5, 217, 219, 235, 242, 251, 261, 266-7, 271, 278, 290
Seminary, *see also* college 34, 42, 68, 72, 84, 93, 129-130, 159, 215, 219, 233, 254, 287
Seng, Joseph 131, 133, 134
Shanghai 77, 107, 108, 117, 123, 134, 163, 185
Sheehan, Samuel 198, 212, 215, 217, 220
Sientaochen 118, 124, 127, 134
Sisters 18, 25, 43, 72, 83, 94, 98, 109-14, 115-8, 121-122, 127-9, 132-3 146, 151, 154, 158, 159-60, 167, 182, 194, 198, 205, 213, 235, 247-8, 254, 265, 274, 284-5, 290, 293-4
Society of St. Columban 14, 32, 46, 48, 49, 52, 56-67, 68, 71, 93, 100, 114, 129, 164, 167, 186, 193, 214, 230, 265, 289
Spanish 186-9, 201, 216, 218
Spirit-worship 259, 264, 272
Starvation, *see also* floods, refugees 113, 127, 155, 157, 175, 243, 255
Statistics 22-3, 76, 95, 99-100, 120, 135, 138, 141, 148, 156, 250, 292
St Joseph's Sheaf 33
Stuart, James 269-70, 275-7
Student Catholic Action 198, 200, 213
Taoism 38, 149-50
Tierney, Cornelius 62-3, 95, 141, 144
Times 33

Translation of the Bible 25, 219, 239, 261, 286, 292
Treaty ports, *see also* unequal treaties 87
Tribal people 216, 221-2, 259, 281
True principles of Catholicism 226
Tsu Feng Chin, John 185
Unequal treaties 86, 107
US 38, 42, 43, 67-70, 100, 110, 153, 158, 168, 190, 193, 207, 210, 213, 239, 240, 245, 248, 257-62, 275
Usher, Patrick 257, 265-87
Van Rossum, William 76
Vicariate, *see also* prefecture 25, 29, 42-5, 67, 72, 75, 80, 82, 119, 140, 152, 179
Vincentian, Lazarist 33, 38, 51, 95, 106, 146, 175, 217
Virgins 122, 127-8, 154
Visiting the poor, sick 95, 111, 117, 158
Walsh, William J. 45-7, 50-1
War 39, 43, 71, 76, 81, 87, 108, 123, 126, 132, 143, 144-5, 152-4, 161, 171, 189, 206-11, 238, 245, 273
Women, needs and role 41, 112-3, 116-8, 126, 127-9, 146-7, 234, 284
Wuchang 88, 106, 107, 126
Wuhan 107, 126, 132,
Yang, James 159, 174-5
Yu, Thomas 159-60, 176
Yukiang 138
Zambales 221-3
Zhang, Peter 126-7, 131, 133-4
Zhou Jishi 159, 164, 172, 306